T0332161

CONSTRAINT HANDLING RULES

Constraint Handling Rules (CHR) is both a theoretical formalism based on logic and a practical programming language based on rules. This book, written by the creator of CHR, describes the theory of CHR and how to use it in practice. It is supported by a website containing teaching materials, online demos, and free downloads of the language.

After a basic tutorial, the author describes in detail the CHR language, beginning with its syntax and semantics. Guaranteed properties of CHR programs such as concurrency and analysis for desirable properties such as termination are discussed next. The author then compares CHR with other formalisms and languages and illustrates how it can capture their essential features. In the last part, some larger programs are introduced and analyzed in detail.

The book is ideal for graduate students and lecturers, and for more experienced programmers and researchers, who can use it for self-study. Exercises with selected solutions, and bibliographic remarks are included at the ends of chapters. The book is the definitive reference on the subject.

THOM FRÜHWIRTH is a Professor in the Faculty of Computer Science at the University of Ulm, Germany. He is the creator of the programming language CHR and the main author of two books on constraint programming and reasoning.

Constraint Handling Rules

THOM FRÜHWIRTH
University of Ulm, Germany

CAMBRIDGE
UNIVERSITY PRESS

CAMBRIDGE
UNIVERSITY PRESS

University Printing House, Cambridge CB2 8BS, United Kingdom

One Liberty Plaza, 20th Floor, New York, NY 10006, USA

477 Williamstown Road, Port Melbourne, VIC 3207, Australia

314-321, 3rd Floor, Plot 3, Splendor Forum, Jasola District Centre, New Delhi - 110025, India

79 Anson Road, #06-04/06, Singapore 079906

Cambridge University Press is part of the University of Cambridge.

It furthers the University's mission by disseminating knowledge in the pursuit of education, learning and research at the highest international levels of excellence.

www.cambridge.org
Information on this title: www.cambridge.org/9780521877763

First published 2009

A catalogue record for this publication is available from the British Library

Library of Congress Cataloging in Publication data
Frühwirth, Thom, 1962–
Constraint handling rules / Thom Frühwirth.
p. cm.
ISBN 978-0-521-87776-3 (hardback)
1. Constraint programming (Computer science) 2. Logic programming. 3. Declarative programming. I. Title.
QA76.612.F77 2009
005.1′16–dc22

2009018859

ISBN 978-0-521-87776-3 Hardback

Additional resources for this publication at www.cambridge.org/9780521877763

About the author

Thom Frühwirth is the creator of the programming language Constraint Handling Rules (CHR). He is also the main author of two books on constraint programming and reasoning. On these subjects, he has published more than 120 research papers.

Thom Frühwirth obtained his PhD in Computer Science at the Technical University of Vienna in 1990 after a one-year research grant at the State University of New York. Then he was a researcher at the European Computer Industry Research Centre in Munich. In 1996, he joined the Ludwig Maximilians University in Munich, where he became assistant professor in 1998. During that time he held visiting positions at the universities of Pisa, Monash Melbourne, PUC Rio de Janeiro, and at the CWI research center in Amsterdam. Since 2002, he has been an associate professor at the University of Ulm, Germany.

To those from whom I learned
Georg Gottlob
David S. Warren
Ehud Shapiro
To Andrea Walter, the love of my life

I see a great future for very systematic and very modest programming languages.
Edsger W. Dijkstra

Contents

Preface

The more constraints one imposes, the more one frees oneself.

Igor Stravinsky

CHR has taken off. After five dedicated workshops, two special journal issues, and hundreds of related research articles, it was time to write this book about CHR.

About this book

This book is about programming with rules. It presents a rule-based constraint programming language called CHR (short for Constraint Handling Rules). While conceptually simple, CHR embeds the essential aspects of many rule-based and logic-based formalisms and can implement algorithms in a declarative yet highly effective way. The combination of information propagation and multiset transformation of relations in a concurrent, constraint-based language makes CHR a powerful declarative tool for knowledge representation and reasoning. Over the last decade CHR has not only cut its niche as a special-purpose language for writing constraint solvers, but has matured into a general-purpose language for computational logic and beyond.

This intermediate-level book with a gentle introduction and more advanced chapters gives an overview of CHR for readers of various levels of experience. The book is addressed to researchers, lecturers, graduate students, and professional programmers interested in languages for innovative applications. The book supports both self-study and teaching. It is accompanied by a website at `chr.informatik.uni-ulm.de`.

In short, this book concentrates on the basics of CHR while keeping in mind dozens of research papers. In 2009, there will be a companion book on recent advances in CHR and a survey article in a journal. A book on implementation of CHR and a collection of classical CHR papers is also planned.

Underlying concepts

CHR relies on three essential concepts: rules, declarativity, and constraints.

Rules are common in everyday life. The formalization of these rules goes back more than 2000 years to the syllogisms of the Greek philosopher Aristotle, who invented logic this way. Nowadays, rule-based formalisms are ubiquitous in computer science, from theory to practice, from modeling to implementation, from inference rules and transition rules to business rules.

Rules have a double nature, they can express monotonic static causal relations on the basis of logic, but also nonmonotonic dynamic behavior by describing state changes. Executable rules are used in declarative programming languages, in program transformation and analysis, and for reasoning in artificial intelligence applications. Such rules consist of a data description (pattern) and a replacement statement for data matching that description. Rule applications cause transformations of components of a shared data structure (e.g. constraint store, term, graph, or database).

Matured rule-based programming has experienced a renaissance due to its applications in areas such as business rules, the semantic web, computational biology, medical diagnosis, software verification, and security. Commonplace uses of rules are in insurance and banking applications, for mail filtering and product configuration.

Declarativity means to describe knowledge about entities, their relationships and states, and to draw inferences from it to achieve a certain goal, as opposed to procedural or imperative programs that give a sequence of commands to compute a certain result. Declarative program constructs are often related to an underlying formal logic.

Declarativity facilitates program development (specification, implementation, transformation, combination, maintenance) and reasoning about programs (e.g. correctness, termination, complexity). Declarative programming also offers solutions to interaction, communication, distribution, and concurrency of programs.

Constraint reasoning allows one to solve problems by simply stating constraints (conditions, properties) which must be satisfied by a solution of the problem. A special program (the constraint solver) stores, combines, and simplifies the constraints until a solution is found. The partial solutions can be used to influence the run of the program that generates the constraints.

Programming by asserting constraints makes it possible to model and specify problems with uncertain or incomplete information and to solve combinatorial problems, such as scheduling and planning. The advantages of constraint-based programming are declarative problem modeling on a solid mathematical basis and propagation of the effects of decisions expressed as additional constraints. The conceptual simplicity and efficiency of constraint reasoning leads to executable specifications, rapid prototyping, and ease of maintenance.

Constraint Handling Rules (CHR)

CHR is both a theoretical *formalism* (like term rewriting and Petri nets) related to first-order logic and linear logic, and a practical *programming language* (like Prolog and Haskell) based as rules. CHR tries to bridge the gap between theory and practice, between logical specification and executable program by abstraction through constraints and the concepts of computational logic. By the notion of constraint, CHR does not distinguish between data and operations, its rules are both descriptive and executable.

CHR is a declarative concurrent committed-choice constraint logic *programming language* consisting of guarded rules that transform multisets of constraints (relations, predicates). CHR was motivated by the inference rules that are traditionally used in computer science to define logical relationships and arbitrary fix-point computations in the most abstract way.

Direct *ancestors of CHR* are logic programming, constraint logic programming, and concurrent committed-choice logic programming languages. Like these languages, CHR has an operational semantics describing the execution of a program and a declarative semantics providing a logical reading of the program which are closely related. Other influences were multiset transformation systems, term rewriting systems, and, of course, production rule systems. CHR embeds essential aspects of these and other rule-based systems such as constraint programming, graph transformation, deductive databases, and Petri nets, too.

In CHR, one distinguishes two main kinds of rules. *Simplification rules* replace constraints by simpler constraints while preserving logical equivalence, e.g. $X{\leq}Y{\land}Y{\leq}X \Leftrightarrow X{=}Y$. *Propagation rules* add new constraints that are logically redundant but may cause further simplification, e.g. $X{\leq}Y{\land}Y{\leq}Z \Rightarrow X{\leq}Z$. Together with $X{\leq}X \Leftrightarrow \mathtt{true}$, these rules encode the axioms of a partial order relation. The rules compute its transitive closure and replace $\leq$ by equality ($=$) whenever possible.

Multi-headed rules allow us to express complex interactions in a compact way. They provide for implicit iteration instead of cumbersome looping constructs. In other words, CHR supports a topological view of structured data. Components can be accessed directly by just mentioning them in the rule head. CHR also allows for recursive descent where one walks through data.

CHR is appealing for applications in *computational logic*: logical theories are usually specified by implications and logical equivalences that correspond to propagation and simplification rules. On the meta-level, given the transformation rules for deduction in a calculus, its inference rules map to propagation rules and replacement rules to simplification rules. In this context, CHR integrates deduction and abduction, bottom-up and top-down execution, forward and backward chaining, tabulation and integrity constraints.

Algorithms are often specified using inference rules, rewrite rules, sequents, proof rules, or logical axioms that can be written directly in CHR. Starting from such an executable specification, the rules can then be refined and adapted to the specifics of the application. Yet, CHR is no theorem prover, but an efficient programming language: CHR uses formulas to derive new information, but only in a restricted syntax (e.g. no negation) and in a directional way (e.g. no contrapositives) that makes the difference between the art of proof search and an efficient programming language.

The use of CHR as a *general-purpose programming language* is justified by the following observation: given a state transition system, its transition rules can readily be expressed with simplification rules. In this way, CHR accounts for the double nature (causality versus change) of rules. *Statefulness* and declarativity are reconciled in the CHR language. Dynamics and changes (e.g. updates) can be modeled, possibly triggered by events, and handled by actions (that can all be represented by constraints). CHR allows for explicit state (constraints, too), so that the efficiency of imperative programs can be achieved.

CHR programs have a number of *desirable properties* guaranteed and can be analyzed for others. Every algorithm can be implemented in CHR with best known time and space complexity, something that is not known to be possible in other pure declarative programming languages. The efficiency of the language is empirically demonstrated by recent optimizing CHR compilers that compete well with both academic and commercial rule-based systems and even classical programming languages.

Any CHR program will by nature implement an anytime (approximation) and online (incremental) algorithm. Confluence of rule applications and operational equivalence of programs are decidable for terminating CHR programs. We do not know of any other programming language in practical use where operational equivalence is decidable. CHR does not have bias towards sequential implementation. A terminating and confluent CHR program can be run in parallel without any modification and without harming correctness. This property is called declarative concurrency (logical parallelism).

CHR does not necessarily impose itself as a new programming language, but as a language extension that blends in with the syntax of its *host language*, be it Prolog, Lisp, Haskell, C, or Java. In the host language, CHR constraints can be posted and inspected; in the CHR rules, host language statements can be included.

CHR has been used for such *diverse applications* as type system design for Haskell, timetabling for universities, optimal sender placement, computational linguistics, spatio-temporal reasoning, chip card verification, semantic web information integration, computational biology, and decision support for cancer diagnosis. Commercial applications include stockbroking, optical network design, injection mould design, and test data generation.

If asked what distinguishes CHR from similar programming languages and formalisms, the quick answer is that CHR is both a theoretical formalism and a practical programming language. CHR is the synthesis of multiset transformation, propagation rules, logical variables, and built-in constraints into one conceptually simple language with a foundation in logic and with formal methods for powerful program analysis.

Contents

This book has three parts. The first part is a tutorial on CHR. The second part formally defines syntax and semantics of CHR, its properties and their analysis. The third part presents CHR programs and applications to which the analysis of Part II is applied. We present exercises and selected solutions for the chapters that contain practical programs in Parts I and III of this book.

In **Part I**, the CHR tutorial tells you how to write CHR programs in one of the recent CHR libraries, how CHR rules look, and how rules are executed. A wealth of small but expressive example programs, often consisting of just one rule, are discussed in detail. The behavior of CHR implementations is explained, and different programming styles are exhibited: CHR as database language, for multiset transformation, for procedural algorithms, and for constraint solving. Special emphasis is placed on graph-based algorithms. The properties of the programs are discussed informally, and this foreshadows their thorough analysis in Part II of the book.

In **Part II**, the syntax and semantics of CHR are formally introduced. We distinguish between a declarative semantics that is based on a logical reading of the rules and an operational semantics that describes how rules are applied. Several widely used variants of both types of semantics are given.

In the next chapter, guaranteed properties of CHR are discussed. The anytime algorithm property means that we can interrupt the program at any time and restart from the intermediate result. The online algorithm property means that we can add additional constraints incrementally, while the program is running. We then discuss declarative concurrency (also called logical parallelism). Last but not least, we show that CHR can implement any algorithm with best known time and space complexity.

Chapter 5 discusses termination, confluence, operational equivalence, and time complexity: since CHR is Turing-complete, termination is undecidable. Confluence of a program guarantees that a computation has the same result no matter which of the applicable rules are applied. Confluence for terminating CHR programs is decidable. Nonconfluent programs can be made confluent by completion, which is introduced next. Modularity of termination and confluence under union of programs is discussed. Then, we give a decidable, sufficient, and necessary syntactic condition for operational equivalence of terminating and confluent programs. Finally, a meta-theorem to predict the worst-case time complexity of a class of CHR programs is given.

In the last chapter of this part, CHR is compared to other formalisms and languages by embedding them in CHR. It is shown that essential aspects of

- logic-based programming, deductive databases, concurrent constraints
- production rules, event–condition–action rules, business rules
- multiset, term, and graph-rewriting, and Petri nets

can be covered by suitable fragments of CHR.

Part III analyzes the programs from the CHR tutorial and a number of larger programs in more detail and more formally. The programs solve problems over finite and infinite domains of values: propositional satisfaction problems (Boolean algebra), syntactic equations over rational trees, and linear polynomial equations, implement the graph-based constraint algorithms of arc and path consistency, and the global lexicographic order constraint. We also directly implement description logic (extended with rules), which is the formal basis of ontology languages of the semantic web. We give a program for the classical union-find algorithm with optimal time and space complexity. We parallelize the algorithm and generalize it for efficient equation solving. We use it in an efficient syntactic equation solver. All programs in this part are elegant, concise, and effective.

The book ends with an extensive list of references and an index.

Further information and software

The web page of this book offers teaching material such as slides and further exercises along with many links. It can be found via the comprehensive CHR website at `chr.informatik.uni-ulm.de`. The CHR site features access to research papers, software for download, programming examples, and descriptions of applications and projects. More than 1000 papers mentioning CHR are listed, many of them with links. There are lists of selected papers, ordered by topic, recency, and author. Tutorial notes and slides can be found as well.

More than a dozen free implementations of CHR exist. They are available in most Prolog systems, several in Haskell, and in more mainstream programming languages such as Java and C. Many can be downloaded for free from the CHR website. CHR is also available as WebCHR for online experimentation with dozens of example programs, including most from this book. So you can try out CHR from work, home, or any internet cafe. Last but not least there is the mailing list `CHR@listserv.cc.kuleuven.ac.be` for beginners' questions, discussion, and announcements concerning CHR.

Acknowledgments or how CHR came about

I came up with CHR during the first weeks at the European Computer Industry Research Centre in Munich in January 1991. Soon, Pascal Brisset implemented the first CHR compiler in Prolog. This was after an inspiring year with a Fulbright grant at SUNY at Stony Brook with David S. Warren, where I met Patreek Mishra and Michael Kifer, and after a research visit to Ehud Shapiro at the Weizmann Institute, where I met Moshe Vardi.

For the next five years or so, I had research papers introducing CHR rejected, even though there was some isolated interest and encouragement from people in the logic programming, constraint programming, and term rewriting community.

Out of frustration I started to work on temporal reasoning until, in 1995, Andreas Podelski invited me to contribute to the Spring School in Theoretical Computer Science in Chatillon with CHR. The breakthrough came when Slim Abdennadher provided the formal basis for the advanced semantics of CHR and essential CHR properties like confluence and operational equivalence and when Christian Holzbaur wrote an optimizing CHR compiler that would become the de-facto standard for a decade. All this cumulated in the invitation of Peter Stuckey to submit a CHR survey to a special issue of the *Journal of Logic Programming* in 1998, which became the main reference for CHR, leading to several hundred citations.

Since then, quite a few people have contributed to the success of CHR, too many to thank them all by name, but let me just mention a few more of them. I was lucky again when Tom Schrijvers picked up CHR and within a few short years created the currently most active CHR research group at K.U. Leuven. He has also edited special journal issues on CHR, organizes CHR workshops, and maintains the CHR website.

I would also like to thank my PhD students in Ulm, Marc Meister, Hariolf Betz, and Frank Raiser. They not only advanced the state of the art in CHR, they also helped me tremendously to deal with the downsides of academic life by sharing the burden. Together with Jon Sneyers and Ingi Sobhi, they provided detailed comments for parts of this book. I finally want to thank the reviewers of research papers that laid the ground for this book for their helpful comments.

Hariolf Betz pointed me to the Chinese character that became the CHR logo. CHR can be interpreted not only as an acronym for "Chinese HoRse". The Chinese character written "CHR" in the Yale transcription of Mandarin is derived from the character for horse but depending on the context, it can also mean *to speed, to propagate, to be famous*.

My first sabbatical semester gave me time to start this book. It would not have been written without public domain software such as the operating system Linux and Latex for typesetting. It would not have been published in this form without the friendly people from Cambridge University Press and the typesetters from India. I doubt that I could have written the book at home or at my workplace. So special thanks to Oliver Freiwald, who gave me some work space in his insurance agency, to Marianne Steinert there, and to the people from the Caritas social project coffee shop where during my sabbatical I had lunch and a lot of coffee, proofread the manuscript, and met my students for discussions.

Figures

Part I
CHR tutorial

We present the essentials of the Constraint Handling Rules (CHR) programming language by the use of examples in this Tutorial part.

The first chapter **Getting started** is a step-by-step introduction to CHR based on simple examples.

The second chapter **My first CHR programs** introduces some simple, but concise and effective, CHR programs. We discuss basic properties of CHR programs in an informal way: anytime and online algorithm property, correctness, confluence, concurrency, and complexity. The formal analysis of these programs is deferred to Part III.

Exercises and selected solutions are given for the practical programming chapters in Parts I and III. More exercises can be found online.

1
Getting started

This chapter is a basic introduction to CHR using simple examples. They introduce the types of rules used in CHR, their behavior and basic ingredients of the language such as logical variables and built-in constraints. Last but not least, we define the concrete syntax of CHR and we informally describe how CHR executes its rules.

In this book, we will use the *concrete syntax* of CHR with Prolog as the host language in the practical programming parts and mathematical *abstract syntax* in the formal Part II.

1.1 How CHR works

For programming, we recommend using a CHR implementation from K.U. Leuven, since they are currently the most recent and advanced. The CHR rules themselves will also be executable in other Prolog implementations of CHR and with minor modifications in K.U. Leuven JCHR, an implementation of CHR in Java and in the K.U. Leuven CHR library for C.

When we write a CHR program, we can mix host language statements and CHR code. The CHR-specific part of the program consists of declarations and rules.

1.1.1 Propositional rules

We start programming in CHR with rules that only involve *propositions*, i.e. constraints without arguments. Syntactically, constraints are similar to procedure calls.

Example 1.1.1 (Weather) Everybody talks about the weather, and we do as well.

3

Declarations. They introduce the CHR constraints we are going to define by the rules. They are specific to the implementation and the host language. Later in this book, we will usually skip the declarations and concentrate on the rules.

We introduce three CHR constraints named `rain`, `wet`, and `umbrella` with the following declaration:

```
:- module(weather, [rain/0]).
:- use_module(library(chr)).

:- chr_constraint rain/0, wet/0, umbrella/0.
```

In the first line, the optional Prolog module declaration puts the CHR program into a module named `weather`, which exports only the mentioned constraint `rain/0`. The *functor* notation `c/n` defines the name (`c`) and number of arguments (`n`) of a constraint $c(t_1, \ldots, t_n)$. In the host language Prolog and its CHR libraries, function symbols (including constants) start with lower-case letters.

The second line of the declaration makes sure that the CHR library is loaded before any CHR-specific code. CHR constraints must be declared using the `chr_constraint` keyword before they are defined and used by rules. In the declaration, for each CHR constraint, at least its name and arity (number of arguments taken) are given, optional specifications are the input/output mode and the type of the arguments.

Rules. Any kind of constraint-handling rule has an optional name, a left-hand side (l.h.s.) called the *head* together with an optional *guard*, and a right-hand side (r.h.s.) called the *body*. There are three kinds of rules. The head, guard, and body of a rule consist of constraints.

The following two CHR rules encode statements about rain:

```
rain ==> wet.
rain ==> umbrella.
```

The first rule says "If it rains, then it is wet". The second rule can be read as "If it rains, then we need an umbrella". Both rules have a head consisting of the constraint `rain`. The bodies are `wet` and `umbrella`, respectively. There are no guards. These rules are so-called *propagation rules*, recognizable by `==>`. These kind of rules do not remove any constraints, they just add new ones.

Queries. Computation of a CHR program is initiated by posing a *query*. The rules of the program will be applied to the query until exhaustion, i.e. until no more change happens. The rule applications will manipulate the query by removing CHR constraints and by adding constraints. The result of the computation is called the *answer*, it simply consists of the remaining constraints.

If we pose the query `rain`, the answer will be `rain, wet, umbrella` (not necessarily in that order).

In Prolog CHR implementations, the query is typically entered at the command line prompt followed by a dot. After the computation has finished, the answer is displayed.

Top-down execution. If we write instead the two simplification rules

```
rain <=> wet.
rain <=> umbrella.
```

then the answer to `rain` will be just `wet`. The first rule is applied and removes `rain`.

Rules are tried in textual order, in a top-down fashion, and so only the first rule will ever be applied in our example. In general, whenever more than one rule application is possible, one rule application is chosen. A rule application cannot be undone (unlike Prolog). We thus say that CHR is a *committed-choice language*.

With propagation rules, we can draw conclusions from existing information. With simplification rules, we can simplify things, as we will see. Simplification rules can also express *state change*, i.e. *dynamic behavior* through updates.

Example 1.1.2 (Walk) Assume we describe a walk (a sequence of steps) by giving directions, `left, right, forward, backward`. A description of a walk is just a sequence of these CHR constraints, and of course, multiplicities matter. Note that the order in which the steps are made is not important to determine the position reached. With simplification rules, we can model the fact that certain steps (like `left` and `right`) cancel each other out, and thus we can simplify a given walk to one with a minimal number of steps that reaches the same position.

```
left, right <=> true.
forward, backward <=> true.
```

So the walk `left, forward, right, right, forward, forward, backward, left, left` posed as a query yields as answer the simplified and shorter walk `left, forward, forward`.

1.1.2 Logical variables

Declarative programming languages such as CHR feature a special kind of variables. These so-called *logical variables* are similar to mathematical unknowns and variables in logic. A logical variable can be either *unbound* or *bound*. A bound variable is indistinguishable from the value it is bound to. A bound logical variable cannot be overwritten with another value (but it can be bound to the same value again). We call languages with such variables *single-assignment* languages, while more traditional languages like Java and C feature *destructive (multiple) assignment* where the value of a variable can be overwritten.

In Prolog CHR implementations, variable names start with an upper-case letter. The underscore symbol denotes an unnamed variable.

Example 1.1.3 (Men and women) Computer science textbooks always have an example involving people of the two sexes. In our case, we have several men, e.g. `male(joe)`, ..., and several women `female(sue)`, ... at a dancing lesson. So we have the CHR constraints `male` and `female`. The two constraints have one argument, the name of the person of that sex. We want to assign men and women for dancing. This can be accomplished by a simplification rule with two head constraints:

```
male(X), female(Y) <=> pair(X,Y).
```

The variables of the rule are X and Y, they are placeholders for the actual values from the constraints that match the rule head. The scope of a variable is the rule it occurs in. Given a query with several men and women, the rule will pair them until only persons of one sex remain. Clearly the number of pairs is less than the number of men and women.

Types of rules. If we replace the simplification rule by a propagation rule, we can compute all possible pairings, since the `male` and `female` constraints are kept.

```
male(X),  female(Y) ==> pair(X,Y).
```

Now the number of pairs is quadratic in the number of people. Propagation rules can be expensive, because no constraints are removed and thus every combination of constraints that match the rule head may lead to a rule application.

There may also be a dance where a single man dances with several women, and this can be expressed by a *simpagation rule*:

```
male(X) \ female(Y) <=> pair(X,Y).
```

In this type of CHR rule, the constraints left of the backslash \ are *kept* but the remaining constraints of the head, right of the backslash, are *removed*.

It is worth experimenting with queries where men and women are in different orders to understand how CHR rules execute.

Example 1.1.4 (Family relationships I) The following propagation rule named mm expresses that the mother of a mother is a grandmother. The constraint grandmother(joe,sue) reads as "The grandmother of Joe is Sue". The use of variables in the rule mm should be obvious.

```
mm @ mother(X,Y), mother(Y,Z) ==> grandmother(X,Z).
```

The rule allows us to derive the grandmother relationship from the mother relationship. For example, the query mother(joe,ann), mother(ann,sue) will propagate grandmother(joe,sue) using rule mm.

1.1.3 Built-in constraints

In CHR, we distinguish two kinds of constraints: *CHR constraints*, which are declared in the current program and defined by CHR rules, and *built-in constraints* (short: *built-ins*), which are predefined in the host language or imported CHR constraints from some other module.

On the left-hand side of a rule, CHR and built-in constraints are separated into head and guard, respectively, while on the right-hand side, the body, they can be freely mixed. The reason is that the head and guard constraints are treated differently when the rule is executed, as we will see soon.

Example 1.1.5 (Family relationships II) The mother of a person is unique, she or he has only one mother.

Syntactic equality. In mathematical terms, the mother relation is a function, the first argument determines the second argument. We can write a simpagation rule that enforces this *functional dependency*:

```
dm @ mother(X,Y) \ mother(X,Z) <=> Y=Z.
```

The rule makes sure that each person has only one mother by equating the variables standing for the mothers. We use the *built-in syntactic equality* =. The constraint Y=Z makes sure that both variables have the same value, even if it is yet unknown. We may actually safely and correctly assume that, in the remainder of the computation, the occurrences of one variable are replaced by (the value of) the other variable in the equation.

For example, the query `mother(joe,ann), mother(joe,ann)` will lead to `mother(joe,ann)` (the built-in constraint `ann=ann` is simplified away, because it is always true).

Failure. The query `mother(joe,ann), mother(joe,sue)` will fail, because then Joe would have two different mothers, and the rule `dm` for mother will lead to the syntactic equality `ann=sue`. This built-in equality cannot be satisfied, it fails. The built-in has acted as a test now. Failure aborts the computation (it leads to the answer `no` in most Prolog systems).

Variables in queries and head matching. In CHR, the current constraints must *match* the rule head that serves as a pattern (unlike Prolog). The query constraints may contain variables and the matching is successful as long as these variables are not bound by the matching.

In the query `mother(A,B), mother(B,C)` we will see in the answer also `grandmother(A,C)` by rule `mm`. On the other hand, no rule is applicable to the query `mother(A,B), mother(C,D)`. We may, however, add a built-in equality constraint to the query, i.e. `mother(A,B), mother(C,D), B=C`. Then we also get `grandmother(A,D)`. If we add `A=D` instead, the mother relations are matched the other way round by the head of the `mm` propagation rule and we get `grandmother(C,B)`.

If we add `A=C`, the rule `dm` will apply and add `B=D`, so the complete answer will be `mother(A,B), mother(C,D), A=C, B=D`.

We now give a CHR programming example that involves simple arithmetic built-ins.

Example 1.1.6 (Mergers and acquisitions) Let us move to the commercial world of companies. A large company will buy any smaller company. We use a CHR constraint `company(Name,Value)`, where `Value` is the market value of the company.

Guards. This rule describes the merge–acquisition cycle that we can observe in the real world:

```
company(Name1,Value1), company(Name2,Value2) <=> Value1>Value2 |
            company(Name1,Value1+Value2).
```

The meaning of the arithmetic comparison `Value1>Value2` in the guard should be obvious. A guard basically acts as a test or precondition on the applicability of a rule. Only built-in constraints are allowed in a guard. These built-ins should be simple tests, i.e. the same constructs that occur in conditions of the host language.

For readability of the rule, we have used an in-lined arithmetic expression, `Value1+Value2`, inside a CHR constraint. This works in a similar notation for the host language Java, for the host language Prolog we would have to use the built-in is to evaluate the arithmetic expression:

```
company(Name1,Value1), company(Name2,Value2) <=> Value1>Value2 |
              Value is Value1+Value2, company(Name1:Name2,Value).
```

After exhaustive application of these rules to some companies, only a few big companies will remain, because the rule is applicable in one way or another to any two companies with different market value. If one company remains, we have a monopoly, otherwise we have an oligopoly. All remaining companies will have the same value.

1.2 CHR programs and their execution

We formally introduce the concrete syntax of CHR and we informally introduce the operational semantics of the language.

1.2.1 Concrete syntax

The CHR-specific part of a CHR program consists of declarations and rules. Declarations are implementation-specific, for details consult your manual.

Rules. There are three kinds of constraint-handling rules, which can be seen from the following EBNF grammar. Terminal symbols are in single quotes. Expressions in square brackets are optional. The symbol | (without quotes) separates alternatives.

```
Rule --> [Name '@']
         (SimplificationRule | PropagationRule | SimpagationRule) '.'

SimplificationRule --> Head             '<=>' [Guard '|'] Body
PropagationRule    --> Head             '==>' [Guard '|'] Body
SimpagationRule    --> Head '\' Head '<=>' [Guard '|'] Body

Head            --> CHRConstraints
Guard           --> BuiltInConstraints
Body            --> Goal

CHRConstraints --> CHRConstraint | CHRConstraint ',' CHRConstraints
BuiltInConstraints -->   BuiltIn | BuiltIn ',' BuiltInConstraints
Goal            --> CHRConstraint | BuiltIn | Goal ',' Goal

Query           --> Goal
```

A `Head` is a comma-separated sequence of `CHRConstraints`. The `Guard` consists of `BuiltInConstraints`. The symbol ' | ' separates the guard (if present) from the body of a rule. (The symbol is inherited from early concurrent languages and should not be confused with the ' | ' used in the EBNF grammar.) The `Body` of a rule is a `Goal`. A `Goal` is a comma-separated sequence of built-in and CHR constraints. In simpagation rules, the backslash symbol '\' separates the head of the rule into two parts. A `Query` is simply a goal.

Basic built-in constraints. With Prolog as the host language, we use the following minimal set of predefined predicates as built-in constraints. Some of them we have already discussed in the introductory examples of this chapter. Built-in constraints may be used for auxiliary computations in the body of a rule, such as arithmetic calculations. Built-in constraints that are tests are typically used in the guard of rules. They can either *succeed* or *fail*. We give the name of the built-in and, preceded by ' / ', the number of its arguments.

- The most basic built-in constraints:
  `true/0` always succeeds.
  `fail/0` never succeeds, i.e. always fails.

- Testing if variables are bound:
  `var/1` tests if its argument is an unbound variable.
  `nonvar/1` tests if its argument is a bound variable.

- Syntactical identity of expressions (infix notation used):
  `=/2` makes its arguments syntactically identical by binding variables if necessary. If this is not possible it fails.
  `==/2` tests if its two arguments are syntactically identical.
  `\==/2` tests if its two arguments are syntactically different.

- Computing and comparing arithmetic expressions (infix notation used):
  `is/2` binds the first argument to the numeric value of the arithmetic expression in the second argument. If this is not possible it fails.
  `</2,=</2,>/2,>=/2,=:=/2,=\=/2` test if both arguments are arithmetic expressions whose values satisfy the comparison.

Because `=/2` and `is/2` bind their first arguments, they should never be used in guards. The built-ins `==/2` and `=:=/2` should be used instead. (However, some CHR compilers silently replace the former with the latter in guards.) On the other hand, tests will only occur in rule bodies to ensure that a condition that must hold, actually holds.

1.2.2 Informal semantics

We describe the behavior of current sequential implementations according to the so-called *refined operational semantics* of CHR. A formal description can be found in Section 3.3.4. Parallel, experimental, and future implementations may apply the rules in different ways. However, these will still respect the more general *abstract operational semantics* (cf. Section 3.3.3).

A CHR constraint is both an *active operation* and *passive data*. The constraints in a goal are processed from *left to right*. When a CHR constraint is encountered, it is evaluated like a procedure call, i.e. it checks the applicability of the rules it appears in. Such a constraint is called an *active constraint*. One tries and applies rules in the order they are written in the program, i.e. top-down and from left to right. If, at the moment, no rule is applicable that would remove the active constraint, it becomes passive data and is put into the constraint store. The *constraint store* is a data structure for constraints. The constraint is now called *passive*. Passive constraints become active code again if the environment (context) changes, concretely if their variables get bound.

There are several computational phases when the active constraints consider a CHR rule. These phases coincide with the constituents of a rule, namely head, guard, and body.

Head matching. For each rule, one of its head constraints is matched against the active constraint. Matching succeeds if the constraint is an instance of the head, i.e. the head serves as a pattern. The matching may bind variables in the head, but not those in the active constraint. If matching succeeds and the rule has more than one head constraint, the constraint store is searched for *partner constraints* that match the other head constraints.

Head constraints are searched from left to right, except for the ones in simpagation rules. In them, the constraints to be removed are tried *before* the head constraints to be kept (this is done for efficiency reasons). If the matching succeeds, the guard is checked.

If there are several head constraints that match the active constraint, the rule is tried for each such matching. If there is no successful matching, the active constraint tries the next rule.

Guard checking. A guard is a precondition on the applicability of a rule. The guard is basically a test that either succeeds or fails. If the guard succeeds, the rule is applied. If the guard fails, the active constraint tries the next head matching.

Body execution. If a rule is applied, we say it *fires*. If the firing rule is a simplification rule, the matched constraints are removed from the store and the rule body is executed. Similarly for a firing simpagation rule, except that the constraints that matched the head part preceding the backslash '\' are kept. If the firing rule is a propagation rule, the body is executed without removing any constraints. It is remembered that the propagation rule fired, so it will not fire again with the same constraints. According to the rule type, we say that the constraints matching the rule head are either *kept* or *removed* constraints. When the active constraint has not been removed, the next rule is tried.

1.3 Exercises

Compare the following CHR programs, which each consist of *one* of the given rules, based on their answers to the suggested queries.

1.1 Single-headed rules:

```
p <=> q.
p ==> q.
```

Multi-headed rules:

```
p , q <=> true.
p \ q <=> true.
```

Use some queries containing p and/or q.

1.2 Simplification rules with logical variables and syntactic equality:

```
p(a) <=> true.
p(X) <=> true.
p(X) <=> X=a.
p(X) <=> X=a | true.
p(X) <=> X==a | true.
```

Propagation rules with logical variables and syntactic equality:

```
p(a) ==> true.
p(X) ==> true.
```

```
p(X) ==> X=a.
p(X) ==> X=a | true.
p(X) ==> X==a | true.

p(X) ==> q(X).
p(a) ==> q(X).
p(a) ==> q(a).
p(X) ==> q(Y).
```

Queries: (a) p(a), (b) p(b), and (c) p(C).

1.3 Arithmetic comparison:

```
p(X) <=> X>1 | q(X).
p(X) ==> X>1 | q(X).
p(X) ==> X>1 | fail.
p(X) ==> X=<1.
```

Queries: (a) p(0), (b) p(1), (c) p(2), and (d) p(A).

1.4 Multi-headed rules, conjunctions in head and body, unary constraints:

```
p(X), q(X) <=> r(X).
p(X), q(Y) <=> X==Y | r(X).
p(X), q(Y) <=> X=Y, r(X).
p(X) \ q(X) <=> r(X).
```

Queries: (a) p(a), q(a), (b) p(a), q(b), (c) p(a), q(a), q(b), and (d) p(a), q(b), q(a).

1.5 Multi-headed rules, conjunctions in head and binary constraints in body:

```
c1 @ c(X), c(X) <=> q(X,X).
c2 @ c(X), c(Y) <=> r(X,Y).
c3 @ c(X), c(X) ==> q(X,X).
c4 @ c(X), c(Y) ==> r(X,Y).
```

Queries: (a) c(a), (b) c(a), c(a), (c) c(a), c(b), (d) c(X), c(X), (e) c(X), c(Y), and (f) c(X), c(Y), X=Y.

Selected answers:

```
c1 @ c(X), c(X) <=> q(X,X).
(d) q(X,X)
(e) c(X), c(Y)
(f) Y = X, q(X,X)
```

```
c2 @ c(X), c(Y) <=> r(X,Y).
(d) r(X,X)
(e) r(Y,X)
(f) Y = X, r(X,X)


c3 @ c(X), c(X) ==> q(X,X).
(d) c(X), c(X), q(X,X), q(X,X)
(e) c(X), c(Y)
(f) Y = X, c(X), c(X), q(X,X), q(X,X)


c4 @ c(X), c(Y) ==> r(X,Y).
(d) c(X), c(X), r(X,X), r(X,X)
(e) c(X), c(Y), r(Y,X), r(X,Y)
(f) Y = X, c(X), c(X), r(X,X), r(X,X)
```

1.6 Binary constraints:

```
q1 @ p(X,Z), q(Z,Y) <=> q(X,Y).
q2 @ q(Z,Y), p(X,Z) <=> q(X,Y).
q3 @ p(X,Z), q(Z,Y) ==> q(X,Y).
q4 @ q(Z,Y), p(X,Z) ==> q(X,Y).
q5 @ p(X,Z) \ q(Z,Y) <=> q(X,Y).
q6 @ q(Z,Y) \ p(X,Z) <=> q(X,Y).
```

Queries: (a) p(a,b), q(b,c), (b) p(A,B), q(B,C), (c) p(A,B),
q(B,C), p(D,A), (d) p(X,C), p(Y,C), q(C,A), and (e) p(Y,C),
p(X,C), q(C,A).

Selected answers:

```
q1 @ p(X,Z), q(Z,Y) <=> q(X,Y).
(b) q(A,C)
(c) q(D,C)


q2 @ q(Z,Y), p(X,Z) <=> q(X,Y).
(b) q(A,C)
(c) q(D,C)


q3 @ p(X,Z), q(Z,Y) ==> q(X,Y).
(b) p(A,B), q(B,C), q(A,C)
(c) p(A,B), q(B,C), q(A,C), p(D,A), q(D,C)
```

```
q4 @ q(Z,Y), p(X,Z) ==> q(X,Y).
```
(b) p(A,B), q(B,C), q(A,C)
(c) p(A,B), q(B,C), q(A,C), p(D,A), q(D,C)

```
q5 @ p(X,Z) \ q(Z,Y) <=> q(X,Y).
```
(b) p(A,B), q(A,C)
(c) p(A,B), p(D,A), q(D,C)

```
q6 @ q(Z,Y) \ p(X,Z) <=> q(X,Y).
```
(b) q(B,C), q(A,C)
(c) q(B,C), q(A,C), q(D,C)

1.4 Origins and applications of CHR

CHR [Frü98, HF00, FA03, AFH05, FMS06, SWSK08] has many roots and combines their features in an attractive way, enabling powerful applications.

Origins. Prolog and Logic programming (LP) [Kow86, CR93], constraint logic programming (CLP) [Hen91, JM94, JL87, MS98, FA03, RBW06] and concurrent committed choice logic programming (CC) [Mah87, Ued88, Sha89, Sar93] are direct ancestors of CHR. CHIP was the first CLP language to introduce feasible constructs (demons, forward rules, conditionals) [DHS+88, Hen89] for user-defined constraints. These various constructs have been generalized into and made uniform by CHR.

CHR adapts concepts from term rewriting systems (TRS) [BN98] for program analysis. Augmented term rewriting was used in the functional language Bertrand [Lel88] to implement constraint-based algorithms.

Other influences for the design of CHR were the General Abstract Model for Multiset Manipulation (GAMMA) [BCM88, BM93], the Chemical Abstract Machine (CHAM) based on it [BB92], and, of course, production rule systems like OPS5 [BFKM85], but also integrity constraints and event–condition–action rules found in relational and deductive database systems.

Executable rules with multiple head constraints were also proposed in the literature to model parallelism and distributed agent processing as well as logical objects [BCM88, AP90] and for constraint solving [Gra89].

In comparison to all these languages, the combination of multiple heads, propagation rules, and logical variables with built-in constraints is unique to CHR.

Applications. Frequent applications of CHR can be found in particular in the areas of temporal reasoning, agent-based systems, semantic web, and type systems. Commercial applications include stockbroking, optical network design, injection mold design, and test data generation. Much more information than here can be found in the recent survey on CHR [SWSK08] and online at the CHR web pages.

Scheduling and timetabling are popular constraint-based applications, and this also holds for CHR [AM00]. Based on [Frü94], CHR has been used for spatio-temporal reasoning [ET96, ET98], where it is applied to robot path planning. An extension of the event calculus [SK95] called GRF, including different time scales and continuous processes, was implemented in CHR [Don93].

PMON is a logic for dynamic systems [San94]. A PMON scenario description consists of observations holding at time points, action laws defining change, schedule statements for actions, and axioms expressing inertia. The CHR implementation is described in [Bja96]. The logic and its implementation have evolved into [MD06].

The agent-based system FLUX is implemented in CHR [Thi05]. Its application FLUXPLAYER [ST07] won the General Game Playing competition at the AAAI conference in 2006. Other applications in multi-agent systems (and abductive reasoning) are, for example, [SBB02, ADT$^+$04].

For the semantic web, the integration and combination of data from different information sources is an important issue that can be handled with CHR [BG98, BTH04]. The Cuypers Multimedia Transformation Engine [GOH01] supports the automatic generation of Web-based presentations adapted to the user's needs.

The most successful application for CHR is in the design, protyping, and analysis of advanced type systems for the functional programming language Haskell [SS05]. Type reconstruction is performed for functional and logic programs in [SB06]. Finally, a flow-based approach for a variant of parametric polymorphism in Java is based on CHR in [CCKP06].

2

My first CHR programs

In this chapter, we introduce some simple, but concise and effective CHR programs. Often these programs consist just of one rule. We discuss basic properties of CHR programs which we introduce in an informal way. These properties are the anytime and online algorithm property, logical correctness, rule confluence, declarative concurrency, and worst-case time complexity. The programs in this section will be formally analyzed for these properties in Part III.

We will sometimes give longer examples of computations as a sequence of goals, one per line. We may underline the constraints involved in a rule application if it helps to understand the computation.

2.1 CHR as a database language

We can use CHR as an information store, as a simple *deductive database*, where database relations are modeled as CHR constraints which are maintained in the constraint store. Each database tuple corresponds to an instance of the constraint. The query contains (or generates) the tuples of the database as CHR constraints. Database queries, views, integrity constraints, and deductive database rules can be formulated as CHR propagation rules. This leads to the deduction of new and additional data constraints, i.e. tuples.

Example 2.1.1 (Family relationships III) We stay with the family relationships from Example 1.1.4. Mothers and fathers are parents and siblings are people who have the same parent:

```
mother(X,Y) ==> parent(X,Y).
father(X,Y) ==> parent(X,Y).
parent(X,Z), parent(Y,Z) ==> sibling(X,Y).
```

Given the information
```
mother(hans,mira), mother(sepp,mira), father(sepp,john),
```
the first two propagation rules will derive the parent relationships
```
parent(hans,mira), parent(sepp,mira), parent(sepp,john)
```
and from this the last propagation rule will add the sibling constraints:
```
sibling(hans,sepp), sibling(sepp,hans).
```

To avoid two sibling constraints being generated for every pair of siblings, we can use the simpagation rule:

```
sibling(X,Y) \ sibling(Y,X) <=> true.
```

We may also want to talk about grandparents, great-grandparents and so on. We call these ancestors. In mathematical terms, the ancestor relation is the *transitive closure* of the parent relation. It can be implemented by the following propagation rules. The first rule says that a parent is an ancestor, the second rule says the ancestor of a parent is also an ancestor.

```
parent(X,Y) ==> ancestor(X,Y).
parent(X,Y), ancestor(Y,Z) ==> ancestor(X,Z).
```

Transitive closure is discussed extensively in Section 2.4.1.

Example 2.1.2 (Crossword) In CHR, one rule suffices to solve crossword problems. A word is represented as a sequence of letters that form the arguments of the CHR constraint word/n, where n is the length of the word. Examples are word(n,o), word(d,o,g), word(b,o,o,k).

The crossword problem is encoded as a sequence of word constraints whose arguments are variables. Each variable corresponds to a field in the crossword and the same variable is used if it is shared between a horizontal and vertical word. These word constraints form the head of a propagation rule, while the rule body just outputs the values found for the variables, e.g. with the help of an auxiliary CHR constraint as below. For example,

```
word(A,B,C,D), word(E,F,G), word(A,E,H)... ==>
                          solution(A,B,C,D,E,F,G,H).
```

A query with all possible words for crossword puzzles will be large, so we may store the words in one large rule of the form words <=> word(n,o), word(d,o,g),... and just use the CHR constraint words in the query.

2.2 Multiset transformation

The following CHR programs consist essentially of one constraint representing active data. Pairs of such constraints are rewritten by a single simplification rule. Often, the rule can be written more compactly as a simpagation rule where one of the constraints is kept and the other is removed and possibly replaced by an updated one. Similar, but less concise programs exist in other rule-based approaches, namely production rule systems (see Section 6.1) and the General Abstract Model for Multiset Manipulation (GAMMA) model of computation (see Section 6.2.2).

The first program computes the minimum of a set of numbers and it sets the stage for other programs, that follow the same structure in their presentation.

2.2.1 Minimum

We compute the minimum of a multiset of numbers n_i, given as the query `min(n_1)`, `min(n_2)`, ..., `min(n_k)`. We interpret `min(n_i)` to mean that the number n_i is potentially the minimum, that it is a *candidate* for the minimum value.

```
min(N) \ min(M) <=> N=<M | true.
```

The simpagation rule takes two `min` candidates and removes the one with the larger value. It keeps going until only one, the smallest value, remains as a single `min` constraint. The program illustrates the use of multi-headed rules instead of explicit loops or recursions for iteration over data. This keeps the program code extremely compact and makes it easier to analyze. The rule corresponds to the intuitive algorithm that when we are to find the minimum from a given list of numbers, we just cross out larger numbers until one, the minimum, remains.

We will give computations as the sequence of goals resulting from rule applications. For clarity we sometimes underline the constraints that are involved in a rule application.

A possible computation would be (where constraints involved in a rule application are underlined):

min(1), min(0), min(2), min(1)
min(0), min(2), min(1)
min(0), min(1)
min(0)

Program properties. In the above example we used the top-down rule
application order and the left-to-right goal processing order of current sequential CHR implementations. Here is a computation with another order of rule
applications:

<u>min(1)</u>, min(0), <u>min(2)</u>, min(1)
<u>min(1)</u>, min(0), <u>min(1)</u>
<u>min(0)</u>, <u>min(1)</u>
min(0)

In the above two example computations for the query min(1), min(0),
min(2), min(1), the answers were the same. Actually, the answer will
always be the same, i.e. the minimum value, no matter in what order the
rules are applied to any pair of constraints. We call this property *confluence*,
and it will be defined in Section 5.2 and discussed for the examples here in
Chapter 7.

Without changing the program, rules can be applied in parallel to different
parts of the query. This is referred to as *logical parallelism* or *declarative
concurrency* and discussed in Section 4.3.

<u>min(1)</u>, <u>min(0)</u>,   <u>min(2)</u>, <u>min(1)</u>
<u>min(0)</u>,   <u>min(1)</u>
min(0)

We arrive at the answer in fewer computation steps.

The program is terminating because the rule removes a CHR constraint
and does not introduce new ones. Therefore, the number of rule applications
is one less than the number of min constraints. We can apply a rule in
constant time. Given any two min constraints, we can always apply the
rule – either in one pairing order or the other. Therefore the complexity of
this small program is linear in the number of min constraints, i.e. linear in
the size of the query. Termination and complexity analysis are defined and
discussed in Section 5.1 and Section 5.6, respectively.

We can also stop the computation at *any time* and observe the current
store as an intermediate answer. We can then continue by applying rules
to this store without the need to recompute from scratch and no need to
remember anything about how we arrived at the current store. If we stop
again, we will observe another intermediate answer that is closer to the final
answer than the one before. By closer we mean here that the store has
fewer min constraints, i.e. fewer candidates for the final minimum. The
intermediate answers approximate more and more closely the final answer.
This property of a CHR program is called the *anytime algorithm property*

and it is discussed in Section 4.1. Note that by this description, an anytime algorithm is also an *approximation algorithm*.

Now assume that while the program runs, we add a min constraint. It will eventually participate in the computation in that the rule will be applied to it. The answer will be correct, as if the newly added constraint had been there from the beginning but ignored for some time. This property of a CHR program is called *incrementality* or the *online algorithm property*, and it is discussed in Section 4.2.

Abstract semantics. So far we have assumed that the min constraints contain given values. In that case, the guard acts as a test that compares two such values. In general, under the *abstract operational semantics* of CHR, even though not necessarily in a given implementation, the guard is made out of built-in constraints that hold if they are logically implied by the current store. While in current practical implementations of CHR, a guard check will give an error or silently fail if unbound variables occur in it, the same guard check may succeed under the abstract semantics.

For example, the query min(A), min(B), A=<B will reduce to min(A), A=<B, because we know that A=<B and that is exactly what the guard asks for. Similarly, the query min(A), min(B), A<B will reduce to min(A), A<B. Finally, the query min(A), min(A) will reduce to min(A). But the query min(A), min(B) will not reduce, because we know nothing about the relationship of the unknown values A and B.

Operational equivalence. Now consider what happens if we modify the program in that we strengthen the guard. If we replace N=<M by N<M, multiple occurrences (duplicates) of the final minimum constraint will no longer be removed. If we replace N=<M by N=M, we will just remove duplicates. Both rules taken together have the same behavior as our initial rule, provided we work with known values.

```
min(N) \ min(M) <=> N<M | true.
min(N) \ min(M) <=> N=M | true.
```

Under the abstract semantics, it turns out that the two rules are weaker than the single initial rule. Consider the previous examples. Most of them still work, but the query min(A), min(B), A=<B will not reduce at all, because the built-in constraint A=<B is too weak to imply one of the guards of the two rules, A<B or A=B. We say that these two programs are not *operationally equivalent*. Operational equivalence is discussed in Section 5.5.1. However, the programs are logically equivalent. The logical reading of rules as formulas is the *declarative semantics* as discussed in Section 3.4.

Program variations. If we want to use this rule for the minimum in a larger program, we may be faced with some pragmatical issues.

First, we may want to compute the minimum from values that occur in constraints that should not be removed. Then it suffices to add a propagation rule that generates a `min` constraint for each value we want to consider, e.g. `c(...,X,...)  ==> min(X)`.

Second, we may want to trigger the computation at a certain moment. It suffices to add an *auxiliary dummy constraint* to the rule, say `findmin`, that triggers the computation:

```
findmin, min(N) \ min(M) <=> N=<M | true.
```

The constraint `findmin` can also be used to return the resulting minimum using a second rule, so that we do not pick up a minimum candidate of an intermediate answer by mistake:

```
findmin, min(N) <=> ismin(N).
```

This assumes that `findmin` is executed last, *after* all `min` constraints have been added. We may also return the minimum in `findmin`:

```
findmin(Min), min(N) <=> Min=N.
```

Third, we may want to compute several minima from different sources and need to distinguish them. It suffices to add an identifier to the `min` constraint and modify the minimum rule so that it refers only to constraints with the same identifier:

```
min(Id,N) \ min(Id,M) <=> N=<M | true.
```

In general, this technique of adding an explicit identifier to each constraint can be used to localize computations, i.e. to implement *local constraint stores*.

2.2.2 Boolean Exclusive Or

Similar to the minimum, we can implement the Exclusive Or (XOR) operation of propositional logic. There is a multiset of `xor` constraints denoting the input, and we are to compute the output as a single remaining `xor` constraint. The truth values *true* and *false* are represented by the numbers 1 and 0, respectively. According to the truth table for exclusive or, we come up with the four rules:

```
xor(0), xor(0) <=> xor(0).
xor(0), xor(1) <=> xor(1).
```

```
xor(1), xor(0) <=> xor(1).
xor(1), xor(1) <=> xor(0).
```

Clearly, one of the second and third rules is redundant, as it just differs in the order of the head constraints. We can also generalize the first and last rules into one rule, provided the arguments are always of the correct type (truth values):

```
xor(X),  xor(X) <=> xor(0).
xor(1) \ xor(0) <=> true.
```

These rules say that in order to compute the result of an exclusive or, it suffices to replace pairs of identical constraints by `xor(0)` and to remove all `xor(0)` if there is a `xor(1)` constraint, in any order we like.

One can show that the program is confluent. For example, to the query `xor(1), xor(1), xor(0)` we can either apply twice the first rule or first the second rule and then the first rule. In both cases, the answer is `xor(0)`.

We can also see that if we apply the first rule to exhaustion before applying the second rule, we will be left either with a single constraint `xor(1)` or `xor(0)` or with two different constraints `xor(1), xor(0)`. With this rule application order the second rule is applied at most once only.

Note that simplifying the second rule to
```
xor(0) <=> true.
```
would be incorrect, since a query like `xor(0), xor(0)` would then have the wrong answer, just `true`. However, we can generalize the second rule into `xor(X) \ xor(0) <=> true`. Then to a query `xor(0), xor(0)` both rules are applicable. But in both cases, the answer is the correct `xor(0)`. With the generalized rule, the query `xor(X), xor(X), xor(X)` reduces to `xor(X)` while with the original rule, we get `xor(0), xor(X)`.

The properties of the `xor` program (confluence, termination, complexity, concurrency, ...) are discussed in detail in Section 7.1.2.

Of course, such a minimalistic encoding only works for associative and commutative operations. A general way to implement Boolean constraints will be discussed in Section 8.1.

2.2.3 Greatest common divisor

We implement maybe the oldest known nontrivial algorithm still in use. It was given by Euclid around 300 BC. The next rule computes the greatest common divisor of natural numbers n_i, written as $gcd(n_i)$. The remaining nonzero gcd constraint contains the resulting answer.

```
gcd(N) \ gcd(M) <=> 0<N,N=<M | gcd(M-N).
```

As an example, consider a query `gcd(12)`, `gcd(8)` and its computation (new constraints are added to the right):

```
gcd(12),gcd(8)
gcd(8), gcd(4)
gcd(4), gcd(4)
gcd(4), gcd(0)
```

The condition `0<N` in the guard ensures that constraints with value 0 are ignored. It improves the usability of the program if we clean up the gcd constraints with value zero:

```
gcd(0) <=> true.
```

As an example, consider a query `gcd(7)`, `gcd(12)` and its computation:

```
gcd(7), gcd(12)
gcd(7), gcd(5)
gcd(5), gcd(2)
gcd(2), gcd(3)
gcd(2), gcd(1)
gcd(1), gcd(1)
gcd(1), gcd(0)
gcd(1)
```

We can improve the efficiency of the program by replacing the subtraction in the rule body by the arithmetic modulo operation:

```
gcd(N) \ gcd(M) <=> 0<N,N=<M | gcd(M mod N).
```

The previous example needs fewer computation steps now:

```
gcd(7), gcd(12)
gcd(7), gcd(5)
gcd(5), gcd(2)
gcd(2), gcd(1)
gcd(1), gcd(0)
gcd(1)
```

Of course, the gcd programs also work for several gcd candidates. For example, the gcd of `gcd(94017)`, `gcd(1155)`, `gcd(2035)` is `gcd(11)`. If the arithmetic operations permit it, the code also works for rational numbers. It will not work for floating point numbers due to rounding errors, which can cause incorrect answers or even nontermination.

Termination is ensured for natural numbers as arguments of **gcd**, since L will always be strictly smaller than M but cannot become negative due to the guard condition. The program is confluent for its intended use with known numbers, but not in general (cf. Section 7.1.3).

Program variation: binary gcd. The gcd computation can be speeded up using the so-called *binary gcd algorithm*. Since the gcd of an odd and an even number cannot be even, we can divide the even number by 2 until it becomes odd. This behavior can be achieved by adding this rule in front of the **gcd** computation rule (// is used for integer division):

```
gcd(M) \ gcd(N) <=> odd(M), even(N) | gcd(N//2).
```

The presence of **gcd(M)** ensures that there is at least one odd number. In this case, the gcd algorithm becomes logarithmic even in the subtraction version: the new rule is immediately applicable after the original subtraction gcd rule, since the difference of two odd numbers is always even.

In a preprocessing step, the binary gcd algorithm divides all numbers by 2 until one of them is odd. So there will always be at least one odd number. With the resulting power of two, we later multiply the gcd. To implement a similar idea, we represent numbers by a product of an odd number with a power of 2:

```
gcd(0,A) <=> true.
gcd(N,A) <=> 0<N,even(N) | gcd(N//2,A).
gcd(N,A) \ gcd(M,B) <=> 0<N,N=<M,odd(N),odd(M) |
                        gcd(M-N, min(A,B)).
```

2.2.4 Prime numbers Sieve of Eratosthenes

We implement the algorithm known as the Sieve of Eratosthenes, but without any particular sifting order. Given some numbers, the rule just removes multiples of each of the numbers.

```
sift @ prime(I) \ prime(J) <=> J mod I =:= 0 | true.
```

We feed the rule a sequence of prime number candidates consisting of all numbers from 2 up to N, i.e. prime(2),prime(3),prime(4),...,prime(N). The candidates react with each other such that each number absorbs multiples of itself. When we feed it all integers up to a given bound starting from 2, all composite numbers will be removed after exhaustive application of the rule, so that only prime numbers remain.

A possible computation would be

```
prime(7), prime(6), prime(5), prime(4), prime(3), prime(2)
prime(7), prime(5), prime(4), prime(3), prime(2)
prime(7), prime(5), prime(3), prime(2)
```

The **sift** rule can be seen as a specialization of the efficient modulo-operator version gcd rule (cf. Section 2.2.3) where we require that the result of the modulo operation is zero, i.e. L=0. The rule is also similar to that for the minimum in that it compares two numbers and removes one of them. But unlike the minimum, the rule is not applicable to arbitrary pairs of prime number candidates.

As before, the program has the desirable properties that are typical for CHR. For example, the program is terminating, since it removes constraints without adding new ones. Prime number candidates can be added while the program runs, and intermediate results contain fewer and fewer false primes.

Generating numbers. To generate the prime candidates, we may use the auxiliary CHR constraint upto:

```
upto(1) <=> true.
upto(N) <=> N>1 | prime(N), upto(N-1).
```

To the same effect, we can use the **prime** constraint itself:

```
prime(N) ==> N>2 | prime(N-1).
```

Both rule variants generate the prime candidates in descending order. While for the answer the order does not matter due to confluence, it matters for efficiency. Ascending order is preferable, because smaller prime candidates increase the chance that the **sift** rule is applicable. We can fix upto by exchanging the recursive call with the generation of the prime:

```
upto(N) <=> N>1 | upto(N-1), prime(N).
```

We cannot fix the variation using **prime** itself this way.

2.2.5 Exchange sort

We can sort an array by exchanging values at positions that are in the wrong order. Given an unsorted array as a sequence of constraints of the form a(Index,Value), i.e. a(1,A1),...,a(n,An), this simplification rule sorts in this way:

```
a(I,V), a(J,W) <=> I>J, V<W | a(I,W), a(J,V).
```

This rule replaces a pair of constraints by another pair, which in effect is an update.

For example, consider the query

```
a(0,1), a(1,7), a(2,5), a(3,9), a(4,2)
a(0,1), a(1,5), a(2,7), a(3,2), a(4,9)
a(0,1), a(1,5), a(2,2), a(3,7), a(4,9)
a(0,1), a(1,2), a(2,5), a(3,7), a(4,9)
```

In a sorted array, it holds for each pair $a(I,V)$, $a(J,W)$ where $I>J$ that $V>=W$. The rule ensures that this indeed holds for every such pair by exchanging the values if necessary. So if the rule is not applicable any more, the resulting array must be sorted.

The rule terminates because the exchange of values cannot continue forever, since each rule application (and thus exchange) corrects the order relationship of the exchanged pair of values and maybe others, but cannot introduce more new wrong orderings. The program is confluent for queries with known numbers, but not in general.

2.2.6 Newton's method for square roots

Newton's iteration is an approximation method for the value of polynomial expressions relying on derivatives. We would like to compute the square root of a positive number. As can be computed by Newton's method, the approximations for square roots are related by the formula $G_{i+1} = (G_i + X/G_i)/2$.

Since CHR programs already implement anytime, i.e. approximation, algorithms, the implementation in CHR is straightforward. We assume that the answer is returned as a CHR constraint. sqrt(X,G) means that the square root of X is approximated by G. This rule computes the next approximation (where the infix operator / denotes division):

```
sqrt(X,G) <=> abs(G*G/X-1)>0 | sqrt(X,(G+X/G)/2).
```

For simplicity, we have inlined the arithmetic expression (G+X/G)/2 (instead of using an explicit built-in is/2 when Prolog is the host language). The query is just sqrt(GivenNumber,Guess). Both numbers must be positive, and if no guess is known, we may take 1. The guard stops its application if the approximation is exact. This is unlikely in practice when floating point numbers are used due to rounding errors. We replace 0 in the guard by a sufficiently small positive number ϵ.

Since the quality of approximation is often in the eye of the beholder, we may implement a more interesting, *demand-driven* version of the algorithm.

An approximation step is performed *lazily*, only on demand, which is expressed by the constraint `improve(Expression)`.

```
improve(sqrt(X)), sqrt(X,G) <=> sqrt(X,(G+X/G)/2).
```

Of course the constraint `improve` can be extended with a counter or combined with a check for the quality of the approximation.

2.3 Procedural algorithms

We now employ a more traditional style of programming, where constraints are relations that resemble procedures as they are used in imperative programming languages. Results of a computation are not returned as constraints as before, but as values of variables that are bound. As we will see with the example of Fibonacci numbers, CHR supports different programming styles and it is easy to change between them. The classical procedural union-find algorithms and their variants are discussed in Chapter 10.

2.3.1 Maximum

We define a CHR constraint `max`, where `max(X,Y,Z)` means that the maximum of X and Y is Z:

```
max(X,Y,Z) <=> X=<Y | Z=Y.
max(X,Y,Z) <=> Y=<X | Z=X.
```

The first rule states that `max(X,Y,Z)` can be simplified to Z=Y when it holds that X=<Y. Analogously for the second rule.

To the goal `max(1,2,M)` the first rule is applicable and it reduces to M=2. The goal `max(1,2,3)` fails due to the inconsistent built-in constraint 3=2. To the goal `max(1,1,M)` both simplification rules are applicable, and in both cases the answer is M=1. Indeed, the program is confluent as we will discuss in Section 7.2.1.

The program is terminating, since the bodies of its rules contain only built-in constraints.

2.3.2 Fibonacci

The nth Fibonacci number is defined inductively as follows:

$$fib(0) = fib(1) = 1; fib(n) = fib(n-1) + fib(n-2) \text{ for } n \geq 2$$

The ratio between two subsequent Fibonacci numbers approximates the Golden ratio.

When we implement this definition in CHR, we translate the functional notation of *fib* into a relational notation, and the equivalence becomes a simplification rule. (For a general approach to translating functional into relational notation called *flattening*, see Section 6.2 on embedding term rewriting systems in CHR.)

Top-down evaluation. For our problem, *top-down evaluation* results in a recursive approach where we start from the highest Fibonacci number. This approach to reasoning, where we start with a goal and proceed with smaller and smaller subgoals, is also called *goal-driven* and *backward-chaining*.

The CHR constraint `fib(N,M)` holds if the Nth Fibonacci number is M.

```
f0 @ fib(0,M) <=> M=1.
f1 @ fib(1,M) <=> M=1.
fn @ fib(N,M) <=> N>=2 | fib(N-1,M1), fib(N-2,M2), M is M1+M2.
```

The three rules are a direct translation of the definition. For example, the query `fib(8,A)` yields `A=89`, the query `fib(12,233)` succeeds, the query `fib(11,233)` fails, the query `fib(N,233)` delays.

As is well known, such a direct implementation has exponential time complexity because of the double recursion that recomputes the same Fibonacci numbers over and over again in different parts of the recursions.

Adding tabulation and memorization. We would like to store the results of Fibonacci numbers that we have already computed and look them up to avoid computing the same Fibonacci numbers several times. This approach is called *memorization (memoing)* or *tabulation (tabling)*. Since CHR constraints are both procedures (operations) and data, it is easy to change the rules accordingly. We just have to turn the three simplification rules into propagation rules, so that the left-hand side constraints are kept. In this way the result of the computation will be kept in the constraint store as data.

The rule for the look-up of already computed Fibonacci numbers has to come first, so that it is applied before we compute in the usual way using the expensive recursive definition.

```
mem @ fib(N,M1) \ fib(N,M2) <=> M1=M2.
```

```
f0 @ fib(0,M) ==> M=1.
f1 @ fib(1,M) ==> M=1.
fn @ fib(N,M) ==> N>=2 | fib(N-1,M1), fib(N-2,M2), M is M1+M2.
```

The rule `mem` for look-up enforces the functional dependency between input and output of the Fibonacci relation, in other words it uses the fact that `fib` defines a function. Remember that a simpagation removes the currently active constraint if it has a choice. The query `fib(8,A)` now returns *all* Fibonacci numbers up to 8:

`fib1(0,1), fib1(1,1), fib1(2,2),..., fib1(7,21), fib1(8,34).`

The effect of memorization is dramatic: while the original rules have exponential complexity, the new version has only linear complexity, because each Fibonacci number is only computed once. Since the rule body is executed from left to right, the second recursive call is just a look-up using the `mem` rule. Actually, the `mem` rule does more than just looking up computed results, in effect it merges two computations that must have the same result into one, even if both computations are still ongoing.

Bottom-up evaluation. Another way of computing the Fibonacci numbers efficiently is using only data and computing larger numbers from smaller ones. Reasoning *bottom-up* starts from the given facts and proceeds towards the given goal. The approach is therefore also called *forward-chaining* and *data-driven*.

Basically, it suffices to reverse the head and body of the top-down rules for Fibonacci:

`fn @ fib(N1,M1), fib(N2,M2) ==> N2=:=N1+1 | fib(N2+1,M1+M2).`

Since reversing the rules `f0` and `f1` does not give well-formed CHR rules (they do not have a head), we add the first two Fibonacci numbers in the query, `fib(0,1),fib(1,1)`. Of course, the resulting computation is infinite, and in order to observe the results, we have to add a rule in front such as:

`fib(N,M) ==> write(fib(N,M)).`

Termination. The computation can be made finite by introducing an upper bound `Max`. The query `fib_upto(Max)` will produce all Fibonacci numbers up to `Max`. The constraint `fib_upto(Max)` is also used to introduce the first two Fibonacci numbers.

```
f01@ fib_upto(Max) ==> fib(0,1), fib(1,1).
fn @ fib_upto(Max), fib(N1,M1), fib(N2,M2) ==>
                    Max>N2, N2=:=N1+1 | fib(N2+1,M1+M2).
```

A version that is faster than any one discussed so far can be achieved with a tiny change in the previous program: we turn the propagation rule into a simpagation rule that only keeps the (last) two Fibonacci numbers (we do not need more information to compute the next one).

```
fn @ fib(Max), fib(N2,M2) \ fib(N1,M1) <=>
                Max>N2, N2=:=N1+1 | fib(N2+1,M1+M2).
```

We have exchanged the order of the two `fib` constraints in the head so that the simpagation rule removes the smaller Fibonacci number.

Procedural style version. Since we now keep only the two last Fibonacci numbers, we can merge the three constraints of the head of the `fn` rule into one constraint, and the same for the three constraints that will be present after the rule has been applied (the two kept constraints from the head and the new one from the body). The resulting code is the most efficient:

```
f01@ fib(Max) <=> fib(Max,1,1,1).
fn @ fib(Max,N,M1,M2) <=> Max>N | fib(Max,N+1,M2,M1+M2).
```

2.3.3 Depth first search in trees

In a binary tree the data at the nodes is ordered such that every node in the left subtree is smaller than its parent node and every node in the right subtree is larger than its parent note. We can represent a binary tree by a nested term `node(Data, Lefttree, Rightree)`, where empty trees are denoted by `nil`. The *operation constraint* `dfsearch(Tree,Data)` searches the tree for given data.

```
empty @ dfsearch(nil,X) <=> false.
found @ dfsearch(node(N,L,R),X) <=> X=N | true.
left  @ dfsearch(node(N,L,R),X) <=> X<N | dfsearch(L,X).
right @ dfsearch(node(N,L,R),X) <=> X>N | dfsearch(R,X).
```

This illustrates that CHR allows for recursive descent where one walks through the data.

We can also choose another *granularity* of the data representation, where a node is represented by a CHR constraint and a sequence of such constraints represents the tree. We have to add a unique identifier to each node in the tree and to the `dfsearch` constraint.

```
empty @ nil(I) \ dfsearch(I,X) <=> fail.
found @ node(I,N,L,R) \ dfsearch(I,X) <=> X=N | true.
```

```
left  @ node(I,N,L,R) \ dfsearch(I,X) <=> X<N | dfsearch(L,X).
right @ node(I,N,L,R) \ dfsearch(I,X) <=> X>N | dfsearch(R,X).
```

Actually, we can access the data directly by just mentioning it in the head
of the rule. We abandon the tree data structure and just use a unary CHR
constraint `node(N)`:

```
found @ node(N) \ search(N) <=> true.
empty @ search(N) <=> fail.
```

This illustrates that CHR also supports a topological view of structured
data. Components can be accessed directly by just mentioning them in the
rule head.

2.3.4 Destructive assignment

In a declarative programming language, bound variables cannot be updated
or overwritten. However, in CHR it is possible to simulate the *destructive
(multiple) assignment* of procedural and imperative programming languages
by using recursion in CHR. The original constraint with the old value is
removed and a constraint of the same type with the new value is added. An
optimizing CHR compiler can translate this type of recursion into inplace
updates. Hence destructive assignment can be simulated in constant time.
This is not known to be possible in other pure declarative languages and is
a source of the effectiveness of CHR (cf. Section 4.4), as demonstrated by
an optimal implementation of the union-find algorithm in Chapter 10.

For example, we can store variable name–value pairs in the CHR constraint `cell/2` and use the CHR constraint `assign` to assign to a variable
a new value. This rule expresses the desired update:

```
assign(Var,New), cell(Var,Old) <=> cell(Var,New).
```

Variables are introduced by a `cell` constraint. To access and read the value
of the variable, we use the constraint `cell/2` directly in the rule head that
needs the value.

Note that in CHR, the update in the form of the new `cell` constraint may
trigger further computation. A rule may become applicable (again) that
refers to a suitable `cell` constraint. This behavior results in a *data-driven*
computation.

As usual with destructive updates, the order of the updates matters. A
program consisting of this rule does not have the confluence property and
thus cannot be run in parallel without modifications. This rule is also

a canonical example where the standard first-order declarative semantics (cf. Section 3.4) does not reflect the intended meaning.

2.4 Graph-based algorithms

We implement algorithms that work on a generic class of relations, namely graphs. A *graph* is a binary relation over nodes. We discuss transitive closure, shortest paths, partial order constraints, grammar parsing, and ordered merging and sorting algorithms.

2.4.1 Transitive closure

Transitive closure is an essential operation that occurs in many algorithms, e.g. in graph algorithms, automated reasoning, and inside constraint solvers. The transitive closure R^+ of a binary relation R is the smallest transitive relation that contains R. The relation xR^+y holds iff there exists a finite sequence of elements x_i such that $xRx_1, x_1Rx_2, \ldots, x_{n-1}Rx_n, x_nRy$ holds.

For example, if R is the parent relation, then its transitive closure R^+ is the ancestor relation. If R is the relation between cities connected by direct trains, then R^+ also contains cities reachable by changing trains.

We can depict the relation R as a *directed graph*, where there is a directed edge (arc) from node (vertex) x to node y iff xRy holds. The transitive closure then corresponds to all paths in the graph. The *length of the path* is the number of edges in the path.

We implement the relation xRy as edge constraint e(X,Y) and its transitive closure xR^+y as path constraint p(X,Y).

```
p1 @ e(X,Y) ==> p(X,Y).
pn @ e(X,Y), p(Y,Z) ==> p(X,Z).
```

The implementation in CHR uses two propagation rules that compute the transitive closure *bottom-up*. In the first rule p1, for each edge, a corresponding path is added. The rule reads: if there is an edge from X to Y then there is also a path from X to Y. The second rule pn extends an existing path with an edge in front. It reads: if there is an edge from X to Y and a path from Y to Z then there is also a path from X to Z.

For example, the query e(1,2),e(2,3),e(2,4) adds the path constraints p(1,4), p(2,4), p(1,3), p(2,3), p(1,2). The query e(1,2), e(2,3), e(1,3) will compute p(1,3) *twice*, because there are two ways to go from node 1 to node 3, directly or via node 2.

If we drop the distinction between edges and paths in the transitive closure program, then we can drop rule p1.

```
p(X,Y), p(Y,Z) ==> p(X,Z).
```

Termination. The program does not terminate given a cyclic graph as input. Consider the query e(1,1), where infinitely many paths p(1,1) are generated by rule pn. There are various compiler optimizations and options that avoid the repeated generation of the same constraint, but here we are interested in a source-level solution that works in any current implementation.

Duplicate removal. Termination can be restored by removing duplicate path constraints before they can be used. In other words, we would like to enforce a *set-based semantics* for path constraints. This ensures termination, since in a given finite graph, there can only be a finite number of different paths.

With a simpagation rule we can remove multiple occurrences of a constraint, i.e. *duplicates* (copies); in our case:

```
dp @ p(X,Y) \ p(X,Y) <=> true.
```

This duplicate removal works only if the rule comes first in the program. It also relies on the fact that CHR implementations apply simpagation rules in the right way: they first try to remove the new constraint and keep the old one.

Candidates. There is also a direct and declarative way for a terminating transitive closure program that does not rely on rule order. Having the nodes of the graph also at hand as unary constraint, n, one simply generates all *candidates* for all possible paths, cp, and uses simpagation rules.

```
n(X) ==> cp(X,X).
n(X), n(Y) ==> cp(X,Y).
```

```
e(X,Y) \ cp(X,Y) <=> p(X,Y).
e(X,Y), p(Y,Z) \ cp(X,Z) <=> p(X,Z).
```

Note that the first rule is necessary, since the two n constraints in the head of the second rule can only match different constraints in CHR. The cp constraints remaining after exhaustive application of the rules are those for which *no* path exists, so they form the negation of the path constraint.

For example, the query `n(1)`, `n(2)`, `n(3)`, `e(1,2)`, `e(2,3)` adds the paths `p(1,2)`, `p(2,3)`, `p(1,3)` and a constraint `cp` between all other six pairs of nodes. If we add a cycle to the query `e(3,1)`, all pairs of nodes become paths and no `cp` constraint will be left.

Reachability: single-source and single-target paths. We may specialize the transitive closure rules so that only paths that reach a given single target node are computed. We simply add the target node as a constraint:

```
target(Y), e(X,Y) ==> p(X,Y).
target(Z), e(X,Y), p(Y,Z) ==> p(X,Z).
```

However, this does not work if we want to fix the source node in the same way:

```
source(X), e(X,Y) ==> p(X,Y).
source(X), e(X,Y), p(Y,Z) ==> p(X,Z).
```

The reason is that in the second rule we need a path from Y to Z to be extended, but we only produce paths starting in X. If we exchange the edge and path constraints so that we add an edge at the end of an existing path, then we can add a restriction to a source node as simply as before:

```
source(X), e(X,Y) ==> p(X,Y).
source(X), p(X,Y), e(Y,Z) ==> p(X,Z).
```

Note that any path constraint produced will have the same node as the first argument, that given in the source constraint. Thus, we can simplify the code as follows:

```
p(X) \ p(X) <=> true.
source(X), e(X,Y) ==> p(Y).
      p(Y), e(Y,Z) ==> p(Z).
```

If we replace `source(X)` by `p(X)`, the second rule is not needed any longer. Analogously, we can do this for the single-target node program.

Shortest paths. Let us add an argument to the path constraint that stores the length of the path. When we adapt the duplicate removal rule, we keep the shorter path. This also ensures termination. The path propagated from an edge has length 1. A path of length n extended by an edge has length $n + 1$.

```
p(X,Y,N) \ p(X,Y,M) <=> N=<M | true.
e(X,Y) ==> p(X,Y,1).
e(X,Y), p(Y,Z,N) ==> p(X,Z,N+1).
```

For example, the query e(X,X) reduces to p(X,X,1). For the query e(X,Y),
e(Y,Z), e(X,Z), the answer is e(X,Y), e(Y,Z), e(X,Z), p(X,Z,1),
p(Y,Z,1), p(X,Y,1).

These rules can be generalized to compute shortest distances. Initial
distances are given in the edge constraint. It suffices to replace the constant
1 by the additional distance D:

```
p(X,Y,N) \ p(X,Y,M) <=> N=<M | true.
e(X,Y,D) ==> p(X,Y,D).
e(X,Y,D), p(Y,Z,N) ==> p(X,Z,N+D).
```

2.4.2 Partial order constraint

The classical CHR introductory example is the constraint solver for the
partial order constraint leq (usually written $\leq$). We use infix notation for
the binary constraint leq.

```
duplicate     @ X leq Y \ X leq Y <=> true.

reflexivity   @ X leq X <=> true.
antisymmetry  @ X leq Y , Y leq X <=> X=Y.
transitivity  @ X leq Y , Y leq Z ==> X leq Z.
```

The CHR program implements duplicate removal, and the axioms reflexivity,
antisymmetry, transitivity in a straightforward way. The rule **reflexivity**
removes occurrences of constraints that match X$\leq$X. The rule **antisymmetry**
means that if we find X$\leq$Y as well as Y$\leq$X in the current goal, we can replace
them by the logically equivalent X=Y. The rule **transitivity** propagates
constraints. It adds the logical consequence X$\leq$Z as a redundant constraint,
but does not remove any constraints.

The program can be seen as using the transitive closure rules from Section 2.4.1, where both e and p are replaced by leq, and with rules for
reflexivity and antisymmetry added. Propagation rules are useful, as the
query A leq B, C leq A, B leq C illustrates:

A leq B, C leq A, B leq C
A leq B, C leq A, B leq C, C leq B
A leq B, C leq A, B=C
A=B, B=C

The first two constraints cause the rule **transitivity** to fire, which adds
C leq B to the query. This new constraint together with B leq C matches
the rule head **antisymmetry**, X leq Y, Y leq X. So the two constraints are

replaced by B=C. Since B=C makes B and C equivalent, the rule `antisymmetry` applies to the constraints `A leq B`, `C leq A`, simplifying them to A=B. Now the query contains no more CHR constraints, no more rule application is possible. The program has solved `A leq B`, `C leq A`, `B leq C` and produced the answer `A=B`, `B=C`. Starting from a circular relationship, we have found out that the three variables must be the same.

2.4.3 Grammar parsing

A *(formal) grammar* is defined by *(grammar) (production) rules* of the form `LHS -> RHS`, where each side of the rule is a sequence of symbols. There are two kinds of symbols, *terminal symbols* corresponding to characters in the string, and *nonterminal symbols* standing for sets of strings. Nonterminals are defined by grammar rules. The `LHS` of a rule must contain at least one nonterminal.

In a *context-free grammar*, the `LHS` of each grammar rule is a single nonterminal. Let `A`, `B`, `C` stand for nonterminals, and `T` for a terminal symbol. A context-free grammar is in *Chomsky normal form* if the grammar rules are of the form `A->T` or `A->B*C`.

The *Cocke–Younger–Kasami (CYK) algorithm* parses a string according to a given context-free grammar in Chomsky normal form. This bottom-up algorithm can be seen as a specialization of transitive closure and inherits its properties. The algorithm is also an example of *dynamic programming*.

We will represent the string to be parsed as a *graph chain* of terminal symbols by extending edge constraints `e` by an additional argument for the terminal. A *parse* is just a restricted transitive closure computed *bottom-up* from the string where the path constraint `p` is extended by an additional argument for the nonterminal that is successfully parsed with the subchain.

```
duplicate   @ p(A,I,J) \ p(A,I,J) <=> true.
terminal    @ A->T, e(T,I,J) ==> p(A,I,J).
nonterminal @ A->B*C, p(B,I,J), p(C,J,K) ==> p(A,I,K).
```

With the `duplicate` rule, the program terminates also in the presence of cyclic strings.

Parse tree. We can extend the rules to construct a *parse tree*. With each (partial) parse `p` we store the information from which subparses and which grammar rule it came from. Since no subparses are ever removed, the parse tree information from the subparses can be looked up in the subparses and there is no need to store them in the new parse. (This corresponds to the backpointer approach in imperative languages.) We just have to store in an additional argument of p the arguments from the rule head that do not occur in the rule body. For the `terminal` rule we store T, for the `nonterminal` rule we store B and C as well as J:

```
duplicate    @ p(A,I,J,P) \ p(A,I,J,P) <=> true.
terminal     @ A->T, e(T,I,J) ==> p(A,I,J,t(T)).
nonterminal @ A->B*C, p(B,I,J,P1), p(C,J,K,P2) ==>
                              p(A,I,K,nt(B*C,J)).
```

Generalizations. If there are several definitions for a nonterminal (when it occurs on the l.h.s. of grammar rules), we say that the grammar is *non-deterministic (ambiguous)*, otherwise it is called *deterministic*. Ambiguous grammars will give rise to several possible parses for a given (sub)chain, and thus to a forest of (partial) parse trees. The bottom-up approach taken will produce all possible parses simultaneously. We can also simultaneously parse several strings, even if they share substrings.

We can generalize the algorithm to work with other types of grammars. For example, *regular grammars* just allow grammar rules of the form A->T or A->T*C, i.e. the first symbol on the RHS must be a terminal symbol. It suffices to replace the first p by e in the `nonterminal` rule.

If the grammar rules are fixed, we may compile them away. For example, for each grammar rule of the form A->B*T*C we generate a rule instance:

```
'A->B*T*C' @ p(B,I,J), e(T,J,K), p(C,K,L) ==> p(A,I,L).
```

Given an arbitrary grammar, we just need to chain the path and edge constraints in the CHR rule that corresponds to the sequence of nonterminal and terminal symbols in the grammar rule.

2.4.4 Ordered merging and sorting

To represent a *directed edge (arc)* from node A to node B, we use a binary CHR constraint written in infix notation, A -> B. We use a *chain* of such arcs to represent a sequence of values that are stored in the nodes, e.g. the sequence 0,2,5 is encoded as 0 -> 2, 2 -> 5.

Ordered merging. We assume ordered chains with node values in ascending order. So A -> B now implies that A=<B. We also say that B is the *(immediate) successor* of A.

The following one-rule program performs an ordered merge of two chains by zipping them together, provided they start with the same (smallest) node.

A -> B \ A -> C <=> A<B,B<C | B -> C.

For example, consider the query 0->2, 0->5. It will result in 0->2, 2->5 after one rule application. Given A -> B and A -> C, we add the arc B -> C. In terms of the inequalities that these arcs imply, the arc A -> C now is redundant due to transitivity and is thus removed. The rule in a sense undoes *transitive closure*. It flattens out a *branch* in a graph.

The code works like a zipper. In the rule, A denotes the current position where there is a branch. During computation, all nodes up to A have already been merged, now the successors of A in the two chains are examined. The arc from A to B, the smaller of the two successor nodes of A, is kept, since B must be the immediate successor of A. The second arc is replaced by an arc from B to C. If the first chain is not finished yet, the new branch will be at B now. The rule applies again and again until there is no more branch left because at least one of the chains is used up. (The chains can have different length.)

For example, consider the computation:

0 -> 2, 2 -> 5, 0 -> 3, 3 -> 7.
0 -> 2, 2 -> 5, 2 -> 3, 3 -> 7.
0 -> 2, 3 -> 5, 2 -> 3, 3 -> 7.
0 -> 2, 2 -> 3, 3 -> 5, 5 -> 7.

(The constraints in the answer may not necessarily be sorted in that way.)

Termination and correctness. Applying the rule will not change the number of arcs and the set of involved node values. The nodes on the right of an arc will not change, too. Only a node on the left of an arc may be replaced by a larger node value. Since there is only a finite number of values, the program terminates.

The query consists of two ordered chains with a common first and smallest node. During computation the chains will share a longer and longer common prefix. The application of the rule maintains the invariant that

- the set of values does not change
- the individual arcs are ordered
- the graph is connected
- from the smallest node, all other nodes are reachable
- along all paths, node values are in ascending order.

If the rule is not applicable anymore, there are no more branches in the graph (except for duplicate arcs). So each value has a unique immediate successor. Therefore each path from the smallest node must contain all values in ascending order. Thus the two chains have been merged. There is only one chain, and that chain is ordered.

Duplicate removal. Duplicate values are ignored by the rule due to its guard, as they occur as arcs of the form `A->A`. Also duplicate arcs of the form `A->B, A->B` are ignored. To remove duplicate values and duplicate arcs, we may add the two rules:

```
A -> A   <=> true.
A -> B \ A -> B <=> true.
```

The rule for duplicate arcs can be made redundant when we slightly generalize the guard of our initial merge rule:

```
A -> B \ A -> C <=> A<B, B=<C | B -> C.
```

Concretely, from `A->B, A->B`, the merge rules now produces `A->B, B->B`. The arc `B->B` can be removed by the rule for duplicate values.

Sorting. We can now perform an ordered merge of two chains that are in ascending order. But the merge rule also works with more than two chains. It will actually merge them simultaneously. Based on this observation, we can implement a merge sort algorithm. If we want to sort a set of values, we take a chain of length one for each value. These are arcs of the form `0 -> V`, where `0` is assumed to be a given smallest (dummy) value and `V` is a value. For example, we can have the computation to sort `2, 5, 1, 7`:

```
0 -> 2, 0 -> 5, 0 -> 1, 0 -> 7.
0 -> 2, 2 -> 5, 0 -> 1, 0 -> 7.
1 -> 2, 2 -> 5, 0 -> 1, 0 -> 7.
1 -> 2, 2 -> 5, 0 -> 1, 1 -> 7.
1 -> 2, 2 -> 5, 0 -> 1, 2 -> 7.
1 -> 2, 2 -> 5, 0 -> 1, 5 -> 7.
```

The resulting chain has the ordered values `0, 1, 2, 5, 7`. Applied repeatedly to a left node, the merge rule will find that node's immediate successor. As before, the answer is a single ordered chain of arcs.

In its generality, the code turns a certain type of graph into an ordered chain. Any graph of ordered arcs, where all nodes can be reached from a single root node, can be sorted.

Our one-rule sorting program has quadratic complexity (when indexing is used), an optimal lin-log complexity version is discussed in the analysis section (Section 7.1.5).

2.5 Exercises

2.1 Given some cities as propositional CHR constraints, write some propagation rules that can express which city can be reached directly from which other city. What is the answer to a query that consists of a city? How do you avoid nontermination?

Now use unary CHR constraints of the form `city(NameOfCity)`. What becomes simpler, what not?

Use a set of CHR constraints `direct (City1,City2)` to implement the propagation rules.

Answer:

```
ulm \ ulm <=> true.
...
ulm ==> munich.
munich ==> ulm.
munich ==> salzburg.
...
```

All cities reachable from the city in the query are computed. The duplicate removal rule avoids nontermination.

```
city(A) \ city(A) <=> true.
...
city(ulm) ==> city(munich).
city(munich) ==> city(ulm).
city(munich) ==> city(salzburg).
...
```

Simpagation rules for each city can be merged into one. Propagation rules become more verbose.

```
city(A) \ city(A) <=> true.
...
direct(City1,City2), city(City1) ==> city(City2).
...
```

2.2 Represent colors as propositional CHR constraints `red, blue, ...` Write simplification rules that describe the result of mixing two primary colors. Observe what happens if you have all three primary colors, in different orders, in the query. How do you ensure that the answer is always the same, say `brown`?

Answer:

```
red, blue <=> violet.
red, yellow <=> orange.
blue, yellow <=> green.
red, blue, yellow <=> brown.
```

Confluence can be regained by additional rules, e.g.

```
violet, yellow <=> brown.
```

2.3 In an example from geometry, assume that lines are given by variables (or constants) and that CHR constraints express the relationships between two lines, `parallel` and `orthogonal`. Write propagation rules that derive further such relationships from the given relationships. Ensure termination.

Answer:

```
parallel(L1,L2) \ parallel(L1,L2) <=> true.
(see 2.7)
parallel(L1,L2), parallel(L2,L3) ==> parallel(L1,L3).
orthogonal(L1,L2), orthogonal(L2,L3) ==> parallel(L1,L3).
...
```

2.4 Compute the factorial of a number n, given `fact(1)`,...,`fact(n)`.

Answer:

```
fact(N), fact(M) <=> fact(N*M).
```

2.5 Extend the prime numbers program to factorize numbers.

2.6 What happens if the exchange sort rule is run backwards, i.e. head and body are exchanged?

2.7 The exchange sort rule shall be restricted to considering only neighboring array entries.

Answer:

```
a(I,V), a(J,W) <=> I=:=J+1, V<W | a(I,W), a(J,V).
```

By a similar reasoning as before we can still be sure that the final array will be sorted.

2.8 What does the exchange sort rule do with array constraints where value and index are exchanged, i.e. `a(Value, Index)`?

2.9 Add several natural numbers. Write numbers in successor notation, i.e. `s(s(0))` denotes the number 2. Use two CHR constraints, `add` for each number to add, and `sum` for the resulting sum of all the numbers.

Our query then has the form `add(V1),...,add(Vn),sum(0)`. In the rules consider one `add` constraint at a time. If it contains zero, delete it, because it cannot change the sum. If it is not zero, it is the successor of some number `X`, and so move one successor symbol to the sum.

Answer:

```
add(0) <=> true.
add(s(X)), sum(Y) <=> add(X), sum(s(Y)).
```

The second rule applies until all `add` constraints contain zero, at which point they will be deleted and only the output remains with the sum.

2.10 Compute the number of days in a given year. The calculation is based on the modulo operation for the year and rules to find out if the given year is a leap year. For example, consider the years 1991, 2000, 2004.

Answer:

```
days(Y,D) <=> days(Y mod 4, Y mod 100, Y mod 400, D).

days(Ym4, Ym100, 0, D) <=> D=366.
days(Ym4, 0, Ym400, D) <=> Ym400>0 | D=365.
days(0, Ym100, Ym400, D) <=> Ym100>0 | D=366.
days(Ym4, Ym100, Ym400, D) <=> Ym4>0, Ym400>0 | D=365.
```

2.11 In the Newton approximation of the square root, extend the constraint `improve` with a counter.

2.12 Like the Newton approximation of the square root, implement the approximation of the reciprocal using the formula $G_{i+1} = 2G_i - XG_i^2$.

2.13 Binomial coefficients (Pascal's triangle) can be computed based on the double recursive definition (in functional notation):

$cb(n, k) :=$
if $k = 0$ or $k = n$ then 1
if $k > 0$ and $k < n$ then $cb(n - 1, k) + cb(n - 1, k - 1)$

where $0 \leq k \leq n$. Use a CHR constraint `cb(N,K,B)` and experiment with top-down and bottom-up implementations in analogy to the Fibonacci example.

2.14 Consider the program for transitive closure. What happens if we replace p(X,Y) in the first propagation rule of the original program by p(X,X)? What happens in the program variations?

2.15 Consider the program for transitive closure. To ensure termination, we may have the idea to avoid applications of the second propagation rule when it produces some path again. The same path is produced again if X=Y. Similarly, if Y=Z, we will produce a path that can already be produced by the first propagation rule. Is this sufficient to ensure termination?

Answer: We add a guard to the original propagation rule:

e(X,Y), p(Y,Z) ==> X$\neq$Y,Y$\neq$Z | p(X,Z).

However this alone is not enough to guarantee termination, as soon as we have more than one cycle in the graph. Consider e(1,2), e(2,3), e(3,1), e(2,1).

2.16 Consider the program for computing path lengths. What happens if we replace the guard N=<M of the modified duplicate elimination rule by N=M?

Answer: For the query e(X,Y), e(Y,Z), e(X,Z) the answer will be p(X,Z,1), p(X,Z,2), p(Y,Z,1), p(X,Y,1). The answer shows that there are two paths of different length from node X to node Z. The duplicate rule only removes paths that are also identical in the length. But this now causes nontermination, since e.g. already e(X,X) has infinitely many paths with different lengths from X to X itself (we essentially just count the path lengths up).

2.17 For a car routing application, where nodes correspond to cities, extend the edge constraint e by a third argument that contains the distance between the two cities. Adapt the shortest path program accordingly.

2.18 Consider the program for transitive closure, modified for single sources or target nodes. What happens if there are several target and/or source nodes?

2.19 Based on the program for transitive closure, implement rules for the single-source shortest path computation.

Answer: Specialize the propagation rule with source/1 and extend to shortest paths:

source(X),e(X,Y) ==> p(X,Y,1).
source(X),p(X,Y,N),e(Y,Z) ==> p(X,Z,N+1).

2.20 In a connected Eulerian graph, there exists a path that traverses all nodes. Write a simple program to check if a graph is Eulerian. It suffices to check if each node has the same number of incoming and outgoing edges.

Answer:

```
e(X,Y) ==> e_in(X,Y), e_out(X,Y).
e_in(X,Y), e_out(Y,Z) <=> true.
```

The graph is Eulerian, if no auxiliary edges `e_in` and `e_out` are left.

2.21 Take your last name with `leq` constraints from the partial order example program in Section 2.4.2 between succeeding characters written as variables. For example, the name *Fruehwirth* translates to the query

```
F leq R, R leq U, U leq E, E leq H, H leq W, W leq I,
I leq R, R leq T, T leq H
```

and leads to the answer

```
F leq E, H=E, I=E, R=E, T=E, U=E, W=E.
```

2.22 Define a grammar that admits Gertrud Stein's repetitive sentences about roses, "a rose is a rose", "a rose is a rose is a rose", ... where the terminal symbols are the words in such a sentence.

2.23 Write a rule for admitting grammar rules of the form `A->empty`, where the special symbol `empty` stands for the empty string. These types of rules are usually allowed for regular languages. This extension does not change the expressitivity.

2.24 What happens to the merge sort rule if the guard is weakened to allow the rule to be applicable to `A->A` arcs?

```
A -> B \ A -> C <=> A<B, B<C | B -> C.
```

Answer: If the rule guard allows `A=B`,

```
A -> B \ A -> C <=> A=<B, B<C | B -> C.
```

then the query `A -> A, A -> C` removes and adds `A -> C` again and again. The query does not terminate.

2.25 Consider the classical *Hamming's problem*, which is to compute an ordered ascending chain of all numbers whose only prime factors are 2, 3, or 5. The chain starts with the numbers

$1, 2, 3, 4, 5, 6, 8, 9, 10, 12, 15, 16, 18, 20, 24, 25, \ldots$

Two neighboring numbers later in the chain are 79164837199872 and 79254226206720.

Generate the infinite sequence of Hamming numbers using the merge sort rule with duplicate removal.

The idea for solving this problem is based on the observation: any element of the chain can be obtained by multiplying a previous number of the chain with 2, 3, or 5. The only exception is the initial number 1.

Define a nonterminating process `hamming(N)` that will produce the numbers as elements of the infinite chain starting with value N. We multiply the number N with 2, 3, and 5, and merge them using merge sort. Once we have done this, we know that the successor of N in the chain must be determined, and we can move along the arc starting in N to recursively call `hamming` with that new value.

Answer: To the rules for merge sort we add the following pair of rules:

```
hamming(X) <=> X->X*2, X->X*3, X->X*5, next(X).
X->A \ next(X) <=> writeln(X), hamming(A).
```

Part II
The CHR language

In this formal part of the book, we define the syntax and semantics of the CHR programming language. We will actually define several operational and several declarative semantics. We introduce guaranteed properties of CHR programs such as incrementality and concurrency. We then analyze CHR programs for desired properties such as termination and confluence.

Last but not least we show how to embed essential aspects of other rule-based and graph-based formalisms such as term rewriting, Petri nets, and constraint programming in CHR.

When we present theorems and the like, we will only give the proof idea, detailed proofs can be found in the respective research papers.

3

Syntax and semantics

The *syntax* of a formal language states how the constituents of a language are to be combined to form valid expressions. The abstract description of what it means to execute a certain programming language statement is semantics, we call this the *operational semantics*. The *declarative semantics*, on the other hand, describes the meaning without referring to a way of executing the language. Often, the operational semantics is given by a transition system and the declarative semantics is given in terms of logic.

We wish the operational and declarative semantics to correspond to each other. *Soundness* means that what we compute is correct with regard to the declarative semantics. *Completeness* means that we compute everything that the declarative semantics can prove. Because the logic behind the declarative semantics is too powerful (undecidable), completeness typically cannot be fully achieved.

3.1 Preliminaries

We define logical expressions, their syntactic equality as well as constraint systems and transition systems.

3.1.1 Syntactic expressions

The signature of a first-order-logic language (such as CHR) consists of a set of variables $\mathcal{V}$, a set of function symbols Σ, and a set of predicate symbols Π. Function and predicate symbols are associated with an *arity*, i.e. the number of *arguments* they take. For a symbol f with arity n we use the notation f/n and call this a *functor*. Function symbols with arity zero are called *constants*; predicate symbols with arity zero are called *propositions*.

49

A *term* is a variable or a *function term* of the form $f(t_1, \ldots, t_n)$ where $f/n \in \Sigma$ and each argument t_i is a term. (If $n = 0$ we speak of constants.) An *atomic formula (atom)* is of the form $p(t_1, \ldots, t_n)$ where $p/n \in \Pi$. (If $n = 0$ we speak of propositions.) Terms and atomic formulas as well as sets, multisets, and sequences (lists) are called *(logical) expressions*.

A *ground expression* is an expression that does not contain any variables. A variable is ground if it is bound to a ground term.

3.1.2 Substitution, variants, and equality

A *substitution* θ is a finite function from variables to terms written as $\theta = \{X_1/t_1, \ldots, X_n/t_n\}$, where each $X_i \neq t_i$. We say X_i is *bound (instantiated)* (to t_i). An unbound variable is *free*. We say that a variable is *fixed (determined)* if it is bound to or equivalent to a ground term. If E is an expression and θ a substitution, then $E\theta$ is the expression obtained by simultaneously replacing each occurrence of a variable X_i in E by the term t_i, for each $X_i/t_i \in \theta$. $E\theta$ is called an *instance* of E. We also say that $E\theta$ *matches* E – with *matching substitution* θ. If the expression E is a set or multiset, we can freely reorder the elements of the set so that a matching is possible.

If E and F are expressions, then E and F are *variants* of each other if one is an instance of the other. Variants can be obtained by a bijective renaming of variables. A *renamed apart* expression F of an expression E is a variant of E which has no variables in common with E. A *fresh variant* of an expression contains only new variables that do not occur elsewhere.

Unification (cf. Section 9.4) makes expressions syntactically equivalent by substituting terms for variables. A *unifier* of two expressions E and F is a substitution θ for which $E\theta = F\theta$.

The following classical theorem establishes the relation between syntactic equations and substitutions.

Theorem 3.1 Given two expressions A and B and a substitution $\theta = \{X_1/t_1, \ldots, X_n/t_n\}$, then

$$\forall \theta \; A = B\theta \leftrightarrow (X_1 = t_1 \wedge \cdots \wedge X_n = t_n \rightarrow A = B).$$

An equation of the form $\{p_1, \ldots, p_n\} = \{q_1, \ldots, q_m\}$ is shorthand for $p_1 = q_1 \wedge \ldots \wedge p_n = q_n$ (where the elements of the sets can be permuted) if $n = m$ and for *false* otherwise.

3.1.3 Constraint systems

Constraints are distinguished predicates of first-order logic. Constraint systems take a data type together with its operations and interpret the resulting expressions as constraints. Typically, these constraint systems use the universal data types of numbers to represent scalar data and terms to represent structured data.

A *constraint system* consists of a set of constraint symbols, a set of values called the *domain* and a logical theory CT called *constraint theory* describing the constraints. CT must be nonempty, consistent, and complete. A (constraint) theory CT is *complete*, if for every constraint c either $CT \models \forall c$ or $CT \models \forall \neg c$ holds. CT must include an axiomatization of syntactic equality $=$ together with *true* and *false*. The proposition *true* always holds and *false* never holds. (*false* corresponds to the built-in `fail` of the ISO Prolog Standard.) As usual, $\forall F$ denotes the universal closure of a formula F.

An *atomic constraint* is an atomic formula whose predicate symbol is a constraint symbol. A *constraint* is a conjunction of atomic constraints. The empty conjunction of constraints is equivalent to *true*.

Let the substitution θ map the variables in a constraint C to values of the domain of the associated constraint system. Then θ is a *solution* for C if $C\theta$ holds in the constraint system, i.e. $CT \models C\theta$. A constraint C is *satisfiable (consistent)* if it has a *solution*; otherwise it is *unsatisfiable (inconsistent)*. Two constraints C_1 and C_2 are *(logically) equivalent*, denoted $CT \models \forall(C_1 \leftrightarrow C_2)$, if and only if they have the same solutions.

Two reasoning problems are associated with a constraint: the *satisfaction problem*, i.e. determining whether there exists at least one solution, and the *solution problem*, i.e. determining a particular solution. An algorithm for determining the satisfiability of a constraint is called a *decision procedure* and an implementation also computing the constraint's solution is called a *(constraint) solver*. A solver will typically also simplify constraints.

3.1.4 Transition systems

A transition system is the most abstract way to capture the essence of computation which is change. It is basically a binary relation over states. With such a transition, one can proceed from one state to the next as prescribed by the transition relation.

Definition 3.2 *A (state) transition system (reduction system) T is a pair of the form $T = (S, \mapsto)$ where S is a set of states (configurations) and*

$\mapsto$ *is a binary relation on states,* $\mapsto \subseteq S \times S$*, the* transition (reduction) relation.

A transition system is deterministic *if there is at most one transition from every state, i.e. the transition relation is a partial function; otherwise it is* nondeterministic.

The reachability relation $\mapsto^*$ *is the reflexive transitive closure of* $\mapsto$*.*

Initial states *and* final states *are nonempty subsets of the set of states. Every state* s_i *from which no transition is possible is* final.

A derivation *is a sequence of states* $s_0, s_1, \ldots$*, often written* $s_0 \mapsto s_1 \mapsto \ldots$ *, such that* $s_0 \mapsto s_1 \wedge s_1 \mapsto s_2 \wedge \ldots$ *A derivation is* finite (terminating) *if its sequence is finite, otherwise it is* infinite (diverging, nonterminating)*. The* derivation length *is the number of transitions in a derivation.*

A computation *of* s_0 *is a derivation that starts with an initial state* s_0 *and ends in a final state or is infinite.*

Depending on context, a transition (reduction) is also called a derivation step *or* computation step*.*

The set of states (and the transition relation) may be finite, countably infinite, or infinite. Initial and final states do not need to be disjoint sets. If no initial states are given, all states are initial. Final states can include other states than those that have no successor.

Example 3.1.1 The set of states are the tuples $S = \{(t, p, a, b) \mid 0 \le t, a, b \le 90, p \in \{A, B\}\}$. Initial states are $\{(0, A, 0, 0), (0, B, 0, 0)\}$ and final states are of the form $(90, p, a, b) \in S$.

$$(t, A, a, b) \mapsto (t + 1, A, a+1, b)$$
$$(t, A, a, b) \mapsto (t + 1, A, a, b)$$
$$(t, A, a, b) \mapsto (t + 1, B, a, b)$$
$$(t, B, a, b) \mapsto (t + 1, B, a, b+1)$$
$$(t, B, a, b) \mapsto (t + 1, B, a, b)$$
$$(t, B, a, b) \mapsto (t + 1, A, a, b)$$

While this example will not satisfy real soccer fans, it faithfully models the progression of the goal count over the time of play: the first component of the state is a counter for the minutes that have passed, the second component denotes which team is in possession of the ball, the third and fourth components are the goal counts of the respective teams. After each minute in the game, the ball will either score for the current team, stay with the current team, or pass on to the opponent team. The soccer example is highly nondeterministic, as we expect from a game where no bribery is involved.

The well-known induction principle can be generalized to transition systems.

Definition 3.3 *Let $s_0, s_1, \ldots$ be a computation in a transition system $(\mathcal{S}, \mapsto)$ and let P be a property, called* invariant, *defined over states.*

If the base case $P(s_0)$ *holds and the* induction hypothesis *"$P(s_n)$ implies that $P(s_{n+1})$" holds for all transitions $s_n \mapsto s_{n+1}$ then $P(s_n)$ holds for all states in the derivation.*

For example, we can show by structural induction that the goal score is always less than or equal to 90 in our soccer example: let the invariant $P((t, p, a, b))$ be $t \leq 90$. P clearly holds for the initial states, i.e. the base case holds. By definition, in all other states we have that $0 < t \leq 90$, and all transitions increment the value of t by one. In the final states, $t = 90$. Therefore the induction hypothesis holds and thus the claim holds.

3.2 Abstract syntax

We distinguish between two different kinds of constraints: *built-in (pre-defined) constraints* which are provided by the host language, and *CHR (user-defined) constraints* which are defined by the rules of a CHR program. This distinction allows us to embed and utilize constraints from given constraint solvers. It also allows for side-effect-free host language statements as built-in constraints. In other words, a built-in constraint can be an arbitrary logical relation that can be effectively solved and simplified. Built-in constraint solvers are considered as black boxes whose behavior is trusted and that do not need to be modified or inspected. We assume these solvers are correct, terminating, and confluent. Following Section 3.1.3, built-in constraints are assumed to include *true*, *false*, and syntactic equality $=$. The constraint theory of the built-ins is denoted by $\mathcal{CT}$.

Definition 3.4 *A CHR program P is a finite set of rules. There are three kinds of rules, simplification rules, propagation rules, and simpagation rules. They consist of built-in and CHR constraints. Their syntax is defined in Figure 3.1.*

In the rules, r *is an optional, unique identifier (name) of a rule, the* (multi-) head (left-hand side, l.h.s.) E, *or* E_1 *and* E_2, *is a nonempty conjunction of CHR constraints, the optional* guard (neck) C *is a conjunction of built-in constraints, and the* body (right-hand side, r.h.s.) G *is a goal. A goal is a conjunction of built-in and CHR constraints.*

Built-in constraint:	C, D	$::=$	$c(t_1, \ldots, t_n) \mid C \wedge D, \; n \geq 0$
CHR constraint:	E, F	$::=$	$e(t_1, \ldots, t_n) \mid E \wedge F, \; n \geq 0$
Goal:	G, H	$::=$	$C \mid E \mid G \wedge H$
Simplification rule:	SR	$::=$	$r @ E \Leftrightarrow C \mid G$
Propagation rule:	PR	$::=$	$r @ E \Rightarrow C \mid G$
Simpagation rule:	SPR	$::=$	$r @ E_1 \backslash E_2 \Leftrightarrow C \mid G$
CHR rule:	R	$::=$	$SR \mid PR \mid SPR$
CHR program:	P	$::=$	$\{R_1 \ldots R_m\}, m \geq 0$

Fig. 3.1. Abstract syntax of CHR programs and rules

The guard may be omitted from a rule, this is as if the guard "true |" was present. A query *is a goal.*

Based on this syntax, we define some essential concepts involving variables and CHR constraints of the rules.

Definition 3.5 *The* local variables *of a rule are the variables that do not occur in the rule head. A local variable will be automatically and uniquely generated by the system while the program runs. A CHR rule is* range-restricted *if it has no local variables. A CHR program is range-restricted if all its rules are range-restricted.*

The head constraints of a simplification rule and the head constraints E_2 of a simpagation rule are called removed constraints. *The other head constraints, i.e. those of a propagation rule and E_1 of a simpagation rule, are called* kept constraints.

A CHR constraint is defined *in a CHR program if it occurs in the head of a rule in the program. A CHR constraint is* used *in a CHR program if it occurs in the body of a rule in the program.*

Generalized simpagation rule notation. In the following, we often consider both simplification and propagation rules as special cases of *generalized simpagation rules* of the form

$$E_1 \setminus E_2 \Leftrightarrow C \mid G$$

where E_1 are the kept head constraints and E_2 are the removed head constraints, the guard is C and the body is G. If E_1 is empty, then the rule is equivalent to the simplification rule $E_2 \Leftrightarrow C \mid G$. If E_2 is empty, then the rule is equivalent to the propagation rule $E_1 \Rightarrow C \mid G$. At least one of E_2 and E_1 must be nonempty.

Multiset and sequence notation. The use of first-order logic conjunction as notation emphasizes the close ties of CHR to logic. This conjunction, however, should be understood purely syntactically. Depending on the semantics, it will be interpreted as logical operator, multiset, or sequence forming operator. The empty set is denoted by $\emptyset$. The infix operator $\uplus$ will be used for multiset union. When we treat multisets as sequences, we nondeterministically choose an order for the objects in the multiset. We will use *list* notation for sequences. Thus a *sequence* is either empty, written [], or of the form $[H|T]$ with first element H and remaining (sub)sequence T. The infix operator $+$ denotes sequence concatenation.

3.3 Operational semantics

The operational semantics describes how a program is executed. We have given an informal semantics of CHR in Section 1.2.2. Here we define the operational semantics of CHR by a state transition system. States represent conjunctions of CHR and built-in constraints. A transition corresponds to a rule application.

Starting from a given initial state, CHR rules are applied exhaustively or until a contradiction occurs. A simplification rule replaces instances of the CHR constraints matching its head by its body provided the guard holds. A propagation rule instead adds its body without removing any constraints. A simpagation rule is a hybrid rule that removes only a specified part of the constraints it matches.

We will actually define three operational semantics, with decreasing degree of abstraction. While the first one basically manipulates conjunctions of constraints, the last operational semantics closely follows the behavior of current sequential CHR implementations.

3.3.1 Very abstract semantics

Let P be a CHR program for the CHR constraints and CT be a constraint theory for the built-in constraints. The very abstract operational semantics of CHR is given by a nondeterministic state transition system where the states and the transition relation are defined as follows.

States. States are just goals.

Definition 3.6 *A state is a conjunction of built-in and CHR constraints. An* initial state *(initial goal) is an arbitrary state. A* final state *is one where no transition is possible anymore.*

Note that in the states, the multiplicity of the conjuncts (i.e. atomic constraints) in a conjunction matters, even though logical conjunction is idempotent. We make use of commutativity and associativity of logical conjunction, however. Therefore, we can freely permute the conjuncts in a conjunction.

States can be understood as set comprehensions, i.e. intentional set definitions. A state $E \wedge D$, where E are CHR constraints and D are built-in constraints, stands for the potentially infinite set of ground instances of E, $\{E \mid D\}$. With the help of built-in constraints we can perform computations with possibly infinitely many ground instances.

Transitions. We use rules in head normal form (HNF), where each argument of a head constraint is a unique variable. A rule is put into HNF by replacing its head arguments t_i with a new variable V_i and adding the equations $V_i = t_i$ to its guard. A transition corresponds to a rule application. In Figure 3.2, the transition relation is formally defined. Upper-case letters H_1, H_2, C, B, G stand for (possibly empty) conjunctions of constraints.

Apply
$$(H_1 \wedge H_2 \wedge G) \mapsto_r (H_1 \wedge C \wedge B \wedge G)$$
if there is an instance with new local variables $\bar{x}$ of a rule named r in P,
$$r @ H_1 \backslash H_2 \Leftrightarrow C \mid B$$
$$\text{and } \mathcal{CT} \models \forall (G \rightarrow \exists \bar{x} C)$$

Fig. 3.2. Transition of the very abstract operational semantics of CHR

The CHR transition system for the very abstract semantics is nondeterministic, because in a state, several rules may be applicable. Whenever more than one rule application is possible in a state, one rule application is chosen nondeterministically. This choice cannot be undone, it is *committed-choice*.

An instance (with new local variables $\bar{x}$) of a rule named r from the CHR program P is *applicable* if its head constraints occur in the state and if the *applicability condition* $\mathcal{CT} \models \forall (G \rightarrow \exists \bar{x} C)$ holds. (The notation $\bar{x}$ denotes a set of variables subjected to a quantifier.) The applicability condition checks if the guard C is logically implied (entailed) by the built-in constraints appearing in G. Since $\mathcal{CT}$ only refers to built-in constraints, only the built-in constraints of G are relevant for the applicability condition.

Table 3.1. *Example computation under the very abstract semantics*

	$\text{gcd}(6) \wedge \text{gcd}(9)$
$\longmapsto_{gcd1}$	$\underline{\text{gcd}(6)} \wedge \underline{\text{gcd}(3)}$
$\longmapsto_{gcd1}$	$\underline{\text{gcd}(3)} \wedge \underline{\text{gcd}(3)}$
$\longmapsto_{gcd1}$	$\underline{\text{gcd}(0)} \wedge \text{gcd}(3)$
$\longmapsto_{gcd2}$	$\text{gcd}(3)$

Since this implication checking is more general than simply testing C as condition, rules are more often applicable in this semantics than in current CHR implementations (cf. Example 2.2.1).

If an applicable rule is applied, the CHR constraints H_1 are kept, but the CHR constraints H_2 are removed from the state. The guard C of the rule and its body B are added to the resulting state. The guard C is added, because it may contain variables that also occur in the body B of the rule (and not in the head). A built-in constraint in the body does not act as a test, but asserts (enforces) a certain relation.

Note that CHR constraints can be added and removed by a rule application, while built-in constraints are always added. So the built-ins *monotonically* accumulate information, while the CHR constraints behave *nonmonotonically* in general. Since new variables can be added through the rule body, the accumulation of built-in constraints can in general proceed forever.

Example 3.3.1 Consider the gcd program of Section 2.2.3 in generalized simpagation rule notation.

```
gcd1 @ \ gcd(I) ⇔ I=0 | I=0.
gcd2 @ gcd(I) \ gcd(J) ⇔ J>=I | gcd(J−I).
```

Table 3.1 shows a computation for the query gcd(6) ∧ gcd(9) that leads to the answer gcd(3). For readability, we underline the constraints that are involved in a rule application. No more transitions are possible after the last state, so this is the final state.

3.3.2 CHR with disjunction

The operational semantics of CHR exhibits nondeterminism in the choice of constraints from a state and in the choice of a rule that should be applied to these constraints. These choices are performed by the system and it commits to them. Ideally, these choices should not matter for the result of a computation. Even though the choice of a rule can influence the result, one possible result should be as good as any other result. (The property of confluence (cf. Section 5.2) ensures that.) It is enough to know one result. We therefore speak of *don't-care nondeterminism* that is involved in these choices.

There are situations, however, where we would like to try out several choices, and each of them covers a different case. This kind of nondeterminism is called *don't-know nondeterminism*. In CHR it is usually provided by the host language, e.g. by the built-in *backtrack search* of Prolog and by search libraries in Java. In all Prolog implementations of CHR, the *disjunction* of Prolog can be used in the body of CHR rules.

The semantics of this extension was formalized in the language $CHR^\vee$. Note that any Horn clause (Prolog) program can be directly converted into an equivalent $CHR^\vee$ program (cf. Section 6.3).

Syntax. The part of the syntax of $CHR^\vee$ that is an extension over the syntax of CHR (Figure 3.1) is given in Figure 3.3. It concerns the goals, where logical disjunctions are now allowed.

$$\text{Goal:} \quad G, H \quad ::= \quad C \mid E \mid G \wedge H \mid G \vee H$$

Fig. 3.3. Extended goal syntax for $CHR^\vee$

Configurations. In the extended transition system for $CHR^\vee$, we operate on configurations instead of states. A *configuration* is a disjunction of CHR states, $s_1 \vee s_2 \vee \ldots \vee s_n$ (i.e. a goal where we emphasize disjunctions on the outermost level). Each state in a configuration represents an independent branch of a tree. A configuration is *failed* if all its states have inconsistent built-in constraints. An *initial configuration* is an initial state. A *final configuration* consists of final states only.

Transitions. We can apply the original transitions to single states. In addition, we have the transition for configurations (cf. Figure 3.4). The **Split** transition can always be applied to a configuration in which a state contains a disjunction. It leads to a *branching* in the derivation: the state is split into a disjunction of two states, each of which is processed independently. With this new transition, we construct trees of states rather than sequences of states. Every inner node has two children, one for each disjunct generated. Such trees are called *search trees*. Disjunction is considered to be associative and commutative but not idempotent, just as conjunction. The **Apply** transition applies to a disjunct, i.e. a state inside a configuration. Our previous definitions apply to paths in this search tree.

Split
$$((H_1 \lor H_2) \land G) \lor S \mapsto_\lor (H_1 \land G) \lor (H_2 \land G) \lor S$$

Apply
$$(H_1 \land H_2 \land G) \lor S \mapsto_r (H_1 \land C \land B \land G) \lor S$$
if there is an instance with new variables $\bar{x}$ of a rule named r in P,
$$r @ H_1 \backslash H_2 \Leftrightarrow C \mid B$$
$$\text{and } \mathcal{CT} \models \forall (G \to \exists \bar{x} C)$$

Fig. 3.4. CHR$^\lor$ transitions

Example 3.3.2 The maximum relation from Section 2.3.1 can be implemented in CHR$^\lor$ using a disjunction for the two cases:

max(X,Y,Z) $\Leftrightarrow$ (X$\leq$Y $\land$ Y=Z) $\lor$ (Y$\leq$X $\land$ X=Z).

A max constraint in a query will reduce to the disjunct. For the query max(1,2,M) the first disjunct simplifies to M=2 while the second disjunct leads to a failed state. For the query max(1,2,3) both disjuncts fail. For the query max(1,1,M) both disjuncts reduce to M=1.

3.3.3 Abstract semantics ω_t

The transition system for the very abstract semantics (cf. Section 3.3.1) is so abstract that it does not care much about termination. The trivial reasons for nontermination are states with inconsistent built-in constraints and propagation rules. The same propagation rule can be applied again and again, since additional built-in constraints cannot invalidate an applicability condition that holds. Also, because a false formula implies any formula, the applicability condition trivially holds for inconsistent built-in constraints. In that case, too many rules can be applied, leading to a result with contradictions or to nontermination. The very abstract semantics also does not give an effective means to find the rule instance that is needed to apply a rule. The *abstract operational semantics* of CHR addresses these issues. In addition, in its states it distinguishes between yet unprocessed, CHR and built-in constraints.

The abstract semantics is also called *standard*, *theoretical*, or *high-level* operational semantics. We adopt the ω_t version of the abstract operational semantics which is equivalent to previous formulations of the semantics, but closer in formulation to the refined operational semantics (to be introduced next).

Trivial nontermination. In a failed state, any rule is applicable. This is because the built-in constraints are inconsistent and therefore trivially the rule applicability precondition is satisfied. Since the built-in constraints are accumulated monotonically, a failed state can only lead to another failed state, ad infinitum. It therefore makes sense to identify all failed states and declare them as final states.

If a generalized simpagation rule does not remove any constraints, it represents a propagation rule. Such a rule can be applied again and again. One remedy is a *fair* rule selection strategy that does not ignore a possible rule application infinitely often. With this approach we still do not know how often a propagation rule will be applied.

There are basically two more practical ways to avoid repeated application of propagation rules: either they are not applied a second time to the same constraints or they are not applied if they add constraints that have been added before. Since in CHR, we can remove CHR constraints, the second option would mean keeping track of all removed CHR constraints. Clearly, this is not feasible in general. Therefore the first option is chosen, where we keep track of all CHR constraints to which propagation rules have been applied. This information is called a *propagation history*.

Rules and constraints. Under the view of abstract semantics, the head and body of a rule are no longer conjunctions but multisets of atomic constraints. The guard is a conjunction as before.

To distinguish multiple occurrences (copies, duplicates) of CHR constraints, they are extended by a unique identifier. We use the notation $c\#i$ for a CHR constraint c with identifier i, which is a natural number. We call $c\#i$ a *numbered constraint*. We introduce the functions $chr(c\#i) = c$ and $id(c\#i) = i$, and extend them to sequences and sets of numbered CHR constraints in the obvious way.

States. States now have several components that contain the constraints and additional information.

Definition 3.7 *A ω_t state is a tuple of the form $\langle G, S, B, T \rangle_n^{\mathcal{V}}$.*

- *The* goal *(store) G is a multiset of constraints which contains all constraints to be processed.*

- *The* CHR *(constraint) store S is a set of numbered CHR constraints that can be matched with rules in a given program P.*
- *The* built-in *(constraint) store B is a conjunction of built-in constraints that has been passed to the built-in constraint solver.*
- *The* propagation history T *is a set of tuples (r, I), where r is the name of a rule and I is the sequence of the identifiers of the constraints that matched the head constraints of r.*
- *The* counter n *represents the next free integer that can be used as an identifier for a CHR constraint.*
- *The* sequence $\mathcal{V}$ *contains the variables of the initial goal.*

In short, G contains the constraints that remain to be dealt with, S and B are the CHR and built-in constraints, respectively, that have been processed so far. The propagation history T contains information on which (propagation) rules have been applied to which constraints. Since $\mathcal{V}$ does not change during execution, it will usually be omitted.

Definition 3.8 *Given an* initial goal *(query, problem, call) G with variables $\mathcal{V}$, the* initial state *is $\langle G, \emptyset, true, \emptyset \rangle_1^{\mathcal{V}}$.*

A state $\langle G, S, B, T \rangle_n^{\mathcal{V}}$ with inconsistent built-in constraints $(CT \models \neg \exists\, B)$ is called failed. *A state with consistent built-in constraints and empty goal store $(G = \emptyset)$ is called* successful. *The remaining kinds of states have no special name.*

A final state *is either a successful state where no transition is possible anymore or a failed state. Given a final state $\langle G, S, B, T \rangle_n^{\mathcal{V}}$, its (conditional or qualified)* answer *(solution, result) is the conjunction $\exists \bar{y}(chr(S) \wedge B)$, where $\bar{y}$ are the variables not in ν.*

A failed state leads to an answer with inconsistent built-in constraints. Therefore the answer of any failed state is logically equivalent to *false*.

Transitions. The abstract operational semantics ω_t is based on the three transition rules given in Figure 3.5.

- In the **Solve** transition, the built-in solver adds a built-in constraint from goal G to the built-in constraint store B. The resulting built-in store is simplified, which is indicated by the logical condition $CT \models \forall((c \wedge B) \leftrightarrow B')$. How far the simplification goes is left unspecified. In the worst case, the result is just the original conjunction of the new constraint with the old store.
- The **Introduce** transition adds a CHR constraint to the CHR store S and numbers it with the next free integer n. The counter is incremented to $n+1$.

- The **Apply** transition chooses a rule named r from the program P for which constraints matching its head exist in the CHR store S, and whose guard g is logically implied by the built-in store B under the matching and applies that rule. If an **Apply** transition occurs, we say that the corresponding CHR rule is *applied (fired, executed)*.

Let us discuss the essential **Apply** transition in more detail. When we use a rule from the program, we will rename its variables apart from the program and the current state. A fresh variant of a rule $r @ H_1' \backslash H_2' \Leftrightarrow g \,|\, C$ with new variables $\bar{x}$ is *applicable* to CHR constraints H_1 and H_2 if the applicability condition $CT \models \exists(B) \wedge \forall(B \rightarrow \exists \bar{x}(chr(H_1)=H_1' \wedge chr(H_2)=H_2' \wedge g))$ holds.

The applicability condition first ensures that the built-in constraint store B is satisfiable. It then checks, given the built-in constraints, whether H_1 and H_2 match the head constraints H_1' and H_2' of the rule using the equations $chr(H_1)=H_1' \wedge chr(H_2)=H_2'$. Since the variables from the rule $\bar{x}$ are existentially quantified and the variables from the state are universally quantified, the (simplified) equations correspond to a matching (cf. Theorem 3.1). Under this matching, it is checked if the guard g is logically implied (entailed) by the built-in constraints B under the constraint theory CT. In addition, the condition $(r, id(H_1)+id(H_2)) \notin T$ checks that the propagation history does not contain an entry for the identifiers of the CHR constraints matching the head of the chosen rule.

If an applicable rule is applied (i.e. when it fires), the constraints H_1 are kept, but the constraints H_2 are removed from the CHR store. The equations $chr(H_1)=H_1' \wedge chr(H_2)=H_2'$ and the guard g are added to the built-in constraint store. The body C of the rule is added to the goal store and the propagation history is updated by adding $(r, id(H_1)+id(H_2))$. (In practice, we only need to store this information for generalized simpagation rules that correspond to propagation rules. Entries in the propagation history can be garbage-collected in an implementation if the involved CHR constraints have been removed in the meantime.)

Definition 3.9 *A finite computation is* successful *if its final state is successful and it is* (finitely) failed *if its final state is failed. If the computation has no final state, it is* nonterminating.

Example 3.3.3 Consider the gcd program last mentioned in Section 3.3.1. We explicitly adapt the rule syntax to the abstract semantics in that we use multisets of constraints instead of conjunctions.

```
gcd1 @ ∅ \ {gcd(0)} ⇔ true | true.
gcd2 @ {gcd(I)} \ {gcd(J)} ⇔ J>=I | {K is J−I, gcd(K)}.
```

Solve

$$\langle \{c\} \uplus G, S, B, T \rangle_n \mapsto_{solve} \langle G, S, B', T \rangle_n$$

where c is a built-in constraint and $CT \models \forall((c \wedge B) \leftrightarrow B')$.

Introduce

$$\langle \{c\} \uplus G, S, B, T \rangle_n \mapsto_{introduce} \langle G, \{c\#n\} \cup S, B, T \rangle_{(n+1)}$$

where c is a CHR constraint.

Apply

$$\langle G, H_1 \cup H_2 \cup S, B, T \rangle_n \mapsto_{apply\ r}$$

$$\langle C \uplus G, H_1 \cup S, chr(H_1) = H_1' \wedge chr(H_2) = H_2' \wedge g \wedge B, T \cup \{(r, id(H_1) + id(H_2))\} \rangle_n$$

where there is a fresh variant of a rule named r in P with variables $\bar{x}$ of the form

$$r @ H_1' \backslash H_2' \Leftrightarrow g \mid C$$

where $CT \models \exists(B) \wedge \forall(B \rightarrow \exists \bar{x}(chr(H_1) = H_1' \wedge chr(H_2) = H_2' \wedge g))$ and $(r, id(H_1) + id(H_2)) \notin T$.

Fig. 3.5. Transitions of the abstract operational semantics ω_t

Table 3.2. *Example computation under the abstract semantics ω_t*

	$\langle \{gcd(6), gcd(9)\}, \emptyset \rangle_1$
$\mapsto_{introduce}$	$\langle \{\overline{gcd(9)}\}, \{gcd(6)\#1\} \rangle_2$
$\mapsto_{introduce}$	$\langle \emptyset, \{gcd(6)\#1, gcd(9)\#2\} \rangle_3$
$\mapsto_{apply\ gcd2}$	$\langle \{K_1 \text{ is } 9-6, gcd(K_1)\}, \{gcd(6)\#1\} \rangle_3$
$\mapsto_{solve}$	$\langle \{gcd(3)\}, \{gcd(6)\#1\} \rangle_3$
$\mapsto_{introduce}$	$\langle \emptyset, \{gcd(6)\#1, gcd(3)\#3\} \rangle_4$
$\mapsto_{apply\ gcd2}$	$\langle \{K_2 \text{ is } 6-3, gcd(K_2)\}, \{gcd(3)\#3\} \rangle_4$
$\mapsto_{solve}$	$\langle \{gcd(3)\}, \{gcd(3)\#3\} \rangle_4$
$\mapsto_{introduce}$	$\langle \emptyset, \{gcd(3)\#3, gcd(3)\#4\} \rangle_5$
$\mapsto_{apply\ gcd2}$	$\langle \{K_3 \text{ is } 3-3, gcd(K_3)\}, \{gcd(3)\#3\} \rangle_5$
$\mapsto_{solve}$	$\langle \{gcd(0)\}, \{gcd(3)\#3\} \rangle_5$
$\mapsto_{introduce}$	$\langle \emptyset, \{gcd(3)\#3, gcd(0)\#5\} \rangle_6$
$\mapsto_{apply\ gcd1}$	$\langle \emptyset, \{gcd(3)\#3\} \rangle_6$

Table 3.2 shows again the computation for the query $gcd(6) \wedge gcd(9)$. For readability, we usually apply the resulting variable bindings to all constraints of the state. For the sake of brevity, only G, S, and n are shown, while B, T, and $\mathcal{V}$ have been omitted from the states. The constraints that are involved

in a transition have been underlined for clarity. No more transitions are possible after the last state, so it is the final state.

3.3.4 Refined operational semantics ω_r

The abstract operational semantics of CHR leaves two main sources of non-determinism: the order in which constraints of a goal are processed and the order in which rules are applied (rule scheduling). Current sequential CHR implementations execute goals from left to right and apply rules top-down in the textual order of the program. CHR constraints in a goal are now processed one by one. Currently executing constraints basically behave like a procedure call. This behavior has been formalized in the *refined operational semantics* ω_r of CHR. It was proven to be a concretization of the abstract operational semantics. The refined operational semantics allows the programmer to use more programming idioms and to maximize efficiency at the cost of losing logical properties and declarative concurrency.

Rules and constraints. A CHR program is now a sequence of rules, and the head and body of a rule are considered sequences of atomic constraints. A number is associated with every atomic head constraint, called the *occurrence*. Head constraints are numbered per functor, starting from 1, in top-down order from the first rule to the last rule, and from left to right. However, removed head constraints in a simpagation rule are numbered before kept head constraints.

Example 3.3.4 The gcd program in Section 2.2.3 now looks like this:

```
gcd1 @ [] \ [gcd(0)_1] ⇔ true | true.
gcd2 @ [gcd(I)_3] \ [gcd(J)_2] ⇔ J>=I | [K is J−I, gcd(K)].
```

The **gcd** constraints have been numbered according to the scheme described above.

Definition 3.10 *An* active (occurrenced) *CHR constraint $c\#i{:}j$ is a numbered constraint that should only match with occurrence j of constraint c in a given CHR program P. We extend the function chr to remove occurrence numbers as well, i.e. $chr(c\#i{:}j) = c$.*

States. A ω_r *state* is a tuple $\langle A, S, B, T \rangle_n^{\mathcal{V}}$ where A, S, B, T and n represent the goal, CHR store, built-in store, propagation history, and next free identity number respectively, as in the abstract semantics. Except that the goal

G in the first component of a state has been refined into the *(execution, call, activation, goal) stack A*. It is a *sequence* of built-in and CHR constraints, numbered CHR constraints, and active CHR constraints. Since the goal stack A is now a sequence and not a multiset, we are no longer free to pick any constraint from it. Unlike in the abstract operational semantics, the same numbered constraint may simultaneously appear in both the stack A and the store S.

The notions of initial and final states, successful and failed states, and computations are analogous to those of the abstract semantics.

Transitions. In the refined semantics, constraints in a goal are executed from left to right. Each atomic CHR constraint is basically executed like a procedure call. A constraint under execution is called *active*. The active constraint tries all rules in the textual order of the program.

To try a rule, the active constraint is matched against a head constraint of the rule with the same constraint symbol. If matching partner constraints are found in the store, if the guard check succeeds under the resulting matching, and if the propagation history permits it, the rule applies (fires) and the constraints in its body are executed from left to right.

As with a procedure, when a rule fires, other CHR constraints might be executed and, when they finish, the execution returns to finding rules for the current active constraint. (This approach is used because it corresponds closely to that of the stack-based programming languages to which CHR is typically compiled.)

If the active constraint has not been removed after trying all rules and executing all applicable rules, it will be removed from the stack but be kept in the CHR constraint store. Constraints from the store will be reconsidered (woken) if newly added built-in constraints further constrain variables of the constraint.

The *wake-up policy* of an implementation is a function $wakeup(S, c, B)$ that defines which CHR constraints of S are woken by adding the constraint c to the built-in store B. We say that these constraints are *woken (triggered)* by c. One never wakes constraints that have become ground (i.e. that only contain fixed (determined) variables that are bound to ground terms). In practice, only CHR constraints which may potentially cause a rule to fire are woken. This is the case if the newly added built-in constraint further constrains variables of the constraint. If the same built-in constraints are added a second time, this should not wake any CHR constraints.

The behavior of CHR under the refined semantics ω_r is formalized in the transition system given in Figure 3.6 and explained below.

- The transition **Solve+Wake** now in addition reconsiders CHR constraints for rule applications according to the *wake-up policy* by adding these constraints on top of the stack. These constraints will eventually become active again (via the **Reactivate** transition).

- In the **Activate** transition, a CHR constraint c (that has never been active before) becomes active (with first occurrence 1) and is also introduced into the CHR constraint store. This transition increments the counter n for identifiers. This transition corresponds to the **Introduce** transition of the abstract semantics. We say that the constraint is *added (introduced, posted, called, executed, asserted, imposed)* and becomes active.

- In the **Reactivate** transition, c is a CHR constraint which was woken and re-added to A by **Solve+Wake** but has not been active yet and now becomes active again. The constraint will reconsider all rules of the program in which it occurs. We say the constraint is *woken (triggered, reconsidered, resumed, re-executed)* and becomes active.

- If an **Apply** transition occurs, we say that the corresponding CHR rule is *applied (fired, executed)*. An active constraint is only allowed to match against the constraint in the head of a rule with the same occurrence number. Thus, a rule can only fire if the number of the current active constraint appears in the rule head. If the active constraint matches a removed constraint, it is removed, if it matches a kept constraint, it is kept and remains active.

- In the **Default** transition, the current active constraint cannot be matched against the associated rule and proceeds to the next occurrence in the rules of the program.

- In the **Drop** transition, when there are no more occurrences since all existing ones have been tried thanks to transition **Default**, the currently active constraint is removed from the stack, but stays in the CHR constraint store. We say the constraint is *delayed (suspended, sleeping, waiting)* and becomes *passive (stored)*.

Example 3.3.5 Reconsider the gcd program as given in Example 3.3.4. Table 3.3 shows a computation for the query gcd(6) $\wedge$ gcd(9) under ω_r. As in the example before, only A, S, and n are shown.

Relating abstract and refined semantics. The refined operational semantics ω_r is an instance of the abstract operational semantics ω_t. We can give an abstraction which maps states of ω_r to states of ω_t and ω_r derivations to ω_t derivations while preserving termination. The abstraction

Solve+Wake

$$\langle [c|A], S, B, T\rangle_n \mapsto_{solve+wake} \langle wakeup(S, c, B) + A, S, B', T\rangle_n$$

where c is a built-in constraint and $\mathcal{CT} \models \forall((c \wedge B) \leftrightarrow B')$.

Activate

$$\langle [c|A], S, B, T\rangle_n \mapsto_{activate} \langle [c\#n{:}1|A], \{c\#n\} \cup S, B, T\rangle_{(n+1)}$$

where c is a CHR constraint.

Reactivate

$$\langle [c\#i|A], S, B, T\rangle_n \mapsto_{reactivate} \langle [c\#i{:}1|A], S, B, T\rangle_n$$

where c is a CHR constraint.

Apply

$$\langle [c\#i{:}j|A], H_1 \cup H_2 \cup S, B, T\rangle_n \mapsto_{apply} r$$
$$\langle C + H + A, H_1 \cup S, chr(H_1) = H_1' \wedge chr(H_2) = H_2' \wedge B, T \cup \{(r, id(H_1) + id(H_2))\}\rangle_n$$

where the jth occurrence of a CHR constraint with the same functor as c is in the head $H_1' \backslash H_2'$ of a fresh variant of a rule in program P of the form

$$r \ @ \ H_1' \setminus H_2' \Leftrightarrow g \mid C$$

where $\mathcal{CT} \models \exists(B) \ \wedge \ \forall(B \rightarrow \exists \bar{x}(chr(H_1) = H_1' \wedge chr(H_2) = H_2' \wedge g))$ and $(r, id(H_1) + id(H_2)) \notin T$. $H = [c\#i{:}j]$ if the occurrence for c is in H_1' and $H = []$ if the occurrence is in H_2'.

Drop

$$\langle [c\#i{:}j|A], S, B, T\rangle_n \mapsto_{drop} \langle A, S, B, T\rangle_n$$

where there is no occurrence j for c in P.

Default

$$\langle [c\#i{:}j|A], S, B, T\rangle_n \mapsto_{default} \langle [c\#i{:}j+1|A], S, B, T\rangle_n$$

if no other transition is possible in the current state.

Fig. 3.6. Transitions of the refined operational semantics ω_r

simply removes numbered and active constraints from the stack A in states and removes transitions between states which become identical after the abstraction.

Definition 3.11 *The abstraction function α on states is defined as*

$$\alpha(\langle A, S, B, T\rangle_n^{\mathcal{V}}) = \langle G, S, B, T\rangle_n^{\mathcal{V}},$$

where the unordered multiset G contains all atomic constraints of the sequence A except for active and numbered CHR constraints.

The abstraction function α on derivations is defined as

$$\alpha(s_1 \mapsto s_2 \mapsto \ldots) = \begin{cases} \alpha(s_1) \mapsto \alpha(\ldots) & \text{if } \alpha(s_1) = \alpha(s_2) \\ \alpha(s_1) \mapsto \alpha(s_2) \mapsto \alpha(\ldots) & \text{otherwise.} \end{cases}$$

Table 3.3. *Example computation under the refined semantics* ω_r

	$\langle [\text{gcd}(6), \text{gcd}(9)] \ , \ \emptyset \rangle_1$
$\longmapsto_{activate}$	$\langle [\text{gcd}(6)\#1 : 1, \text{gcd}(9)] \ , \ \{\text{gcd}(6)\#1\} \rangle_2$
$\longmapsto_{default}$	$\langle [\text{gcd}(6)\#1 : 2, \text{gcd}(9)] \ , \ \{\text{gcd}(6)\#1\} \rangle_2$
$\longmapsto_{default}$	$\langle [\text{gcd}(6)\#1 : 3, \text{gcd}(9)] \ , \ \{\text{gcd}(6)\#1\} \rangle_2$
$\longmapsto_{default}$	$\langle [\text{gcd}(6)\#1 : 4, \text{gcd}(9)] \ , \ \{\text{gcd}(6)\#1\} \rangle_2$
$\longmapsto_{drop}$	$\langle [\text{gcd}(9)] \ , \ \{\text{gcd}(6)\#1\} \rangle_2$
$\longmapsto_{activate}$	$\langle [\text{gcd}(9)\#2 : 1] \ , \ \{\text{gcd}(6)\#1, \text{gcd}(9)\#2\} \rangle_3$
$\longmapsto_{default}$	$\langle [\text{gcd}(9)\#2 : 2] \ , \ \{\text{gcd}(6)\#1, \text{gcd}(9)\#2\} \rangle_3$
$\longmapsto_{apply} \text{gcd2}$	$\langle [K_1 \text{ is } 9 - 6, \text{gcd}(K_1)] \ , \ \{\text{gcd}(6)\#1\} \rangle_3$
$\longmapsto_{solve+wake}$	$\langle [\text{gcd}(3)] \ , \ \{\text{gcd}(6)\#1\} \rangle_3$
$\longmapsto_{activate}$	$\langle [\text{gcd}(3)\#3 : 1] \ , \ \{\text{gcd}(6)\#1, \text{gcd}(3)\#3\} \rangle_4$
$\longmapsto_{default}$	$\langle [\text{gcd}(3)\#3 : 2] \ , \ \{\text{gcd}(6)\#1, \text{gcd}(3)\#3\} \rangle_4$
$\longmapsto_{default}$	$\langle [\text{gcd}(3)\#3 : 3] \ , \ \{\text{gcd}(6)\#1, \text{gcd}(3)\#3\} \rangle_4$
$\longmapsto_{apply} \text{gcd2}$	$\langle [K_2 \text{ is } 6 - 3, \text{gcd}(K_2), \text{gcd}(3)\#3 : 3] \ , \ \{\text{gcd}(3)\#3\} \rangle_4$
$\longmapsto_{solve+wake}$	$\langle [\text{gcd}(3), \text{gcd}(3)\#3 : 3] \ , \ \{\text{gcd}(3)\#3\} \rangle_4$
$\longmapsto_{activate}$	$\langle [\text{gcd}(3)\#4 : 1, \text{gcd}(3)\#3 : 3] \ , \ \{\text{gcd}(3)\#3, \text{gcd}(3)\#4\} \rangle_5$
$\longmapsto_{default}$	$\langle [\text{gcd}(3)\#4 : 2, \text{gcd}(3)\#3 : 3] \ , \ \{\text{gcd}(3)\#3, \text{gcd}(3)\#4\} \rangle_5$
$\longmapsto_{apply} \text{gcd2}$	$\langle [K_3 \text{ is } 3 - 3, \text{gcd}(K_3), \text{gcd}(3)\#3 : 3] \ , \ \{\text{gcd}(3)\#3\} \rangle_5$
$\longmapsto_{solve+wake}$	$\langle [\text{gcd}(0), \text{gcd}(3)\#3 : 3] \ , \ \{\text{gcd}(3)\#3\} \rangle_5$
$\longmapsto_{activate}$	$\langle [\text{gcd}(0)\#0 : 1, \text{gcd}(3)\#3 : 3] \ , \ \{\text{gcd}(3)\#3, \text{gcd}(0)\#5\} \rangle_6$
$\longmapsto_{apply} \text{gcd1}$	$\langle [\text{gcd}(3)\#3 : 3] \ , \ \{\text{gcd}(3)\#3\} \rangle_6$
$\longmapsto_{default}$	$\langle [\text{gcd}(3)\#3 : 4] \ , \ \{\text{gcd}(3)\#3\} \rangle_6$
$\longmapsto_{drop}$	$\langle [] \ , \ \{\text{gcd}(3)\#3\} \rangle_6$

The abstraction function produces a valid and correct derivation under the abstract semantics.

Theorem 3.12 For all ω_r derivations D, $\alpha(D)$ is a ω_t derivation.

If D is a terminating computation, then $\alpha(D)$ is a terminating computation.

Proof. The first claim is shown by induction on the derivation length and case distinction according to the possible transitions in the refined semantics ω_r.

The second claim is proven by showing that a (reachable) final state is mapped onto a final state by the abstraction function.

Considering arbitrary derivations from a given goal, termination (and confluence) under the abstract semantics are preserved under the refined semantics, but not the other way round.

While it fixes the constraint and rule order for execution, the refined operational semantics is still *nondeterministic*. First, in the **Solve+Wake** transition, the order in which constraints are added to the stack by the wake-up-policy function is left unspecified. The second source of nondeterminism is the *matching order* in the **Apply** transition, where we do not know which partner constraints (H_1 and H_2) from the store may be chosen for the transition, if more than one possibility exists. With this remaining nondeterminism, we capture the behavior of most CHR implementations, including optimizations.

3.4 Declarative semantics

The declarative semantics associates a program with a logical theory. This logical reading should coincide with the intended meaning of the program. A declarative semantics facilitates nontrivial program analysis, foremost for correctness, program transformation, and composition of programs.

3.4.1 First-order logic declarative semantics

The logical reading of a CHR program consists of the logical reading of its rules (defining the CHR constraints) and of its built-in constraints.

Logical reading of rules. A rule logically relates head and body provided the guard is true. A simplification rule means that the head is true if and only if the body is true. A propagation rule means that the body is true if the head is true. The propagation rule denotes an implication. Thus the naming of *head* and *body* is in the wrong order. Still, CHR uses that naming convention due to its roots in Prolog.

Definition 3.13 *The* logical reading (meaning) *of the three types of rules is as follows:*

Simplification rule: $H \Leftrightarrow C \mid B$ $\qquad \forall (C \to (H \leftrightarrow \exists \bar{y} \, B))$
Propagation rule: $\quad H \Rightarrow C \mid B$ $\qquad \forall (C \to (H \to \exists \bar{y} \, B))$
Simpagation rule: $\quad H_1 \backslash H_2 \Leftrightarrow C \mid B$ $\;\; \forall (C \to ((H_1 \wedge H_2) \leftrightarrow (H_1 \wedge \exists \bar{y} \, B)))$

The sequence $\bar{y}$ contains those local variables that appear only in the body B of the rule.

The logical reading of a simplification rule or simpagation rule is a logical equivalence provided the guard holds. For a propagation rule it is an implication provided the guard holds.

Example 3.4.1 The logical reading of the order relation program in Example 2.4.2 is straightforward and very similar to the program itself:

```
(duplicate)     ∀ X,Y    (X≤Y ∧ X≤Y ⇔ X≤Y)
(reflexivity)   ∀ X      (X≤X ⇔ true)
(antisymmetry)  ∀ X,Y    (X≤Y ∧ Y≤X ⇔ X=Y)
(transitivity)  ∀ X,Y,Z  (X≤Y ∧ Y≤Z ⇒ X≤Z)
```

The duplicate rule states the tautology (due to idempotence of logical conjunction) that X≤Y ∧ X≤Y is logically equivalent to X≤Y. The reflexivity rule states that X≤X is logically true. The antisymmetry rule means X≤Y ∧ Y≤X is logically equivalent to X=Y. The transitivity rule states that the conjunction of X≤Y and Y≤Z implies X≤Z. All variables are universally quantified.

Logical reading and equivalence of programs. For the declarative semantics of a program, we also have to take the meaning of the built-in constraints into account.

Definition 3.14 *The logical reading of a CHR program P is $\mathcal{P}, CT$, the conjunction of the logical reading of the rules in P, denoted by $\mathcal{P}$, and of the constraint theory CT that defines the built-in constraint symbols used in P.*

We can also define what logically equivalent programs are.

Definition 3.15 *Let P_1 and P_2 be CHR programs and let CT be the appropriate constraint theory. P_1 and P_2 are logically equivalent iff their logical meanings $\mathcal{P}_1$ and $\mathcal{P}_2$ are equivalent:*

$$CT \models \mathcal{P}_1 \leftrightarrow \mathcal{P}_2.$$

Before we write a program, we can specify the intended meaning of the program as logical theory. Then CHR programs can be formally verified on the basis of their declarative semantics. We say that the program is logically correct if its logical reading is the consequence of a given logical specification.

Definition 3.16 *A logical specification T for a CHR program P is a consistent theory for the CHR constraints in P. A program P is logically correct with respect to specification T iff*

$$T, CT \models \mathcal{P}.$$

By this definition, $\mathcal{P}$ need not cover all consequences of $\mathcal{T}$, since the consequence relation holds only in one direction.

Logical reading of states. The logical reading of a state is basically the conjunction of its constraints. Thus, the logical reading of a state in the very abstract semantics is just the state itself. For the abstract and refined semantics we define it as follows.

Definition 3.17 *The* local variables *of a state are the variables not in* $\mathcal{V}$.

The logical reading (meaning) *of an* ω_t *state or an* ω_r *state of the form* $\langle G, S, B, T \rangle_n^{\mathcal{V}}$ *is the formula*

$$\exists \bar{y} \, (G \wedge chr(S) \wedge B),$$

where $\bar{y}$ *are the local variables of the state.*

Empty sequences, sets, or multisets are interpreted as *true*. The variables in $\mathcal{V}$ are not quantified. Remember that the function *chr* removes the identifiers and occurrence numbers from atomic CHR constraints. The local variables in a state come from the local variables of rules that are introduced by their application. The definition coincides with that of a query for initial states and that of an answer for final states, see Definition 3.8.

Equivalence of states. With the definition of the logical reading of states we can talk about their logical equivalence. However, a slightly stricter notion of equivalence is useful, where we take into account the multiset character of CHR constraints and consider all failed states as equivalent. The idea is that to equivalent states, the same rules should be applicable. When we view states as set comprehensions, this amounts to requiring that the states define the same set of ground CHR constraints.

Definition 3.18 *Two states of the very abstract semantics* $s_i = (B_i \wedge C_i)$ ($i{=}1, 2$), *where* B_i *are built-in constraints,* C_i *are CHR constraints, and with local variables* $\bar{y}_i$ *that have been renamed apart, are* (state-)equivalent, *written* $s_1 \equiv s_2$, *iff*

$$\mathcal{CT} \models \forall(\exists \bar{y}_1 B_1 \leftrightarrow \exists \bar{y}_2 B_2) \wedge \forall(B_1 \rightarrow \exists \bar{y}_2(C_1{=}C_2)) \wedge \forall(B_2 \rightarrow \exists \bar{y}_1(C_1{=}C_2)).$$

Two ω_t *(or* ω_r*) states* $s_i = \langle G_i, C_i, B_i, T_i \rangle_n^{\mathcal{V}}$ ($i{=}1, 2$), *with local variables* $\bar{y}_i$ *that have been renamed apart and where* $D_i = (\tau(G_i), \tau(C_i), alive(\tau(C_i), \tau(T_i)))$, *with* τ *a renaming of the numeric CHR constraint identifiers, are* (state-)equivalent, *iff*

$$\mathcal{CT} \models \forall(\exists \bar{y}_1 B_1 \leftrightarrow \exists \bar{y}_2 B_2) \wedge \forall(B_1 \rightarrow \exists \bar{y}_2(D_1{=}D_2)) \wedge \forall(B_2 \rightarrow \exists \bar{y}_1(D_1{=}D_2)).$$

The function alive(C, T) returns the subset of tuple entries in T that only contain identifiers from C.

The global variables of the states are universally quantified, the local variables are existentially quantified. The first condition $\forall(\exists \bar{y}_1 B_1 \leftrightarrow \exists \bar{y}_2 B_2)$ ensures logical equivalence of the built-in constraints in the two states. The second and third conditions make sure that CHR constraints and propagation histories are syntactically equivalent up to renaming of local variables and modulo the instantiation of determined variables as prescribed by the built-in constraints. The similarity of these conditions with the application condition of the operational semantics is not accidental. The function $alive(C, T)$ cleans up the propagation history by deleting entries that contain identifiers of CHR constraints that have been removed (they do not occur in C anymore). The function τ renames constraint identifiers so that corresponding CHR constraints and propagation histories become syntactically equivalent. If both states are failed, the conditions are trivially satisfied. The definition also implies that the states are logically equivalent.

We may also say that two states under the very abstract semantics are equivalent if they are syntactically equivalent modulo permutation of atomic CHR constraints, instantiation of variables determined by the built-in constraints, renaming of local variables, logical equivalence of built-in constraints, and failure.

For example, the two states with the logical reading $q(X) \wedge X = a$ and $\exists Y q(a) \wedge X = Y \wedge Y = a$ are equivalent. The state $q(a)$ is not equivalent to these states. However, if X is not a global variable, then the resulting three formulas $\exists X q(X) \wedge X = a$, $\exists X, Y q(a) \wedge X = Y \wedge Y = a$, and $q(a)$ are equivalent. However, the state $q(a) \wedge q(a)$ is not equivalent to these states.

Soundness and completeness

In the ideal case, the operational and declarative semantics should coincide, i.e. we would like to have soundness and completeness results between the two semantics. However, completeness cannot be fully achieved, because the logic behind the declarative semantics is too powerful (undecidable).

Still, the soundness and completeness theorems for CHR semantics show that operational and declarative first-order-logic semantics are strongly related. However, some additional conditions are necessary to improve on the completeness. These results are based on the fact that the transitions for CHR preserve the logical reading of states, i.e. all states in a derivation are logically equivalent.

Solve

$$\mathcal{CT} \models (\exists \bar{y}(c \wedge G \wedge chr(S) \wedge B) \leftrightarrow_{solve} \exists \bar{y}(G \wedge chr(S) \wedge B'))$$
where c is a built-in constraint and $\mathcal{CT} \models \forall((c \wedge B) \leftrightarrow B')$.

Introduce

$$\mathcal{CT} \models (\exists \bar{y}(c \wedge G \wedge chr(S) \wedge B) \leftrightarrow_{introduce} \exists \bar{y}(G \wedge c \wedge chr(S) \wedge B))$$
where c is a CHR constraint.

Apply

$$\mathcal{CT} \models (\exists \bar{y}(G \wedge chr(H_1) \wedge chr(H_2) \wedge chr(S) \wedge B) \leftrightarrow_{apply\ r}$$
$$\exists \bar{y}, \bar{x}, \bar{y}'(C \wedge G \wedge chr(H_1) \wedge chr(S) \wedge chr(H_1){=}H_1' \wedge chr(H_2){=}H_2' \wedge g \wedge B))$$
and there is a rule named r in P with logical reading

$$\forall \bar{x}(g \rightarrow ((H_1' \wedge H_2') \leftrightarrow \exists \bar{y}'(H_1' \wedge C)))$$

where $\bar{x}, \bar{y}'$ are the variables of the rule with $\bar{y}'$ the variables that only occur in the body, and $\mathcal{CT} \models \forall \exists(B) \wedge (B \rightarrow \exists \bar{x}, \bar{y}'(chr(H_1){=}H_1' \wedge chr(H_2){=}H_2' \wedge g))$.

Fig. 3.7. Logical reading of ω_t transitions

The following results apply to the abstract operational semantics w_t and first-order-logic declarative semantics. In the following, let P be a CHR program and G be a goal.

Lemma 3.19 If C is the logical reading of a state appearing in a derivation of the goal G, then

$$\mathcal{P}, \mathcal{CT} \models \forall (C \leftrightarrow G).$$

Proof. The proof is by structural induction over the transitions considering their logical reading. If we replace the states, the rules, and the rule applicability condition in the transitions of the abstract operational semantics ω_t of CHR by their logical reading, we will get the formulas given in Figure 3.7. In the figure, the variables $\bar{y}$ are those variables of the state that do not occur in $\mathcal{V}$ and $\bar{x}, \bar{y}'$ are the variables of the rule. We can then show that the preconditions of the transitions imply that the states in a transition are logically equivalent.

For a given goal, all states in a computation are logically equivalent to each other.

Lemma 3.20 For the logical reading C_1 and C_2 of two states in a computation of G,

$$\mathcal{P}, \mathcal{CT} \models \forall (C_1 \leftrightarrow C_2).$$

Proof. Immediately from Lemma 3.19.

In the soundness and completeness results for CHR, there is no need to distinguish between successful and failed computations.

Theorem 3.21 (Soundness) If G has a computation with answer C then

$$\mathcal{P}, \mathcal{CT} \models \forall\, (C \leftrightarrow G).$$

Proof. Immediately from Lemma 3.19.

Theorem 3.22 (Completeness) Let G be a goal with at least one finite computation and C be a goal. If $\mathcal{P}, \mathcal{CT} \models \forall\, (C \leftrightarrow G)$, then G has a finite computation with answer C' such that

$$\mathcal{P}, \mathcal{CT} \models \forall\, (C \leftrightarrow C').$$

Proof. Immediately from Theorem 3.21.

The completeness theorem does not hold if G has no finite computations.

Example 3.4.2 Let P be the CHR program

p $\Leftrightarrow$ p.

Let G be p. It holds that $\mathcal{P}, \mathcal{CT} \models$ p $\leftrightarrow$ p since $\mathcal{P}$ is $\{\text{p} \leftrightarrow \text{p}\}$. However, G has only infinite computations, so there is no answer we can use.

The soundness theorem (Theorem 3.21) can be specialized to failed computations.

Corollary 3.23 (Soundness of failed computations) If G has a failed computation, then

$$\mathcal{P}, \mathcal{CT} \models \neg \exists G.$$

Proof. By Theorem 3.21.

However, an analogous completeness result, that is, the converse of Corollary 3.23, does not hold in general.

Example 3.4.3 Let P be the CHR program

p $\Leftrightarrow$ q.
p $\Leftrightarrow$ *false*.

$\mathcal{P}, \mathcal{CT} \models \neg$q, but q has no failed computation.

Thus, the completeness theorem (Theorem 3.22) is weak, especially for failed computations.

Example 3.4.4 The discrepancy between operational and declarative semantics lies in the additional reasoning power of first-order logic. Let P be the CHR program

```
a ⇔ b.
a ⇔ c.
```

From the logical reading of the program $\mathcal{P}, \mathcal{CT}$ follows, for example, $a \leftrightarrow b$, $a \leftrightarrow c$, but also $b \leftrightarrow a$, $b \leftrightarrow c$, $a \leftrightarrow b \wedge c$, and $a \wedge b \leftrightarrow b \wedge c$, actually any logical equivalence between nonempty conjunctions consisting of a, b, and c holds. However, the only computations possible are $a \mapsto b$, $a \mapsto c$, as well as $b \mapsto^0 b$, and $c \mapsto^0 c$.

A stronger completeness result can be given for programs with a consistent logical reading and data-sufficient goals.

Definition 3.24 *A goal is* data-sufficient *if it has a computation ending in a final state of the form* $\langle \emptyset, \emptyset, B, T \rangle_n^\mathcal{V}$.

So there are no CHR constraints in the final state.

Theorem 3.25 (Stronger completeness of failed computations) Let P be a CHR program with a consistent logical reading and G be a data-sufficient goal. If $\mathcal{P}, \mathcal{CT} \models \neg \exists G$ then G has a failed computation.

Proof. By Theorem 3.21, by consistency and the fact that a final state contains only built-in constraints, because G is data-sufficient.

We will see that the confluence property introduced in Section 5.2 will further improve soundness and completeness results for CHR (see Section 5.2.7).

3.4.2 Linear logic declarative semantics

The classical logic declarative semantics does not suffice when CHR is used as a general-purpose concurrent programming language. Rules about distribution, objects, or agents involve nonmonotonicity, e.g. dynamic updates and state changes caused by actions or method calls, as opposed to rules for declarative constraint solving that model equivalence and implication of constraints. First-order logic cannot handle change without resorting to auxiliary constructions like adding time-stamps to predicates. In CHR, we can model changes by removing and adding CHR constraints. Thus, CHR implementations of such algorithms do not have the intended first-order-logic reading (cf. Chapter 10).

This problem has led to the development of an alternative declarative semantics. It is based on *linear logic* that can model resource consumption (it also embeds classical logic). Also, the linear logic semantics for CHR$^\vee$ preserves the clear distinction between don't-care and don't-know nondeterminism in CHR$^\vee$ by mapping it to the dualism of internal and external choice in linear logic. The resulting soundness and completeness theorems are stronger than those of the classical first-order predicate logic declarative semantics.

Intuitionistic linear logic. We will limit our focus to a commonly used segment of linear logic, called intuitionistic linear logic. The syntax of intuitionistic linear logic is given in Figure 3.8.

$$L ::= p(\bar{t}) \mid L \multimap L \mid L \otimes L \mid L \& L \mid L \oplus L \mid !L \mid \exists x.L \mid \forall x.L \mid \top \mid 1 \mid 0$$

Fig. 3.8. Syntax of intuitionistic linear logic

The atoms $p(\bar{t})$ of (intuitionistic) linear logic are generally considered to represent resources rather than formulas. These atoms may be consumed during the process of reasoning.

The $\otimes$ *("times") conjunction* (multiplicative conjunction) is similar to conjunction in classical logic. The formula $A \otimes B$ denotes the resource that is available iff both A and B are available. Multiplicities matter, the atomic formula (A) is *not* equivalent to the formula $(A \otimes A)$. The *constant 1* represents the empty resource and is the neutral element of $\otimes$. It corresponds to *true* in first-order logic.

Linear implication $\multimap$ *("lollipop")* differs from classical implication. The precondition is consumed when used in reasoning. A formula $A \multimap B$ (*"consume A yielding B"*) means that we can replace one instance of a resource A (that we dispose of) for one instance of a resource B. Note that the formula $(A \multimap B)$ is a resource itself, and as such is used up when applied.

The *!* *("bang") modality* marks stable facts or unlimited resources. Thus, a *banged* resource is *not consumed* during reasoning.

Linear logic distinguishes between internal and external choice, i.e. between decisions that can be made during the process of reasoning and decisions of undetermined result (e.g. those enforced by the environment).

The $\&$ *("with") conjunction* (additive conjunction) expresses *internal* choice. The formula $A \& B$ (*"either A or B"*) does imply A or B. However, it does *not* imply $A \otimes B$. The *constant* $\top$ *("top")* is the neutral element of &.

The $\oplus$ *disjunction* expresses *external* choice. The formula $A \oplus B$ in itself neither implies A alone nor B alone. It is similar to classical disjunction. The *constant 0* represents failure. It is the neutral element of $\oplus$.

Intuitionistic linear logic semantics. Figure 3.9 summarizes the intuitionistic linear logic semantics of CHR. The operator $.^L$ represents translation into linear logic. The main differences to the classical first-order-logic semantics of CHR are the interpretation of CHR constraints as linear resources and of built-in constraints as embedded intuitionistic formulas, as well as the logical reading of CHR rules as expressing linear implication rather than logical equivalence.

Built-in constraints:	$true^L$	$::=$	1
	$false^L$	$::=$	0
	$c(\bar{t})^L$	$::=$	$!c(\bar{t})$
CHR constraints:	$e(\bar{t})^L$	$::=$	$e(\bar{t})$
Goals:	$(G \wedge H)^L$	$::=$	$G^L \otimes H^L$
	$(G \vee H)^L$	$::=$	$G^L \oplus H^L$
Configuration:	$(S \vee T)^L$	$::=$	$S^L \oplus T^L$
Simpagation rule:	$(E \backslash F \Leftrightarrow C \| G)^L$	$::=$	$!(\forall\, (C^L \multimap (E^L \otimes F^L \multimap E^L \otimes \exists \bar{y} G^L)))$
CHR program:	$\{R_1 \dots R_m\}^L$	$::=$	$R_1^L \otimes \dots \otimes R_m^L$

Fig. 3.9. Linear logic declarative semantics P^L of a $CHR^\vee$ program

Constraints are mapped to $\otimes$ conjunctions of their atomic constraints, atomic built-in constraints are banged. As a result, built-in constraints are treated as unlimited resources similar to first-order logic. The constraint theory $\mathcal{CT}$, which we require to be of intuitionistic logic, is translated from the first-order-logic theory according to the *Girard's Translation*. Disjunctions are mapped to $\oplus$ disjunctions.

$CHR^\vee$ rules are mapped to linear implications between head and body, instead of classical logic equivalence. It means that consuming (part of) the head produces the body. Also, linear logic implication is not commutative, its direction of reasoning cannot be reversed. This clearly models the operational semantics of (simplification) rules more faithfully then classical logic does. As before, the variables $\bar{y}$ are those that only appear in the body G of a rule. The formula for the rule is banged, since it is to be used more than once. Finally, a $CHR^\vee$ program is translated into a $\otimes$ conjunction of the translation of its rules.

Example 3.4.5 As an example for an inconsistent first-order-logic reading, consider a coin-throw simulator defined by the two rules:

```
throw(Coin) ⇔ Coin = head
throw(Coin) ⇔ Coin = tail
```

The program handles the constraint `throw(Coin)` by committing to one of the rules, thereby equating either `head` or `tail` with the variable `Coin`. Its classical declarative semantics is:

$$\forall(throw(Coin) \leftrightarrow (Coin{=}head)) \wedge (throw(Coin) \leftrightarrow (Coin{=}tail)).$$

From this we can conclude $(Coin{=}head) \leftrightarrow (Coin{=}tail)$ and therefore *head=tail*, i.e. both sides of our coin are equal. This statement is not consistent with the intuitive idea of a coin throw. The program describes a course of action. The logical reading misinterprets it as a description of stable facts.

In contrast, the linear logic reading is:

$$!\forall(throw(Coin){\multimap}!(Coin{=}head))\otimes!(throw(Coin){\multimap}!(Coin{=}tail)).$$

This is logically equivalent to:

$$!\forall(throw(Coin){\multimap}!(Coin{=}head)\&!(Coin{=}tail)).$$

This formula reads as "Of course, consuming $throw(Coin)$ produces: choose from $Coin{=}head$ and $Coin{=}tail$". In other words, we can replace $throw(Coin)$ with either $Coin{=}head$ or $Coin{=}tail$ but not both at the same time, i.e. a *committed choice* takes place.

Example 3.4.6 Consider the destructive assignment rule from Section 2.3.4:

`assign(Var,New) ∧ cell(Var,Old) ⇔ cell(Var,New).`

The classical logical reading of the rule,

$$\forall(assign(Var, New) \wedge cell(Var, Old) \Leftrightarrow cell(Var, New)),$$

stipulates that the variable `Var` has the old and new value simultaneously, since it is logically equivalent to

$$\forall(assign(Var, New) \wedge cell(Var, Old) \Leftrightarrow cell(Var, Old) \wedge cell(Var, New)).$$

In contrast, the linear logic reading is:

$$!\forall(assign(Var, New) \otimes cell(Var, Old) \multimap cell(Var, New)).$$

This reads as "Of course, consuming `assign(Var,New)` and `cell(Var,Old)` produces `cell(Var,New)`". This reading properly reflects the dynamics of the destructive update.

Example 3.4.7 Consider the classical declarative semantics of the constraint `prime` from Section 2.2.4:

$$\forall((M \bmod N = 0) \rightarrow (prime(M) \wedge prime(N) \leftrightarrow prime(N))).$$

The logical formula actually says that "a number is prime, if it is a multiple of another prime number", i.e. a composite number. This is not the intended meaning. The prime constraints initially represent candidates for primes. Only upon completion of the calculation do they represent the actual primes. Classical first-order logic has no straightforward means to express this dynamics.

The linear logic reading for the constraint `prime` is as follows:

$$!\forall(!(M \bmod N = 0) \multimap (prime(M) \otimes prime(N) \multimap prime(N))).$$

This reads as "Of course, consuming `prime(M)` and `prime(N)` where (M mod N = 0) produces `prime(N)`". This reading properly reflects the dynamics of the filtering that leads to prime numbers.

Example 3.4.8 Next we deal with birds and penguins.

```
bird ⇔ albatross ∨ penguin.
penguin ∧ flies ⇔ false.
```

The first rule says that a bird may either be an albatross or a penguin. In the second rule, an integrity constraint is given, stating that a penguin cannot fly.

Here the first-order logical reading is correct:

$$(bird \leftrightarrow albatross \vee penguin) \wedge (penguin \wedge flies \leftrightarrow false).$$

The linear logic reading of this CHR$^\vee$ program is the logical formula

$$!(bird \multimap albatross \oplus penguin) \otimes !(penguin \otimes flies \multimap 0).$$

This interpretation is indeed faithful to the operational semantics of CHR$^\vee$ as it logically implies the formula

$$bird \otimes flies \multimap albatross \otimes flies.$$

A conjunction of `bird` and `flies` can be mapped to a conjunction of `albatross` and `flies`.

This is also a simple classic example of default reasoning and abductive reasoning. *Abducibles* are predicates that are only partially defined by integrity constraints. We can implement abducibles as CHR constraints and integrity constraints as CHR rules. In the example, `flies` is an abducible.

Soundness and completeness. Concerning soundness, our approach is analogous to that used in the classical framework. We rely on Lemma 3.26, which proves that any configuration in a derivation is linearly implied by the logical reading of the initial configuration.

In the following, let P be a CHR$^\vee$ program, P^L be its linear logic reading, and $!CT^L$ be the constraint theory for the built-in constraints. Let S_0 be an initial configuration and let S_n and S_m be configurations. The turnstile symbol $\vdash$ denotes deducability w.r.t. the sequent calculus of intuitionistic linear logic.

Lemma 3.26 If S_n appears in a derivation of S_0 in P then

$$P^L, !CT^L \vdash \forall(S_0^L \multimap S_n^L).$$

Proof. The proof is analogous to the respective proof in the classical logic case.

From this lemma, Theorem 3.27 follows directly.

Theorem 3.27 (Soundness) If S_0 has a computation with final configuration S_n^L in P, then

$$P^L, !CT^L \vdash \forall \left(S_0^L \multimap S_n^L\right).$$

Proof. The proof is analogous to the respective proof in the classical logic case.

We have a rather strong completeness theorem. The theorem and its proof are different to the classical logic case.

Theorem 3.28 (Completeness) If

$$P^L, !CT^L \vdash \forall \left(S_0^L \multimap S_n^L\right)$$

then there is a configuration S_m in a finite prefix of a derivation of S_0 such that

$$!\mathcal{CT}^L \vdash S_m^L \multimap S_n^L.$$

Proof. The first element of the proof is to use *restricted* sequents. In a restricted sequent, every logical reading $(!\rho)$ of a CHR$^\vee$ rule is substituted by a finite number of formulas of the form $(1\&\rho)$. The number of CHR$^\vee$ rule applications is not strictly determined, but limited. We prove this by defining a set of transformation rules that transform a sequent calculus proof tree of our original sequent into a formal proof of the restricted sequent.

We then show that we can apply CHR$^\vee$ transformations to the initial configuration S_0, such that the logical reading of the resulting configuration also implies $\bar{S}_n^L$. This is easy to show for the transitions **Solve** and **Split**. In the case that none of those are applicable, we show that either a formula $(1\&\rho)$ in the transformed sequent corresponds to an applicable CHR$^\vee$ rule, or that we have already found the configuration $\bar{S}_m$. We do this by induction over the sequents of a formal proof. The finite number of subformulas of the form $(1\&\rho)$ implies that we can derive $\bar{S}_m$ with a *finite* derivation.

Theorem 3.28 means that the logical deduction in our segment of linear logic closely follows the operational semantics of CHR. If an initial configuration S_0 logically implies a configuration S_n under the logical reading of the program then it is operationally possible to reach a configuration S_m that implies S_n under the constraint theory. This is different from the classical logic semantics, where we have logical equivalence between the two configurations only under the logical reading of the program. Here, for every state in S_m, there is a state in S_n such that they differ *only* in their built-in constraints. Note that the computation $S_0 \mapsto^* S_m$ is explicitly finite.

The semantics implicitly defines an interesting segment of intuitionistic linear logic, consisting of all sequents of the form $!\mathcal{CT}^L, P^L \vdash \forall \left(S_0^L \multimap S_n^L \right)$. For any such sequent, it is a necessary condition for its provability that a finite number of *modus ponens* applications in the logic – corresponding to rule applications – can simplify it to a sequent of the form $!\mathcal{CT}^L \vdash S_m^L \multimap S_n^L$ whose proof can be performed in classical intuitionistic logic. Furthermore, if the *modus ponens* applications and a proof for $!\mathcal{CT}^L \vdash S_m^L \multimap S_n^L$ are known, they can be used to construct a proof for $!\mathcal{CT}^L, P^L \vdash \forall \left(S_0^L \multimap S_n^L \right)$.

3.5 Bibliographic remarks

The original operational semantics for CHR was published in [Frü95]. It is the most general operational semantics in that every derivation possible in any of the other semantics is also true in this semantics. In [Abd97], Abdennadher extended it to the abstract semantics with a token store as propagation history for propagation rules in order to avoid trivial nontermination. This semantics was extended to the so-called refined semantics of CHR [DSdlBH04], which is closest to the execution strategy used in most current implementations of CHR. CHR was extended with disjunction in the language CHR$^\vee$ in [AS97, AS98].

The soundness and completeness theorems relating the operational and first-order-logic CHR semantics are due to [AFM99]. The linear-logic semantics of CHR occurs in [BF05]. Linear logic is introduced in [Gir87, Gir95].

More semantics. The paper [DGM05] introduces an abstract fix-point semantics for CHR which characterizes the input/output behavior in terms of built-in constraints of a CHR program and which is *and*-compositional: it allows us to retrieve the semantics of a conjunctive query from the semantics of its conjuncts. Such a semantics can be used as a basis to define incremental and modular program analysis and verification tools. Because CHR features multiple head constraints, a trace-based semantics is used that collects the missing head constraints as assumptions.

The paper [SSR07] presents a set-based refined operational semantics for CHR which enables efficient integration with tabling. The semantics addresses the trivial nontermination problem of propagation rules but avoids the use of a propagation history. CHRd is an implementation of this semantics that uses a distributed constraint store that can be directly represented in tables. The language is used for the verification of concurrent object-oriented systems and reachability analysis of real-time systems.

The refined operational semantics with priorities for CHR^{rp} [KSD07b] is used to extend CHR with rule priorities. Concurrent and parallel CHR semantics rely on the monotonicity property of CHR and are thus introduced in Section 4.3 after defining that property. In the extension of probabilistic CHR [FdPW02], applicable rules have a (weighted) chance of firing. Another noteworthy extension is adaptive CHR [Wol01], where CHR constraints and their consequences can be retracted dynamically using justifications.

Another approach to a declarative semantics that covers the dynamic aspects of CHR is based on *transaction logic* [MDR07]. Transaction logic extends first-order logic with a declarative account of state changes by extending it with the notion of sequences of formulas. It also allows us to link the declarative and operational semantics with a formal statement within transaction logic. In this way we can reason about the states of a computation inside the logic itself.

4

Properties of CHR

Real-world applications have to interact with their environment and be sufficiently fast for real-time computation, and thus concurrent, anytime, online algorithms are an asset.

A CHR program will automatically implement algorithms with these desirable properties due to the properties of its operational semantics. The *anytime (approximation) algorithm property* means that we can interrupt the execution of a program at any time, observe an approximation to the result and restart from that intermediate result. The *online (incremental) algorithm property* means that we can add additional constraints while the program is running without the need to recompute from scratch. *Concurrency* means that rules can be applied in parallel to separate (even certain overlapping) parts of a goal.

Unless otherwise noted, we use the very abstract semantics in this chapter to avoid clutter and technicalities of the abstract semantics.

The results in this chapter carry over to the refined operational semantics with some limitations only. In particular, programs written with the refined semantics in mind may give wrong results when executed in parallel. However, if a program has the confluence property (cf. Section 5.2), programs executing under the refined semantics basically also have the three properties (anytime, online, concurrent) discussed in this chapter.

4.1 Anytime approximation algorithm property

In an *anytime algorithm* we can interrupt the execution of a program at any time, observe an approximation to the result and continue from that intermediate result without the need to recompute from scratch. The intermediate results from successive interrupts better and better approximate the final result. Thus, an anytime algorithm is also an *approximation algorithm*.

Anytime algorithms are useful to guarantee response times for real-time and embedded systems or when hard problems are solved.

In CHR, we can interrupt the computation after any rule application, and the intermediate result is the current state of the computation. These states are meaningful, since they have a logical reading. We can then continue by applying rules to this state without the need to recompute from scratch. The intermediate states approximate the final state, since during the computation, more and more built-in constraints are added and the CHR constraints are simplified further and further. In a sense, this property is trivial, since the state of a transition system contains all information needed for the computation and since the transitive closure of the transition relation is trivially transitive.

Example 4.1.1 Consider a computation with the partial order constraint from Example 2.4.2. We use $\leq$ instead of $=<$ from now on. Clearly we may stop at any state of the following computation, observe the intermediate state and proceed in the same way as without interrupting:

$$\begin{aligned}
&\underline{A\leq B} \wedge \underline{B\leq C} \wedge C\leq A \mapsto && \text{(transitivity)} \\
&A\leq B \wedge B\leq C \wedge \underline{C\leq A} \wedge \underline{A\leq C} \mapsto && \text{(antisymmetry)} \\
&\underline{A\leq B} \wedge \underline{B\leq C} \wedge A{=}C \mapsto && \text{(antisymmetry)} \\
&A{=}B \wedge A{=}C
\end{aligned}$$

At the time of writing, no CHR implementation directly provides the support for interrupting the computation and adding constraints while the program runs, but the program's rules can be instrumented to support this behavior.

In current CHR implementations we can usually just observe the logical reading of a state, but not the state itself. This makes a difference for the abstract and refined operational semantics, where the propagation history, the location of the constraints in the components of the state and the resulting distinction between CHR constraints and their numbered and active instances is lost.

In the abstract semantics, if we use the logical reading of an intermediate state as initial goal for continuing the computation, then there exists a sequence of **Solve** and **Introduce** transitions that reconstructs the state up to renaming of identifiers and without the propagation history. From this state, the same transitions are possible as from the original state. Thus there exists a computation that proceeds in the same way as without interrupting.

For the refined semantics, the transition system is deterministic and may not reconstruct the intermediate state we stopped in. But confluence (Section 5.2) can still guarantee that the answers are the same.

4.2 Monotonicity and online algorithm property

The *monotonicity property* of CHR means that if a transition is possible in a state, then the same transition is possible in any larger state (that contains additional information in the form of constraints). In other words, adding constraints to a state cannot inhibit the applicability of a rule. In the very abstract semantics, a state is just a goal, i.e. a conjunction of constraints.

Lemma 4.1 Let A be a state and D be a state.

$$\begin{array}{llll} \text{If} & A & \mapsto & B \\ \text{then} & A \wedge D & \mapsto & B \wedge D \end{array}$$

Proof. If we add constraints to a state, the only change in the **Apply** transition happens in the applicability condition $CT \models \forall\, (G \rightarrow \exists \bar{x} C)$, where the new constraints now are included as $CT \models \forall\, ((G \wedge D) \rightarrow \exists \bar{x} C)$. Clearly, if the former condition holds, then so does the latter.

Example 4.2.1 Consider again the computation of the partial-order constraint from Example 2.4.2. The same computation is possible, no matter whether the constraint $C \leq A$ is added at the beginning or later during the computation.

$$\begin{array}{ll} \dfrac{A{<}B \wedge B{<}C \mapsto}{A{\leq}B \wedge B{\leq}C \wedge \underline{A{\leq}C}} \quad \wedge\ \underline{C{\leq}A}\ (\text{added}) \mapsto & (\text{transitivity}) \\[4pt] \overline{A{\leq}B \wedge B{\leq}C \wedge \underline{A{=}C}} \mapsto & (\text{antisymmetry}) \\[4pt] \dots \end{array}$$

For the abstract semantics given in this book, we can restate the lemma as follows. Roughly, to a nonfailed state, we can add suitable constraints to the first three components and remove entries from the propagation history as long as the built-in constraint store stays consistent.

Lemma 4.2 Given two nonfailed ω_t states

$$A = \langle G, S, B, T \rangle_n^{\mathcal{V}} \text{ and } D = \langle G', S', B', T' \rangle_m^{\mathcal{V}'},$$

where the states do not share local variables and where $B \wedge B'$ is consistent, then the combined state

$$\langle G \uplus G'_{+n}, S \cup S'_{+n}, B \wedge B', T'' \rangle_{n+m}^{\mathcal{V} \cup \mathcal{V}' \cup \mathcal{V}''},$$

where the subscript $+n$ for E in E_{+n} increments the identifier numbers from the numbered CHR constraints in E by n, where T'' is a subset of $T \cup T'_{+n}$, and $\mathcal{V}''$ are arbitrary variables, admits the same transitions as the state A.

Proof. In the transition system for the abstract semantics ω_t (Figure 3.5), all transitions update the contents of the components of a state in a way that is still possible in the combined state. The remainder of the proof is analogous to Lemma 4.1.

In the refined semantics, the goal G is turned into an activation stack A, so that we can only add constraints *at the end* of that sequence and must observe the restrictions for numbered and active constraints that can occur in a state. This means that given two states, there are two different ways of combining them. In general, there is no single combined state from which transitions of both states are possible.

The monotonicity property implies that constraints can be processed incrementally in CHR, giving rise to an online algorithm behavior; and that computations can be composed concurrently (cf. Section 4.3).

The *online (incremental) algorithm property* thus means that we can add additional constraints while the program is running without the need for redoing the computation from scratch. The program will behave as if the newly added constraints were present from the beginning of the computation but had been ignored so far. Incrementality is useful for constraint solving and interactive, reactive, and control systems, in particular for agent programming.

4.3 Declarative concurrency and logical parallelism

One of the main features of CHR is its inherent concurrency. We can interpret conjunction as a parallel operator and we will use the *interleaving semantics* for concurrency in CHR.

4.3.1 Processes, concurrency, and parallelism

Processes (depending on context and level of abstraction, also called threads, tasks, activities, agents) are the main notion in concurrent and distributed programming. Processes are programs that are executed independently but can interact with each other. Such programs are called *concurrent*. Processes can either execute local actions or *communicate* and *synchronize* by sending and receiving messages. The communicating processes build a *process network* which can change dynamically.

Concurrency allows for logically independent computations, thus supporting the modular design of independent components that can be composed together. *Parallelism* allows for computations that happen simultaneously, thus hopefully improving performance.

Concurrency can be implemented in a parallel or sequential way. A parallel implementation requires hardware that executes several processes at the same time, simultaneously. A sequential implementation uses interleaving of different concurrent computations, so that each gets a share of computation time. The *interleaving semantics* of concurrency is defined by the fact that for each possible parallel computation, there exists a sequential interleaving with the same result. It means that a parallel computation step can be simulated by a sequence of sequential computation steps.

Concurrency and distribution are easier with declarative programming languages, since they are compositional: different computations can be composed into one without unintended interference. So the programming, analysis, and reasoning techniques for programs still apply. In imperative languages concurrent computations may lead to conflicting updates with unpredictable results (e.g. consider executing the destructive assignments x:=5 and x:=7 in parallel). In concurrent constraint languages like CHR, unintended interference will always lead to failure and thus does not go unnoticed (e.g. consider the equations x=5 and x=7).

In CHR, concurrently executing processes are CHR constraints that communicate via a shared built-in constraint store. The built-in constraints take the role of (partial) messages and variables take the role of communication channels. Usually, communication is asynchronous. Running processes are atomic CHR constraints that by their rules check (in the guard) and place (in the body) built-in constraints on shared variables.

4.3.2 Parallelism in CHR

We now define two notions of CHR parallelism, weak and strong: intuitively, in a parallel execution of a CHR program, rules can be applied to separate parts of a problem in parallel. This is possible due to the *monotonicity property* of CHR: adding constraints to a state cannot inhibit the applicability of a rule. CHR rules can be applied in parallel to separate not only parts of a goal, but also overlapping parts, provided the *overlap* is not removed by any rule. (Clearly we cannot apply two rules in parallel that remove the same CHR constraint.) For the interleaving semantics, we have to come up with structural (program-independent) rules such that if $A \overset{\scriptscriptstyle\mapsto}{\mapsto} B$ in parallel, then there exists a sequential(ized) execution $A \mapsto^+ B$. Concurrency for CHR can, for example, be implemented with a locking mechanism or by a high-level program transformation.

A subclass of CHR programs, namely those that are *confluent*, can be executed in parallel without change, even when they were written with the refined semantics in mind.

In the following, let A, B, C, D, and E be conjunctions of arbitrary constraints. We denote a parallel transition by the relation $\overset{\scriptscriptstyle\mapsto}{\mapsto}$.

Weak parallelism. We allow parallel rule applications to separate parts of a problem. This can be defined by the following structural (program-independent) transition rule.

Definition 4.3 (Weak parallelism)

$$
\begin{array}{lll}
\text{If} & A & \mapsto & B \\
\text{and} & C & \mapsto & D \\
\text{then} & A \wedge C & \overset{\scriptscriptstyle\mapsto}{\mapsto} & B \wedge D
\end{array}
$$

We can justify *weak parallelism* as a consequence of the monotonicity (Lemma 4.1), which we call *trivial confluence*. It allows us to compose two computations and parallelize them by the interleaving semantics.

Corollary 4.4 (Trivial confluence)

$$
\begin{array}{lll}
\text{If} & A & \mapsto & B \\
\text{and} & C & \mapsto & D \\
\text{then} & A \wedge C & \mapsto S \mapsto & B \wedge D
\end{array}
$$

where S is either $A \wedge D$ or $B \wedge C$.

Proof. The final transition is a trivial consequence of the monotonicity (Lemma 4.1).

There are two ways to see this corollary: rule applications on separate parts of a goal can be exchanged. Rule applications from different goals can be composed. The result only holds for the (very) abstract semantics, but not for the refined semantics which has limited monotonicity.

With weak parallelism, a constraint can be used at most once in a simultaneous computation. To use a constraint means to involve it in a rule application. So we cannot apply several propagation rules simultaneously to the same constraints.

Example 4.3.1 Remember the `min` program from Section 2.2.1, where $\leq$ is a built-in constraint:

`min(N) \ min(M) ⇔ N≤M | `*`true`*`.`

The rule of `min` can be applied in parallel to different parts of the query, as already shown in that section:

$$\frac{\underline{\texttt{min(1)} \wedge \texttt{min(0)}} \quad \wedge \quad \underline{\texttt{min(2)} \wedge \texttt{min(3)}}}{\underline{\texttt{min(0)}} \quad \wedge \quad \underline{\texttt{min(2)}} \mapsto} \overset{\mapsto}{}$$
$$\texttt{min(0)}$$

One rule instance is applied to the constraints `min(1)` $\wedge$ `min(0)`, the other to `min(2)` $\wedge$ `min(3)`.

Example 4.3.2 Consider the partial-order constraint from Section 2.4.2, where $\leq$ is a CHR constraint used instead of `=<`:

```
duplicate     @ X≤Y ∧ X≤Y ⇔ X≤Y.
reflexivity   @ X≤X ⇔ true.
antisymmetry @ X≤Y ∧ Y≤X ⇔ X=Y.
transitivity @ X≤Y ∧ Y≤Z ⇒ X≤Z.
```

We can apply the antisymmetry rule and the transitivity rule in parallel in the derivation:

$$\frac{\underline{A{\leq}B} \wedge \underline{C{\leq}A} \wedge \underline{B{\leq}C} \wedge \underline{B{\leq}A}}{A{=}B \wedge C{\leq}A \wedge B{\leq}C \wedge B{\leq}A} \overset{\mapsto}{}$$

The antisymmetry rule is applied to $A{\leq}B \wedge B{\leq}A$, the transitivity rule to $B{\leq}C \wedge C{\leq}A$.

The weakness of weak parallelism is that it is too strict: for example, it does not allow the application of propagation rules to overlapping parts of the state, even though this would do no harm. It even does not allow us to share built-in constraints for the guard check of parallel rule applications.

Strong parallelism. The definition of *strong parallelism* shows that there is more potential for parallelism in CHR than working on separate parts of the problem.

Definition 4.5 (Strong parallelism)

$$\begin{array}{lll} \text{If} & A \wedge E & \mapsto & B \wedge E \\ \text{and} & C \wedge E & \mapsto & D \wedge E \\ \text{then} & A \wedge E \wedge C & \overset{\mapsto}{\mapsto} & B \wedge E \wedge D \end{array}$$

We allow parallel rule applications to overlapping parts, provided the *overlap* E is kept. With weak parallelism, we would need two copies of the constraints E or E would have to be empty otherwise.

Strong parallelism can be justified by the properties of trivial confluence and monotonicity.

Corollary 4.6 (Trivial confluence with context)

$$
\begin{array}{llll}
\text{If} & A \wedge E & \mapsto & B \wedge E \\
\text{and} & C \wedge E & \mapsto & D \wedge E \\
\text{then} & A \wedge C \wedge E & \mapsto S \mapsto & B \wedge D \wedge E
\end{array}
$$

where S is either $A \wedge D \wedge E$ or $B \wedge C \wedge E$.

Proof. The transitions are consequences of the monotonicity of CHR.

Propagation rules only add CHR constraints, so any CHR constraints they match can be in the overlap. Simpagation rules do not remove some of the constraints they match, so these can be in the overlap as well. Simplification rules remove all the CHR constraints they match, so they cannot be involved in an overlap.

A CHR constraint can be used several times if it is kept in all its matchings, or once if it is removed. So we can apply several propagation rules simultaneously to the same constraints. A simpagation rule may remove an arbitrary number of constraints simultaneously in one concurrent computation step.

Example 4.3.3 The rules of `min` can be applied in parallel to overlapping parts of the query. The CHR constraint `min(1)` matches the kept head constraint of the simpagation rule, while `min(2)` and `min(3)` match in parallel two different instances of the head constraint to be removed.

$\underline{\texttt{min(1)}} \wedge \texttt{min(0)} \wedge \underline{\texttt{min(2)}} \wedge \underline{\texttt{min(3)}} \overset{\mapsto}{\mapsto}$
$\underline{\texttt{min(1)}} \wedge \underline{\texttt{min(0)}} \mapsto$
$\texttt{min(0)}$

If we had chosen the constraint `min(0)` to be kept, we could have computed the minimum in one parallel computation step.

Example 4.3.4 Consider once again the partial-order constraint $\leq$ and the parallel computation where we first apply the transitivity rule and then the antisymmetry rule, each three times in parallel:

$$\frac{A{\leq}B \land B{\leq}C \land \ C{\leq}A \overset{\longmapsto}{}}{A{\leq}B \land B{\leq}C \land C{\leq}A \land A{\leq}C \land B{\leq}A \land C{\leq}B \overset{\longmapsto}{}}$$
$$A{=}B \land B{=}C \land A{=}C$$

The first parallel transition is only possible with strong parallelism, but not with weak, since several propagation rules are applied to the same constraints simultaneously.

Stronger parallelism. Can we implement even stronger parallelism, where rules are allowed to remove constraints from the overlap? The next example shows that in such a case we may get an incorrect behavior that is not covered by the interleaving semantics. For example, consider the simpagation rule for `min`

`min(N) \ min(M)` $\Leftrightarrow$ `N≤M |` *true*.

and the goal `min(1)` $\land$ `min(1)`. There are two competing rule instances for application: one tries to match the two constraints in the given order, the other in reversed order. So if we apply both rules simultaneously, both constraints will be removed. This is not correct and also not allowed by weak or strong parallelism, because we removed constraints from the overlap.

Implementation with locking. Parallelism in CHR can be implemented with a *locking mechanism* that applies to atomic CHR constraints. Rules lock CHR constraints that match their head with some unique identifier.

We can implement weak parallelism as follows: when a rule is about to be applied, it will first try to lock all constraints it matches. Locking of a constraint fails if it is already locked by another rule. If locking fails, we release our locks and try to redo the rule application. If all head constraints are successfully locked, the rule is applied. Kept constraints are unlocked before executing the rule body.

We can implement strong parallelism as follows: an applicable rule will first try to lock its removed head constraints only. On rule application, the kept head constraints must not be locked by any rule. In that way, kept constraints can be used by several rules simultaneously. When the rule is applied, no unlocking is necessary since locked constraints are removed.

The locking mechanism can avoid deadlocks and cyclic behavior using standard algorithms for these problems, e.g. by using time-stamps to give earlier rule application attempts higher priority than later ones.

Programs under the refined semantics. While any CHR program can be run in parallel in the (very) abstract semantics, we may get unexpected or even incorrect results for programs written with the refined semantics in mind. If such programs rely crucially on the order of rules in the program text and the order of constraints in the goal, parallel execution will garble these orders. Trivial confluence (Corollary 4.4) does not hold in the refined semantics, because the combination of states is not a symmetric operation (Lemma 4.2).

Example 4.3.5 Consider the destructive assignment rule from Section 2.3.4:

`assign(Var,New)` $\wedge$ `cell(Var,Old)` $\Leftrightarrow$ `cell(Var,New)`.

If the query `cell(x,2)` $\wedge$ `assign(x,1)` $\wedge$ `assign(x,3)` is executed in parallel, it is undetermined which update through `assign` comes first.

Here the *confluence* property (cf. Section 5.2) comes to the rescue: in confluent programs, the order in which the rules are applied does not matter for the result. This also implies that the order of the constraints in a goal does not matter. Thus, a confluent program can always be run in parallel without change of the program behavior (even when it was written with the refined semantics in mind).

Therefore we can rewrite programs to make them less dependent on the refined semantics by making them confluent with the help of confluence analysis (Section 5.2) to find the problematic rules (and with *completion* (Section 5.3) to introduce new rules).

4.4 Computational power and expressiveness

CHR machines are a fragment of the CHR language, analogous to RAM and Turing machines. CHR machines are characterized by the built-in constraints (at least *true*, *false*, $=$, and $\neq$) and the queries they allow. CHR, RAM, and Turing machines can simulate each other in polynomial time, thus establishing that CHR is Turing-complete. More importantly, every algorithm can be implemented in CHR without performance penalty, with best known time and space complexity. This is not known to be possible in other pure declarative programming paradigms such as logic programming (e.g. Prolog), term rewriting (e.g. Maude), and functional programming (e.g. Haskell). Thus CHR is the first declarative language for which the "optimal complexity" result can be demonstrated within the pure part of the language, i.e. without imperative extensions to the language.

We need some simple arithmetic built-in constraints for our CHR machine.

```
i(L,L1,add,B,A), m(B,Y) \ m(A,X), c(L) <=> Z is X+Y, m(A,Z), c(L1).
i(L,L1,sub,B,A), m(B,Y) \ m(A,X), c(L) <=> Z is X-Y, m(A,Z), c(L1).
i(L,L1,mult,B,A), m(B,Y) \ m(A,X), c(L)<=> Z is X*Y, m(A,Z), c(L1).
i(L,L1,div,B,A), m(B,Y) \ m(A,X), c(L) <=> Z is X/Y, m(A,Z), c(L1).

i(L,L1,move,B,A), m(B,X) \ m(A,Y), c(L) <=> m(A,X), c(L1).
i(L,L1,imove,B,A), m(B,C), m(C,X) \ m(A,Y), c(L) <=> m(A,X), c(L1).
i(L,L1,movei,B,A), m(B,X), m(A,C) \ m(C,Y), c(L) <=> m(C,X), c(L1).
i(L,L1,const,B,A) \ m(A,X), c(L) <=> m(A,B), c(L1).

i(L,L1,jump,A) \ c(L) <=> c(A).
i(L,L1,cjump(R),A), m(R,X) \ c(L) <=> X ==  0 | c(A).
i(L,L1,cjump(R),A), m(R,X) \ c(L) <=> X =\= 0 | c(L1).

i(L,L1,halt) \ c(L) <=> true.
```

Fig. 4.1. RAM machine simulation in CHR

Definition 4.7 *A sufficiently strong* constraint theory *CT defines at least the built-in constraints* $true, false, =, \neq,$ *and the standard arithmetic operations* $+, -, *, /$ *over integers.*

The CHR (machine) program in Figure 4.1 depicts the simulation of a standard RAM machine in CHR with a sufficiently strong constraint theory. A memory cell with address A and value V is represented as CHR constraint m(A,V). The program counter pointing to the instruction at program line L is represented as c(L). A program instruction has the form i(L, L1, I, D1, D2), where L is the line number of the instruction, L1 is the number of the next program line, I is the name of the instruction and the remaining arguments D1 and D2 are the arguments of the instruction, i.e. addresses or line numbers. Depending on the instruction, one or both arguments D1 and D2 may be omitted.

A query consists of program instructions, memory cells, and the program counter set to the line number of the first instruction. In the RAM machine simulation, the instruction at line L pointed to by the program counter is executed, thereby accessing and possibly updating the memory m and updating the program counter c (to L1 by default). The essential aspect here is that these updates (destructive assignment) are effectively simulated in CHR by removing and adding CHR constraints for m and c.

Now we can say that any algorithm can be implemented efficiently in CHR.

Theorem 4.8 Given a sufficiently strong constraint theory CT, there exists a CHR (machine) program which can simulate in $O(T + P + S)$ time and $O(P + S)$ space a T-time, S-space RAM machine with a program of P lines.

Proof. We use the CHR program for the simulation of RAM machines as given in Figure 4.1. The reading of the program instructions and the initial memory cells from the memory takes $O(P + S)$ time and space. Each instruction of the RAM machine can be executed in constant time by a single rule application. This introduces the parameter T into the time complexity.

These theoretical results can be effectively realized in recent CHR implementations of K.U. Leuven.

Corollary 4.9 For every (RAM machine) algorithm which uses at least as much time as it uses space, a CHR program exists which can be executed in the K.U. Leuven CHR system, with time and space complexity within a constant factor from the original complexities.

Proof. The proof is based on showing that the CHR RAM machine simulator of Figure 4.1 can be simulated on a RAM machine without increase of time and space complexity.

Of course, we still have to worry whether algorithms can be expressed in a natural and elegant way and about the constant factors. Practical experience with the CHR implementation of classical algorithms like union-find, shortest paths, and Fibonacci heaps indicates that conciseness and elegance can be achieved even for imperative algorithms.

Empirical evidence also shows that the run-time penalty for CHR is indeed a constant factor in comparison to implementations in lower-level imperative languages. The observed slow-down over C is now within an order of magnitude (as for some other highly optimized declarative languages). This applies at least to recent optimizing CHR compilers of K.U. Leuven.

4.5 Bibliographic remarks

The lemma for the monotonicity property of CHR was first stated and proven for a variant of the abstract semantics in [AFM99, FAM96].

The notion of *logical parallelism* was coined in [BM93] for this type of well-behaved parallelism. A similar property was called *declarative concurrency* in [RH04].

In concurrent constraint programming languages, e.g. in CHR, in the CC framework [SR90, SRP91] and OZ [Smo95], the interleaving semantics approach was taken for concurrency. Although well known, the concurrency property of CHR has scarcely been exploited for parallel execution until the recent past when [Frü05] proposed a parallel execution model for CHR.

Concurrency can be implemented in its sequential version by a program transformation [Mei07]. Also, promising genuine parallel implementations of CHR in Haskell do exist [LS08]. These papers feature first experiments that show a potential for practical speed-up by parallelization of CHR programs that can be linear (and in one case super-linear).

The theoretical results about optimal time and space complexity of CHR [SSD05b] can be effectively realized in recent CHR implementations of K.U. Leuven [SD04]. The implementation of Fibonacci heaps in CHR can be found in [SSD06]. Empirical efficiency experiments occur in [SSD05b, Frü02b].

5

Program analysis

One advantage of a declarative programming language is the ease of formally sound program analysis. Properties like confluence and program equivalence have been investigated for CHR. These properties are decidable for terminating programs.

Since CHR is Turing-complete, termination is undecidable. Still, establishing termination for CHR programs can be straightforward, if simplification and propagation rules occur by themselves mainly.

Confluence means that it does not matter for the result which of the applicable rules are applied in a computation. The result will always be the same. Even if the computation itself is nondeterministic, in confluent programs, the relation between initial and final state, between query and answer, is a function and thus deterministic. For terminating CHR programs, there is a decidable, sufficient, and necessary test for confluence. Confluence implies consistency of the logical reading of the program. It improves the soundness and completeness results between the operational and declarative semantics. We have already discussed that confluent programs enjoy declarative concurrency and logical parallelism. So confluent programs can be run in parallel without change (cf. Section 4.3).

There is also a decidable, sufficient, and necessary test for operational equivalence of CHR programs. We do not know of any other programming language in practical use that admits such a test.

Unless otherwise noted, we use the very abstract semantics in this chapter to avoid clutter and technicalities of the abstract semantics. Not all results carry over to the refined semantics.

5.1 Termination

We start with an obvious definition.

Definition 5.1 *A CHR program is* terminating, *if there are no infinite computations.*

Since CHR is Turing-complete (Section 4.4), termination is undecidable. In particular, termination analysis is difficult for nontrivial interactions between simplification and propagation rules and has to rely on the refined operational semantics of CHR.

One way to show termination is to prove that in each rule, the rule head is strictly larger than the rule body in some well-founded termination order.

Definition 5.2 *An order $\gg$ is* well-founded *if it has no infinite descending chains $t_1 \gg t_2 \gg \ldots \gg t_n \gg \ldots$*

A (CHR) termination order *is a well-founded order on CHR states.*

In this section, we use the $>$ relation between natural numbers as the basis of the termination order. We prove termination under the abstract operational semantics of CHR programs that contain only simplification rules by using so-called rankings that map logical expressions to natural numbers. Rankings also give upper bounds for worst-case derivation lengths.

5.1.1 Rankings

A commonly used termination order are *polynomial interpretations* adapted from term rewriting systems (TRS). They map terms and constraints to natural numbers using a polynomial function. Instances of this mapping are also called measure function, norm, *ranking*, or level mapping in the literature.

A ranking is an arithmetic function that maps terms and formulas to integers and thus induces an order over integers. It is inductively defined on the function symbols, constraint symbols, and logical connectives (in our case, conjunction only). The resulting order on formulas is total. It is well-founded if it has a smallest value for the formulas under consideration.

Of particular interest are ranking functions that are linear polynomials, where the rank of a logical expression is defined by a linear positive combination of the rankings of its arguments. These functions are simple but seem sufficient to cover common constraint solver programs written in CHR.

Definition 5.3 *Let f be a function or constraint symbol of arity n ($n \geq 0$) and let t_i ($1 \leq i \leq n$) be terms. A (linear polynomial) CHR ranking (function) defines the rank of the expression $f(t_1, \ldots, t_n)$ as follows:*

$$rank(f(t_1, \ldots, t_n)) = a_0^f + a_1^f * rank(t_1) + \ldots + a_n^f * rank(t_n)$$

where the a_i^f are integers.

For each formula B we require $rank(B) \geq 0$.

For each built-in C we impose $rank(C) = 0$.

The rank of a conjunction is the sum of the ranks of its conjuncts: $rank((A \wedge B)) = rank(A) + rank(B)$.

An arithmetic expression $rank(s) > rank(t)$ is an order constraint.

Definition 5.4 *The (syntactic) size of a term can be expressed as the ranking:*

$$size(f(t_1, \ldots, t_n)) = 1 + size(t_1) + \ldots + size(t_n).$$

For example, the size of the term f(a,g(b,c)) *is 5. The size of* f(a,X) *is $2 + size(X)$ with $size(X) \geq 0$. This allows us to conclude that the term* f(g(X),X) *is larger in size than* f(a,X)*, since $2 + 2 * size(X) \geq 2 + size(X)$, no matter what term X stands for.*

A ranking for a CHR program will have to define the ranks of CHR and built-in constraints. The rank of any built-in is 0, since we assume that their termination is established. A built-in constraint may imply order constraints between the ranks of its arguments (interargument relations), such as $s = t \rightarrow rank(s) = rank(t)$, where s and t are terms.

In an extension to the usual approaches for termination analysis of logic-based programs and term rewriting systems (TRS), we have to define the rank of a conjunction of constraints. If the rank of a conjunction is the sum of the ranks of its conjuncts, the worst-case derivation length can properly be reflected by the ranking. Such a ranking function also takes into account that conjunctions of CHR constraints are associative and commutative, but not idempotent.

Definition 5.5 *Let rank be a CHR ranking function. The ranking (condition) of a simplification rule $H \Leftrightarrow G \mid B$ is the formula*

$$\forall \, (C \rightarrow rank(H) > rank(B)),$$

where C is the conjunction of the built-in constraints in the rule.

The intuition behind the definition of a ranking condition is that the built-in constraints C in the rule will imply order constraints that can help us to establish that $rank(H) > rank(B)$. The precondition C consists of the built-in constraints from the guard and from the body, since they both avoid nontermination: if the constraints in the guard do not hold, the rule is not applicable. If the built-in constraints in the body do not hold, the application of the rule leads to an inconsistent, thus final, state. (This does not necessarily hold under the refined semantics, where the order of constraints in the body matters.)

Example 5.1.1 Consider the constraint **even** that ensures that a positive natural number is even. We write numbers in successor notation, i.e. `s(s(0))` denotes the number 2.

`even(s(N)) ⇔ N=s(M)∧even(M).`

The rule says that if the argument of **even** is the successor of some number N, then the predecessor of this number M must be even in order to ensure that the initial number `s(N)` is even.

The query **even(N)** delays. The query **even(0)** delays as well. To the query **even(s(N))** the rule is applicable, the answer is `N=s(M)`, **even(M)**. The query **even(s(0))** will fail after application of the rule, since `0-s(M)` is unsatisfiable.

A suitable polynomial interpretation is

$$rank(even(N)) = size(N)$$

The resulting (simplified) ranking condition for the rule is

$$N = s(M) \rightarrow size(s(N)) > size(M).$$

The ranking condition is satisfied.

5.1.2 Program termination

To ensure well-foundedness of the termination order using polynomial interpretations, queries must be sufficiently known.

Definition 5.6 *A goal G is* bounded *if the rank of any instance of G is bounded above by a constant.*

The rank of a ground (variable-free) term is always bounded. Typically, in bounded goals, variables only appear in positions which are ignored by the ranking.

In Example 5.1.1, the value of the polynomial interpretation for **even** can only be computed, if its argument is a ground term. So the ranking is bounded for ground terms only. Indeed, a query that is not bounded may lead to nontermination, e.g. consider the query **even(N),even(s(N))**.

The next theorem tells us how to prove CHR program termination. One basically shows that the rank of the removed constraints is greater than the rank of the constraints added in the body.

Theorem 5.7 Let P be a CHR program containing only simplification rules together with a ranking. If the ranking condition holds for each rule in P, then P is terminating for all bounded goals.

Proof. Besides showing well-foundedness by boundedness, we have to show that the rank of the source state in a transition under the very abstract semantics is strictly larger than the rank of the resulting successor state, i.e. $A \mapsto_r B$ implies $rank(A) > rank(B)$.

Without loss of generality, consider a state $H' \wedge D$ and a simplification rule $(H \leftrightarrow G \mid B)$ with ranking condition $C \rightarrow rank(H) > rank(B)$. Applying the rule to the state $H' \wedge D$ will lead to the state $(H{=}H') \wedge G \wedge B \wedge D$. We show that $rank(H' \wedge D) > rank((H{=}H') \wedge G \wedge B \wedge D)$.

We know that $rank(G){=}0$, $rank(H{=}H'){=}0$, since G and $H{=}H'$ are built-in constraints, and that $(H{=}H') \rightarrow rank(H){=}rank(H')$ by definition.

Since $C \rightarrow rank(H) > rank(B)$, we have that $C \rightarrow$
$rank(H' \wedge D){=}rank(H'){+}rank(D){=}rank(H){+}rank(D) >$
$0{+}0{+}rank(B){+}rank(D){=}rank(((H{=}H') \wedge G \wedge B \wedge D))$
where C is contained in the target state.

Since termination is undecidable for CHR, a suitable ranking with suitable order constraints cannot be found automatically.

5.1.3 Derivation lengths

Since the rank of a state decreases with each rule application, the rank of a query gives us an upper bound on the number of rule applications (derivation steps), i.e. derivation lengths. Consider Example 5.1.1, where the rank of the argument of **even** decreases by 2 with each rule application.

Theorem 5.8 Let P be a CHR program containing only simplification rules together with a ranking. If the ranking condition holds for each rule in P, then the worst-case derivation length D for a bounded goal G in P is bounded by the rank of G if we stop at failed states:

$$D(G) \leq rank(G).$$

Proof. From the proof of Theorem 5.7 we know that given a derivation step $G \mapsto G_1$ it holds that $rank(G) > rank(G_1)$ if G_1 is not failed. Since ranks are natural numbers, we can rewrite this as $rank(G) \geq rank(G_1)+1$. For $G \mapsto^n G_n$, we have that $rank(G) \geq rank(G_n)+n$. Since ranks are nonnegative, this implies the desired $rank(G) \geq n$.

5.2 Confluence

The confluence property of a program guarantees that any computation for a goal results in the same final state no matter which of the applicable rules are applied. Confluence as a consequence also ensures that the order of rules in a program and the order of constraints in a goal does not matter for the result. There is a decidable, sufficient, and necessary test for confluence for terminating programs that returns the conflicting rule applications.

5.2.1 Minimal states

When analyzing properties of CHR programs – such as confluence and operational equivalence – that involve infinitely many possible states of computations, we can often restrict ourselves to a finite number of so-called *minimal states*. For each rule, there is a minimal, most general state to which it is applicable.

Definition 5.9 *The* minimal state of a rule *is the conjunction of the head and the guard of the rule.*

Removing any constraint from the minimal state would make its rule inapplicable. Adding constraints to the minimal state cannot inhibit the applicability of the rule because of the monotonicity property of CHR (cf. Lemma 4.1). All other states to which the rule is applicable contain their minimal state in the following sense:

Lemma 5.10 Given a minimal state $H_1' \wedge H_2' \wedge C$ of a generalized simpagation rule r and a state S to which the rule r is applicable, there exists a goal G' such that $H_1' \wedge H_2' \wedge C \wedge G' \equiv S$. We say that S contains the minimal state.

 Proof. Let the state be $H_1 \wedge H_2 \wedge G$ and let the minimal state be $H_1' \wedge H_2' \wedge C$. Assume their variables are disjoint. Since according to the **Apply** transition, $H_1 \wedge H_2$ must be an instance of $H_1' \wedge H_2'$ and G must imply C under this instance, it suffices to extend the minimal state to the state $H_1' \wedge H_2' \wedge H_1'{=}H_1 \wedge H_2'{=}H_2 \wedge C \wedge G$. This state is equivalent to the state

$H_1 \wedge H_2 \wedge G$ when we existentially quantify all variables from the minimal state.

As a consequence, the logical reading of each state to which a rule is applicable implies the logical reading of its minimal state (under a suitable variable renaming).

5.2.2 Joinability

We adapt and extend the terminology and techniques of term rewriting systems. A straightforward translation of the results in TRS was not possible, because the CHR formalism gives rise to phenomena not appearing in term rewriting systems, such as conjunctions of relations instead of nested terms, logical variables, built-in constraints, and propagation rules (see the comparison of TRS and CHR in Section 6.2).

The following basic definitions apply to any transition system. We first define when two derivations lead to the same result. In the case of CHR, we use the equivalence relation on states to define what same results are.

Definition 5.11 *Two states S_1 and S_2 are* joinable *if there exist states S_1', S_2' such that $S_1 \mapsto^* S_1'$ and $S_2 \mapsto^* S_2'$ and $S_1' \equiv S_2'$.*

Given a state with two derivations starting from it that eventually reach two different states, we are interested if equivalent states can be reached from them (Figure 5.1).

Definition 5.12 *A CHR program is* confluent *if for all states S, S_1, S_2:*

$$\text{If } S \mapsto^* S_1, S \mapsto^* S_2 \text{ then } S_1 \text{ and } S_2 \text{ are joinable.}$$

A CHR program is well-behaved *if it is terminating and confluent.*

5.2.3 Confluence test

To analyze confluence of a given CHR program we cannot check joinability starting from any possible state, because in general there are infinitely many such states. For terminating programs, one can restrict the joinability test to a finite number of most general states, the so-called overlaps. These are states where more than one rule is applicable. An *overlap* consists of the *minimal states*, i.e. the heads and guards, of the rules. Overlaps can be extended to any larger state by adding constraints, i.e. to any state where several rules are applicable that may lead to different states.

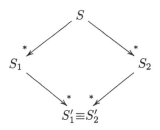

Fig. 5.1. Confluence diagram

Two rules are overlapped by merging their minimal states by equating at least one head constraint from one rule with one from the other rule. For each *overlap*, we consider the two states resulting from applying one or the other rule. These two states form a so-called *critical pair*. One tries to *join* the states in the critical pair. If the critical pair is not *joinable*, we have found a counterexample for confluence of the program.

Definition 5.13 *Let R_1 be a simplification or simpagation rule and R_2 be a (not necessarily different) rule, whose variables have been renamed apart. Let $H_i \wedge A_i$ be the conjunction of the head constraints, C_i be the guard and B_i be the body of rule R_i ($i = 1, 2$). Then a (nontrivial) overlap (critical ancestor state) S of rules R_1 and R_2 is*

$$S = (H_1 \wedge A_1 \wedge H_2 \wedge (A_1{=}A_2) \wedge C_1 \wedge C_2),$$

provided A_1 and A_2 are nonempty conjunctions and the built-in constraints are satisfiable, $\mathcal{CT} \models \exists((A_1{=}A_2) \wedge C_1 \wedge C_2)$.

Let $S_1{=}(B_1 \wedge H_2 \wedge (A_1{=}A_2) \wedge C_1 \wedge C_2)$ and $S_2{=}(H_1 \wedge B_2 \wedge (A_1{=}A_2) \wedge C_1 \wedge C_2)$. Then the tuple (S_1, S_2) is a critical pair *(c.p.) of R_1 and R_2.*

A critical pair (S_1, S_2) is joinable, *if S_1 and S_2 are joinable.*

The critical pair results from applying the rules to the overlap, i.e. $S \mapsto S_1$ using rule R_1 and $S \mapsto S_2$ using rule R_2.

Clearly, joinability of critical pairs is a necessary condition for confluence. Joinability can only be destroyed if one rule inhibits the application of the other rule. This is only the case if one rule removes constraints that are to be matched with the head of the other rule. Hence critical pairs from two propagation rules are always joinable. To possibly inhibit each other's application, at least one rule must not be a propagation rule and the two rules must overlap. If a critical pair is not joinable, we have found a counterexample for the confluence of the program.

5.2.4 Joinability for confluence

Theorem 5.16 gives a decidable, sufficient, and necessary condition for confluence of a terminating CHR program. We show that joinability of critical pairs is not only a necessary but also a sufficient condition for confluence in the case of terminating programs.

For the theorem we take a detour via a weaker notion of confluence. Local confluence requires that the different states are reached with *one* derivation step each.

Definition 5.14 *A CHR program is* locally confluent *if for all states* S, S_1, S_2:

> *If* $S \mapsto S_1, S \mapsto S_2$ *then* S_1 *and* S_2 *are joinable.*

The point is that local confluence and confluence coincide for terminating programs according to Newman's Lemma for arbitrary reduction systems.

Lemma 5.15 A terminating reduction system is confluent iff it is locally confluent.

Theorem 5.16 A terminating CHR program is confluent iff all its critical pairs are joinable.

    Proof.   Because of Newman's Lemma 5.15 it suffices to prove local confluence.

    The if direction: assume that we are in state S where there are two (or more) possibilities of transitions:

$$S \mapsto S_1 \text{ and } S \mapsto S_2.$$

We investigate all pairs of possible transitions and show that S_1 and S_2 are joinable. We show that equivalent states can be reached by further transitions. We distinguish two cases: either two rules apply to different parts of the state S or the two transitions involve two rule applications which overlap. In the first case, we use the monotonicity Lemma 4.1 and the resulting trivial confluence Corollary 4.4. In the second case, where there is an overlap, there must exist critical pairs that can be extended to states S_1 and S_2 by adding constraints and updating the propagation history without losing joinability.

The only-if direction we prove by contradiction. We assume that we have a locally confluent CHR program with a c.p. that is not joinable. We construct a state in which the rule applications lead to the states of the nonjoinable critical pair. Since the program is locally confluent the states must be joinable. This results in a contradiction.

The theorem gives a decidable characterization of confluent terminating CHR programs: joinability of a given critical pair is decidable because programs are terminating and by construction there are only finitely many critical pairs.

5.2.5 Examples

Clearly, CHR programs containing either only propagation rules or single headed simplification rules that do not overlap are trivially confluent.

Example 5.2.1 Let P be the CHR program from Example 3.4.3:

p $\Leftrightarrow$ q.
p $\Leftrightarrow$ *false*.

From the single overlap p of the two rules we can construct the critical pair (q, *false*) that consists of final states that are not joinable. Hence the program is not confluent.

Example 5.2.2 Consider the coin-throw Example 3.4.5:

    throw(Coin) $\Leftrightarrow$ Coin = head.
    throw(Coin) $\Leftrightarrow$ Coin = tail.

The only overlap is (after simplifying for readability)

$$\text{throw(Coin)}$$

and it leads to the critical pair

$$(\text{Coin=head}, \text{Coin=tail})$$

These two states are final and different. Thus, they are not joinable.

Example 5.2.3 The simple program consisting of a single rule

p(X) $\wedge$ q(Y) $\Leftrightarrow$ *true*.

is not confluent, as an overlap of the rule with itself, p(X)∧q(Y1)∧q(Y2), shows. This overlap leads to the critical pair (q(Y1), q(Y2)), where Y1 and Y2 are different variables from the overlap. To see it more clearly, consider an instance of the overlap, e.g. p(1) ∧ q(a) ∧ q(b). An analogous situation arises from the other nontrivial overlap p(X1)∧p(X2)∧q(Y).

Clearly nonjoinability does not arise with the rule

p(X) ∧ q(Y) ⇔ X=Y | *true*.

which requires that the arguments of the CHR constraints are the same.

Example 5.2.4 Consider the destructive assignment rule from Section 2.3.4 and Example 4.3.5:

assign(Var,New) ∧ cell(Var,Old) ⇔ cell(Var,New).

Analogously to Example 5.2.3 above, we have a nonjoinable overlap assign (Var,New1) ∧ assign(Var,New2) ∧ cell(Var,Old) resulting in either cell (Var,New1) or cell(Var,New2) depending on the order of the assignment constraints.

Example 5.2.5 Consider the two rules for the maximum relation as CHR constraint from the example program in Section 2.3.1:

max(X,Y,Z) ⇔ X ≤ Y | Y = Z.
max(X,Y,Z) ⇔ Y ≤ X | X = Z.

The only overlap of the two rules is

$$\text{max}(X, Y, Z) \wedge X \leq Y \wedge Y \leq X$$

and it leads to the critical pair

$$(Y{=}Z \wedge X \leq Y \wedge Y \leq X, X{=}Z \wedge X \leq Y \wedge Y \leq X)$$

The states of the c.p. are equivalent to $X{=}Y \wedge Y{=}Z$ and thus joinable.

Example 5.2.6 We implement a CHR constraint merge/3 for merging two unordered lists into one list as soon as the elements of the input lists arrive. Thus, the order of elements in the final list can differ from computation to computation.

merge([],L2,L3) ⇔ L2=L3.
merge(L1,[],L3) ⇔ L1=L3.
merge([X|R1],L2,L3) ⇔ L3=[X|R3] ∧ merge(R1,L2,R3).
merge(L1,[Y|R2],L3) ⇔ L3=[Y|R3] ∧ merge(L1,R2,R3).

There are eight critical pairs. For readability, we identify variables that are equated when constructing the overlap. The critical pair coming from the overlap of the first two rules is

```
([]=L1 ∧ L2=[] ∧ L2=L3, []=L1 ∧ L2=[] ∧ L1=L3).
```

This critical pair is joinable, because both states are already equivalent to the state `L1=[]∧L2=[]∧L3=[]`.

The c.p. stemming from the third and fourth rules is not joinable, however:

```
([X|R1]=L1 ∧ L2=[Y|R2] ∧ L3=[X|R3] ∧ merge(R1,L2,R3),
 [X|R1]=L1 ∧ L2=[Y|R2] ∧ L3=[Y|R3] ∧ merge(L1,R2,R3)).
```

A query like `merge([a],[b],L)` can either result in putting `a` before `b` in the output list `L` or vice versa, depending on which rule is applied. Hence, as expected, the `merge` program is not confluent. The result of a computation, i.e. the order of elements in the merged list, is not uniquely determined.

Example 5.2.7 Recall the program for $\leq$ from Example 4.3.2:

```
duplicate @    X≤Y ∧ X≤Y ⇔ X≤Y.
reflexivity @  X≤X ⇔ true.
antisymmetry @ X≤Y ∧ Y≤X ⇔ X=Y.
transitivity @ X≤Y ∧ Y≤Z ⇒ X≤Z.
```

Consider the rules for reflexivity and antisymmetry. We overlap them completely according to Figure 5.2. The resulting c.p. is joinable. The example also shows that multiplicities matter in CHR.

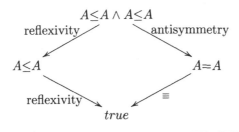

Fig. 5.2. Joinable overlap of reflexivity and antisymmetry rules

Now consider the overlap of the transitivity rule and the antisymmetry rule that comes from equating their first, left-most head constraints, i.e.

where $A_1 = A_2 = (X \leq Y)$. This overlap is

$$X \leq Y \wedge Y \leq Z \wedge Y \leq X$$

and leads to the c.p.

$$(X \leq Y \wedge Y \leq X \wedge Y \leq Z \wedge X \leq Z, X = Y \wedge X \leq Z)$$

It is joinable. There is a computation beginning with the first state of the c.p. which results in a state that is equivalent to the second state of the c.p.:

$$\underline{X \leq Y} \wedge \underline{Y \leq X} \wedge Y \leq Z \wedge X \leq Z \qquad \longmapsto_{antisymmetry}$$
$$\underline{Y \leq Z} \wedge \underline{X \leq Z} \wedge X = Y \qquad \longmapsto_{duplicate}$$
$$X \leq Z \wedge X = Y$$

The `duplicate` rule is applicable since the built-in $X = Y$ makes the two CHR constraints in the state syntactically equivalent.

5.2.6 Confluence test for the abstract semantics

So far we have considered the very abstract semantics. If we extend our results to the abstract semantics, we have to consider the propagation history when propagation rules are involved in the construction of a critical pair. In the states of the c.p., the propagation history is chosen so that we are not allowed to apply propagation rules that only involve constraints that were already present in the overlap. This choice is motivated by the minimality criterion for these states. It covers the case where all propagation rules have already been applied to the constraints of the CHR store before the overlap was reached.

Given an overlap $S \wedge B$, where S are the CHR constraints and B are the built-in constraints, we associate with the overlap the ω_t state $\langle \emptyset, S', B, \emptyset \rangle_n^{\mathcal{V}}$, where S' are n consistently numbered CHR constraints such that $S = chr$ (S'), and $\mathcal{V}$ contains all variables of the overlap.

In the ω_t states of the resulting critical pair, the propagation histories are set to $prop(S')$. The function $prop(S')$ returns a propagation history that contains an entry for each propagation rule of the program with each valid combination of constraints from S'.

Example 5.2.8 Consider the CHR program where r1 is a propagation rule:

```
r1 @ p ⇒ q.
r2 @ r∧q ⇔ true.
r3 @ r∧p∧q ⇔ s.
r4 @ s ⇔ p∧q.
```

As shown in Figure 5.3 (where we abstract states to their logical readings), in case (1) computations starting with state r∧p∧q lead to the final state p∧q no matter which rules are applied.

In case (2) the computation of r∧p uses r1 to reach state r∧p∧q. Since the propagation rule r1 has already been applied to p before the overlap was reached, it cannot be reapplied if a propagation history is used. So after application of rule r2 to the overlap we get the final state p. If we apply rule r3 instead, we reach the state s. From this state we can proceed to p∧q with rule r4. A new p is introduced in this state to which propagation rule r1 is applicable. However, no matter which rule we apply, we cannot remove q to join this state with the other state p. This is because we cannot introduce a constraint r which would be necessary to remove q. Hence nonjoinability results and confluence is violated.

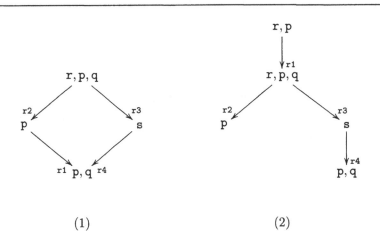

Fig. 5.3. Violated confluence in larger state

We can detect the nonconfluence using the appropriate propagation history. We consider the overlap r∧p∧q of rules r2 and r3, the associated ω_t state $\langle \emptyset, \{r\#1, p\#2, q\#3\}, true, \emptyset \rangle_4^{\emptyset}$, and its resulting critical pair, where $prop(\{r\#1, p\#2, q\#3\}) = \{(r1, [2])\} = T$,

$$(\langle \{true\}, \{p\#2\}, true, T\} \rangle_4^{\emptyset}, \langle \{s\}, \emptyset, true, T\} \rangle_4^{\emptyset},).$$

The first state of the c.p. immediately leads to the final state $\langle \emptyset, \{p\#2\}, true, T \rangle_4^\emptyset$, since the propagation history does not allow application of the propagation rule **r1**. However, derivations starting from the second state of the c.p. will reach, after application of rule **r4**, the state $\langle \emptyset, \{p\#5, q\#6\}, true, T \cup \{r^4, [4]\} \rangle_7^\emptyset$. As explained before, we cannot reach a state just consisting of p from this state.

5.2.7 Properties of confluent programs

Consistency. The operational notion of confluence has an impact on the declarative semantics as well, as the theorem shows.

Theorem 5.17 Let P be a *range-restricted* CHR program. If P is confluent, then its logical reading $\mathcal{P}, \mathcal{CT}$ is consistent.

Proof. We define the notion of *computational equivalence* $\rightleftharpoons^*$ as reflexive, *symmetric*, and transitive closure of the transition relation $\mapsto$. Two states are computationally equivalent if they can be reached by going forward and backward in the computation. By induction on the length of the equivalence $true \rightleftharpoons^* false$ we show that it cannot exist for confluent programs since the intermediate states of the equivalence must be joinable.

We then show that if $true \rightleftharpoons^* false$ does not hold for a range-restricted program, then there exists a ground interpretation for $\mathcal{P}, \mathcal{CT}$ that consists of ground built-in constraints C with $\mathcal{CT} \models C$ and ground CHR constraints G with $G \rightleftharpoons^* true$. This ground interpretation does not contain $false$ and therefore $\mathcal{P}, \mathcal{CT}$ is consistent.

Of course, this does not necessarily mean that the logical reading is also the intended meaning. For example, the prime number program in Section 2.2.4 is confluent (Section 7.1.4), but its classical declarative semantics is flawed (Section 3.4.7).

The program p $\Leftrightarrow$ *true*, p $\Leftrightarrow$ *false* is not confluent and has an inconsistent logical reading. The program p $\Leftrightarrow$ q, p $\Leftrightarrow$ *false* is not confluent but has a consistent logical reading. The program p $\Leftrightarrow$ q, q $\Leftrightarrow$ *false* is confluent and has a consistent logical reading.

Soundness and completeness revisited. We can improve on soundness and completeness if a CHR program is confluent and terminating. This is because every computation for a given goal has the same answer (up to equivalence of states).

Theorem 5.18 (Strong soundness and completeness) Let P be a well-behaved (terminating and confluent) CHR program and let C, C', C'', and G be goals. Then the following statements are equivalent:

(a) $P, CT \models \forall\, (C \leftrightarrow G)$.
(b) G has a computation with answer C' such that $P, CT \models \forall\, (C \leftrightarrow C')$.
(c) Every computation of G has an answer C'' such that $C' \equiv C''$ and $P, CT \models \forall\, (C \leftrightarrow C'')$.

Proof. We prove a cyclic chain of implications between these statements to show their logical equivalence.
"(a) $\Rightarrow$ (b)" by Theorem 3.22.
"(b) $\Rightarrow$ (c)" by confluence and termination.
"(c) $\Rightarrow$ (a)" by Theorem 3.21.

The restriction to terminating programs means that every computation is finite. The restriction to confluence means that all computations for a given goal lead to equivalent states. So statement (b) implies statement (c), which is not the case for programs that are not well-behaved.

The corollary gives a significantly improved soundness and completeness result for failed computations.

Corollary 5.19 (Soundness and completeness of failure) Let P be a range-restricted, well-behaved CHR program and G be a data-sufficient goal. Then the following statements are equivalent:

(a) $P, CT \models \neg \exists G$.
(b) G has a failed computation.
(c) Every computation of G is failed.

Proof. By Theorems 5.18, 5.17, and 3.25.

Example 5.2.9 The program

```
p ⟺ q.
p ⟺ false.
q ⟺ false.
```

is confluent, terminating, and the goal p data-sufficient. It holds that P, $CT \models \neg \exists p$ and every computation of p is failed.

The program

```
p ⟺ q.
p ⟺ false.
```

is not confluent but terminating. While $\mathcal{P}, \mathcal{CT} \models \neg\exists p$, not every computation of p is finitely failed: with the first rule, the query p has the successful answer q.

The program

p $\Leftrightarrow$ p.
p $\Leftrightarrow$ *false*.

is confluent, but not terminating. While $\mathcal{P}, \mathcal{CT} \models \neg\exists p$, not every computation of p is finitely failed: with only the first rule, the query p does not terminate.

Since there is a combinatorial explosion in the number of critical pairs with program size, in practice it is important to filter out trivial nonjoinable critical pairs that either stem from overlaps that are not possible for allowed queries or that we would like to consider equivalent for our purposes. Another issue is confluence under the refined semantics. For example, the program p $\Leftrightarrow$ *true*, p $\Leftrightarrow$ *false* is confluent under the refined semantics, but not confluent under the abstract semantics.

5.3 Completion

Completion is the process of adding rules to a nonconfluent program until it becomes confluent. These rules are generated from critical pairs. In contrast to other completion algorithms, in CHR we generally need more than one rule to make a critical pair joinable: a simplification rule and a propagation rule. The generation of these rules is not always possible. When completion generates a rule, it joins a c.p., but it may also introduce new nonjoinable critical pairs. Completion tries to continue introducing rules until the program becomes confluent. This process may not be terminating.

5.3.1 Completion algorithm

The completion algorithm is specified by a set of inference rules. The generation of CHR rules from a critical pair is provided by the following function.

The function *orient* tries to generate a simplification and a propagation rule from a given critical pair under a given termination order (cf. Section 5.1). The function does not apply if rules cannot be generated, the function is partial.

Definition 5.20 *Let* $\gg$ *be a termination order. Let* $(E_i \wedge C_i ,\ E_j \wedge C_j)(i, j \in \{1, 2\})$ *be a nonjoinable critical pair, where* E_i, E_j *are CHR constraints and* C_i, C_j *are built-in constraints. The partial function* orient $\gg$ *applies to the*

set of the two states in the critical pair $\{E_1 \wedge C_1,\ E_2 \wedge C_2\}$ *if* $E_1 \wedge C_1 \gg E_2 \wedge$
C_2, *if* E_1 *is a nonempty conjunction, and if* E_2 *is a nonempty conjunction*
or $\mathcal{CT} \models C_2 \to C_1$. *It returns a set of rules:*

$$\{E_1 \Leftrightarrow C_1 \mid E_2 \wedge C_2,$$
$$E_2 \Rightarrow C_2 \mid C_1\}$$

where the propagation rule is generated only if $\mathcal{CT} \not\models C_2 \to C_1$.

The propagation rule ensures that the built-ins of both states in the critical pair are enforced. The conditions of the function are carefully chosen so that it does not apply if the two states in the c.p. cannot be ordered by $\gg$ or if rules with empty head would result. In addition, we do not add redundant propagation rules ($\mathcal{CT} \models C_2 \to C_1$).

The completion algorithm for CHR maintains a set C of critical pairs (as sets) and a set P of rules. These sets are manipulated by four inference rules (Figure 5.4). We write $(C, P) \longmapsto (C', P')$ to indicate that the pair (C', P') can be obtained from (C, P) by an application of an inference rule.

Simplification:	If $S_1 \mapsto S_1'$ then $(C \cup \{\{S_1, S_2\}\}, P) \longmapsto (C \cup \{\{S_1', S_2\}\}, P)$
Deletion:	If S_1 and S_2 are joinable then $(C \cup \{\{S_1, S_2\}\}, P) \longmapsto (C, P)$
Orientation:	If $orient \gg (\{S_1, S_2\}) = R$ then $(C \cup \{\{S_1, S_2\}\}, P) \longmapsto (C, P \cup R)$
Introduction:	If (S_1, S_2) is a c.p. of P not in C then $(C, P) \longmapsto (C \cup \{\{S_1, S_2\}\}, P)$

Fig. 5.4. Inference rules of completion

Completion starts with a given program P and its set of nonjoinable critical pairs S, i.e. (S, P). We can then apply the inference rules in the order given in Figure 5.4 until exhaustion or failure: the rule *Simplification* replaces a state in a c.p. by its successor state. When applied to exhaustion, we only work with final states. The rule *Deletion* removes the joinable critical pairs. The rule *Orientation* removes a (nonjoinable) c.p. from C and adds new rules to P, as computed by the partial function *orient*. If the function does not apply, the inference is not possible. We apply this rule once. We then compute all critical pairs between the new rules and the current rules of the program P using inference rule *Introduction*.

If the final state is $(\emptyset, P')$, we have succeeded and P' is the completed program, otherwise we have failed. Completion fails if nonjoinable critical pairs cannot be oriented. In such a c.p., either states cannot be ordered or they consist of different built-in constraints only. In the first case, the termination order may be to blame, in the second case, the program has an inconsistent logical reading. Completion may also not terminate, this is the case when new rules produce critical pairs, which require again new rules, and so on. Sometimes a different termination order may lead to termination.

5.3.2 Examples

In the examples, we use a simple generic termination order where built-in constraints are the smallest, atomic CHR constraints are ordered by their symbols, and conjunctions of CHR constraints are larger than their conjuncts.

Example 5.3.1 Consider the CHR program

p ⇔ q.
p ⇔ *false*.

This program is not confluent since p leads to the c.p. (q, *false*). The inference rules *Simplification* and *Deletion* do not apply. The rule *Orientation* adds, via the function $orient_\gg$, the rule q ⇔ *false* to the program. A propagation rule is not produced since $CT \models false \rightarrow true$. Rule *Introduction* does not apply, since there is no overlap between the new rule (with head q) and the old rules of the program. So completion terminates successfully with the program

p ⇔ q.
p ⇔ *false*.
q ⇔ *false*.

Example 5.3.2 In the ≤ solver from Example 2.4.2, we introduce a < constraint by adding just one rule about the contradiction between these two types of inequalities:

(inconsistency) $X \leq Y \wedge Y < X$ ⇔ *false*

The resulting program is not confluent, as can be seen by an overlap with the antisymmetry rule of ≤:

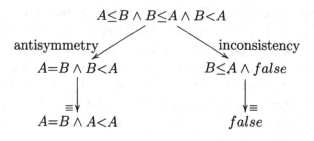

Completion uses the states in the nonjoinable critical pair to derive the rule

$$X<X \Leftrightarrow X{=}Y \mid false,$$

which can be simplified to the rule

$$X<X \Leftrightarrow false,$$

which means that we have discovered irreflexivity of $<$.

Example 5.3.3 In the program, the constraint `min(X,Y,Z)` stands for $min(X,Y) = Z$ and `X leq Y` for the partial-order constraint $X{\leq}Y$:

```
min1 @ min(X,X,Z)  ⇔  X=Z.
min2 @ min(X,Y,X)  ⇔  X leq Y.
min3 @ min(X,Y,Z) ∧ min(X,Y,Z1)  ⇔  min(X,Y,Z) ∧ Z=Z1.
```

We choose an instance of the generic termination order where `min` $\gg$ `leq`.

The overlap `min(X,X,Z)`$\wedge$`X=Y`$\wedge$`X=Z` of the rules `min1` and `min2` results in the critical pair

$$(\texttt{X leq X}, \texttt{X=X})$$

This c.p. becomes joinable after the inference rule *Orientation* of completion adds rule `r1`,

```
r1 @ X leq X  ⇔  true.
```

The two critical pairs between rules `min1` and `min3` are joinable.

Another c.p. comes from the overlap of rule `min2` with the first head constraint of `min3`,

$$(\min(X, Y, X) \wedge X{=}Z, X \texttt{ leq } Y \wedge \min(X, Y, Z)).$$

The c.p. is joined by the completion algorithm with rule `r2`:

```
r2 @ X leq Y ∧ min(X,Y,Z) ⇔ X leq Y ∧ X=Z.
```

An analogous c.p. comes from the overlap of `min2` with the second head constraint of `min3`. This c.p. is already joinable due to rule `r2`. A nonjoinable c.p. comes from this new rule, the overlap of rule `min2` and the second head constraint of `r2`. It leads to rule `r3`,

```
r3 @ X leq Y ∧ X leq Y ⇔ X leq Y.
```

The new rules `r1`, `r2`, and `r3` reveal some interesting properties of `leq` and `min`. The completed program with all rules `min1`, `min2`, `min3` as well as `r1`, `r2`, `r3` is terminating and confluent.

The next example shows that it is not sufficient to add just simplification rules in order to join a nonjoinable critical pair.

Example 5.3.4 Given the following CHR program, where $\geq$ and $\leq$ are built-in constraints, let $p \gg r \gg q$ in the generic termination order:

```
r1 @ p(X,Y) ⇔ X ≥ Y ∧ q(X,Y).
r2 @ p(X,Y) ⇔ X ≤ Y ∧ r(X,Y).
```

The program is not confluent, since the c.p. stemming from **r1** and **r2**

$$(X \geq Y \wedge q(X,Y), \quad X \leq Y \wedge r(X,Y))$$

is not joinable. Completion inserts the two rules

```
r3 @ r(X,Y) ⇔ X ≤ Y | q(X,Y) ∧ X ≥ Y.
r4 @ q(X,Y) ⇒ X ≥ Y | X ≤ Y.
```

The computations show that it is necessary to add the propagation rule **r4** to the program. Consider the query **p(X,Y)**. A computation using rule **r2** is

	$p(X,Y)$
$\mapsto$*Apply r2*	$r(X,Y) \wedge X \leq Y$
$\mapsto$*Apply r3*	$q(X,Y) \wedge X = Y$
$\mapsto$*Apply r4*	$q(X,Y) \wedge X = Y$

The application of propagation rule **r4** does not change the answer. However, the computation for **p(X,Y)** using rule **r1** needs the propagation rule **r4** to result in the same answer:

	$p(X,Y)$
$\mapsto$*Apply r1*	$q(X,Y) \wedge X \geq Y$
$\mapsto$*Apply r4*	$q(X,Y) \wedge X = Y$

In the next example, completion fails because a c.p. cannot be oriented.

Example 5.3.5 Given the CHR program

```
r1 @ p(X,Y) ⇔ X ≥ Y ∧ q(X,Y).
r2 @ p(X,Y) ⇔ X ≤ Y ∧ q(Y,X).
```

the program is not confluent, since the c.p. stemming from **r1** and **r2**

$$(X \geq Y \wedge q(X,Y), \quad X \leq Y \wedge q(Y,X))$$

is not joinable. However, there is no termination order that can order this critical pair, as can be seen from the rule that would result from function *orient*:

rf @ q(Y,X) ⇔ X ≤ Y | q(X,Y) ∧ X ≥ Y.

5.3.3 Correctness

When the completion algorithm terminates successfully (without leaving critical pairs), the returned program is confluent and terminating, and moreover it has the same meaning as the original program. For the proof of the correctness theorem to go through, every rule has to satisfy a syntactic condition: the program has to be range-restricted, i.e. the rules have no local variables. The reason for this restriction is that completion could put an occurrence of a local, i.e. existentially quantified, variable in the head of a rule it generates. However, the variables of the head are defined to be universally quantified in the logical reading.

We can now state our correctness theorem for completion of CHR programs.

Theorem 5.21 Let P be a *range-restricted* CHR program that is terminating with respect to a termination order $\gg$ and let C be the set of nonjoinable critical pairs of P. If, for inputs (C, P) and $\gg$, completion succeeds with $(\emptyset, P')$, then program P' is

(a) terminating with respect to $\gg$,
(b) confluent, and
(c) logically equivalent to P.

Proof.

(a) P is terminating and any rule that we add respects the termination order $\gg$. Therefore, P' is terminating.
(b) Since P' is terminating, for confluence it suffices to show that all its critical pairs are joinable. During completion, we have generated all critical pairs. They were either joinable or we joined them by introducing an appropriate rule.
(c) To show that P' and P are logically equivalent, we show that each rule we add is a logical consequence of P. Let (S_1, S_2) be a critical pair. Let $T_1 = E_1 \wedge C_1$ and $T_2 = E_2 \wedge C_2$ be final states in the computations beginning with S_1 and S_2, respectively. W.l.o.g. assume $T_1 \gg T_2$. The function *orient*$_\gg (T_1, T_2)$ = returns $R = \{E_1 \Leftrightarrow C_1 \mid E_2 \wedge C_2, E_2 \Rightarrow C_2 \mid C_1\}$ in the general case.

Since (S_1, S_2) is a c.p. of some overlap S, the states T_1 and T_2 must have the same meaning by Lemma 3.20:

$$\mathcal{P}, \mathcal{CT} \models \forall((E_1 \wedge C_1) \leftrightarrow (E_2 \wedge C_2)).$$

(There are no local variables, since P is range-restricted.)

We deduce that $\forall(C_1 \rightarrow (E_1 \leftrightarrow (E_2 \wedge C_2)))$ holds, which is the logical reading of the simplification rule in R. We also deduce that $\forall(C_2 \rightarrow (E_2 \rightarrow C_1)$ holds, which is the logical reading of the propagation rule in R.

Example 5.3.6 To illustrate the need for the range-restrictedness condition, consider the fragment of a program that is not range-restricted due to the first rule given:

```
p  ⇔  q(X).
p  ⇔  true.
```

The unary constraint q is an arbitrary property that does not hold for all possible values. The c.p. is $(q(X), true)$. It can only be oriented so that this rule results:

```
q(X)  ⇔  true.
```

However, the logical reading of this rule contradicts the meaning of q, since now it holds for all possible values.

5.3.4 Failing completion and inconsistency

A failing completion can exhibit inconsistency of the given program.

Theorem 5.22 Let P be a CHR program and $\mathcal{CT}$ a complete theory for the built-in constraints. If completion fails and a remaining nonjoinable critical pair consists only of built-in constraints that are not logically equivalent, then the logical meaning of P is inconsistent.

Proof. Let (C_1, C_2) be the critical pair. We prove the claim by contradiction. Assume that $\mathcal{P}$ is consistent. Then $\mathcal{P}, \mathcal{CT}$ is consistent. By Lemma 3.20,

$$\mathcal{P}, \mathcal{CT} \models \forall\, (\exists \bar{x}_1 C_1 \leftrightarrow \exists \bar{x}_2 C_2),$$

where $\bar{x}_1, \bar{x}_2$ are the local variables of the states. Since C_1 and C_2 are built-in constraints, it follows that $\mathcal{CT} \models \forall\, (\exists \bar{x}_1 C_1 \leftrightarrow \exists \bar{x}_2 C_2)$ holds ($\mathcal{CT}$ is by definition complete). But then the two states C_1 and C_2 must be joinable, because they are equivalent under $\equiv$.

The most simple example for this theorem is the program $\{$p $\Leftrightarrow$ $true$, p $\Leftrightarrow$ $false\}$.

Example 5.3.7 Consider the program

```
p(X)  ⇔  q(X).
p(X)  ⇔  true.
q(X)  ⇔  X>0.
```

Now there is a critical pair for q, (X>0, $true$) that cannot be oriented, because the states contain only different built-in constraints. Completion fails and the c.p. indicates an inconsistent program according to our theorem.

Example 5.3.8 Let P be the following CHR program (trying to implement the constraint max(X,Y,Z) from Example 2.3.1). Note that there is a typo in the body of the second rule, since Y should have been Z. The built-in constraints are $\leq$ and $=$.

```
r1 @ max(X,Y,Z) ⇔ X ≤ Y | Z = Y.
r2 @ max(X,Y,Z) ⇔ Y ≤ X | Y = X.
```

The c.p.

$$(Z = Y \wedge X \leq Y \wedge Y \leq X, \quad Y = X \wedge X \leq Y \wedge Y \leq X)$$

stemming from r1 and r2 is not joinable and completion fails. The program is not consistent.

The logical meaning of this program is the theory

$$\forall \ X,Y,Z \ (X \leq Y \ \rightarrow \ (\text{max}(X,Y,Z) \ \leftrightarrow \ Z = Y))$$
$$\forall \ X,Y,Z \ (Y \leq X \ \rightarrow \ (\text{max}(X,Y,Z) \ \leftrightarrow \ Y = X))$$

together with a constraint theory describing $\leq$ as an order relation and $=$ as syntactic equality. The logical meaning is not a consistent theory. This can be exemplified by the atomic formula max(1,1,0), which is logically equivalent to 0=1 (and therefore $false$) using the first formula. Using the second formula, however, max(1,1,0) is logically equivalent to 1=1 (and therefore $true$). This results in $\mathcal{P}, \mathcal{CT} \models false \leftrightarrow true$.

5.3.5 Program specialization by completion

The upcoming examples show that completion can be used to specialize programs and their CHR constraints.

Example 5.3.9 We define the binary CHR constraint $<$ as a special case of the constraint $\leq$ from Example 2.4.2. We assume inequality $\neq$ is built-in.

r5 @ X $\leq$ Y $\Leftrightarrow$ X $\neq$ Y | X $<$ Y.

The resulting program loses confluence. With an instance of the generic termination order where $(\leq) \gg (<)$, completion inserts the two rules

r6 @ X $<$ Y $\wedge$ Y $<$ X $\Leftrightarrow$ X $\neq$ Y | *false*.
r7 @ X $<$ Y $\wedge$ X $<$ Y $\Leftrightarrow$ X $\neq$ Y | X $<$ Y.

Rule **r6** comes from a c.p. of **r2** and **r5**,

$$(X = Y \wedge X \neq Y, \quad X < Y \wedge Y \leq X \wedge X \neq Y).$$

Rule **r7** comes from a c.p. of **r4** and **r5**,

$$(X \leq Y \wedge X \neq Y, \quad X < Y \wedge Y \leq X \wedge X \neq Y).$$

Rule **r6** implements the antisymmetry of $<$ and **r7** idempotence of conjunction by duplicate removal.

The next example shows that completion can also derive definitions of recursively defined constraints.

Example 5.3.10 The classical Prolog predicate append(L1,L2,L3) holds if the concatenation of list L1 and list L2 is list L3. We implement **append** as CHR constraint by the two rules

r1 @ append([],L,L) $\Leftrightarrow$ *true*.
r2 @ append([X|L1],Y,[X|L2]) $\Leftrightarrow$ append(L1,Y,L2).

The program is confluent since there are no critical pairs. When we add the rule

r3 @ append(L1,[],L3) $\Leftrightarrow$ new(L1,L3).

to define a special case of **append**, confluence is destroyed. Using completion, one can generate a program for **new** (that does not refer to **append** anymore):

r4 @ new([],[]) $\Leftrightarrow$ *true*.
r5 @ new([A|B],[A|C]) $\Leftrightarrow$ new(B,C).

Rule **r4** joins the c.p. of rules **r1** and **r3**, rule **r5** joins the c.p. of rules **r2** and **r3**. Completion has uncovered that append(L1,[],L3) holds exactly if L1 and L2 are the same list, as checked by the generated recursive constraint **new**.

The next example shows how completion can be used to provide generic answers, even if a constraint cannot further be simplified. This retains some of the power of logic languages such as Prolog, where several answers can be given using backtrack search. At the same time, we can avoid infinitely many answers. The built-ins are $=$ and $\neq$.

Example 5.3.11 The classical Prolog predicate `member` as a CHR constraint is defined by the rules

r1 @ member(X,[]) ⇔ *false*.
r2 @ member(X,[H|T]) ⇔ X = H | *true*.
r3 @ member(X,[H|T]) ⇔ X ≠ H | member(X,T).

Using CHR, the query member(X,[1,2,3]) delays (no rule is applicable), while Prolog generates three answers X=1, X=2, and X=3. If we add

r4 @ member(X,[1,2,3]) ⇔ answer(X).

then the resulting program is not confluent. If we apply completion (Figure 5.5), the Prolog answers are represented by a set of four rules:

a1 @ answer(1) ⇔ *true*.
a2 @ answer(2) ⇔ *true*.
a3 @ answer(3) ⇔ *true*.
a4 @ answer(X) ⇔ X ≠ 1 ∧ X ≠ 2 ∧ X ≠ 3 | *false*.

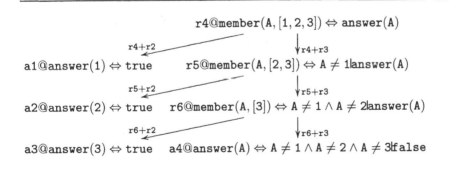

Fig. 5.5. Answer rules generated for Example 5.3.11

Example 5.3.12 Consider append again from Example 5.3.10. Using CHR, the query append(X,[b|Y],[a,b,c|Z]) delays. Prolog generates an infinite number of answers, starting with

```
X = [a], Y = [c|Z])
X = [a,b,c], Z = [b|Y]
X = [a,b,c,X1], Z = [X1,b|Y]
X = [a,b,c,X1,X2], Z = [X1,X2,b|Y] ...
```

If we apply completion to the two rules of **append** together with the rule

```
r3 @ append(X,[b|Y],[a,b,c|Z]) ⟺ answer(X,Y,Z).
```

we obtain the rules

```
a1 @ answer([a],[c|Z],Z) ⟺ true.
a2 @ answer([a,b,c],Y,[b|Y]) ⟺ true.
a3 @ answer([a,b,c,H|L],Y,[H|L2]) ⟺ answer([a,b,c|L],Y,L2).
```

Rule **a1** corresponds to the first answer X = [a], Y = [c|Z] of the corresponding Prolog program and **a2** to the second answer. Rule **a3** represents the remaining infinitely many answers of Prolog in a finite form.

5.4 Modularity of termination and confluence

A programmer will often modify and combine existing programs. For CHR, some possibilities are: flat composition by program merging (union) taking the union of all rules; hierarchical composition using modules by turning some CHR constraints into built-in constraints of another CHR program; and extending arbitrary solvers with CHR.

We are interested in flat composition in this section and how it effects well-behavedness under the abstract operational semantics. In this semantics, any computation that was possible in one of the programs will also be possible in the union of the programs, because adding rules to a program cannot inhibit the application of existing rules.

By *modularity (of a program property)* we mean that the property is preserved under the union of programs. We denote program union by the set union operator ∪. Indeed, the union of the programs could lose termination or confluence, and thus their well-behavedness. Hence these properties are not modular in general.

Example 5.4.1 Consider a terminating program with a single rule {a ⟺ b} and another terminating program with a rule {b ⟺ a}. The union of the two programs, {a ⟺ b, b ⟺ a}, is not terminating (but confluent).

Consider a confluent program P_1 {a ⟺ b} and a confluent program P_2 {a ⟺ c}. The union {a ⟺ b, a ⟺ c} is terminating, but not confluent, since a computation for a may result in either b or c depending on the committed choice of the rule.

We have seen that well-behavedness is not preserved under union of programs. We can either repair unions of programs that are not well-behaved by modifying rules or try to find syntactic criteria for classes of programs where well-behavedness is modular.

Modular classes of CHR programs. For the definitions of constraint circularity and variable sharing, propagation rules are considered as recursive simplification rules, where the head is repeated in the body.

Definition 5.23 *We define:*

- *c is a* constraint of a CHR program P *if it is either a CHR constraint whose constraint symbol is defined in P or a built-in constraint whose constraint symbol occurs in P. (CHR constraints that are only used in P are not included.)*
- *The CHR programs P_1 and P_2 are* nonoverlapping *if P_1 and P_2 do not have any defined CHR constraints in common.*
- *P_1 and P_2 are* circular *if P_1 defines CHR constraints that are used in P_2 and vice versa.*
- *Given a goal (query) G, a variable is P_1, P_2-shared if it occurs in constraints of P_1 and in constraints of P_2.*

Note that nonoverlapping programs may have common CHR constraints and common built-in constraints (by definition, at least syntactic equality) and common function symbols.

For preserving termination, a syntactic class of programs that would be of practical use is hard to find. This is not surprising, since termination is undecidable. However, we are able to show that the union of noncircular terminating programs is terminating for queries where all shared variables have finite domains. A variable over a finite domain can only take its values from a finite set of ground terms (usually constants). Furthermore, the union of confluent nonoverlapping programs is always confluent. Thus, noncircular nonoverlapping program union is modular if shared variables have finite domains.

5.4.1 Modularity of termination

Termination is nonmodular due to circular definitions in the union of programs or shared variables in queries.

For modularity, we are interested in the union of programs that are not circular. Noncircularity does not imply a hierarchy among the constraint programs, since both programs can still define and use common CHR symbols as long as the common symbols are not defined and used at the same time in both programs.

In other words, noncircularity holds if at least one intersection of defined symbols in one and used symbols in the other program is empty. So in at least one of the programs, all used CHR constraint symbols are not defined in the other program. It also means that a CHR constraint that is defined in both programs can only be defined recursively in one of the programs.

From Example 5.4.1 we can already see that circular definitions of CHR constraints can lead to nontermination. Even if two terminating programs do not have common CHR constraint symbols, and thus are noncircular, their union may not be terminating.

Example 5.4.2 Consider the two programs P_1 and P_2:

$P1$: `c(f(X))` $\Leftrightarrow$ `X=g(Y)` $\wedge$ `c(Y).`
$P2$: `d(g(Y))` $\Leftrightarrow$ `Y=f(Z)` $\wedge$ `d(Z).`

Any goal (of finite size) terminates in each of the two programs, e.g. to the goals `c(A)` and `c(g(A))` no rules are applicable, the goal `c(f(A))` reduces to `A=g(Y)` $\wedge$ `c(Y)`, the goal `c(f(f(A))` fails, the goal `c(f(g(A))` reduces to `c(A)`, and so forth. Despite the terminating programs, the goal `c(f(X))` $\wedge$ `d(X)` does not terminate in the union of the programs. This is due to P_1, P_2-shared variables and common function symbols.

`c(f(X))` $\wedge$ `d(X)`	$\longmapsto_{P_1}$
`X=g(Y)` $\wedge$ `c(Y)` $\wedge$ `d(g(Y))`	$\longmapsto_{P_2}$
`X=g(f(W))` $\wedge$ `Y=f(W)` $\wedge$ `c(f(W))` $\wedge$ `d(W)`	$\longmapsto_{P_1}$ ...

Even if there are no common symbols in the program text, we may run into nontermination due to P_1, P_2-shared variables.

Example 5.4.3 The previous example can be rewritten such that instead of common function symbols one uses built-in constraints to the same effect:

$P1$: `c(FX)` $\Leftrightarrow$ `f1(FX,X)` | `g1(X,Y)` $\wedge$ `c(Y).`
$P2$: `d(GY)` $\Leftrightarrow$ `g2(GY,Y)` | `f2(Y,Z)` $\wedge$ `d(Z).`

where $f1(X,Y)$ and $f2(X,Y)$ are both defined as $X = f(Y)$ in the constraint theory for the built-in constraints and $g1(X,Y)$ and $g2(X,Y)$ are both defined as $X = g(Y)$. There are no common symbols in the CHR program itself, but only in the constraint theory. Any goal terminates in each of the two programs, but the goal `c(FX)` $\wedge$ `f1(FX,X)` $\wedge$ `d(X)` does not terminate in the union of the programs.

Here a constraint from one program implies a guard constraint in the other program and vice versa. It is hard to rule out such circularity, since the programs must communicate via shared variables and built-in constraints that are imposed on them.

The nontermination problem persists for P_1, P_2-shared variables, even if we only allow rules that do not introduce new variables.

Example 5.4.4 Here we assume built-in arithmetic constraints over natural numbers:

$P1$: c(X,N) $\Leftrightarrow$ f(X,N) | g(X,N) $\wedge$ c(X,N+1).
$P2$: d(Y,N) $\Leftrightarrow$ g(Y,N) | f(Y,N+1) $\wedge$ d(Y,N+1).

where $f(X,N)$ is defined as $X \bmod 2^N = 0 \wedge X > N \wedge N > 0$ in the constraint theory and $g(X,N)$ is defined as $X \bmod 3^N = 0 \wedge X > N \wedge N > 0$.

Note that for each value of N, both built-in constraints have an infinite number of solutions, and also any conjunction of them, in particular $f(X,N) \wedge g(X,N)$. Moreover, $f(X,N+1)$ implies $f(X,N)$ and $g(X,N+1)$ implies $g(X,N)$, but constraints f and g never imply each other.

Any goal terminates in each of the two programs, but the goal c(X,N)$\wedge$ f(X,N)$\wedge$d(X,N) does not terminate in the union of the programs: the goal reduces to g(X,N)$\wedge$f(X,N)$\wedge$d(X,N)$\wedge$c(X,N+1), which in turn reduces to g(X,N)$\wedge$f(X,N+1)$\wedge$d(X,N+1)$\wedge$c(X,N+1), to which the rule of P_1 applies again and so on ad infinitum.

Summarizing, as soon as there are common symbols, no matter if they are CHR constraints, built-in constraints, or function symbols (even when only shared in the built-in constraint theories), termination is at stake for program union – due to circularity in programs or shared variables in queries.

However, if we restrict the domains (possible values) of the P_1, P_2-shared variables to be finite, termination is modular for noncircular CHR program union. Then there cannot be an infinite number of stricter and stricter constraints for these variables.

Theorem 5.24 Let P_1 and P_2 be two well-behaved CHR programs. If P_1 and P_2 are noncircular then $P_1 \cup P_2$ is terminating if P_1, P_2-shared variables in queries are defined over finite domains only.

Proof. First we prove our result for nonoverlapping programs, then for the general case.

Nonoverlapping case. There is one program, say P_2, that does not use constraints from the other program, say P_1. We prove our claim by contradiction. Assume there is an infinite computation. We can describe any computation as a sequence of alternating subcomputations in P_1 and P_2. In an infinite computation there must be an infinite number of such alternations, because the subcomputations taking place in one program are finite since the programs are terminating.

Actually, for nontermination, the subcomputation in one program must be triggered infinitely often by a constraint from the other program.

Since P_1 and P_2 are noncircular and nonoverlapping, there are no CHR constraints from P_2 that could trigger a rule in P_1. So the reason for an infinite computation can only be an infinite number of tighter and tighter built-in constraints that are produced and checked in the subcomputations for P_1 and for P_2. But since all P_1, P_2-shared variables have a finite domain, they can only be further constrained a finite number of times, because each tighter constraint has to remove at least one tuple from the solution space of the shared variables.

General case. We rewrite the two overlapping noncircular programs in such a way that they are nonoverlapping. All rules for CHR symbols that are defined in both programs are put into the program that has used CHR symbols defined in the other program. Now any computation involving previously commonly defined symbols will take place in that program. The other program never produces constraints involving those symbols. By definition, the transferred rules will use constraints from the original program only. Removal of rules cannot introduce nontermination. Addition of rules that introduce only symbols not defined in the program cannot introduce nontermination. Hence termination is still ensured in both programs, because we are back to the first case where there are no common defined CHR symbols, i.e. to the case of nonoverlapping programs.

Example 5.4.5 The *finite domain constraint* X in D means that the variable X takes its value from the given finite list D (cf. Chapter 8). Reconsider Example 5.4.4:

$P1$: c(X,N) $\Leftrightarrow$ f(X,N) | g(X,N) $\wedge$ c(X,N+1).
$P2$: d(Y,N) $\Leftrightarrow$ g(Y,N) | f(Y,N+1) $\wedge$ d(Y,N+1).

where $f(X, N)$ is defined as $X \bmod 2^N = 0 \wedge X > N \wedge N > 0$ in the constraint theory and $g(X, N)$ is defined as $X \bmod 3^N = 0 \wedge X > N \wedge N > 0$.

The two programs are noncircular. The query c(X,N) $\wedge$ f(X,N) $\wedge$ d(X,N) does not terminate. Variables X and N are P_1, P_2-shared. Adding a finite domain constraint for them results in a terminating query, e.g.

X in [2,4,6,8] $\wedge$ N in [1,2] $\wedge$ c(X,N)$\wedge$ f(X,N)$\wedge$d(X,N)

leads to a state where the domains are reduced to single values

X in [6] $\wedge$ N in [1] $\wedge$ g(X,N)$\wedge$f(X,N)$\wedge$d(X,N)$\wedge$c(X,N+1).

The next state contains the built-in constraint f(X,N+1), but f(6,2) does not hold, so the computation fails.

5.4.2 Modularity of confluence

The union of two nonoverlapping well-behaved programs is always well-behaved if the union is terminating.

Theorem 5.25 Let P_1 and P_2 be two well-behaved CHR programs. Let the union of the two programs, $P_1 \cup P_2$, be terminating. If P_1 and P_2 are nonoverlapping then $P_1 \cup P_2$ is confluent.

Proof. To show that $P_1 \cup P_2$ is confluent, we only have to show that all critical pairs of $P_1 \cup P_2$ are joinable, since $P_1 \cup P_2$ is assumed to be terminating. We distinguish three cases: the set of critical pairs of $P_1 \cup P_2$ consists of (a) all critical pairs stemming from two rules appearing in P_1, (b) all critical pairs stemming from two rules appearing in P_2, and (c) all critical pairs stemming from one rule appearing in P_1 and one rule appearing in P_2.

(a) P_1 is well-behaved, thus all critical pairs stemming from two rules appearing in P_1 are joinable. Therefore, these critical pairs are also joinable in $P_1 \cup P_2$.

(b) Analogous to case (a).

(c) Critical pairs from rules of different programs can only exist if the heads of the rules have at least one constraint in common. This is not possible, since P_1 and P_2 are nonoverlapping.

Example 5.4.6 Consider the nonconfluent union of Example 5.4.1, which is {a $\Leftrightarrow$ b, a $\Leftrightarrow$ c}. The two programs both define a.

On the other hand, the union of the two well-behaved programs $P_1 = $ {a $\Leftrightarrow$ b} and $P_2 = $ {b $\Leftrightarrow$ c} is still confluent, since P_1 and P_2 are non-overlapping.

Once termination of the union has been established, we can use our confluence test to check if the union of well-behaved programs is confluent again. Since P_1 and P_2 are already confluent, for confluence of their union it suffices to check only those critical pairs coming from rules in different programs (cf. the proof of Theorem 5.25). In other words, the confluence test can be made incremental in the addition of rules.

5.5 Operational equivalence

A fundamental and hard question in programming language semantics is when two programs should be considered equivalent. For example, correctness of program transformation can be studied only with respect to a notion of equivalence. Also, if modules or libraries with similar functionality are used together, one may be interested in finding out if program parts in different modules or libraries are equivalent. In the context of CHR, this case arises frequently when constraint solvers are combined.

We embark on a strict notion of program equivalence. Operational equivalence means that given two programs, for any given query, its computations in both programs lead to the same answer. There is a decidable, sufficient, and necessary syntactic condition for operational equivalence of *well-behaved* (terminating and confluent) CHR programs. As far as we know, CHR is the only programming language in practical use with a decidable test for operational equivalence.

5.5.1 *Operational equivalence of programs*

We now formally define operational equivalence of two programs by the fact that for any given (initial) state, equivalent states can be reached by computations in both programs.

Definition 5.26 *Let the notation* $\mapsto_P$ *denote a transition using program* P.

Two CHR programs P_1 *and* P_2 *are operationally equivalent if all states are* P_1, P_2-*joinable.*

A state S *is* P_1, P_2-*joinable iff there are computations* $S \mapsto^+_{P_1} S_1$ *and* $S \mapsto^+_{P_2} S_2$ *such that* $S_1 \equiv S_2$ *or* S *is a final state in both programs.*

There is a straightforward test for operational equivalence of well-behaved CHR programs: the minimal states of all rules in both programs are each executed as queries in both programs, and for each minimal state, the computations must reach equivalent states in both programs.

Theorem 5.27 Two well-behaved programs P_1 and P_2 are *operationally equivalent* iff all minimal states of the rules in P_1 and P_2 are P_1, P_2-joinable.

Proof. The proof uses so-called macro-steps of a computation. These are conveniently chosen nonempty, finite subcomputations from a minimal state to its final state which are contained in a given state.

Let r be a CHR rule with head H and guard C and let $(H \wedge C) \mapsto^+ B$ be a minimal state computation, where B is a final state. Let $H' \wedge G$ be a goal and let r be applicable to H'. A *macro-step* of a goal $H' \wedge G$ is a computation of the form $(H' \wedge G) \mapsto^+ (B \wedge H{=}H' \wedge G)$.

We then prove by induction over the number of macro-steps that the final states of any given goal G computing in P_1 and P_2, respectively, are equal. The proof uses the fact that the number of macro-steps for a given goal is the same in both programs. Furthermore, since P_1 and P_2 are confluent, any computation for the goal G in any of the two programs will lead to the same answer.

Example 5.5.1 We would like to know if these two CHR rules defining the CHR constraint `max` (see also Section 2.3.1 and Example 5.2.5) with different guards,

```
max(X,Y,Z) ⇔ X≤Y | Z=Y.
max(X,Y,Z) ⇔ Y<X  | Z=X.
```

are operationally equivalent with these two rules:

```
max(X,Y,Z) ⇔ X<Y  | Z=Y.
max(X,Y,Z) ⇔ Y≤X | Z=X.
```

Already the minimal state of the first rule of the first program, `max(X,Y,Z)` $\wedge$ `X≤Y`, shows that the two programs are not operationally equivalent. The state can reduce to `Z=Y` in the first program, but is a final state for the second program, since `X≤Y` does not imply any of the guards in the second program. The two programs are logically equivalent, however.

5.5.2 Operational equivalence of constraints

The notion of operational equivalence can be too strict. For example, states that involve (auxiliary) CHR constraints defined in one program only are not P_1, P_2-joinable in general. Therefore, we investigate operational equivalence of CHR constraints that are implemented in different programs with different signatures. We will give a decidable sufficient syntactic condition for constraints defined in well-behaved CHR programs.

As for operational program equivalence, we compare states reached from minimal states when they are executed in the two given programs. However, we only consider minimal states that contain the given common CHR constraint we want to compare and those constraints that can be reached from it using rule applications. Since reachability is very likely to be undecidable, we can only give a sufficient, but not a necessary, condition. The approach can be extended from one to several common constraints.

Definition 5.28 *Let c be a CHR constraint (symbol). A c-state is a state where all CHR constraints have the symbol c.*

Let c be a CHR constraint defined in two CHR programs P_1 and P_2. P_1 and P_2 are operationally *c-equivalent if all c-states are P_1, P_2-joinable.*

The next example shows that for our test we not only have to consider minimal c-states, but also those states that can be reached from these c-states. There may be larger states in which the programs differ, even if they contain just c-constraints.

Example 5.5.2 Let P_1 be the CHR program

```
p(a) ⇔ s.
p(b) ⇔ r.
s∧r ⇔ true.
```

Let P_2 consist only of the first two rules:

```
p(a) ⇔ s.
p(b) ⇔ r.
```

It is not sufficient for operational p-equivalence to consider the minimal states for CHR constraint p, p(a) and p(b). In P_1 the conjunction p(a) ∧ p(b) leads to *true*, but in P_2 it leads just to s∧r. Clearly, if we include the minimal state(s) for s and r, which is just s∧r, different program behavior will be observed.

Before we can give a sufficient syntactic condition for operational c-equivalence, we introduce an approximation of reachability between constraints in a computation called dependency.

Definition 5.29 *Let c, c′, and d be CHR constraint symbols. A CHR constraint (symbol) c* directly depends *on d if there is a rule that defines c and uses d. Then the* dependency *relation is the reflexive transitive closure of direct dependency.*

Given two CHR programs, P_1 and P_2, a c-dependent CHR constraint is a constraint that depends on c in both programs P_1 and P_2.

The upcoming definition and theorem are analogous to those for operational equivalence of programs, except that joinability is not a necessary condition anymore.

Definition 5.30 *The c-minimal states are the minimal states of two CHR programs P_1 and P_2 that only contain c-dependent CHR constraints.*

Theorem 5.31 Let c be a CHR constraint defined in two well-behaved CHR programs P_1 and P_2. Then P_1 and P_2 are operationally c-equivalent if all c-minimal states are P_1, P_2-joinable.

Proof. Analogous to Theorem 5.27.

We now give an example of operationally c-equivalent CHR programs.

Example 5.5.3 The constraint sum(List,Sum) holds if Sum is the sum of elements of a given list List. Let P_1 be the CHR program

```
sum([],Sum) ⇔ Sum=0.
sum([X|Xs],Sum) ⇔ sum(Xs,Sum1) ∧ Sum=Sum1+X.
```

The program P_2 implements sum with an auxiliary constraint sum1:

```
sum([],Sum) ⇔ Sum=0.
sum([X|Xs],Sum) ⇔ sum1(X,Xs,Sum).
 sum1(X,[],Sum) ⇔ Sum=X.
 sum1(X,Xs,Sum) ⇔ sum(Xs,Sum1) ∧ Sum=Sum1+X.
```

The sum-minimal states coming from P_1 and P_2 are sum([],Sum) and sum([X|Xs],Sum).

For the sum-minimal state sum([],Sum), the final state is Sum=0 in both P_1 and P_2.

A computation of the sum-minimal state sum([X|Xs],Sum) in P_1 proceeds as follows: sum([X|Xs],Sum) $\mapsto_{P_1}$ sum(Xs, Sum1)$\wedge$Sum=Sum1+X. A computation in P_2 results in the same answer: sum([X|Xs],Sum) $\mapsto_{P_2}$ sum1(X,Xs, Sum) $\mapsto_{P_2}$ sum(Xs, Sum1) $\wedge$ Sum=Sum1+X.

Since all sum-minimal states are P_1, P_2-joinable, P_1 and P_2 are operationally sum-equivalent.

The reason that we can only give a sufficient, but not necessary, condition for operational c-equivalence is that the dependency relation between CHR constraints only approximates the actual set of CHR constraints that occur in states that can be reached from a c-state. The example illustrates this observation.

Example 5.5.4 Let P_1 be the CHR program

```
p(X) ⇔  X>0 | q(X).
q(X) ⇔  X<0 | true.
```

Let P_2 be the program

```
p(X) ⇔  X>0 | q(X).
q(X) ⇔  X<0 | false.
```

P_1 and P_2 are operationally p-equivalent, but the p-minimal state $q(X) \wedge X < 0$ is not P_1, P_2-joinable.

The next example shows that c-equivalence of all constraints considered on their own does not imply operational program equivalence.

Example 5.5.5 Let P_1 be

```
p ⇔ s.
s∧q ⇔ true.
```

let P_2 be

and

```
p ⇔ s.
s∧q ⇔ false.
```

P_1 and P_2 have three common CHR constraints, p, s, and q. s and p are the p-dependent constraints. There are no s-dependent CHR constraints except s itself. Analogously for q. Hence all p-, s-, and q-minimal states are P_1, P_2-joinable, but the programs are not operationally equivalent: s∧q leads in P_1 to *true* and in P_2 to *false*.

Clearly, if we extend the notion of c-equivalence to sets of constraints, the p-, s-, q-minimal states include the indicative state s∧q.

5.5.3 Removal of redundant rules

The union of programs and completion may result in redundant rules. We can use a variation of the operational equivalence test to detect rules that can be removed from a program without changing its operational semantics.

Definition 5.32 *The notation $P \backslash r$ denotes a CHR program P without rule r.*

A rule r is redundant *in a CHR program P iff for all states S: if $S \mapsto_P^* S_1$ then $S \mapsto_{P \backslash r}^* S_2$, such that $S_1 \equiv S_2$.*

Example 5.5.6 Consider the *union* of the two programs defining `max` from Example 5.5.1:

```
r1 @ max(X,Y,Z) ⟺ X<Y | Z=Y.
r2 @ max(X,Y,Z) ⟺ X≥Y | Z=X.
r3 @ max(X,Y,Z) ⟺ X≤Y | Z=Y.
r4 @ max(X,Y,Z) ⟺ X>Y | Z=X.
```

This union contains redundant rules. Rule `r3` can always apply when rule `r1` does, with the same answer, but not vice versa. Hence rule `r1` is redundant, and analogously rule `r4`.

However, our operational equivalence test (according to Theorem 5.27) may not be directly applicable for our redundancy check: if we remove a rule from a well-behaved program, it may become nonconfluent (cf. Section 5.4.2). Thus, we first have to test confluence of the program without the candidate rule for redundancy.

Theorem 5.33 Let P be a well-behaved program. A rule r is *redundant with respect to P* iff $P\backslash r$ is well-behaved and all minimal states of P and $P\backslash r$ are $P, P\backslash r$-joinable.

Proof. *The if direction:* We prove the claim that $P\backslash r$ is well-behaved by contradiction. We assume P is well-behaved, r is redundant, but $P\backslash r$ is not well-behaved. We can distinguish two reasons for this situation:

- Program $P\backslash r$ is not terminating, thus P is also not terminating (cf. Section 5.4.1), which is a contradiction to the fact that P is well-behaved.
- Program $P\backslash r$ is not confluent, thus there exists a state S such that $S \mapsto^*_{P\backslash r} S_1$ and then $S \mapsto^*_{P\backslash r} S_2$, but $S_1 \not\equiv S_2$. Rule r is redundant with respect to P, then by Definition 5.32 there exists a state S_3 such that $S \mapsto^*_P S_3$. Since P is confluent, $S_3 \equiv S_1$ as well as $S_3 \equiv S_2$. This contradicts $S_1 \not\equiv S_2$.

The only-if direction: Now we prove that all minimal states of P and $P\backslash r$ are $P, P\backslash r$-joinable. r is redundant with respect to P. By definition, for all states S, $S \mapsto^*_P S_1$ then $S \mapsto^*_{P\backslash r} S_2$, where $S_1 \equiv S_2$. Therefore, all states are $P, P\backslash r$-joinable.

We can specialize our operational equivalence test for redundancy removal: we just check if the computation due to the candidate rule for redundancy can be performed by the remainder of the program. In other words, some state in the computation for the minimal state of r must be reachable also in $P\backslash r$. We can repeat the process of removing redundant rules to minimize the number of rules in a given program.

Example 5.5.7 Consider the four-rule program for maximum from Example 5.5.6. Note that any subset of the program is still well-behaved. If we try to remove rule r1 we only have to check the minimal state of rule r1, that is max(X,Y,Z)∧X<Y, by running it in both programs:

P: max(X,Y,Z)∧X<Y ↦ X<Y∧Z=Y by rule r1
$P\backslash\{\text{r1}\}$: max(X,Y,Z)∧X<Y ↦ X<Y ∧ Z=Y by rule r3

Since rule r3 enables the same computation step, rule r1 is redundant. In an analogous way, redundancy of rule r4 can be shown. Rule r2, however, is not redundant:

P: max(X,Y,Z)∧X≥Y ↦ X≥Y ∧ Z=X by rule r2
$P\backslash\{\text{r2}\}$: max(X,Y,Z)∧X≥Y ↦̸

In program $P\backslash\{\text{r2}\}$, the minimal state is a final state.

Hence the max program without redundant rules consists of the rules r2 and r3. This program is unique.

Example 5.5.8 Consider rules for a strict order constraint in analogy to the ones for the nonstrict order of Example 2.4.2 (see also Example 5.3.9).

```
duplicate     @ X less Y \ X less Y ⇔ true.
irreflexivity@ X less X ⇔ false.
antisymmetry @ X less Y ∧ Y less X ⇔ false.
transitivity @ X less Y ∧ Y less Z ⇒ X less Z.
```

The **antisymmetry** rule is redundant. Its computation can be performed by applying the **transitivity** rule and then **irreflexivity**. No other rule is redundant.

The program resulting from removing all redundant rules is not necessarily unique, since it may depend on the order in which rules are removed.

Example 5.5.9 Let P be the well-behaved CHR program that results from completion of the program in Example 5.3.1.

```
r1 @ p ⇔ q.
r2 @ p ⇔ false.
r3 @ q ⇔ false.
```

Either rule r1 or rule r2 can be removed to arrive at a program with no redundant rule, but not both. Hence the program for P without redundant rules is not unique.

5.6 Worst-case time complexity

Our semi-automatic worst-case time complexity analysis will be based on semi-naive implementations of CHR under the abstract semantics. Available CHR systems achieve much better complexity results since they implement the refined semantics and feature compiler optimizations such as indexing.

Indexing is based on the observation that usually the head constraints of a rule are connected through common variables (or values). Thus, given one constraint, we only need to search for partner constraints in those constraints that share a variable. Using an index at the argument position of the common variable, one can often find suitable partner constraints in constant time.

The run-time of a CHR program not only depends on the number of rule applications (derivation lengths), but also, more significantly, on the number of rule application *attempts (rule tries)*. We combine the predicted worst-case derivation length with a worst-case estimate of the number and cost of rule tries and the cost of rule applications to obtain a meta-theorem for the worst-case time complexity of simplification rule programs. The number of potential rule applications can be computed automatically from the program text, once a ranking is known.

Example 5.6.1 We continue with Example 5.1.1. We can show that the worst-case time complexity of a single **even** constraint is linear in the derivation length, i.e. its rank. The same observation holds for a query consisting of several ground **even** constraints, where the rank is defined as the sum of the ranks of the individual constraints.

However, things change when we add a second rule:

```
even(s(N)) ⇔ N=s(M)∧even(M).
even(s(X))∧even(X) ⇔ false.
```

In general, the new rule must be tried for *all pairs of* **even** constraints in a query, and again after a computation step of a single **even** constraint with the first rule. Of course in most cases, the rule application attempts (rule tries) will be in vain, but they will cost.

The number of rule tries in a single derivation step is at worst quadratic in the number of **even** constraints in the query. Since the rank of an **even** constraint is at least one, the rank of the query is a bound on the number of constraints. The number of derivation steps is also bounded by the rank of the query. Overall, this yields a semi-naive implementation that is cubic in the rank of the query.

We first consider the worst cost of applying a single rule, which consists of the cost to try the rule on all CHR constraints in the current state and the cost to apply the rule to some CHR constraints in the state. Then we choose the worst rule in the program and apply it in the worst possible state of the derivation. Multiplying the result with the worst-case derivation length gives us the desired upper bound on the worst-case time complexity.

5.6.1 Simplification rules

There are several computational phases when a rule is applied:

Head matching: Atomic CHR constraints in the current state have to be found that match the head constraints of the rule.

Guard checking: Under head matching, it is checked if the current built-in constraints imply the guard of the rule.

Body handling: According to rule type, CHR constraints matching the head are removed. Then the guard and the body with its built-in and CHR constraints are added.

We now give the worst-case time complexity for application of a single rule to given CHR constraints.

Lemma 5.34 Let r be a simplification rule of the form $H \Leftrightarrow G \mid C \wedge B$, where H is a conjunction of n CHR constraints, G and C are built-in constraints, and B are CHR constraints. A *worst-case time complexity of applying the rule r in a state with c CHR constraints* is, in O-notation:

$$O(c^n(O_H + O_G) + (O_C + O_B)),$$

where O_H is the complexity of matching the head H of the rule, O_G the complexity of checking the guard G, O_C the complexity of adding the body built-in constraints C to the state, and O_B the complexity of removing the head and of adding the body CHR constraints B to the state.

Proof. The formula consists of two summands, the first is the cost of trying the rule, the second the cost of applying the rule. In a semi-naive implementation, we compute all possible combinations of n constraints and try to match them to the rule head. Hence, given c constraints in a query and a rule with n head constraints, there are $O(c^n)$ combinations of constraints to try. Each try involves matching the head of the rule with complexity O_H and, if successful, checking the guard with complexity O_G. Then, the cost of handling the rule body, $(O_C + O_B)$, is incurred.

5.6.2 Programs

Now we are ready to give our meta-theorem about the time complexity of simplification rule programs. To compute the time complexity of a derivation, we have to find the worst case for the application of a rule, i.e. the largest number of CHR constraints of any state in a derivation and the most costly rule that could be tried and applied.

Theorem 5.35 Let P be a CHR program containing only simplification rules. Given a query with worst-case derivation length D, the worst-case time complexity of a derivation starting with the given query is:

$$O(D\sum_i((c+D)^{n_i}(O_{H_i}+O_{G_i}) + (O_{C_i}+O_{B_i}))),$$

where the index i ranges over the rules in the program P.

Proof. In the worst case, in each of the D derivation steps, all rules are tried on all combinations of the maximum possible number of head constraints, say c_{max}, and then the most costly rule is applied. Since rule application attempts are independent from each other, we can extend Lemma 5.34 to a set of rules in a straightforward way:

$$O(\sum_i c_{max}^{n_i}(O_{H_i}+O_{G_i}) + \mathbf{Max}_i(O_{C_i}+O_{B_i})),$$

where c_{max} is the worst number of CHR constraints in a derivation from a given query and $\mathbf{Max}_i$ takes the maximum over all i. Since the functions **Max** and $+$ are equivalent in the O-notation, we can replace $\mathbf{Max}_i$ by $\sum_i$. This gives us the complexity for one derivation step.

Multiplying the resulting formula by the derivation length D yields the overall complexity:

$$O(D\sum_i(c_{max}^{n_i}(O_{H_i}+O_{G_i}) + (O_{C_i}+O_{B_i}))).$$

Now we need a bound on $c_{max}^{n_i}$ that only depends on properties of the query, namely c, the number of CHR constraints in the query, and D, the upper bound on the derivation length. There cannot be more than $c + O(D)$ CHR constraints in any state of a derivation starting with the query, because we start from c constraints and there are at most D derivations steps, and each derivation step adds a fixed number of new constraints when applying a rule of the program. After replacing c_{max} by the bound $c + O(D)$, we arrive at the formula of the theorem.

From the meta-theorem it can be seen that the cost of rule tries dominates the complexity of a semi-naive implementation of CHR. Furthermore, it often suffices to take the worst rule of the program to compute the complexity measure.

Typical complexities. We end this section with some general remarks on the complexity of using the constituents of a simplification rule. The cost of syntactic matching O_H is determined by the syntactic size of the head in the given program text. Thus, its time complexity is constant. We assume that the complexity O_B of removing and adding CHR constraints (without applying any rules) is constant in a semi-naive implementation where lists are used to store the CHR constraints.

The complexity of handling built-ins is predetermined by the built-in constraint solvers used. We assume that the time complexity of checking and adding built-in constraints is not dependent on the constraints accumulated so far in the derivation. While this is not true in general, it usually holds because the built-ins that appear in CHR programs are usually simple.

We will also assume constant time for arithmetic operations and quasi-constant time for unification and matching. (This complexity can be achieved with the union-find algorithm.) In the following we will sometimes not distinguish between constant and quasi-constant time.

The complexity of guard checking O_G is usually at most as high as the complexity of adding the respective constraints. The worst-case time complexity of adding built-in constraints O_C is often linear in their size. In many cases, D contains the factor c, so that $c + D$ simplifies to just D.

In summary, this gives a simplified complexity of

$$O(\sum_i (D^{n_i+1}O_{G_i} + DO_{C_i})).$$

We will sometimes use the constant 0 to denote zero time, e.g. for O_G if there is no guard.

Examples for semi-automatic complexity analysis and their comparison with empirical results from benchmarking experiments can be found in Part III. Here we just give a notorious example with very high complexity.

Example 5.6.2 Consider the one-rule program that uses successor notation:

c(s(X)) ⇔ c(X)∧c(X) .

Since removing a successor doubles the number of constraints, only an exponential ranking can prove termination and give an upper bound on the derivation length:

$rank(c(t)) = 2^{size(t)} - 1$
$size(0) = 0$
$size(s(N)) = 1 + size(N)$

By our meta-complexity theorem, the worst-case complexity is exponential in the size of the argument of c (let $n = size(t)$):

$$O(2^n((1 + 2^n)^1(1 + 0) + (0 + 1)) = O(2^n 2^n) = O(4^n).$$

The complexity can be explained by the fact that we will have $O(2^n)$ derivation steps and in each state we will have $O(2^n)$ constraints among which we have to search for one where the rule is still applicable.

5.7 Bibliographic remarks

In this chapter, we have discussed program analysis for CHR. Termination, confluence, and completion analysis of CHR benefits strongly from results in term rewriting systems (TRS) [Der87, BN98].

For CHR programs that mainly use simplification rules, simple well-founded orders are often sufficient to prove termination [Frü00, Frü01, Frü02a]. Theorem 5.7 can be found in [Frü00]. For CHR programs that mainly use propagation rules, results from bottom-up logic programming [GA01] as well as from deductive and constraint databases could apply.

Confluence is presented first in [FAM96]. The main critical-pair confluence Theorem 5.16 can be found in [Abd97, AFM99]. The consistency-by-confluence theorem was published in [AFM99]. Newman's Lemma can be found in [New42].

In [DSS07] the notion of *observable confluence* is introduced, where the states that represent overlaps and critical pairs must satisfy a user-defined invariant (as defined for transition systems in general in Section 3.1.2). Reachability is one possible invariant. The invariant can also be used to restrict oneself to certain allowed (valid) queries and states. The most general states of the critical pairs may not satisfy the required invariant. In that case, larger states containing those states must be tested for joinability. In general, this may lead to an infinite number of states to be tested, and so the confluence test loses decidability.

Completion is introduced in [AF98]. The approach to use completion for computing answer rules turns out to be similar to the ones that related Prolog and TRS computation methods [DJ84, BH92].

In the discussion of modularity, we mentioned several ways of combining CHR programs: flat composition by program union [AF03]; hierarchical composition [SDD+06]; and extending arbitrary solvers [DSdlBH03].

Theorem 5.27 on operational equivalence of well-behaved CHR programs is from [AF99].

In [Frü02b] the meta-theorem for the worst-case time complexity of simplification rule programs is published. Available CHR systems achieve much better complexity results since they implement the refined semantics and feature compiler optimizations such as indexing [Sch05]. As for related work, [GA01, GM02] give several complexity meta-theorems for a hypothetical logical rule-based language that has recently been implemented in CHR with optimal complexity [KSD07a]. They consider mainly propagation rules that must be applied to ground formulas at run-time, while we consider simplification rules that involve unbound variables at run-time and arbitrary built-in constraints.

For program analysis aiming at compiler optimization, an abstract interpretation framework for CHR is introduced in [SSD05a].

6

Rule-based and graph-based formalisms in CHR

We are interested in the relationship of other rule-based formalisms and programming languages to CHR. In particular, we want to know about the principles of embedding essential aspects of them in CHR. We will informally discuss the following formalisms, systems, and language paradigms:

- Rule-based systems such as Production Rules (e.g. OPS5), Event–Condition–Action (ECA) Rules, Business Rules, and the Logical Algorithms (LA) formalism in Section 6.1.
- Rewriting-based and graph-based formalisms such as Term Rewriting Systems (TRS) with a remark on Functional Programming (FP) and on Graph Rewriting Systems (GTS), the General Abstract Model for Multiset Manipulation (GAMMA), and standard and Colored Petri Nets (CPN) in Section 6.2.
- Prolog, a remark on deductive databases, the Constraint Logic Programming (CLP), and the Concurrent Constraint Programming (CC) language framework in Section 6.3.

We cannot give a full account of all these approaches, after all this is a book about CHR. We have to assume some basic knowledge of the approach discussed. The approaches range from theoretically well-researched formalisms like term rewriting and programming language schemes like constraint logic programming to concrete rule-based systems like OPS5. Readers may find the presentation of the formalisms overly simplistic, but this has been done for space reasons and to emphasize the relationship with CHR. We will take the viewpoint of CHR, and this should not be taken as a critique on the other approaches. We also cannot go into the details of the embeddings. When available, we refer to research papers. If not, we present the main idea behind a possible answer to an otherwise unexplored open research question. We think it is still worth presenting all kinds of embeddings in this chapter.

141

It helps to put CHR in perspective and in interaction with formalisms and languages that have a long successful history.

Features of CHR. CHR provides propagation rules and logical variables subject to built-in constraints which are maintained in an implicit global context called constraint store.

It is not clear how to express *propagation rules* directly in the aforementioned approaches while ensuring termination (except for the LA formalism).

CHR manipulates relations considered as constraints which typically contain *unbound logical variables*. Rule-based systems, rewriting-based and graph-based formalisms rely on a *ground representation*, just as any programming language except constraint-based and logic-based languages. Logical variables cannot be represented directly. Expressions are usually considered only once for computation. A rule either does or does not apply to a particular expression. CHR constraints can be woken and reconsidered if new built-in constraints have been added. Without *built-in constraints*, there is also no notion of failure.

Most rule-based systems lack a *declarative semantics*. CHR performs computations justified by classical first-order predicate logic or linear logic. These declarative semantics are closely related to its operational semantics by soundness and completeness results.

Implementations of CHR are typically integrated with their *host language*, other programming languages are typically stand-alone systems.

Positive ground range-restricted CHR. With the exception of constraint programming languages, the aforementioned approaches can be embedded in the *positive ground range-restricted fragment* of CHR. *Positive* means that there are no built-in constraints in the body of rules except *true*. *Ground* means that all queries are ground. *Range-restricted* means that every variable from the guard and body also occurs in the rule head, i.e. there are no local variables.

Groundness, together with range-restrictedness, implies the invariant that every state in a computation will be ground. In this fragment, computations cannot fail and there is no need for the built-in constraint store (provided equations are applied as *substitutions*).

Actually, the condition of range-restriction can be relaxed. We can allow local variables in the rule if they will always become ground (due to solving built-in constraints) whenever the variables in the head are ground.

In this way, we can model auxiliary functions of the rule body as built-in constraints.

Shortcomings of embeddings in CHR. Clearly, a direct embedding in CHR does not cover all aspects of the aforementioned approaches. For example, unlike rule-based systems, CHR has no explicit way to influence the order of rule applications and thus no built-in conflict resolution for choosing rules, even though there are extensions of CHR that have rules with priorities and rules with probabilities. Unlike Prolog and constraint logic programming, CHR does not have disjunction, but the extension of CHR$^\vee$ has. Unlike some graph-based systems, there is no diagrammatic notation for CHR yet.

CHR does not have the nonmonotonic *negation-as-failure* of constraint logic programming and the *negation-as-absence* of rule-based systems. In general, *nonmonotonicity* destroys confluence and classical first-order predicate logic declarative semantics. Still, we show how we can simulate that kind of negation under the refined semantics of CHR.

Advantages of embeddings in CHR. Embedding formalisms and languages in CHR allows for their analysis, comparison, and cross-fertilization using a common platform. When a translated formalism or language is executed in CHR, we immediately get all the advantages of CHR: execution is possible even if some arguments are unknown or partially known as described by built-in constraints. The CHR program then produces a valid abstract run that satisfies the constraints on the variables. CHR execution is incremental, anytime and online, and concurrency comes for free for confluent programs. Termination and confluence can be checked, completion can be performed to regain confluence. Complexity can be semi-automatically estimated. Last but not least, the declarative semantics of CHR relates the approach at hand to a logical theory.

Embedding fragments of CHR. It seems difficult to come up with an embedding of *full* CHR in one of the aforementioned formalisms for the reasons given before. The positive ground range-restricted fragment of CHR without propagation rules can be embedded into rule-based systems as well as rewriting-based and graph-based formalisms as discussed here, but not in (colored) Petri nets, since they are not Turing-complete.

Depending on the overall program, propagation rules can be modeled in rule-based systems, but for their termination, the propagation history has to be made explicit. The exception is the LA formalism, but it has a different operational semantics and the only implementations of it are written in CHR, at the time of writing. The basic pure rewriting-based and graph-based formalisms are likely to require more translation effort for propagation rules.

While constraint-based and logic-based programming languages feature logical variables and built-in constraints, they lack rules with multiple heads and propagation rules. Single-headed simplification rules with logical variables and built-in constraints can be expressed in all other constraint programming languages. Single-headed propagation rules require an explicit propagation history to be carried around. Guard checking in its generality as an implication test is only available in concurrent constraint programming languages.

6.1 Rule-based systems

The programming paradigm of *production rule systems* originates from Artificial Intelligence research. They were the first rule-based systems and are mainly used for expert systems (later called decision support systems and now developed into business rules). These rule systems are procedural and imperative and use a ground representation. They use *destructive assignment* directly and thus lack a declarative logic-based semantics. The implementations often use the RETE and the more efficient TREAT algorithm, while CHR is based on a different approach where active constraints are considered as procedure calls (cf. Section 3.3). This approach is considered faster for a language like CHR. RETE and TREAT work best on slowly changing store and simple rule heads with little sharing (common variables), neither of which is the case for CHR.

ECA rules are an extension of production rules for *active database systems*. ECA rules were a hot research topic in the mid-1990s, in the meantime simple cases have been standardized, e.g. in SQL-3.

The research results on rule-based systems are reused and re-examined for business rules, workflow systems, the *semantic web* (e.g. for enriching web ontologies like OWL, validating web forms, handling privacy preferences, accessing control rules, and knowledge interchange), in Aspect Oriented Programming and in UML (e.g. implicational OCL invariants) and its extensions (e.g. ATL). Rules may also be used for security, to define who is authorized to do what.

Business rules define and constrain the structure and behavior of a business. They lay down the definitions, policies, and procedures that govern how a company operates and interacts with its customers and other companies. They are similar to ECA rules but are employed over the whole workflow in a company.

The LA formalism is basically a hypothetical declarative production rule language. Unlike other rule-based systems, information is never removed, but it can be overshadowed by negative information. In this way, LA is also similar to deductive database languages like Datalog.

6.1.1 Production rule systems

Production rule systems represent knowledge as a set of rules according to the scheme

if *Condition* **then** *Action.*

Production rules are also called reaction rules or stimulus–response rules. There is a *working memory* that stores *facts*, which are also called *working memory elements (WME)*. Facts have an *attribute-value* syntax, i.e. use named attributes (cf. Section 9.5). The *Condition* consists of expression matchings describing facts. The *then-clause* contains actions. *Expression matchings* for facts are *patterns* that involve in-place conditions on attributes. Patterns may be negated, asking for the *absence* of a particular fact. *Actions* are explicit insertion and removal of facts, IO statements and auxiliary functions. Because of the attribute-value syntax and the explicit manipulation of facts, production rules tend to be verbose.

During an execution step, all production rules are identified whose if-clause can be satisfied by facts. One of the applicable rules is chosen during a process called *conflict resolution* and the then-clause of the chosen rule is executed. Conflict resolution can be based on priorities among rules, and it can be static or dynamic. The execution process is called a *recognize–act cycle*. As in CHR, rules are executed till exhaustion.

For embedding production rules in CHR, facts can be translated to CHR constraints where attribute names are encoded by argument positions. Production rules can be translated to CHR simpagation rules, where the if-clause, with pattern and condition separated, form head and guard and where the then-clause forms the body of the CHR rule. Creation, insertion, and removal of facts is implicit in CHR by putting them in the appropriate positions in the head and body of a simpagation rule. For embedding negation-as-absence and conflict resolution, we have to rely on the refined semantics of CHR as discussed in the next sections.

In the following, we use OPS5 as a prototypical example for rule-based systems.

Definition 6.1 *Given an OPS5 production rule named* N *of the form*

(p N LHS --> RHS)

we translate it into a generalized simpagation rule

N @ LHS1 \ LHS2 ⇔ LHS3 | RHS'.

where LHS1 *and* LHS2 *are the patterns of* LHS *and* LHS3 *is the condition of* LHS. LHS1 *contains the patterns for those facts that are not modified in the* RHS. *The body* RHS' *is* RHS *without the actions for removal of facts.*

Some examples illustrate this translation.

Example 6.1.1 The rule for iterative Fibonacci sequence generation in OPS5 is given below:

```
(p next-fib
   (limit ^is <limit>)
   {(fibonacci ^index {<i> <= <limit>}
               ^this-value <v1>
               ^last-value <v2>) <fib>}
     -->
   (modify <fib> ^index (compute <i> + 1)
                 ^this-value (compute <v1> + <v2>)
                 ^last-value <v1>)
   (write (crlf) Fib <i> is <v1>)
)
```

The translation into CHR results in the simplification rule

```
next-fib @ limit(Limit), fibonacci(I,V1,V2) <=> I =< Limit |
        fibonacci(I+1,V1+V2,V1), write(fib I is V1), nl.
```

This rule is similar to the one used for the procedural style version at the end of Section 2.3.2:

```
fn @ fib(Max,N,M1,M2) <=> Max>N | fib(Max,N+1,M2,M1+M2).
```

Example 6.1.2 In OPS5, the greatest common divisor can be computed by these four rules:

```
(p done-no-divisors
(euclidean-pair ^first <first> ^second 1) -->
(write GCD is 1) (halt) )

(p found-gcd
(euclidean-pair ^first <first> ^second <first>) -->
(write GCD is <first>) (halt) )
```

```
(p switch-pair
{(euclidean-pair ^first <first> ^second { <second> > <first>} )
  <e-pair>} -->
(modify <e-pair> ^first <second> ^second <first>)
(write <first> -- <second> (crlf)) )


(p reduce-pair
{(euclidean-pair ^first <first> ^second { <second> < <first> } )
  <e-pair>} -->
(modify <e-pair> ^first (compute <first> - <second>))
(write <first> -- <second> (crlf)) )
```

The direct translation into CHR results in the simplification rules

```
done-no-divisors @ euclidean_pair(First, 1) <=>
        write(GCD is 1).


found-gcd @ euclidean_pair(First, First) <=>
        write(GCD is First).


switch-pair @ euclidean_pair(First, Second) <=>
        Second > First |
        euclidean_pair(Second, First),
        write(First - Second), nl.


reduce-pair @ euclidean_pair(First, Second)) <=>
        Second < First |
        euclidean_pair((First - Second), Second),
        write(First - Second), nl.
```

6.1.2 Negation-as-absence

Production-rule systems allow for negated patterns. They are satisfied if *no* fact satisfies the condition. This notion of asking for absence is similar to *negation-as-failure* in Prolog. This kind of negation has been called *negation-as-absence* in the context of CHR.

The semantics of many rule-based systems has been plagued by this kind of negation and the related problem of reasoning with defaults, since it violates *monotonicity* (cf. Lemma 4.1). So it is not by accident that CHR does not provide such negation as a predefined language construct.

However, there are several ways to implement negation-as-absence in CHR, although it is not encouraged. We may either use a low-level built-in constraint in the guard or use an auxiliary CHR constraint under the refined semantics. The translation schemes we give here can be further refined and can also be extended to cases of multiple and nested negation. Another approach for implementation would be to use the explicit deletion event of ECA rules (cf. Section 6.1.4).

We will use the following three examples to illustrate the translations. The – sign denotes negation-as-absence in OPS5.

Example 6.1.3 To find the minimum among numbers wrapped by num and return it in fact min, we have the OPS5 rule

```
(p minimum
        (num ^val <x>)
        -(num ^val < <x>)
         -->
        (make min ^val <x>)
)
```

Example 6.1.4 In a transitive closure program on graphs, we may have an OPS5 rule to avoid the generation of duplicate paths:

```
(p init-path
        (edge ^from <x> ^to <y>)
        -(path ^from <x> ^to <y>)
        -->
        (make path ^from <x> ^to <y>)
)
```

Negation-as-absence can also be used for *default reasoning*. One assumes the default unless there is evidence to the contrary.

Example 6.1.5 A person is either single or married, where single is to be the default.

```
(p default
        (person ^name <x>)
        -(married ^name <x>)
        -->
        (make single ^name <x>)
)
```

We discuss two approaches for negation-as-absence in CHR and one special case in the following. Given an OPS5 rule, the positive part of the left-hand side (l.h.s.) and the right-hand side (r.h.s.) are translated as before. For simplicity, we assume there is only one negation in the rule to translate.

Built-in constraint in guard. Here a low-level built-in asks the store for the presence of a CHR constraint.

Definition 6.2 *Given an OPS5 production rule with a negated pattern*

```
(p N LHS -Negative --> RHS)
```

we translate it into a generalized simpagation rule

```
N @ LHS1 \ LHS2 ⇔ LHS3 ∧ not Negative' | RHS'.
```

where LHS *contains the positive part of the l.h.s. where* LHS1, LHS2, LHS3, *and* RHS' *are defined as before. The operator* not *negates the result of the test it is applied to.* Negative' *is* Negative *where each pattern for a fact together with its condition is wrapped by a low-level built-in constraint that succeeds if the CHR constraint store contains such a fact.*

If the host language of CHR is Prolog, **not** uses negation-as-failure, and low-level built-in is often called `find_c(onstraint)` or similar.

For minimum finding as in the OPS5 Example 6.1.3 we get:

```
minimum @ num(X) ==> not find_c(num(Y),Y<X) | min(X).
```

For avoidance of duplicate paths in the OPS5 Example 6.1.4 we get:

```
init-path @ e(X,Y) ==> not find_c(p(X,Y),true) | p(X,Y).
```

For Example 6.1.5 we get:

```
default @ person(X) ==> not find_c(married(X),true) | single(X).
```

While this translation is simple, it relies on a low-level built-in which makes the resulting CHR programs hard to analyze.

CHR constraint in head. Here we make use of an auxiliary CHR constraint under the refined semantics of CHR.

Definition 6.3 *Given an OPS5 rule*

```
(p N LHS, -Negative --> RHS)
```

we translate it into three CHR rules (where **check** *is an auxiliary CHR constraint):*

```
N1 @ LHS1 ∧ LHS2 ⇒ LHS3 | check(LHS1,LHS2).
N2 @ Neg1 \ check(LHS1,LHS2) ⇔ Neg2 | true.
N3 @ LHS1 \ LHS2, check(LHS1,LHS2) ⇔ RHS'.
```

Neg1 *contains the patterns and* **Neg2** *contains the conditions of* **Negative.** *The other rule components are as before.*

Given the positive part LHS of the rule, we check for absence of the negative part Negative using the propagation rule N1. If we find what should be absent using rule N2, we remove check and do not apply rule N3 that produces the body. The code relies on the order in which the rules are tried. Thus, confluence is destroyed.

For our three OPS5 examples, this approach results in the CHR rules

```
num(X) ==> check(num(X)).
num(Y) \ check(num(X)) <=> Y<X | true.
num(X) \ check(num(X)) <=> min(X).
```

and

```
e(X,Y) ==> check(e(X,Y)).
p(X,Y) \ check(e(X,Y)) <=> true.
e(X,Y) \ check(e(X,Y)) <=> p(X,Y).
```

and finally

```
person(X) ==> check(person(X)).
married(X) \ check(person(X)) <=> true.
person(X)  \ check(person(X)) <=> single(X).
```

Special case – body in head. In some cases it is safe to use RHS directly instead of check. We assume that the negative part of the rule holds and if not, we repair the situation afterwards. This approach is possible if no facts are to be removed (LHS2 is empty and RHS is RHS'). We can then generate two CHR rules:

```
Nn @ Neg1  RHS' ⇔ Neg2 | true.
Np @ LHS1 ⇒ LHS3 | RHS'.
```

CHR rule Np results from translating the production rule as usual, but ignoring the negative part. Rule Nn removes RHS' in case the negative part is present. The rule has to come first to ensure that RHS' does not trigger another rule.

This special case illustrates that explicit negation-as-absence is not always necessary. Sometimes this type of negation is just used to implement the equivalent of propagation rules in rule-based systems. The results of this translation are shorter and more concise, often incremental and concurrent

CHR programs that can be analyzed more easily. For the three examples, this approach results in

```
min(Y) \ min(X) <=> Y<X | true.
num(X) ==> min(X).
```

and

```
p(X,Y) \ p(X,Y) <=> true.
e(X,Y) ==> p(X,Y).
```

and

```
married(X) \ single(X) <=> true.
person(X) ==> single(X).
```

These are also the programs we would use in CHR (cf. Sections 2.2.1 and 2.4.1 for the first two examples).

6.1.3 Conflict resolution

Conflict resolution can be implemented in CHR for arbitrary CHR rules by delaying the execution of the rule bodies, collecting them, and choosing one among them for execution.

To achieve this, CHR rules are transformed by the following scheme.

Definition 6.4 *Instead of each rule*

```
Head1 \ Head2 ⇔ Guard | Body.
```

we introduce the pair of rules

```
delay @ resolve ∧ Head1 \ Head2 ⇒ Guard |
                        conflictset([rule(Head1,Head2,Body)]).
apply @ Head1 \ Head2 ∧ apply(rule(Head1,Head2,Body)) ⇔
                        Body.
```

and two generic rules to resolve the conflict:

```
collect @ conflictset(L1) ∧ conflictset(L2) ⇔
                        append(L1,L2,L3) ∧ conflictset(L3).
choose  @ resolve ∧ conflictset(L) ⇔
                        choose_rule(L,R) ∧ apply(R) ∧ resolve.
```

where resolve *is an auxiliary CHR constraint to trigger the conflict resolution. The CHR constraint* conflictset *collects the rules in its argument list. The CHR constraint* apply *executes a collected rule.*

When `resolve` becomes active, all applicable rules are collected in the constraint `conflictset` by rules `delay` and `collect`. When there are no more rules, `resolve` proceeds to the last rule `choose` and triggers the application of the rule R (selected with `choose_rule` from the conflict set) using `apply`. After the chosen rule has been applied, `resolve` is called again to initiate the next execution cycle. This approach can be extended to deal with preferences, probabilities and the like that are attached to the individual rules by modifying the constraint `choose_rule`.

6.1.4 Event–condition–action rules

ECA rules are an extension of production rules for active database systems. ECA rules provide the ability to react to events. They generalize various database features like integrity constraints (assertions, invariants), triggers, and view maintenance. ECA rules follow the scheme:

on *Event* **if** *Condition* **then** *Action.*

Events trigger rules. Internal events are caused by database manipulation and retrieval, and by committing and aborting database transactions. External events can be temporal (caused by a timer) or from applications (exceptions and user-defined events). Events can be composed sequentially and by the usual logical operators.

(Pre-)conditions also include database queries. These are satisfied if the result of the query is nonempty. Conditions have to be able to access database tuples as they are before and as they are after some database manipulation (i.e. old and new attribute values).

Actions include database operations, rollback of transactions, call of external applications, including IO and absorption of events. When an event is absorbed, its causing action (e.g. an update) will not be executed. *Postconditions* may be used to check if a rule application led to the desired result.

Technical and semantic questions arise because rules may have different results depending on when they are executed and whether they are applied to single tuples one by one or to sets of matching tuples at once. For the former issue, so-called *coupling modes* are distinguished: applicable rules may be executed immediately (before or after the events they react on), later (deferred) in the same transaction or later (decoupled) outside the current transaction. Results also depend on the application order of rules, on their type of execution (concurrent or sequential), and on commitment and rollback of transactions. As in production rule systems, *conflict resolution* may be necessary if events in different rules are not disjoint.

In the CHR embedding, we make the choices that result in a simple implementation. We model events and database tuples as CHR constraints. Since removal of constraints is implicit in CHR, we define event constraints for manipulation of tuples, namely `insert/1, delete/1, update/2`. An event constraint will never be stored in the constraint store, so the last rule of any ECA rule program should always remove events.

Definition 6.5 *We use the following basic rule scheme, where* C *and* C1 *are tuples and* P *is a tuple pattern:*

```
ins @ insert(C) ⇒ C.
del @ delete(P) \ C ⇔ match(P,C) | true.
upd @ update(P,C1) \ C ⇔ match(P,C) | C1.
```

The built-in match(P,C) *holds if tuple constraint* C *matches pattern* P.

Event constraints are not removed by the rules that define them and that react to them, because we want to be able to trigger ECA rules with them, before and after *their execution. The extra rules for database operation event removal are last in the program:*

```
insert(C) ⇔ true.
delete(C) ⇔ true.
update(C) ⇔ true.
```

These rules destroy confluence.

Example 6.1.6 In this classical example, we want to limit the salary increase of an employee to 10%. This is achieved by an ECA rule that reacts to updates in the salaries. If we add the rule before the rule **upd**, we write

```
update(emp(Name,S1),emp(Name,S2)) <=> S2>S1*(1+0.1) |
                  update(emp(Name,S1),emp(Name,S1*1.1)).
```

If we add the rule after the rule **upd**, we write instead

```
update(emp(Name,S1),emp(Name,S2)) <=> S2>S1*(1+0.1) |
                  update(emp(Name,S2),emp(Name,S1*1.1)).
```

Note the subtle difference in the first argument of the **update** constraint (S1 versus S2) in the bodies of the two rules.

Example 6.1.7 The marital status Example 6.1.5 can be expressed in a database context as follows:

```
insert(person(X)) ==> insert(single(X)).
insert(married(X)), single(X) ==> delete(single(X)).
```

6.1.5 Logical algorithms formalism

The LA formalism defines a hypothetical *bottom-up* logic programming language with deletion of atoms and rule priorities. LA is basically a declarative production rule language. It can also be considered as a deductive database language. LA was designed as a theoretical means for deriving tight complexity results for algorithms described by logical inference rules.

Definition 6.6 *An* LA *program is a set of LA rules. An* LA *rule is of the form*

$$r \, @ \, p : A \to C$$

where r is a rule name, p is a priority, the l.h.s. A is a conjunction of user-defined atoms and syntactic or arithmetic comparisons, the r.h.s. C is a conjunction of user-defined atoms whose variables occur also in A (range-restrictedness). A priority p is an arithmetic expression, whose variables must occur in the first atom of A. If p contains variables, its rule is called dynamic, *otherwise* static. *A positive user-defined atom A_i can be negated, which is written as $del(A_i)$.*

An LA *state is a set of user-defined atoms. In a state, an atom may occur positively, negatively, or both. An* LA *initial state is a ground state. An* LA *rule is applicable to a state if its l.h.s. atoms match atoms from the state such that positive atoms do not occur also negatively and, under this matching, the l.h.s. comparisons hold. Furthermore, the r.h.s. must not be already contained in the state and there must exist no other applicable rule with lower priority. In the l.h.s. matching and the r.h.s. containment test, a set-based semantics for atoms is used.*

Deletion is modeled in LA by adding negated atoms. No atoms are ever removed. We cannot ask for absence of an atom, but we can ask if it was introduced negatively.

LA rules most closely correspond to *positive ground range-restricted* CHR propagation rules. Unlike CHR, a set-based semantics is used, rules have priorities, and atoms can be negative. Negative atoms overshadow positive ones, so to some extent, CHR simplification rules can be simulated. Once a positive atom also occurs negatively, it can never be matched again by a rule l.h.s., while in CHR, removed CHR constraints can be reintroduced again. This behavior of LA may lead to nonconfluent programs. Unlike CHR, the redundancy test for LA rules to avoid trivial nontermination is based on checking if the r.h.s. of the rule has been introduced before. This kind of check is possible, since atoms are never removed in LA.

Embedding LA in CHR. The compilation of LA programs to CHR results in three sets of rules:

- For each LA atom A we introduce simpagation rules for duplicate elimination to enforce the set-based semantics and to overshadow positive occurrences by negative ones:

A \ A $\Leftrightarrow$ *true*.
del(A) \ del(A) $\Leftrightarrow$ *true*.
del(A) \ A $\Leftrightarrow$ *true*.

The last rule causes nonmonotonicity.
- For each LA rule

$$r \ @ \ p{:}A \to C$$

we introduce a CHR propagation rule

$$r{:}p \ @ \ A_1 \Rightarrow A_2 \mid C$$

where A_1 are the atoms of A and A_2 are the comparisons from A.

Several CHR rules are in general needed for one LA rule to enable set-based semantics. Given a translated rule, we generate new rule variants by systematically unifying head constraints in all possible ways. This can be done automatically by completion with all critical pairs between the duplicate elimination rules and each translated LA rule. For example, the LA rule (ignoring priorities and rule names)

a(1,Y) $\wedge$ a(X,2) $\to$ b(X,Y)

is translated into the CHR rule

a(1,Y), a(X,2) ==> b(X,Y).

This also leads to the additional rule due to unifying a(1,Y)=a(X,2):

a(1,2) ==> b(1,2).

- The LA rule scheduler written in CHR uses eager matching similar to the RETE algorithm: partial matches are stored as CHR constraints and are extended by new matching atoms. A partial match is removed if one of its positive atoms has been introduced negatively. For conflict resolution, full matches (applicable rule instances) are inserted into a priority queue and the lowest priority rule is fired.

Example 6.1.8 An LA implementation of Dijkstra's efficient single-source shortest path algorithm is

```
d1 @   1: source(X) → dist(X,0).
d2 @   1: dist(X,N) ∧ dist(X,M) ∧ N<M → del(dist(X,M)).
dn @ N+2: dist(X,N) ∧ edge(X,Y,M) → dist(Y,N+M).
```

In rule d2 the case N=M need not be covered because of the set-based semantics that will remove duplicate atoms. The elegance of the program lies in rule dn that uses the dynamic priority N+2 to schedule rule applications first that deal with shorter distances.

The CHR translation of the LA program is (showing only simpagation rules for dist for brevity):

```
dist(X,N) \ dist(X,N) <=> true.
del(dist(X,N)) \ del(dist(X,N)) <=> true.
del(dist(X,N)) \ dist(X,N) <=> true.

d1:1   @ source(X) ==> dist(X,0).
d2:1   @ dist(X,N), dist(X,M) ==> N<M | del(dist(X,M)).
dn:N+2 @ dist(X,N), edge(X,Y,M) ==> dist(Y,N+M).
```

Compare these rules with the all-pairs shortest path program given in Section 2.4.1.

6.2 Rewriting-based and graph-based formalisms

In this section we discuss the embedding of some classical computational formalisms in CHR. These formalisms are usually considered as a theoretical means and are rarely directly implemented as a programming language. Still, CHR can express and execute essential aspects of these formalisms. Their states can be mapped to CHR constraints and transitions can be mapped to CHR rules. The results are certain types of simplification rules in the *positive ground range-restricted* fragment of CHR.

TRS replace subterms in a given term by other terms until exhaustion. Their analysis (e.g. for termination and confluence) has inspired many related results for CHR. TRS are a basic theoretical formalism that is usually not directly implemented.

Functional programming languages can be seen as related to a syntactic fragment of TRS that is extended with guards, while graph rewriting systems extend TRS from rewriting terms to rewriting graphs. These related formalisms will also be discussed in Section 6.2.1.

GAMMA is an acronym for General Abstract Model for Multiset Manipulation. It is a programming paradigm relying solely on multiset rewriting. We have seen examples of GAMMA-style programming in CHR in Section 2.2 on multiset transformation. GAMMA is the basis of the Chemical Abstract Machine (CHAM). The CHAM has been used to model algebraic process calculi for asynchronous concurrency.

Graph-based diagrammatic formalisms like Petri nets, statecharts, and UML activity diagrams describe computations (activities, processes) by moving control and data tokens along arcs in a graph. Roughly, nodes correspond to states and arcs to transitions. Conditions and assignments that appear as annotations in the graphs can be expressed by additional constraints. Petri nets are typically used to describe and reason about concurrent processes.

6.2.1 Term rewriting systems

TRS consist of rewriting rules that are directed equations between terms. Computation consists of repeatedly replacing, in a given term, a subterm that matches the l.h.s. of a rewrite rule with the r.h.s. of the rule. An initial term is rewritten until a *normal form* is reached where it cannot be rewritten further.

TRS and CHR compared. CHR and TRS seem similar. Both systems repeatedly rewrite a state using rules until exhaustion. Several theoretical results on termination and confluence analysis of CHR were inspired by TRS. Although CHR borrows those notions and techniques from TRS, CHR is in many aspects different from classical TRS (see below). Thus these TRS notions have to be modified and extended accordingly.

In addition to the general differences between other formalisms and CHR as discussed in the introduction to this chapter, we mention here specific differences between standard TRS and CHR.

Syntactically, TRS use a functional notation, while CHR uses a relational notation. In a TRS, all subterms have a particular fixed position in the term, whereas the CHR store is a multiset of constraint relations. TRS rules locally rewrite a single subterm to another one, while several CHR constraints may be manipulated simultaneously using associative–commutative (AC) matching and globally by a single rule.

Standard TRS admit no *guards*. In some extensions of TRS, guards are introduced. They hold if two terms can be rewritten to the same normal form (be joined) by the rewrite rules themselves. In CHR, guards contain built-in constraints only. CHR guards hold if the context of built-in constraints implies them.

Multiple occurrences of variables are allowed on both sides of CHR rules. Variables are allowed to occur only in one side of the rule, in particular variables can be introduced on the r.h.s. of a rule. TRS may have restrictions on occurrences of variables.

Flattening. For the embedding of TRS in CHR, we need the notion of flattening. A term can be *flattened* by performing the opposite of *variable elimination*. Each subterm is replaced by a new variable that is equated with the replaced subterm.

Definition 6.7 *Let* eq *be a binary CHR constraint in infix notation denoting equality. The* flattening function [.] *transforms the atomic equality constraint* X eq T, *where* X *is a variable and* T *is a term, into a conjunction of equations as follows:*

$$[X \text{ eq } T] := \begin{cases} X \text{ eq } T & \text{if T is a variable} \\ X \text{ eq } f(X_1,\ldots,X_n) \wedge (\bigwedge_{i=1}^n [X_i \text{ eq } T_i]) & \text{if } T = f(T_1,\ldots,T_n) \end{cases}$$

where $X_1,\ldots,X_n$ *are new variables.*

Flattening increases the size of the expression only by a constant factor, since we basically introduce an equation with a new variable for each argument of a function symbol.

Embedding TRS in CHR. We simply translate rewrite rules into simplification rules and terms into conjunctions of equations by flattening them.

Definition 6.8 *We translate a rewrite rule*

$$S \rightarrow T$$

into the CHR simplification rule resulting from flattening

$$[X \text{ eq } S] \Leftrightarrow [X \text{ eq } T]$$

where X is a new variable.

Consider the following examples for translating TRS into CHR.

Example 6.2.1 The two rewrite rules define the addition of natural numbers in successor notation.

```
0+Y -> Y.
s(X)+Y -> s(X+Y).
```

The translation into CHR with the help of flattening results in these two simplification rules:

```
T eq T1+T2, T1 eq 0, T2 eq Y <=> T eq Y.
T eq T1+T2, T1 eq s(T3), T3 eq X, T2 eq Y <=>
               T eq s(T4), T4 eq T5+T6, T5 eq X, T6 eq Y.
```

Example 6.2.2 Here is a simple TRS for conjunction in propositional logic as used in the Boolean constraint solver in Section 8.1. X, Y, and Z are propositional variables. The function and(X,Y) stands for X∧Y.

```
and(0,Y) -> 0.
and(X,0) -> 0.
and(1,Y) -> Y.
and(X,1) -> X.
and(X,X) -> X.
```

and its translation into CHR:

```
T eq and(T1,T2), T1 eq 0, T2 eq Y <=> T eq 0.
T eq and(T1,T2), T1 eq X, T2 eq 0 <=> T eq 0.
T eq and(T1,T2), T1 eq 1, T2 eq Y <=> T eq Y.
T eq and(T1,T2), T1 eq X, T2 eq 1 <=> T eq X.
T eq and(T1,T2), T1 eq X, T2 eq X <=> T eq X.
```

The last rule is redundant in TRS, but not so in CHR, where it can apply also if X is an unbound variable.

Completeness, nonlinearity, and structure sharing. A TRS is *linear* if each variable occurs at most once on the l.h.s. and r.h.s. of the rewrite rule. The simple translation by flattening is incomplete if the TRS is not linear. For example, consider the nonlinear rewrite rule and(X,X) -> X. In the CHR translation, we can apply it to the query resulting from the term `and(1,1)` but not to `and(and(0,1),and(0,1))` directly. Implementations of TRS-based systems usually have similar incompleteness.

Completeness can be regained for confluent programs. For nonlinear TRS that are confluent, the introduction of *structure sharing* results in a complete CHR embedding. Structure sharing is implemented by a simpagation rule that enforces *functional dependency*. (The symbol = denotes built-in syntactic equality.)

`fd @ X eq T \ Y eq T <=> X=Y.`

This propagates equality of terms upwards in their equation representation. For example, `Z eq and(X,Y)`, `W eq and(X,Y)` now reduces to `Z eq and(X,Y)`, `W=Z`. The `fd` rule has to come first in the program.

Since the rule `fd` removes equations, other rules may be no longer applicable. In Example 6.2.2, the CHR translation of the rewrite rule `and(X,X) -> X` is the simplification rule `T eq and(T1,T2)`, `T1 eq X`, `T2 eq X <=> T eq X`. It expects two copies of the equations, `T1 eq X` and `T2 eq X`. The remedy is to create variants of the existing CHR rules where head constraints have been unified, so that the rules also apply after the `fd` rule has been applied. This solution is justified as the result of completion with all critical pairs involving the `fd` rule. For our example rule, this results in the additional rule `T eq and(T1,T1)`, `T1 eq X <=> T eq X`.

Functional programming. Functional programming (FP) (with languages such as Haskell and ML) can be seen as a more practical variation of TRS where we have syntactic restrictions on the l.h.s. of a rewrite rule but add built-in functions and guard tests (that are considered as Boolean functions). The main restriction on the l.h.s. is that we have matching only at the outermost redex on the l.h.s., i.e. functions applied to terms interpreted as data.

In the translation, we put back data terms into the arguments of functions. Therefore there is no need to flatten the l.h.s., but equations involving data terms on the r.h.s. have to be turned into built-in syntactic equations.

Definition 6.9 *We translate an FP rewrite rule*

$$S \to G \mid T$$

where G is the guard, into the CHR simplification rule

$$X \text{ eq } S \Leftrightarrow G \mid [X \text{ eq } T]$$

where X is a new variable.

To the CHR program resulting from the translation, we also add rules for treating data and auxiliary functions that are mapped to built-in constraints.

```
X eq T ⇔ datum(T) | X=T.
X eq T ⇔ builtin(T) | c(T,X).
```

where c(T,X) calls the built-in constraint that corresponds to function T and X is its result, for example X=A+B leads to X is A+B.

We can apply the two additional rewrite rules at compile-time to the r.h.s. of the translated CHR rules. We assume so in the examples for translating FP into CHR.

Example 6.2.3 The translation of successor addition results now in

```
T eq 0+Y <=> T eq Y.
T eq s(X)+Y <=> T=s(T4), T4 eq T5+T6, T5 eq X, T6 eq Y.
```

Example 6.2.4 The Boolean conjunction is now translated as follows:

```
T eq and(0,Y) <=> T=0.
T eq and(X,0) <=> T=0.
T eq and(1,Y) <=> T eq Y.
T eq and(X,1) <=> T eq X.
T eq and(X,Y) <=> T eq X.
```

Example 6.2.5 In FP, we can define Fibonacci numbers as follows (cf. Section 2.3.2):

```
fib(0) -> 1.
fib(1) -> 1.
fib(N) -> N>=2 | fib(N-1)+fib(N-2).
```

This results in the CHR simplification rules

```
T eq fib(0) <=> T=1.
T eq fib(1) <=> T=1.
T eq fib(N) <=> N≥2 |
    T is F1+F2, F1 eq fib(N1), N1 is N-1, F2 eq fib(N2), N2 is N-2.
```

Graph transformation systems. Graph transformation systems (GTS) can be seen as a nontrivial generalization of TRS where instead of terms, arbitrary typed graphs are rewritten under a matching morphism. An encoding for GTS production rules in CHR exists, soundness and completeness is proven. GTS joinability of critical pairs can be mapped onto joinability of specific critical pairs in CHR.

6.2.2 Multiset transformation

GAMMA employs a *chemical metaphor*. States in a computation are chemical solutions where floating molecules interact freely according to reaction rules. We can model molecules as CHR constraints (cf. Section 2.2). Reactions can be performed in parallel.

Given a domain D of data elements, a GAMMA program consists of pairs $(c/n, f/n)$ of an n-ary predicate c and an n-ary function f, with arguments ranging over D. The result of applying f is a multiset with data elements from D. Given an initial multiset S of data elements on which to operate, the function f will be applied to a subset of S, $\{x_1, \ldots, x_n\}$, if $c(x_1, \ldots, x_n)$ holds. The result of $f(x_1, \ldots, x_n) = \{y_1, \ldots, y_m\}$ will replace the data elements $x_1, \ldots, x_n$ in S.

Definition 6.10 *We translate each GAMMA pair*

$$(c/n, f/n)$$

into a CHR simplification rule

$$d(x_1), \ldots, d(x_n) \Leftrightarrow c(x_1, \ldots, x_n) \mid f(x_1, \ldots, x_n),$$

where the data elements are wrapped by CHR constraint $d/1$, c/n is a built-in constraint. The function f can be defined by simplification rules of the form

$$f(x_1, \ldots, x_n) \Leftrightarrow G \mid d(y_1), \ldots, d(y_m),$$

where G is a guard.

6.2.3 Petri nets

Petri nets (PN) consist of *places (P)* (∘) in which *tokens* (•) reside. Tokens can move along *arcs* passing through *transitions (T)* (|||) from one place to another. A transition may have several incoming and several outgoing arcs. A transition can only fire if all incoming arcs present tokens. On firing, one token from each incoming arc will be removed and tokens will be presented on all outgoing arcs.

The standard variant of PN, place/transition nets (P/T nets) translates to a small fragment of CHR. This fragment consists just of nullary CHR constraints and simplification rules. Thus we consider a generalization of PN, *colored Petri nets (CPN)*, where tokens can be of different kinds (from a finite set of values called colors), places are typed by the colors they allow, and transitions can be guarded along their arcs with conditions on tokens and their colors and with equations that generate new tokens from old ones. Colors can also stand for numbers or tuples. For both types of Petri nets, soundness and completeness results exist for the translation into CHR.

When CPN are translated to CHR, places are mapped to CHR constraint symbols, tokens to instances of CHR constraints, colors form a *finite domain* and are possible values of variables. Transitions and their arcs are mapped to simplification rules. Incoming (PT-)arc annotations form the rule head, and outgoing (TP-)arc annotations form the rule body, and the transition guard forms the rule guard.

Example 6.2.6 In this classical problem in concurrency, a number of philosophers sit at a round table. Between each philosopher a fork is placed. A philosopher either thinks or eats. In order to eat, a philosopher needs two forks, the one from his left and the one from his right. After a while, an eating philosopher will start to think again, releasing the forks and thus making them available to his neighbors again.

When the problem is modeled as a standard PN, we need places and transitions for the behavior of each philosopher separately (cf. Figure 6.1). In the CPN formulation, places and transitions are generic for any philosopher. The net for three philosophers is shown in Figure 6.2. Each philosopher corresponds to a colored token (a number from 0 to 2). Two philosophers x and y are neighboring if $y = (x+1)$ *mod* 3. Places are think (t), eat (e), and fork (f), transitions go from eat to think (et) and from think to eat (te). The CHR code can be generalized to allow for any *given* number of philosophers by adding a parameter n, but not for arbitrary n, since the number of colors must be finite.

The CPN translates directly into the two simplification rules (the color domains $\{0, 1, 2\}$ for the arguments of t, f, e are omitted from the guard to avoid clutter):

$$te@ \quad t(X), f(X), f(Y) \Leftrightarrow Y = (X+1) \ mod \ 3 \mid e(X).$$
$$et@ \quad e(X) \Leftrightarrow Y = (X+1) \ mod \ 3 \mid t(X), f(X), f(Y).$$

Note that the **et** rule is just the reverse of the **te** rule.

6.3 Constraint-based and logic-based programming

Like CHR, all the languages in this section have logical variables subjected to built-in constraints. Unlike CHR, they do not feature propagation rules and multiple head atoms.

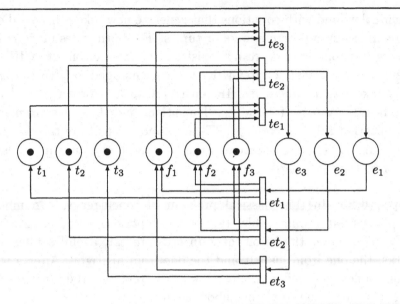

Fig. 6.1. The three dining philosophers problem modeled as a Petri net

Deductive databases. We can also use CHR as a simple deductive *database* as explained in Section 2.1.

A popular deductive database language is Datalog. Only constants are allowed, there are no function symbols, and variables are restricted to have *finite domains*. The rules are *range-restricted*. It evaluates its *Horn clauses* bottom-up. CHR uses propagation rules to evaluate database rules. Bottom-up computation typical for this approach was used in Section 2.3.2 and Section 2.4.1. Formally, deductive databases are covered by the LA formalism (cf. Section 6.1.5).

6.3.1 Prolog and constraint logic programming

Constraint logic programming (CLP) combines the declarativity of logic programming with the efficiency of constraint solving. The logic programming language Prolog (in its pure form) can be understood as CLP where the only built-in constraint is syntactic equality ($=$). Don't-know nondeterminism (by choice of rule or disjunction) is provided in these languages, while don't-care nondeterminism (committed-choice) is typically implemented in a nondeclarative way using the cut operator.

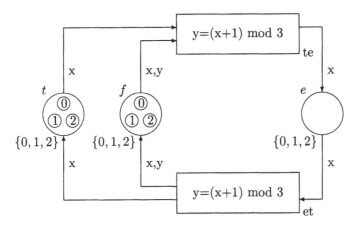

Fig. 6.2. The three dining philosophers problem as a colored Petri net

CHR with disjunction (CHR$^\vee$, cf. Section 3.3.2) provides a declarative formulation of and a clear distinction between don't-care nondeterminism and don't-know nondeterminism. Any Horn clause (CLP) program can be converted into an equivalent CHR$^\vee$ program. One moves CLP head *unification* and clause choices to the body of a single CHR$^\vee$ rule. The required transformation turns out to be Clark's completion of logic programs. In this way, Prolog and similar CLP languages can be embedded in CHR.

Definition 6.11 *A CLP program P is a set of CLP clauses. A CLP (Horn) clause is of the form $A \leftarrow G$, where A is an atom and G is a conjunction of atoms and built-ins.*

(Clark's) completion *of a predicate p/n which is defined by m ($m \geq 0$) clauses*

$$\bigwedge_{i=1}^{m} \forall (p(\bar{t}_i) \leftarrow G_i)$$

is the formula

$$p(\bar{x}) \leftrightarrow \bigvee_{i=1}^{m} \exists \bar{y}_i \, (\bar{t}_i = \bar{x} \wedge G_i)$$

where $\bar{x}$ is a sequence of n new variables, the $\bar{t}_i$ are sequences of n terms, and the $\bar{y}_i$ are sequences of the variables occurring in G_i and t_i.

The CHR translation of a CLP program P considers each predicate p/n in P as a CHR constraint and, for each p/n, contains Clark's completion of p/n written as $CHR^\vee$ simplification rule.

Example 6.3.1 The Prolog predicate `append` was introduced in Example 5.3.10 in the context of completion. Its CLP clauses are:

```
append([],L,L) ← true.
append([X|L1],Y,[X|L2]) ← append(L1,Y,L2).
```

The translated $CHR^\vee$ program for `append` is:

```
append(X,Y,Z) ⇔
    (     X=[]∧Y=L∧Z=L
    ∨     X=[H|L1]∧Y=L2∧Z=[H|L3]∧append(L1, L2, L3) ).
```

We finally compare the expressive power of CLP and CHR using earlier examples.

Example 6.3.2 Consider the prime sieve CHR program from Section 2.2.4:

```
        upto(N) <=> N>1 | M is N-1, upto(M), prime(N).
sift @ prime(I) \ prime(J) <=> J mod I =:= 0 | true.
```

The typical Prolog program for the prime sieve is more contrived, because one explicitly has to maintain a list of prime candidates and use the cut (!) operator to commit to the current clause.

```
primes(N,Ps):- upto(2,N,Ns), sift(Ns,Ps).

upto(F,T,[]):- F>T, !.
upto(F,T,[F|Ns1]):- F1 is F+1, upto(F1,T,Ns1).

sift([],[]).
sift([P|Ns],[P|Ps1]):- filter(Ns,P,Ns1), sift(Ns1,Ps1).

filter([],P,[]).
filter([X|In],P,Out):- X mod P =:= 0, !, filter(In,P,Out).
filter([X|In],P,[X|Out1]):- filter(In,P,Out1).
```

Example 6.3.3 It is interesting to compare the CHR program for all-pair shortest paths from Section 2.4.1:

```
p(X,Y,N) \ p(X,Y,M) <=> N=<M | true.
e(X,Y) ==> p(X,Y,1).
e(X,Y), p(Y,Z,N) ==> p(X,Z,N+1).
```

with the corresponding typical textbook program in Prolog that has to rely on a list of visited nodes and negation-as-failure (**not**) to find the shortest path:

```
p(From,To,Path,N) :- e(From,To,N).
p(From,To,Path,N) :- e(From,Via,1),
                     not member(Via,Path),
                     p(Via,To,[Via|Path],N1),
                     N is N1+1.
shortestp(From,To,N) :- p(From,To,[],N),
                        not (p(From,To,[],N1),N1<N).
```

6.3.2 Concurrent constraint programming

The concurrent constraints (CC) language framework permits both *don't-care and don't-know nondeterminism* (and in its general case subsumes CLP). The languages of the CC framework are the ones closest to CHR. We concentrate on the *committed-choice* fragment of the CC language that is based on don't care nondeterminism just as CHR.

Definition 6.12 *The abstract syntax of a CC program is given by the EBNF grammar*

Declarations	$D ::=$	$p(\tilde{t}) \leftarrow A \mid D, D$
Agents	$A ::=$	$true \mid c \mid \sum_{i=1}^{n} c_i \rightarrow A_i \mid A \| A \mid p(\tilde{t})$

where p is a user-defined predicate symbol, $\tilde{t}$ stands for a sequence of terms, and where c and the c_i's are constraints. Each predicate p is defined by exactly one declaration. A CC program P is a finite set of declarations.

Ask-and-tell. The communication mechanism of CC is based on *ask-and-tell* of constraints that reside in the common constraint store. *Tell* refers to imposing a constraint by adding it to the constraint store. Ask is an inquiry whether a constraint already holds. *Ask* is realized by a logical *entailment* test. It checks whether a constraint is logically implied by the current constraint store. Ask-and-tell can also be seen as generalizations of read and write from values to constraints. The ask-and-tell metaphor generalizes the idea of concurrent data-flow computations, where operations wait until their arguments are known. The ask operation is a *consumer/client* of constraints (even though the constraint will not be removed), the tell operation is a *producer/server* of constraints.

We formally define the operational semantics of CC, since it is the programming paradigm most close to CHR.

Tell
$\langle c, d \rangle \rightarrow \langle true, c \wedge d \rangle$

Ask
$\langle \sum_{i=1}^{n} c_i \rightarrow A_i, d \rangle \rightarrow \langle A_j, d \rangle$ if $\exists j\ CT \models \forall (d \rightarrow c_j)\ (1 \leq j \leq n)$

Composition
$$\frac{\langle A, c \rangle \rightarrow \langle A', c' \rangle}{\begin{array}{l} \langle (A \parallel B), c \rangle \rightarrow \langle (A' \parallel B), c' \rangle \\ \langle (B \parallel A), c \rangle \rightarrow \langle (B \parallel A'), c' \rangle \end{array}}$$

Unfold
$\langle p(\tilde{t}), c \rangle \rightarrow \langle A, \tilde{t} = \tilde{s} \wedge c \rangle$ if $(p(\tilde{s}) \leftarrow A)$ in program P

Fig. 6.3. CC transition rules

Definition 6.13 *The operational semantics of CC is described by a transition system (Figure 6.3). States are pairs consisting of agents and the built-in constraint store.*

*Transition **Tell**: one adds (tells) the constraint c to the common constraint store.*

*Transition **Ask**: don't-care nondeterminism between choices is expressed as $\sum_{i=1}^{n} c_i \rightarrow A_i$. One nondeterministically chooses a constraint c_i which is implied by the current constraint store d, and continues computation with the corresponding agent A_i.*

*Transition **Composition**: the $\parallel$ operator defines concurrent composition of agents.*

*Transition **Unfold**: unfolding replaces an agent $p(\tilde{t})$ by its definition according to its declaration.*

Embedding CC in CHR. CC predicates correspond to CHR constraints, CC constraints correspond to built-in constraints. In CHR, the ask operation belongs in the guard, and the tell operation in the rule body.

Definition 6.14 *CC declarations and asks are translated into single-headed CHR simplification rules and CC agents into CHR goals:*

CC declarations in CHR	$D ::= \ p(\tilde{t}) \Leftrightarrow A \mid D, D$
CC agents in CHR	$A ::= \ true \mid c \mid \mathbf{ask}(\sum_{i=1}^{n} c_i \to A_i) \mid A \wedge A \mid p(\tilde{t})$

We introduce a new CHR constraint symbol **ask** *that takes an ask as argument. For each ask* $A = \sum_{i=1}^{n} c_i \to A_i$ *of a given CC program, we generate* n *simplification rules for CHR constraint* **ask** *of the form*

$$\mathbf{ask}(A) \Leftrightarrow c_i \mid A_i \ (1 \leq i \leq n).$$

Example 6.3.4 The maximum relation from Section 2.3.1 can be implemented in CC as the agent

`max(X,Y,Z) ← (X≤Y → Y=Z) + (Y≤X → X=Z).`

The translation into CHR gives

`max(X,Y,Z) ⇔ ask((X≤Y → Y=Z) + (Y≤X → X=Z)).`

`ask((X≤Y → Y=Z) + (Y≤X → X=Z)) ⇔ X≤Y | Y=Z.`
`ask((X≤Y → Y=Z) + (Y≤X → X=Z)) ⇔ Y≤X | X=Z.`

These rules can be simplified by replacing `ask((X≤Y → Y=Z) + (Y≤X → X=Z))` by `ask_max(X,Y,Z)`.

6.4 Bibliographic remarks

Extensions of CHR by rule priorities [KSD07b], by rules with probabilities [FdPW02], and by disjunction (CHR$^{\vee}$) [AS98] exist. CHR with negation-as-absence is defined and implemented in [WSSD06].

Examples of production rule systems are the classic OPS5 [BFKM85] and the later CLIPS [GR94] for Lisp and then C, as well as the more recent ILOG JRules and the CLIPS-inspired Jess [FH03], both for Java. Unlike CHR, implementations of rule-based systems often use the RETE [For83] and TREAT [Mir87] algorithms.

The LA formalism appears in [GA01, GM02]. In [KSD07a] a direct translation from the theoretical LA language into CHR with rule priorities is given, and a translation into regular CHR. This is the first actual implementation of LA. It achieves the complexity required for the LA meta-complexity theorem to hold.

The programming languages OBJ3 [GKK[+]88], Maude [CDE[+]02], and ELAN [BKK[+]96] implement aspects of a generalization of term rewriting systems called rewriting logic [Mes92]. Last but not least, ACD term rewriting as implemented in the language CADMIUM [DSB06] extends CHR with direct term rewriting capabilities and is used as the basis of the Australian G12 project [SdlBM[+]05]. Typical applications of such TRS languages are theorem proving and modeling.

GAMMA [BCM88, BM93] is an acronym for General Abstract Model for Multiset Manipulation. GAMMA is the basis of the Chemical Abstract Machine (CHAM) [BB92].

In [Rai07] an encoding for graph transformation systems (GTS) [EEUT06] in CHR is given, soundness and completeness is proven. GTS joinability of critical pairs can be mapped onto joinability of specific critical pairs in CHR.

In [Bet07], Petri nets [Pet62] are translated to CHR. It is proven that there is a one-to-one correspondence between colored Petri nets and positive ground range-restricted CHR simplification rules over finite domains.

Prolog and logic programming (LP) [Kow86, CR93], constraint logic programming (CLP) [Hen91, JM94, JL87, MS98, FA03, RBW06], and concurrent committed-choice logic programming (CC) [Mah87, Ued88, Sha89, Sar93] are direct ancestors of CHR. The papers [SR90, SRP91, Sar93] introduce and define the concurrent constraint language (CC) framework. CLP programs are translated into CHR$^\vee$ in [AS98] using Clark's completion [Cla78]. A popular deductive database language is Datalog [CGT89].

Part III

CHR programs and applications

We analyze the programs from the CHR tutorial and then a number of larger programs in more detail and more formally. The programs solve problems over finite and infinite domains of values: propositional satisfaction problems (Boolean algebra), syntactic equations over rational trees and linear polynomial equations, implementing the graph-based constraint algorithms of arc and path consistency, and the global lexicographic order constraint. We also directly implement description logic (extended with rules), which is the formal basis of ontology languages of the semantic web. We give a program for the classical union-find algorithm with optimal time and space complexity. We parallelize the algorithm and generalize it for efficient equation solving. We use it in an efficient syntactic equation solver.

7

My first CHR programs, revisited for analysis

We start by analyzing our first CHR programs from Chapter 2 with the methods from the previous part of this book. In particular, our analyses will consider

- logical reading and program correctness
- termination and complexity
- confluence
- anytime and online algorithm property
- concurrency and parallelism.

Considering complexity, we will discuss both the actual worst-case time complexity achieved by current CHR implementations under the refined semantics and the often crude upper bound from the meta-complexity theorem for CHR that refers to the abstract semantics.

We will analyze our first program for minimum in detail to set the scene. For the remaining programs we will concentrate on the differences from this first program to avoid repetitions. We will leave out some of the easy analyses to avoid tiring details. We will also discuss interesting variations of some of the algorithms.

7.1 Multiset transformation

7.1.1 Minimum

The one-rule CHR program computes the minimum of numbers n_i, given as `min(n_1)`, `min(n_2)`, ..., `min(n_k)`.

```
min(N) \ min(M) <=> N=<M | true.
```

The rule keeps removing larger values until only one, the smallest value, remains. Note that the rule is applicable to any pair of values. The properties of this program have been discussed to some extent already in Section 2.2.1. Concrete example runs are given there.

Logical reading and correctness. The min constraints initially represent *candidates* for the minimum. Only upon completion of the calculation does the actual minimum remain. Classical first-order logic has no straightforward means to express this dynamics. Indeed, the declarative semantics, i.e. the first-order logic reading for the min rule is:

$$\forall (N \leq M \rightarrow (min(N) \wedge min(M) \leftrightarrow min(N))).$$

The formula is logically equivalent to

$$N \leq M \rightarrow (min(M) \leftarrow min(N))$$

and thus says that a number is a minimum if it is larger than another minimum.

The linear logic reading (cf. Section 3.4.2) for the constraint min is

$$!\forall ((N \leq M) \multimap (min(N) \otimes min(M) \multimap min(N))) .$$

This reads as: "Of course, consuming min(N) and min(M) where (N=<M) produces min(N)". This reading properly reflects the dynamics of the minimum computation.

In the following, we will usually give the classical first-order predicate logic reading and omit the linear-logic reading, because it is structurally very similar and linear logic is less known.

We usually prove correctness by contradiction. If the minimum is not correctly computed, then either there are several min constraints left or the single remaining min constraint does not contain the minimum. In the first case, the rule is still applicable. In the second case, we must have removed the minimum value by a rule application. But this is a contradiction, since the rule always removes the larger value.

Termination and complexity. The program is terminating, because the rule removes a CHR constraint and does not introduce new ones. We can apply a rule in constant time to two arbitrary min constraints. The number of rule applications (derivation length) is bounded by the number of min constraints, say n, in the query.

As for worst-case time complexity, the program runs in linear time, $O(n)$ under the *refined CHR semantics*. Since the constraints of a query are executed incrementally from left to right, each active min constraint will immediately react with the only old `min` constraint, and one of them will be removed.

Under the *abstract CHR semantics* the order in which constraints and rules are tried is undetermined. By the CHR meta-complexity Theorem 5.35, the worst-case time complexity of a derivation starting with the given query with n CHR constraints, which has derivation length D, is

$$O(D \sum_i ((n+D)^{n_i}(O_{H_i} + O_{G_i}) + (O_{C_i} + O_{B_i}))),$$

where the index i ranges over the rules in the program P, and n_i is the number of the head constraints in the ith rule and the $O_{H_i}, O_{G_i}, O_{C_i}, O_{B_i}$ are the costs of head matching, guard checking, imposing built-in and CHR constraints of the body, respectively.

In our case, $D = n$, $i = 1$ and $n_1 = 2$, and thus the complexity is cubic in the number of constraints:

$$O(n(n^2(1+0) + (1+0))) = O(n^3).$$

Of course, this worst-case complexity is highly overestimated. It applies to all two-head simpagation rule programs we consider.

Confluence. For given numbers, correctness implies that the result of a computation will always be a single `min` constraint. Thus, the program must be confluent for ground queries. We speak of *ground confluence*, i.e. observable confluence under the invariant of groundness. For the general case, we therefore apply confluence analysis using overlaps and critical pairs.

Since there is only one rule in the program, the rule can only overlap with (a variant of) itself to produce critical pairs. There is one nontrivial full overlap where all head constraints are equated:

```
min(A),min(B), A=<B,B=<A.
```

It is equivalent to the state

```
min(A),min(A), A=B.
```

There are four overlaps where exactly one constraint is shared from the two rule heads (where variables have been renamed conveniently):

```
min(A),min(B),min(C), A=<B,B=<C.
min(A),min(B),min(C), A=<B,B=<C.
min(A),min(B),min(C), A=<B,A=<C.
min(A),min(B),min(C), A=<B,C=<B.
```

We only have to consider the duplicate overlap once in this case.

To the overlap `min(A),min(A), A=B` we can apply the rule in given or reversed order of the `min` constraints. In both cases, this leads to the state `min(A), A=B`. Hence the rule removes duplicates.

The first overlap with three `min` constraints leads to a joinable critical pair:

$$min(A),min(B),min(C), \ A=<B,B=<C$$
$$\diagup \qquad\qquad\qquad \diagdown$$
`min(A),min(B), A=<B,B=<C`   `min(A),min(C), A=<B,B=<C`
$$\diagdown \qquad\qquad \diagup$$
$$min(A), \ A=<B,B=<C$$

Not surprisingly, only the smallest constraint, `min(A)`, is left.

For the next overlap, we get similar confluent computations:

$$min(A),min(B),min(C), \ A=<B,A=<C$$
$$\diagup \qquad\qquad\qquad \diagdown$$
`min(A),min(B), A=<B,A=<C`   `min(A),min(C), A=<B,A=<C`
$$\diagdown \qquad\qquad \diagup$$
$$min(A), \ A=<B,A=<C$$

For the last overlap we get:

$$min(A),min(B),min(C), \ A=<B,C=<B$$
$$| \qquad\qquad\qquad |$$
$$min(A),min(C), \ A=<B,C=<B$$

The computation cannot proceed until the relationship between A and C is known, but in any case, a common state has been reached.

Thus, the `min` program is confluent.

Anytime and online algorithm. The *anytime (approximation)* property means that we can interrupt the program at any time and restart from the intermediate result. If we stop the algorithm between rules, we will see a subset of the initial `min` constraints from which we can restart. These sets always contain the minimum. The intermediate results approximate the final result, because the set of possible minima gets smaller and smaller with each rule application.

The *online (incremental)* property means that we can add additional constraints while the program is running without the need for redoing the computation from scratch. The program is *incremental*, because we can add more `min` constraints at any time and they can immediately react with another `min` constraint.

Concurrency and parallelism. The one-rule CHR program is *well-behaved* (terminating and confluent) and thus can be parallelized rather easily. Under *weak parallelism* (cf. Section 4.3) we apply the instances of the rule to different nonoverlapping parts of a query. The rule can be applied to arbitrary pairs of **min** constraints in parallel, so that the number of **min** constraints is halved in each *parallel computation step*. Given n **min** constraints, we can therefore compute the minimum in $O(log(n))$ time given $n/2$ *parallel processing units (processors)*.

Strong parallelism does not bring an improvement, since for rule matching we would have to search for all values larger than that in the chosen **min** constraint that matches the rule's kept head constraint.

The *cost* of sequential execution is its time complexity, while the cost of parallel execution is the time complexity times the number of processors needed. That cost is $O(nlog(n))$ here, while that of sequential execution is just $O(n)$.

7.1.2 Boolean Exclusive Or

We implemented the Exclusive Or (XOR) operation of propositional logic by two rules.

```
xor(X),  xor(X) <=> xor(0).
xor(1) \ xor(0) <=> true.
```

Most properties of the **xor** program (logical reading and correctness, termination, complexity, online and anytime algorithm property, concurrency) are analogous to that of minimum (**min**).

Logical reading and correctness. The first-order logical reading for the first rule corresponds to the formula $xor(X) \leftrightarrow xor(0)$, which means that all **xor** constraints are equivalent, in particular $xor(1) \leftrightarrow xor(0)$. Therefore we have to resort to the *linear-logic* reading of the program.

A valid query is a conjunction of **xor** constraints whose arguments are either 0 or 1. These arguments should be xored. We can therefore map the CHR conjunction to the **xor** operation. Since both the **xor** operation and the CHR conjunction are associative and commutative but not idempotent, this mapping is correct. Each rule application correctly computes a single **xor** operation. We can show by contradiction that at the end of the computation, exactly one **xor** constraint will be left. From the above observations it follows that that single constraint correctly contains the result of the **xor** operations.

Termination and complexity. The program is terminating, because each rule removes more CHR constraints than it introduces. Given a pair of **xor** constraints, one of the rules will be applicable and this will take constant time. Analogous to **min**, the algorithm runs in linear time under the *refined CHR semantics* and in cubic time under the *abstract CHR semantics*.

Confluence. The overlap **xor(X), xor(X), xor(X)** leads to **xor(0), xor(X)** with the first rule applied in two different ways. The overlap **xor(1), xor(1), xor(0)** occurs twice, once between the first and the second rule, and again between the second rule with itself. In all cases, the state **xor(0)** is reached. Analogously, the overlap **xor(1), xor(0), xor(0)** always leads to **xor(1)**. All critical pairs are joinable, thus the **xor** program is confluent.

Anytime and online algorithm, concurrency and parallelism. If we stop the program between rules, we will see fewer and fewer **xor** constraints. The final result constraint is not necessarily contained in an intermediate state, e.g. consider **xor(1), xor(1)**.

As for **min**, we can apply rules to pairs of **xor** constraints in parallel. Given n **xor** constraints, we can therefore compute the result in $O(log(n))$ time using $n/2$ processors.

7.1.3 Greatest common divisor

The first rule together with one of the rules **sub** or **mod** computes the greatest common divisor of natural numbers n_i, written as **gcd**(n_i).

```
      gcd(0) <=> true.
sub @ gcd(N) \ gcd(M) <=> 0<N,N=<M | gcd(M-N).
mod @ gcd(N) \ gcd(M) <=> 0<N,N=<M | gcd(M mod N).
```

Unless otherwise noted, we restrict ourselves to the **sub** rule, since for the **mod** rule, the results are analogous.

Logical reading and correctness. The first-order logic reading consists of the formulas

$$gcd(0) \leftrightarrow true$$

$$0<N \wedge N=<M \rightarrow (gcd(N) \wedge gcd(M) \leftrightarrow gcd(N) \wedge gcd(M-N)).$$

The latter can also be written as

$$0<N \wedge 0=<M \rightarrow (gcd(N) \wedge gcd(M+N) \leftrightarrow gcd(N) \wedge gcd(M)).$$

For this program, the first-order logical reading suffices. The formulas make conjunctions of **gcd** constraints logically equivalent that have the same gcd. The computation computes the smallest such conjunction: that which contains only a single **gcd** constraint with the gcd of all initial values.

Correctness can be shown in the usual way for Euclid's algorithm. Given termination, we show that all divisors (including the greatest) are preserved under rule application. The numbers N and M are represented as multiples of a chosen divisor, say d, i.e. $N = Ad$ and $M = Bd$. The logical reading of the second rule becomes

$$0{<}Ad \wedge Ad{=}{<}Bd \rightarrow (gcd(Ad) \wedge gcd(Bd) \leftrightarrow gcd(Ad) \wedge gcd(Bd{-}Ad)).$$

Since $gcd(Bd{-}Ad)$ is equivalent to $gcd((B{-}A)d)$, each divisor d remains during the computation until the numbers are the same. Clearly, the gcd is then equivalent to these numbers. Then another application of the **sub** rule produces one **gcd(0)** that is removed and leaves the gcd.

Termination and complexity. Termination is ensured for natural numbers as arguments of **gcd**, since due to the guard condition, the new value will always be strictly smaller than the old M, but cannot become negative.

Given two arbitrary nonnegative **gcd** constraints, a rule is always applicable in constant time. For the rule removing **gcd(0)**, complexity is constant. For the rule **sub**, complexity is *linear* in the larger number, e.g. consider **gcd(10000)**, **gcd(1)**. For the rule **mod** on the other hand, complexity is *logarithmic* in the larger of the two numbers: given two numbers N and M with $N{\leq}M$, the smallest M that yields the largest new value $M \bmod N$ is $N{+}(N{-}1)$. In that case, a rule application brings us from N and $2N{-}1$ to N and $N{-}1$. Thus the larger number decreases at least by a factor of 2 with each rule application.

Actually, the worst case is achieved by giving two neighboring Fibonacci numbers as input (as first proven by Lame in 1844). In that case, the **gcd** constraints produced will go down through all the *Fibonacci numbers*. With such input, the rule **sub** computes the same intermediate results as the rule **mod**.

For more than two **gcd** constraints, the worst-case time complexity has to consider all numbers. For the rule **sub**, the complexity is thus *linear* in the sum of the numbers. For the rule **mod** the complexity is *logarithmic* in the product of the numbers.

Confluence. As argued for min, gcd is also ground confluent. It is, however not confluent in the general case, when arguments are not fully known, a we will see.

The only overlaps are from the recursive rule with itself.

```
gcd(A),gcd(B),         0<A,A=<B, 0<B,B=<A.
gcd(A),gcd(B),gcd(C), 0<A,A=<B, 0<B,B=<C.
gcd(A),gcd(B),gcd(C), 0<A,A=<B, 0<A,A=<C.
gcd(A),gcd(B),gcd(C), 0<A,A=<B, 0<C,C=<B.
```

These overlaps are analogous to those of min. But in contrast to min, th rule for gcd not only removes but also adds a gcd constraint. The confluenc test for these overlaps is left as an exercise. We will, however, exhibit th nonjoinable critical pair:

$$gcd(A),gcd(B),gcd(C),0<A,A=<B,0<C,C=<B$$

```
                    /                              |
gcd(A),gcd(B-A),gcd(C),0<A,A=<B,0<C,C=<B    |
                                                   |
          gcd(A),gcd(B-C),gcd(C),0<A,A=<B,0<C,C=<B
```

The computation cannot proceed until more about the relationship betwee the three numbers A, B, C is known. (Then the computation proceeds t the same state.) But then gcd is not confluent (but ground confluent).

Anytime and online algorithm, concurrency and parallelism. If w stop the algorithm between rules, we will see fewer and fewer gcd constraint involving smaller and smaller numbers, until only one nonzero gcd constrain is left.

If we run disjoint pairs of nonzero gcd constraints in parallel, the com plexity cannot be worse than the overall sequential complexity but als not better than the sequential complexity (i.e. derivation length) for th worst pair (with the largest numbers). Since $O(max(a,b)) = O(a+b)$ the worst-case time complexity for parallel execution is the same as for th sequential one.

In practice, it is very likely that the interactions between different gc constraints will quickly result in small numbers. Indeed, in experiment with a parallel CHR implementation in Haskell, a *super-linear speed-up* wa achieved.

7.1.4 Primes sieve of Eratosthenes

The rule removes multiples in a set of given numbers. If all numbers from 2 to n are given, only prime numbers within this range remain.

```
sift @ prime(I) \ prime(J) <=> J mod I =:= 0 | true.
```

Logical reading and correctness. We discussed the declarative semantics of the constraint `prime` in Section 3.4.2.

For correctness, note that any number that is a multiple of another number is removed. Since the program is confluent, the result is always the same set of numbers. If the numbers from 2 to some n are given, all composite numbers are removed and only the prime numbers in this range remain. A prime number will not be removed, because it is only a multiple of 1 which is not included in the range.

Termination and complexity. Unlike the previous examples, the `sift` rule is not applicable to all pairs of numbers. Thus under the refined semantics, the worst-case time complexity is quadratic in the number of `prime` constraints. Actual run-time can be improved if the prime *candidates* are computed starting from the lower numbers, because they have a higher likelihood to divide other numbers.

Confluence. The one-rule program for `prime` is confluent due to the mathematical properties of divisibility, in particular transitivity. For example, given `prime(I)`, `prime(J)`, `prime(K)` where I is divided by J and J is divided by K, it follows that I is also divided by K. So it does not matter how we apply the `sift` rule, i.e. if I is removed by J or by K. Only `prime(K)` will remain.

The overlaps are analogous to those of the `min` program. For brevity, we write A|B (A divides B) instead of B mod A =:= 0.

```
prime(A),prime(B),            A|B,B|A.
prime(A),prime(B),prime(C),   A|B,B|C.
prime(A),prime(B),prime(C),   A|B,A|C.
prime(A),prime(B),prime(C),   A|B,C|B.
```

The first three overlaps lead to joinable critical pairs, where the subsequent common states contain the single remaining CHR constraint `prime(A)`. For the last overlap `prime(A),prime(B),prime(C)`, A|B, C|B we get:

prime(A),prime(B),prime(C), A|B, C|B
```
        |                        |
```
        prime(A),prime(C), A|B, C|B

Thus the program is confluent.

Anytime and online algorithm, concurrency and parallelism. The first properties are as for `min`.

For parallelism, there is no such simple scheduling as for the previous examples, since the guard of the `sift` rule does not hold for all pairs of `prime` constraints. We have to compute all $O(n^2)$ pairs of prime candidates systematically in $O(n)$ *rounds* (parallel computation steps) with n processors so that no *locking conflicts* occur. We can now apply *strong parallelism* of CHR (cf. Section 4.3) to our advantage: in each round we fix a prime candidate that matches the first head constraint of the `sift` rule and try to apply the rule to all remaining prime candidates by matching them with the second head constraint of the rule. For example, we can first apply `prime(2)` to all other prime candidates using n processors, and then in the next round continue with the next smallest remaining prime candidate, 3, and so on. This will need $O(n)$ rounds. The *cost* in the case of this program is the same as for the sequential execution. We have a maximal, linear parallel speed-up. This was confirmed experimentally.

7.1.5 Exchange sort

Given an array of values of the form `a(1,A₁),...,a(n,Aₙ)`, we sort the array by exchanging values that are in the wrong order.

`a(I,V), a(J,W) <=> I>J, V<W | a(J,V), a(I,W).`

The program for exchange sort differs from the previous one-rule programs in that no constraints are removed, they are just updated.

Logical reading and correctness.

$$I > J \wedge V < W \rightarrow (a(I,V) \wedge a(J,W) \leftrightarrow a(J,V) \wedge a(I,W)).$$

The logical reading above says that all arrays with the same set of values are equivalent and that we can have several values in one array index position. It does not describe the nature of an array and of the preferred order between array elements, because we can apply the logical equivalence in both directions. We have to resort to the linear logic declarative semantics.

In a sorted array, we have that for each pair of elements (a(I,V), a(J,W)) with I>J it holds that V>=W. If there is a pair for which the condition does not hold, the rule is applicable and exchanges the values so that the condition holds. So if the rule is not applicable any more, the resulting array must be sorted.

Termination and complexity. The rule terminates because each rule application corrects the order relationship of the exchanged pair of values and cannot introduce more wrong orderings than right orderings involving the other values. This reasoning can be made concrete by adding a counter to each array entry, which records how many values with larger index position are smaller than the current value. The sum of the counters decreases by at least one with each rule application: the larger value moves to the index position of the smaller value. Due to the exchange, the counter for the smaller value increases by the number of smaller values between the exchanged index positions. But the counter for the larger value will decrease by this number plus one for the exchanged value. The counters of the positions between the two numbers can change too, but the counters can only decrease.

Since the derivation length is quadratic in the number of CHR constraints, and since we have two head constraints, we get by Theorem 5.35

$$O(n^2((n^2)^2(1+1) \; + \; (0+1))) \; = \; O(n^6).$$

Of course, this worst-case complexity is highly overestimated. The exchange sort rule can be applied in constant time, once a pair of array entries in wrong order has been found. In the worst case (when the array is already sorted), we go through all old array entries to look for a partner constraint. Hence each rule application try has a cost of $O(n)$. This is the price for not exchanging values in a systematic way. Since each rule application decreases the number of wrong orders between pairs of values by at least one, there can be at most $O(n^2)$ rule applications. Overall, this gives a cubic worst-case time complexity of

$$O(n^3).$$

We will discuss a simpler and more efficient sorting rule in Section 7.3.4.

Confluence. The program is ground confluent by correctness, but not confluent. The first critical pair is joinable:

```
            a(I,V), a(J,W), a(K,U), I>J,V<W, J>K,W<U
          / I,J                              | J,K
        /              a(I,V), a(K,W), a(J,U), I>J,V<W, J>K,W<U
      /                                      |
a(J,V), a(I,W), a(K,U), I>J,V<W, J>K,W<U     |
      | I,K                                  | I,K
      |              a(K,V), a(I,W), a(J,U), I>J,V<W, J>K,W<U
      |                                      |
a(J,V), a(K,W), a(I,U), I>J,V<W, J>K,W<U     |
      \ J,K                                  | I,J
        \                                    |
          a(K,V), a(J,W), a(I,U), I>J,V<W, J>K,W<U
```

The next two overlaps lead to nonjoinable critical pairs:

```
            a(I,V), a(J,W), a(K,U), I>J,V<W, I>K,V<U
          / I,J                              |
a(J,V), a(I,W), a(K,U), I>J,V<W, I>K,V<U     |
                                             | I,K
                    a(K,V), a(J,W), a(I,U), I>J,V<W, I>K,V<U
```

This critical pair is not joinable. It can be joined once the relationships between J and K as well as W and U are known. In particular, the current critical pair can be joined for ground queries. Then we are basically back to the situation of the first overlap.

```
            a(I,V), a(J,W), a(K,U), I>K,V<U, J>K,W<U
          / I,K                              |
a(K,V), a(J,W), a(I,U), I>K,V<U, J>K,W<U     |
                                             | J,K
                    a(I,V), a(K,W), a(J,U), I>K,V<U, J>K,W<U
```

This situation is analogous to the previous one, the critical pair is not joinable.

Anytime and online algorithm, concurrency and parallelism. The array gets more and more sorted in that the number of pairs in the wrong order decreases with each rule application. We can add additional array entries at any time. The order in which the array entries are added does not matter. The array can have missing index positions, but not duplicate ones.

Like the **prime** sieve program, the exchange sort rule is not applicable to arbitrary pairs of numbers. Unlike previous programs, both CHR constraints are updated when the rule applies. This makes scheduling costly. Only weak parallelism is possible.

Assume n array entries and n processors. We associate an array entry with a processor. To keep the cost of scheduling down, we systematically try all possible pairs of array entries in $O(n)$ parallel computation steps with n pairs each. We call these $O(n)$ steps a *macro-step*, in which all pairings are tried. So each array entry will see all other array entries during a macro-step. Each array entry can react with at most $O(n)$ other array entries. Overall, there are $O(n^2)$ rule applications. We claim that all rule applications can be performed in $O(n)$ macro-steps. So the parallel complexity is quadratic and the cost is cubic, which is the complexity of sequential execution.

7.1.6 Newton's method for square roots

The constraint **sqrt(X,G)** means that the square root of the number X is approximated by G. We start from given positive numbers X and G, our initial guess. In the rule the constant **eps** is greater than but close to zero:

```
sqrt(X,G) <=> abs(G*G/X-1)>eps | sqrt(X,(G+X/G)/2).
```

Logical reading and correctness

$$abs(G * G/X - 1) > \epsilon \rightarrow (sqrt(X,G) \leftrightarrow sqrt(X,(G + X/G)/2)).$$

The logical reading just says that any value approximates the square root. The linear-logic reading better reflects the dynamics of the computation.

Termination and complexity. One can show that after the first iteration (rule application), the value of G will be greater than or equal to the square root of X. If G is the square root, the rule is not applicable anymore, since in the guard, **abs(G*G/X-1)** is zero and **eps** is greater than zero. Otherwise, the rule will be applicable again and G will always decrease between subsequent iterations.

Confluence, anytime and online algorithm, concurrency and parallelism. Since we only have a single rule with a single head constraint, these properties hold in a trivial way. Each rule application brings G closer to the square root of X. Several **sqrt** constraints can run independently in parallel.

7.2 Procedural algorithms

7.2.1 Maximum

Let =< and < be built-in constraints. The CHR constraint `max(X,Y,Z)` means that the maximum of X and Y is Z:

```
max(X,Y,Z) <=> X=<Y | Z=Y.
max(X,Y,Z) <=> Y=<X | Z=X.
```

Logical reading and correctness. The classical logical reading is

$$X \leq Y \rightarrow (max(X,Y,Z) \leftrightarrow Z = Y)$$
$$Y \leq X \rightarrow (max(X,Y,Z) \leftrightarrow Z = X).$$

The formulas are logical consequences of the definition of `max` as

$$max(X,Y,Z) \leftrightarrow (X \leq Y \wedge Z = Y \vee Y \leq X \wedge Z = X),$$

which shows logical correctness.

Termination and complexity. Let n be the number of CHR constraints in a query. In each derivation step, one rule is applied and it will remove one constraint. Hence, there can be at most c derivation steps. In each derivation step, in the worst case, we check each of the at most n constraints in the current state against the given set of rules. Checking or establishing built-in syntactic equality between variables and the constants 0 and 1 can be implemented in constant time. Then checking the applicability of one constraint against one rule can be done in quasi-constant time. Rule application is also possible in quasi-constant time. So the worst-case time complexity of applying the rules is slightly worse than $O(n^2)$. The same complexity is obtained from Theorem 5.35.

Confluence. We have shown confluence of `max` in Examples 5.2.5 and 5.3.8.

Anytime and online algorithm, concurrency and parallelism. For single-headed simplification rules only, these properties hold in a trivial way. Note that one `max` constraint may have to wait for the result of another `max` constraint, e.g. `max(X,Y,Z), max(Y,Z,W)`.

7.2.2 Fibonacci numbers

The CHR constraint `fib(N,M)` holds if the Nth Fibonacci number is M.

```
f0 @ fib(0,M) <=> M=1.
f1 @ fib(1,M) <=> M=1.
fn @ fib(N,M) <=> N>=2 | fib(N-1,M1), fib(N-2,M2), M is M1+M2.
```

Logical reading and correctness. The first-order logic reading

$$fib(0, M) \leftrightarrow M = 1$$

$$fib(1, M) \leftrightarrow M = 1$$

$$N \geq 2 \rightarrow (fib(N, M) \leftrightarrow fib(N-1, M1) \wedge fib(N-2, M2) \wedge M = M1 + M2)$$

also shows correctness since it coincides with the mathematical definition of the `fib` function.

Termination and complexity. Because the first argument of `fib` decreases in each recursive call and recursive calls are only possible with positive first arguments, the rules terminate. As is well known, such a direct implementation has exponential time complexity because of the double recursion that recomputes the same Fibonacci numbers over and over again in different parts of the recursions.

This can be shown by the ranking

$$rank(fib(n, m)) = 2^n.$$

A ranking gives an upper bound on the derivation length. Since rules can be applied in constant time for queries where the first argument of `fib` is given, the complexity is also $O(2^n)$.

If the first argument is not known, complexity may increase depending on the wake-up policy of the implementation under the refined semantics and also under the abstract semantics. A delayed `fib` constraint may be triggered by computing the result of another `fib` constraint. For example, consider the query `fib(B,C)`, `fib(3,B)`. The meta-complexity Theorem 5.35 properly reflects this and gives a quadratic complexity in the derivation length, i.e. $O(4^n)$.

Confluence, anytime and online algorithm, concurrency and parallelism. The program is trivially confluent, since single-headed simplification rules whose heads and guards exclude each other do not have overlaps.

The other properties hold in a trivial way, since the program consists only of single-headed simplification rules.

Memorization version

The program is as follows.

```
mem @ fib(N,M1) \ fib(N,M2) <=> M1=M2.

f0 @ fib(0,M) ==> M=1.
f1 @ fib(1,M) ==> M=1.
fn @ fib(N,M) ==> N>=2 | fib(N-1,M1), fib(N-2,M2), M is M1+M2.
```

Complexity. The memorization version has linear complexity under the refined operational semantics when indexing on the first argument is used, because each Fibonacci number is only computed once. (We ignore the cost of maintaining the propagation history since it is highly implementation-dependent.) Without indexing, the complexity is quadratic because of searching for suitable pairs in rule mem. Theorem 5.35 does not apply because there are propagation rules.

Confluence. There are nontrivial overlaps between the mem rule and each of the propagation rules. Showing joinability actually proves that the propagation rules define a CHR constraint that is a function.

The overlaps, critical pairs, and their computations for joinability are

```
          fib(0,M1), fib(0,M2)
            / mem                  f0
    fib(0,M2), M1=M2    fib(0,M1), M1=1, fib(0,M2)
            | f0                | mem
fib(0,M2), M1=M2, M2=1  ≡  M1=M2, M1=1, fib(0,M2)
```

```
            fib(N,M1), fib(N,M2)
             / mem           fn
fib(N,M2),M1=M2  fib(N,M1),fib(N-1,M3),fib(N-2,M4),M1 is M3+M4,fib(N,M2)
         | fn              | mem
         |     M1=M2,fib(N-1,M3),fib(N-2,M4),M1 is M3+M4,fib(N,M2)
         |            ≡
fib(N,M2),M1=M2,fib(N-1,M5),fib(N-2,M6),M2 is M5+M6
```

Note that the variables M3, M4 and M5, M6 are local variables. The overlap with rule f1 is omitted, it is analogous to the one with f0.

Anytime and online algorithm, concurrency and parallelism. We can execute the two recursive calls in parallel, but this results in no gain, since the mem rule will absorb multiple computations for the same first argument of fib sooner or later.

In theory, no computation steps are redone when restarting a computation at an intermediate state. In practice, however, recomputation may occur in the presence of propagation rules, because the propagation history is not explicit in the state. Due to confluence and the `mem` rule, the additional computations will be absorbed.

Program variations

For the other program variations of `fib`, similar reasoning applies with similar results for the intended use of `fib` as a function with given first argument. The only exception is the rule for the finite bottom-up computation of `fib`,

```
fn @ fib_upto(Max), fib(N1,M1), fib(N2,M2) ==> Max>N2,N2=:=N1+1 |
                                               fib(N2+1,M1+M2).
```

which has quadratic complexity because indexing cannot be utilized between the two `fib` constraints in the head.

7.2.3 Depth-first search in trees

The *operation constraint* `dfsearch(Tree,Data)` searches a binary sorted tree for a given datum.

```
empty @ dfsearch(nil,X) <=> false.
found @ dfsearch(node(N,L,R),X) <=> X=N | true.
left  @ dfsearch(node(N,L,R),X) <=> X<N | dfsearch(L,X).
right @ dfsearch(node(N,L,R),X) <=> X>N | dfsearch(R,X).
```

As for `fib`, all analyzed properties hold in a trivial way, since the program consists only of single-headed simplification rules whose heads and guards exclude each other. The complexity is as usual for binary tree search linear in the depth of the tree.

We can choose another *granularity* of the data representation, where a node is represented by a CHR *data constraint*.

```
empty @ nil(I) \ dfsearch(I,X) <=> fail.
found @ node(I,N,L,R) \ dfsearch(I,X) <=> X=N | true.
left  @ node(I,N,L,R) \ dfsearch(I,X) <=> X<N | dfsearch(L,X).
right @ node(I,N,L,R) \ dfsearch(I,X) <=> X>N | dfsearch(R,X).
```

If the query contains a conjunction of data constraints `nil` and `node` that define a valid binary search tree, the properties are inherited from the previous version of the program. With indexing, complexity is also unaffected. The properties break down for arbitrary states (as for the last version below), e.g. consider a state containing both `nil(I)` and `node(I,N,L,R)`. Unlike the previous version, data constraints (parts of the tree) can be added incrementally, i.e. the online algorithm property holds.

We can also directly access the data by just mentioning it in the rule head.

```
found @ node(N) \ search(N) <=> true.
empty @ search(N) <=> fail.
```

Because of the `empty` rule, all properties except the anytime algorithm property break down. With indexing, the rules can be applied in linear time in the number of constraints in the query.

7.2.4 Destructive assignment

The constraint `assign/2` assigns to a variable `Var` a new value.

```
assign(Var,New), cell(Var,Old) <=> cell(Var,New).
```

With destructive updates, the order of the updates matters. The rule is not confluent (cf. Example 5.2.4) and thus cannot be run in parallel (cf. Example 4.3.5). The rule is also a canonical example where the first-order logical reading does not reflect the intended meaning and a linear-logic semantics is needed (cf. Example 3.4.6).

7.3 Graph-based algorithms

7.3.1 Transitive closure

Let us go back to the basic version of transitive closure from Section 2.4.1.

```
dp @ p(X,Y) \ p(X,Y) <=> true.
p1 @ e(X,Y) ==> p(X,Y).
pn @ e(X,Y), p(Y,Z) ==> p(X,Z).
```

Logical reading and correctness. The rules have an immediate logical reading in first-order logic (FOL) as implications:

$$p(X,Y) \wedge p(X,Y) \leftrightarrow p(X,Y)$$
$$e(X,Y) \rightarrow p(X,Y)$$
$$e(X,Y) \wedge p(Y,Z) \rightarrow p(X,Z).$$

The logical reading of the duplicate removal rule is a tautology of FOL. However, the fact that the transitive closure T is the smallest transitive relation cannot be expressed in FOL, but in the linear-logic reading. The rules actually compute the smallest relation because their application from left to right produces the relation in a bottom-up manner. (A top-down computation would not always terminate.) These observations taken together can prove correctness of the implementation.

Termination and complexity. Under the refined CHR semantics, duplicates are removed by rule dp before the two main propagation rules are applied. This ensures termination, since in a given finite graph, there can only be a finite number of different paths. The program does not terminate under the abstract semantics (for cyclic graphs when the rule dp is applied too late).

Let v be the number of nodes (vertices) in the edge constraints, e be the number of edges, and p be the number of different path constraints. We assume that there are no duplicate edge constraints. Clearly, $v/2 \le e \le p \le v^2$. The rules can be applied in constant time.

Without indexing, an upper bound for the number of propagation rule application attempts is the product of the number of the head constraints that can occur during a computation. Thus rule p1 is tried at most e times and rule pn is tried at most ep times. Rule p1 applies e times. Since the edge and path constraint in the head of rule pn share a variable, only up to $max(ev, vp) = vp$ rule applications are possible (but ep rule tries). Each rule application produces a path constraint that is first subjected to rule dp. Thus this rule is tried up to pvp times. Thus without indexing, the duplicate removal rule dp dominates the complexity, it is $O(vp^2) = O(v^5)$.

The complexity improves when we index constraints on the arguments that contain shared variables in rule heads. Therefore, we index the arguments of the path constraint and on the second argument of the edge constraint. As a result, the upper bounds for rule application attempts and rule applications coincide now. Rule p1 is still tried and applied at most e times. But rule pn is tried and applied at most $max(ev, vp) = vp$ times now. Thus rule dp is tried and applied at most vp times now.

Hence the worst-case time complexity of the program for transitive closure with the indexing optimization is cubic in the number of nodes:

$$O(v^3).$$

This is the optimal complexity for this simple transitive closure algorithm. If there are significantly fewer than $O(v^2)$ paths, the complexity $O(vp)$ is even better. (The best known matrix multiplication algorithms for transitive closure need less time, but still more than quadratic time.)

Confluence. The only nontrivial overlap is between the rules dp and pn.

```
        e(X,Y), p(Y,Z), p(Y,Z)
        / dp              \ pn
e(X,Y), p(Y,Z)    e(X,Y), p(Y,Z), p(Y,Z), p(X,Z)
        \ pn              / dp
        e(X,Y), p(Y,Z), p(X,Z)
```

The program is confluent.

Anytime and online algorithm, concurrency and parallelism. Repeated applications of propagation rules after program interruption do not matter, since confluence and the fd rule remove duplicate paths. We can add edges while the program runs. Starting from it, new path constraints will be introduced.

With strong parallelism, we can apply all applicable propagation rules in parallel. We can apply rule p1 to all edges in parallel to compute all paths of length 1. In the next rounds, we perform all possible applications of the rules dp and pn. Thus, duplicate paths are removed and longer and longer paths are computed. With indexing, the two rules are applied up to vp times. If we do not have enough processors, we can delay some rule applications to later computation steps. Given v processors, we thus claim that we can always apply $O(v)$ rules at once. Thus the parallel complexity is then $O(p) = O(v^2)$. The overall cost is $O(v^3)$.

Program variations

Similar reasoning with similar results applies for the properties of the program variations. The only exceptions are the complexity of single-source (or single-target) path computations and of shortest paths.

Single-source and single-target paths. We can specialize the transitive closure rules so that only paths from a given source node or to a given target node are computed, for example:

```
source(X), e(X,Y) ==> p(X,Y).
source(X), p(X,Y), e(Y,Z) ==> p(X,Z).
```

Complexity. Without indexing, the complexity of the rule application attempts is not affected. But the number of path constraints produced decreases by a factor of v since now $O(p) = O(v)$. Hence the overall worst-case time complexity is $O(v^3)$. With indexing, the number of attempted and successful applications of the second propagation rule is now bounded by v^2, which also determines the overall complexity.

Shortest paths. We have extended the CHR transitive closure program to compute the shortest path lengths between all pairs of nodes.

```
dp @ p(X,Y,N) \ p(X,Y,M) <=> N=<M | true.
e(X,Y) ==> p(X,Y,1).
e(X,Y), p(Y,Z,N) ==> p(X,Z,N+1).
```

Termination and complexity. Even though the program is similar to the transitive closure program, the complexity is worse. In the original transitive closure program, the new active path constraint would always be removed when rule **dp** applied. Now, in the shortest path program, it will only be removed if its path is longer or equal. Otherwise the old path constraint will be removed and computation will continue for the new path constraint (that has a shorter path length). Since work is repeated with a path of shorter length, work can be duplicated at most v times. We may also argue that the number of different path constraints is multiplied by a factor of v, since there are v different possible path lengths for each path. Thus, the worst-case time complexity for an implementation with indexing is $O(ev^2) = O(v^4)$.

For a better complexity result, close to that of transitive closure, i.e. ev, a more clever scheduling of the rule applications is needed. For example, in Dijkstra's algorithm (see also Section 6.1.5) and its extensions to all-pairs shortest paths, computation is always continued with the shortest path computed so far; other path computations are delayed. Compared to transitive closure, there is still an overhead of scheduling the rules accordingly.

7.3.2 Partial order constraint

This classical CHR program introduced in Section 2.4.2 implements a nonstrict partial order relation.

```
duplicate     @ X leq Y \ X leq Y <=> true.
reflexivity   @ X leq X <=> true.
antisymmetry  @ X leq Y , Y leq X <=> X=Y.
transitivity  @ X leq Y , Y leq Z ==> X leq Z.
```

Termination and complexity. The **duplicate** and the **transitivity** rule are analogous to those of transitive closure, i.e. cubic in the number of variables with indexing. The **reflexivity** rule does not change the complexity. With indexing, the `antisymmetry` rule is tried at most $O(v^2)$ times. When the rule is applied, the built-in constraint in the body of the rule will trigger all `leq` constraints that contain the variables X and Y. There are $O(v)$ such constraints in the worst case. In these constraints, one of the variables can be considered to be replaced by the other, so that the overall problem actually gets smaller by one variable. This can happen at most $O(v)$ times. Hence the `antisymmetry` rule can be applied at most $O(v)$ times. So the overhead caused by trying and applying the `antisymmetry` rule is $O(v^2)$ in both cases. Thus the overall complexity is cubic $O(v^3)$.

Remaining properties. Since `leq` is a basic CHR example, we have already discussed its logical reading in Example 3.4.1, confluence in Example 4.3.2, anytime property in Example 4.1.1, online property in Example 4.2.1, and concurrency in Example 4.3.4.

7.3.3 Grammar parsing

The *Cocke–Younger–Kasami (CYK) algorithm* parses a string according to a given context-free grammar in Chomsky normal form. This *bottom-up* algorithm can be seen as a specialization of *transitive closure* and inherits most of its properties. We therefore only discuss confluence and complexity here.

```
duplicate    @ p(A,I,J) \ p(A,I,J) <=> true.
terminal     @ A->T, e(T,I,J) ==> p(A,I,J).
nonterminal @ A->B*C, p(B,I,J), p(C,J,K) ==> p(A,I,K).
```

Termination and complexity. The complexity analysis is analogous to that for transitive closure. We only consider the case with indexing (on the argument positions where shared variables occur in rule heads). Since arguments of the constraints can be associated with *finite domains*, we can simply calculate an upper bound on the number of rule application attempts (and rule applications) as the product of the domain sizes of the variables occurring in the rule head.

The size of the string to parse is the length of the chain that represents the string. A chain has v nodes and $e = v-1$ edges. Let t be the number of terminal symbols and n be the number of nonterminals. Since the grammar rules are contained in our query, we can have them as parameters for complexity (they usually contribute a constant to the complexity). The number of different grammar rules r is bounded from above by $nt + n^3$ (and from below by t and n). We assume that $t \leq n^2$. There are no duplicate grammar rules in a query.

For the `terminal` rule, we thus get the product of the domain sizes for the variables `A`, `T`, `I`, `J`, i.e. $ntvv = ntv^2$ as upper bound on the number of rule applications. For the `nonterminal` rule, we get from variables `A`, `B`, `C`, `I`, `J`, `K` the bound n^3v^3. The `duplicate` rule is tried with each `p` constraint that is produced with each rule application by one of the propagation rules. Since $t \leq n^2$, there are $O(n^3v^3)$ propagation rule applications and thus the same bound applies on `duplicate` rule applications.

Since the program rules can be applied in constant time (with indexing), this gives a cubic complexity of $O(n^3v^3)$.

Confluence. While the program is confluent for its intended use with graph chains representing the expression to be parsed, it is not confluent in general. The critical pair resulting from the overlap between the duplicate and nonterminal rule is not joinable:

```
              A->B*B, p(B,I,I), p(B,I,I)
             / nonterminal              \ duplicate
A->B*B, p(B,I,I), p(B,I,I), p(A,I,I)   A->B*B, p(B,I,I)
             | duplicate
A->B*B, p(B,I,I), p(A,I,I)
```

7.3.4 Ordered merging and sorting

One rule implements a merge sort algorithm. The query contains arcs of the form `0 -> V` for each value `V`, where `0` is assumed to be a given smallest (dummy) value.

`A -> B \ A -> C <=> A<B,B=<C | B -> C.`

Logical reading and correctness. The classical logical reading of the rule is sufficient:

$$A<B \wedge B\text{->}C \rightarrow (A\text{->}B \wedge A\text{->}C \leftrightarrow A\text{->}B \wedge B\text{->}C).$$

Since `A -> B` is to mean $A \leq B$, the logical correctness of the rule can be shown as it is then a logic consequence of the axioms for $\leq$ and $<$:

$$A<B \wedge B \leq C \rightarrow (A \leq B \wedge A \leq C \leftrightarrow A \leq B \wedge B \leq C).$$

Correctness of the algorithm has been discussed when the program was introduced in Section 2.4.4.

Termination and complexity. We first consider the complexity of merging two ordered chains of length n and m. When we index on the first argument of the arc constraint then, given one arc, the second arc constraint for the main rule can be found in constant time. Such a pair of arcs can match the rule in one way or the other. So the rule is applicable to arbitrary pairs of arcs with the same first argument. When two ordered chains are merged, the value A will not reappear in the chains, thus the arc A->B will not be considered again. Thus, each rule application processes one arc constraint. Hence the cost of in-order merging two ordered chains of length n and m is $O(n + m)$ in the worst case.

For sorting, we have given n values as the second argument of arc constraints, where the first argument is fixed to a unique smallest dummy value. Since each value in the first argument can be replaced at most n times by a larger value, the worst-case time complexity is quadratic in n, i.e. $O(n^2)$ (with indexing on the first argument).

Confluence. Since our program is correct and produces a unique ordered chain as a result, we already know it is *ground confluent*.

The overlaps and their joinability checks are analogous to those for the gcd rule of Section 7.1.3. (We can map gcd(N) to X->N and gcd(M-N) to N -> M.) One of the four overlaps is thus not joinable.

```
        X->A,X->B,X->C,  X<A,A=<B,  X<C,C=<B
              /                          |
X->A,A->B,X->C,  X<A,A=<B,  X<C,C=<B      |
                                         |
        X->A,C->B,X->C,  X<A,A=<B,  X<C,C=<B
```

The computation cannot proceed until the relationship between the numbers A and C is known. Then the computation proceeds to the same state. But then our sorting rule is not confluent for nonground queries.

Anytime and online algorithm. Intermediate results will always show an acyclic connected graph with the smallest value as root consisting of longer and longer ordered chains (without branches). We can sort incrementally, new arcs can be added at any time.

Optimal complexity sorting

Complexity can be improved to the optimal complexity of sorting $O(n\ log(n))$ by an optimal order of merging. As in the *merge sort* algorithm we prefer merging chains of the same length. To this end, we precede each chain with its length, written N=>FirstNode. We also add a rule to initiate merging of chains of the same length:

N=>A, N=>B <=> A<B | N+N=>A, A->B.

In the query we now introduce constraints of the form `1=>Vi` instead of arcs for each unique value `Vi`.

This program works only if the number of values `Vi` in the query n is a power of 2. For other n, we have to know when we have seen the last chain. Either a postprocessing phase initiated by an auxiliary *dummy constraint* can merge the remaining chains or it can be inferred from the known number of values n when there are remaining chains to merge using a third rule.

Each chain is prefixed by the constraint `n=>Ai`, where n is always the length of the chain. Since we only merge chains of the same length, their lengths always double. We start with merging n chains of length 1. Pairwise merging them causes a cost of n. In the next round, we merge $n/2$ chains of length 2 with the same overall cost. After $log(n)$ rounds we are done and have a chain of length n. Since the rules can be applied in constant time, the complexity is $O(nlog(n))$.

Concurrency and parallelism. Parallelization is easiest to see for the optimal complexity version. We basically use the same structure of computation as in the proof of optimal complexity. Note that merging two chains itself is strictly sequential. In one round, we can start merging all pairs of chains of the same length. In the next round, we can already start merging the resulting chains of double length, while their tails are still produced. So we need $log(n)$ rounds for merging. In the last round, we are about to merge two chains of size $n/2$. This may result in the need for n more steps, so overall we need $log(n) + n$ steps.

This linear time complexity is also possible with the original version of our sorting algorithm. We just have to use the scheduling that would happen under the optimal version.

Concluding, with n processors, we can sort in parallel in time $O(n)$ and cost $O(n^2)$. A parallel speed-up was confirmed experimentally.

7.4 Exercises

7.1 Check the confluence for the gcd program. The four overlaps are from the recursive rule with itself:

```
gcd(A),gcd(B),        0<A,A=<B, 0<B,B=<A.
gcd(A),gcd(B),gcd(C), 0<A,A=<B, 0<B,B=<C.
gcd(A),gcd(B),gcd(C), 0<A,A=<B, 0<A,A=<C.
gcd(A),gcd(B),gcd(C), 0<A,A=<B, 0<C,C=<B.
```

Answer. The simplified first overlap from above, gcd(A),gcd(B), 0<A, A=B will lead to either gcd(A), gcd(B-A), 0<A,A=B or gcd(A-B), gcd(B), 0<A,A=B. These are the same states since A=B.

The simplified second overlap gcd(A),gcd(B),gcd(C), 0<A,A=<B, B=<C has the two computations:

```
gcd(A),gcd(B),gcd(C),       0<A,A=<B,B=<C % B,C.
gcd(A),gcd(B),gcd(C-B),     0<A,A=<B,B=<C % A,B.
gcd(A),gcd(B-A),gcd(C-B),   0<A,A=<B,B=<C.


gcd(A),gcd(B),gcd(C),       0<A,A=<B,B=<C % A,B.
gcd(A),gcd(B-A),gcd(C),     0<A,A=<B,B=<C % B,C.
gcd(A),gcd(B-A),gcd(C-B),   0<A,A=<B,B=<C.
```

For the overlap gcd(A),gcd(B),gcd(C), 0<A,A=<B,A=<C we get confluent computations:

```
gcd(A),gcd(B),gcd(C),       0<A,A=<B,A=<C % A,C.
gcd(A),gcd(B),gcd(C-A),     0<A,A=<B,A=<C % A,B.
gcd(A),gcd(B-A),gcd(C-A),   0<A,A=<B,A=<C.


gcd(A),gcd(B),gcd(C),       0<A,A=<B,A=<C % A,B.
gcd(A),gcd(B-A),gcd(C),     0<A,A=<B,A=<C % A,C.
gcd(A),gcd(B-A),gcd(C-A),   0<A,A=<B,A=<C.
```

For the overlap gcd(A),gcd(B),gcd(C), 0<A,A=<B, 0<C,C=<B we get a nonjoinable critical pair:

```
gcd(A),gcd(B),gcd(C),     0<A,A=<B, 0<C,C=<B % A,B.
gcd(A),gcd(B-A),gcd(C),   0<A,A=<B, 0<C,C=<B.


gcd(A),gcd(B),gcd(C),     0<A,A=<B, 0<C,C=<B % C,B.
gcd(A),gcd(B-C),gcd(C),   0<A,A=<B, 0<C,C=<B.
```

Hence gcd is not confluent.

7.2 Check confluence for the primes sieve program. In the following, for brevity we write A|B (A divides B) instead of B mod A =:= 0. The overlaps are analogous to those of the min program.

```
prime(A),prime(B),               A|B,B|A.
prime(A),prime(B),prime(C), A|B,B|C.
prime(A),prime(B),prime(C), A|B,A|C.
prime(A),prime(B),prime(C), A|B,C|B.
```

Answer. The simplified first overlap from above, `prime(A)`, `prime(B)`, `A|B,B|A` will lead to either `prime(A)`, `A|B,B|A` or `prime(B)`, `A|B,B|A`. These are the same states since `A|B`, `B|A` implies `A=B`.

The simplified overlap `prime(A),prime(B),prime(C), A|B,B|C` has the following two computations for the critical pair:

```
prime(A),prime(B),prime(C), A|B,B|C % B,C.
prime(A),prime(B),           A|B,B|C % A,B.
prime(A),                    A|B,B|C.

prime(A),prime(B),prime(C), A|B,B|C % A,B.
prime(A),prime(C),           A|B,B|C % B,C.
prime(A),                    A|B,B|C.
```

For the overlap `prime(A),prime(B),prime(C), A|B,A|C` we get similar confluent computations:

```
prime(A),prime(B),prime(C), A|B,A|C % A,C.
prime(A),prime(B),           A|B,A|C % A,B.
prime(A),                    A|B,A|C.

prime(A),prime(B),prime(C), A|B,A|C % A,B.
prime(A),prime(C),           A|B,A|C % A,C.
prime(A),                    A|B,A|C.
```

For the last overlap `prime(A),prime(B),prime(C), A|B, C|B` we get:

```
prime(A),prime(B),prime(C), A|B, C|B
             |                  |
       prime(A),prime(C), A|B, C|B
```

8

Finite domain constraint solvers

In this and the next chapter, algorithms for reasoning in constraint systems, i.e. for solving, simplification, and propagation of constraints, will be presented as logical inference rules that are directly executable in CHR. Unless otherwise noted, these constraint solvers are *well-behaved* (terminating and confluent). For most solvers, we will contrast the worst-case time complexity given by the meta-complexity Theorem 5.35 with empirical results from a preliminary set of test runs. Typically, the observed time complexity has lower exponents than those predicted by the meta-complexity theorem.

There are two main approaches for constraint-solving algorithms, *variable elimination* and *local consistency (local propagation)* techniques. A clear distinction between the two approaches is not always possible. Variable elimination *substitutes* terms for variables. This typically results in solvers defined by rules with recursive calls to the given constraints that contain fewer variables. In the local propagation approach, we derive simple constraints from the given constraints at hand and let the given constraints react to them. Local consistency techniques typically have to be interleaved with *search* to achieve global consistency, i.e. satisfaction-completeness. *(Satisfaction-) completeness* means that the solver can always detect unsatisfiability of allowed constraints.

In this chapter, we deal with constraint solvers for problems where the variables can only take values from a finite domain. Here the solvers try to reduce the set of possible values for a variable, i.e. to remove values from its domain that do not occur in any solution. So finite domain constraint solving proceeds by making domains smaller and smaller. The smallest useful finite domain contains the two truth values of Boolean algebra. We discuss local propagation and variable elimination solvers for this constraint system. Then we discuss two classical generic local propagation methods for finitary problems, arc and path consistency.

8.1 Boolean algebra and propositional logic

Boolean algebra (propositional logic) constraints can be solved by different techniques such as value propagation and variable elimination by resolution. We discuss solvers for either approach here. (A two-rule program for solving ground `xor` constraints has been given in Section 2.2.2.)

8.1.1 Boolean algebra

In this Boolean constraint solver, a *local consistency* algorithm is used. It simplifies one Boolean constraint at a time into one or more syntactic equalities whenever possible. The logical connectives of Boolean algebra are represented as CHR constraints, i.e. in relational form. For example, the logical connective for propositional conjunction is written as the constraint `and(X,Y,Z)`, where $X \wedge Y = Z$.

The complete set of rules for value propagation of conjunction is given below. We have already seen similar rules in Example 6.2.2. The rules are based on the idea that, given a value for one of the variables in one constraint, we try to determine values for other variables it contains.

```
and(X,Y,Z) <=> X=0 | Z=0.
and(X,Y,Z) <=> Y=0 | Z=0.
and(X,Y,Z) <=> Z=1 | X=1,Y=1.
```

We can go beyond propagating values and propagate equalities between variables.

```
and(X,Y,Z) <=> X=1 | Y=Z.
and(X,Y,Z) <=> Y=1 | X=Z.
and(X,Y,Z) <=> X=Y | Y=Z.
```

With equality propagation, the query `and(1,Y,Z)`, `neg(Y,Z)` will reduce to `false`, and this cannot be achieved by value propagation alone.

Termination and complexity. We apply the *meta-complexity Theorem 5.35*. All rules have one head CHR constraint, so $n = 1$. For all rules, (O_H, O_G, O_C, O_B) is $(1, 1, 1, 0)$, i.e. all rule-dependent complexities are constant. By the complexity meta-theorem, this gives $O_{Bool}(c(c^1(1 + 1) + (1 + 0)))$, i.e

$$O_{Bool}(c^2).$$

This worst-case time complexity can actually be reached. Consider the query scheme

```
and(X,X1,X2),and(X,X2,X3),and(X,X3,X4),...,and(X,Xn-1,Xn), X=X1
```

When X=X1, the first and constraint of the query will propagate X1=X2. Since this means that also X=X2, the second and constraint will be simplified and so on. A cascade of equalities is created. At the end, all variables are equal. In each computation step, the variable X is indirectly affected, because the next variable Xi is equated with variable Xi-1 that is already equivalent to X. Thus, all constraints that contain X have to be woken and reconsidered. So in the worst case, we have to go through all and constraints before we find the single constraint that can be simplified next.

If we drop the rules for equality propagation and only keep the rules for value propagation, then linear complexity can be achieved: since variables are bound to values only and not to other variables anymore, a Boolean constraint can only be woken a few times in vain before enough arguments are bound to simplify the constraint.

Experiments show that the order of the (built-in) constraints in the query may strongly influence the run-time. For the and constraint of the Boolean constraint solver, the observed time complexity of the solver was linear:

$$O_{Bool}^{obs}(c).$$

This is because the problems with quadratic complexity are unlikely to appear.

Search. The solver is incomplete. For example, the solver cannot detect inconsistency of and(X,Y,Z),and(X,Y,W),neg(Z,W). (There is no propagation if the arguments of a logical connective are different variables.) For (satisfaction-)completeness, constraint simplification has to be interleaved with search. In finite domain solvers, a so-called *enumeration (or labeling) phase* is introduced that tries possible values for the variables, thus retaining completeness. The generic labeling procedure enum traverses a list of variables.

For Boolean constraints, labeling search tries the values 0 or 1 for each variable using the constraint indomain. Of course, search brings back the inherent exponential complexity of Boolean satisfiability.

```
enum([]) <=> true.
enum([X|L]) <=> indomain(X), enum(L).

indomain(X) <=> (X=0 ; X=1).
```

The semicolon (;) of CHR$^\vee$ (cf. Section 3.3.2) denotes *disjunction* implemented by search.

It is important that the constraint enum is added at the end of a Boolean query. This ensures that we perform a search step (a call to indomain) only, when no other rule is applicable. The execution of indomain will bind a variable and thus trigger further rule applications. After that, enum proceeds recursively with labeling the next variable. We will use enum and variations of indomain also for the remaining Boolean solvers in the next sections.

Now in the query and(X,Y,Z),and(X,Y,W),neg(Z,W),enum([X,Y,Z,W]) we will reach enum without any previous simplification. The labeling routine enum will call indomain for the first variable in the list, X. It will be bound to 0 first. This will wake the two and constraints, and they will simplify to Z=0 and W=0, respectively. As a consequence, neg fails and backtracking tries the second value for X, binding the variable to 1. This now generates the two built-ins Y=Z, Y=W. Since this implies that Z=W, the constraint neg will fail again. Since both possible values for X lead to failure, overall failure is caused and the unsatisfiability of the query is detected.

8.1.2 Boolean cardinality

The cardinality constraint combinator was originally introduced for arbitrary finite domains. In the solver *Card* we adapted cardinality for Boolean variables. The Boolean cardinality constraint card(L,U,BL,N) holds if between L and U Boolean variables in the list BL are equal to 1. N is the length of the list BL.

The cardinality constraint is a so-called *global constraint*. Syntactically, a global constraint is one that admits an arbitrary number of variables as argument. Note that a propositional formula for counting true propositions would have a size that is exponential in the number of involved propositions.

A single Boolean cardinality constraint can express the satisfiability of some logical connectives directly:

- negation card(0,0,[C],1)
- exclusive or (xor) card(1,1,[C1,C2],2)
- nand (negated and) card(0,1,[C1,C2],2)
- at most one card(0,1,[C1,...,Cn],N)
- conjunction card(N,N,[C1,...,Cn],N)
- disjunction card(1,N,[C1,...,Cn],N).

With exclusive or and disjunction we can express *clauses* with conjunctions of cardinality constraints alone. Clauses are a normal form for Boolean constraints discussed in Section 8.1.3.

Boolean cardinality can be implemented by the program

```
triv_sat@ card(L,U,BL,N) <=> L=<0,N=<U | true.
pos_sat @ card(L,U,BL,N) <=> L=N | all(1,BL).
neg_sat @ card(L,U,BL,N) <=> U=0 | all(0,BL).


pos_red @ card(L,U,BL,N) <=> del(1,BL,BL1) |
                            0<U, card(L-1,U-1,BL1,N-1).
neg_red @ card(L,U,BL,N) <=> del(0,BL,BL1) |
                            L<N, card(L,U,BL1,N-1).
```

The rule names `triv_sat`, `pos_sat`, and `neg_sat` stand for trivial, positive, and negative satisfaction, respectively. The rule names `pos_red` and `neg_red` stand for positive and negative reduction, respectively.

In the program, all constraints except cardinality are built-in. The built-in `all(T,L)` binds all elements of the list L to T. The list operation constraint `del(X,L,L1)` deletes the element X from the list L, resulting in the list L1. When `del/3` is used in the guard, it will only succeed if the element to be removed actually occurs in the list.

Termination and complexity. The ranking for `card` relies on the list length:

$$rank(card(L, U, BL, N)) = 1 + length(BL).$$

Termination can be shown if we know that for `del` it holds that

$$del(X, L, L1) \rightarrow length(L) = length(L1) + 1.$$

Let c be the number of CHR constraints in a query and let the rank of atomic constraints be bounded by l. Then the derivation length is linear in the syntactic size of the query in the worst case, $D_{Card} = cl$. Time complexity for the built-ins `del` and `all` is linear in the length of the list, and is constant for the other built-ins. The parameters of the complexity formula, (O_H, O_G, O_C, O_B), of the five rules are $(1, 1, 1, 0), (1, 1, l, 0), (1, 1, l, 0)$, $(1, l, 1, 1)$, and $(1, l, 1, 1)$, respectively. By the meta-theorem, the time complexity is $O(cl((cl)^1 l + l))$, i.e.

$$O(c^2 l^3).$$

In practice, the observed time complexity has lower exponents than those predicted:

$$O^{obs}_{Card}(cl^2).$$

The reason is that a cardinality constraint with given parameters is never woken in vain: it will be woken only when one of its variables is bound to a truth value. But in that case it can always reduce. This reduces the complexity by a factor of *cl*. Experiments confirm this complexity. The order of built-ins influenced the run-time only by a constant factor this time, so complexity is not affected.

8.1.3 Clauses and resolution

Boolean constraint satisfaction problems are conjunctions of Boolean constraints. They are often modeled in *conjunctive normal form (CNF)*. This is a conjunction of clauses, where a clause is a disjunction of literals. Literals are positive or negative atomic propositions (*Boolean, propositional variables*). To clauses we can apply the resolution algorithm that propagates new clauses where variables have been eliminated. However, the old clauses (and the occurrences of the variables) cannot be removed, since otherwise logical correctness would not hold.

Resolution is an inference rule used in calculi for logic. From $(A \lor B)$ and $(\neg A \lor C)$ we can conclude $B \lor C$. When repeated resolution derives the empty *clause*, we know that the initial problem was unsatisfiable. The empty clause can be derived from the contradiction (A) and $(\neg A)$.

In our CHR implementation, a clause is represented as a list of signed Boolean variables. For example, the clause $\neg a \lor b \lor c$ is represented as cl([-A,+B,+C]). The propositional variables in the lists are ordered. The built-in compl(A,B) holds if literal A is the logical complement (negation) of B. We also use some standard operations on lists as built-ins:

member(A,L): element A occurs in list L.
del(A,L1,L2): list L1 without element A is L2.
ounion(L1,L2,L): ordered union of L1 and L2 is L.
sublist(L1,L2): all elements of L1 occur in L2.

The rules for resolution are:

```
empty_clause @ cl([]) <=> false.
tautology    @ cl(L) <=> member(+X,L), member(-X,L) | true.
duplicate    @ cl(L) \ cl(L) <=> true.
```

```
resolution    @ cl(L1), cl(L2) ==> del(+X,L1,L3), del(-X,L2,L4)|
                                    ounion(L3,L4,L), cl(L).
```

Clearly, the `resolution` propagation rule is highly concurrent.

Termination and complexity. Given v variables, we can have exponentially many, $O(3^v)$, different clauses, since each variable can occur positively, negatively, or not at all in a clause. Hence the `resolution` propagation rule can apply at most $O(3^v 3^v) = O(9^v)$ times. The cost of the auxiliary built-ins `member` and `del` adds another factor v to the complexity, which then is $O(v9^v)$.

Program variations

We present some variations on the resolution principle in the next paragraphs.

Subsumption. The method of *subsumption* generalizes the duplicate removal rule `duplicate`:

```
subsumption @ cl(L1) \ cl(L2) <=> sublist(L1,L2) | true.
```

This rule offers more possibilities for removing clauses while retaining logical correctness.

If, after the application of rule `resolution`, the rule `subsumption` becomes applicable, one of the initial clauses will be removed. To treat this special case, we can merge the two rules into one rule for *parental subsumption*:

```
parental_subsumption @ cl(L1) \ cl(L2) <=>
    del(A,L1,L3), del(B,L2,L4), compl(A,B), sublist(L3,L4) |
                                                    cl(L4).
```

This rule is redundant, but may be more effective.

Ordered resolution. This is a restriction of resolution, where resolution is only performed with the leftmost literals of each clause. This approach is still complete, since a set of such ordered clauses where the leftmost variables are all different is always satisfiable. Note the similarity with Fourier's algorithm (cf. Section 9.1.3).

```
ordered_resolution @ cl([+X|L1]), cl([-X|L2]) ==>
                                ounion(L1,L2,L), cl(L).
```

The rules `empty_clause`, `tautology`, and `subsumption` stay as before.

Davis–Putnam procedure (unit resolution). The *Davis–Putnam (DP) procedure (unit resolution)* has been used extensively on satisfiability problems, it is a sound procedure that basically restricts resolution to unit clauses. Unit clauses contain just one literal. Thus the truth value of the propositional variable can be determined. Here is an *incremental* version of the DP procedure. We specialize the **subsumption** rule for unit clauses:

```
unit_subsumption @ cl([A]) \ cl(L) <=> member(A,L) | true.
```

We specialize the **parental_subsumption** rule for unit clauses. The resulting inference rule is called unit propagation.

```
unit_propagation @ cl([A]) \ cl(L) <=> compl(A,B), del(B,L,L1)|
                                        cl(L1).
```

The rules **empty_clause** and **tautology** stay as before. Unit resolution is clearly incomplete, because there are unsatisfiable problems that do not have any unit clauses.

Labeling search for unit resolution. We retain *completeness* for unit resolution by labeling search. We use the generic labeling constraint **enum** and the following specific rule for **indomain** to label the propositional variables.

```
indomain(X) <=> (cl([+X]) ; cl([-X])).
```

Alternatively, we label by the literals in the clauses using an *auxiliary dummy constraint* **label**:

```
label, cl(L) <=> member(A,L), cl([A]), label.
```

The built-in **member** chooses a literal **A** from the clause **L**. With the resulting unit clause **cl([A])** we can do unit resolution. As the constraint **enum**, the constraint **label** has to be added to the end of the query. The removal of **label** in the head and the addition of it again at the end of the body ensures that under the refined semantics, all other rules apply before the labeling rule is applied again.

8.2 Path and arc consistency

The classical artificial intelligence algorithms of path and arc consistency simplify constraint satisfaction problems (CSPs). They can be seen as generalizations of *transitive closure* (cf. Section 2.4.1). We introduce CHR constraint solvers based on these local propagation algorithms in this section.

8.2.1 Constraint networks and operations

We start with some basic definitions.

Definition 8.1 *A* constraint satisfaction problem (CSP) *is a conjunction of constraints over variables whose values range over a given finite domain.*

A binary constraint network *is a CSP where the constraints are binary. The network can be represented by a* directed constraint graph, *where the nodes are the variables (together with their domains) and the arcs are the binary constraints.*

A disjunctive binary constraint (relation) c_{xy} *between two variables X and Y, also written $X \, R \, Y$ and $X \, \{r_1, \ldots, r_n\} \, Y$, is a finite disjunction $(X \, r_1 \, Y) \vee \ldots \vee (X \, r_n \, Y)$, where the r_i are different from each other. The r_i are called* primitive constraints (relations).

The converse *of a primitive constraint r between X and Y is the primitive constraint s that holds between Y and X as a consequence.*

A constraint network is minimal *if each primitive constraint is satisfied in a solution of the network.*

For example, $A \, \{<\} \, B, A \, \{<, >\} \, B, A \, \{<, =, >\} \, B$ are disjunctive binary constraints c_{AB} between A and B. $A \, \{<\} \, B$ is the same as $A < B$, $A \, \{<, >\} \, B$ is the same as $A \neq B$. Finally, $A \, \{<, =, >\} \, B$ does not impose any restrictions on A and B.

Typically, the number p of primitive constraints is finite and they are pairwise disjoint, they exclude each other. We will assume so in the following, unless otherwise noted.

Definition 8.2 *We define two operations on disjunctive binary constraints, intersection $\oplus$ and composition $\otimes$:*

$$R_1 \oplus R_2 = R_3 \text{ iff } I \, R_1 \, J \wedge I \, R_2 \, J \leftrightarrow I \, R_3 \, J,$$

$$R_1 \otimes R_2 = R_3 \text{ iff } I \, R_1 \, K \wedge K \, R_2 \, J \rightarrow I \, R_3 \, J,$$

where R_3 is the smallest representable disjunctive constraint for which the implication holds.

By definition, intersection is associative, commutative, and idempotent. Composition is associative, but not commutative and not idempotent. Composition is a generalization of transitive closure, intersection is a generalization of duplicate removal (idempotence). These operations can be computed by applying the respective operation pairwise to the primitive constraints in the disjunctions. Intersection for disjoint primitive constraints can be implemented by set intersection. Composition for finite number of primitive constraints can be implemented by a table look-up.

8.2.2 Path consistency

Definition 8.3 *A network is* path consistent *if for pairs of nodes (i, j) and all paths $i - i_1 - i_2 \ldots i_n - j$ between them, the direct constraint c_{ij} is at least as tight as the derived constraint along the path, i.e. the composition of constraints $c_{ii_1} \otimes \ldots \otimes c_{i_n j}$ along the path.*

It follows from the definition of path consistency that we can intersect the direct and derived constraint to arrive at a tighter direct constraint. A graph is *complete* if there is a pair of arcs, one in each direction, between every pair of nodes. If the graph underlying the network is *complete* it suffices to repeatedly compute $c_{ij} := c_{ij} \oplus (c_{ik} \otimes c_{kj})$ for each triple of nodes (i, k, j) until a fix-point is reached. This is the basic path consistency algorithm.

For example, given $I \leq K \ \wedge \ K \leq J \ \wedge \ I \geq J$ and taking the triple (i, k, j), $c_{ik} \otimes c_{kj}$ results in $I \leq J$ and the result of intersecting it with c_{ij} is $I = J$. From (j, i, k) we get $J = K$ (we can compute c_{ji} as the *converse* of c_{ij}). From (k, j, i) we get $K = I$. Another round of computation causes no more change, so the fix-point is reached with $I = J \ \wedge \ J = K \ \wedge \ K = I$.

Constraint solver. To avoid technicalities, we assume a complete graph. Thus, in a query, for each pair of variables, there is a disjunctive binary constraint between them. Let the disjunctive binary constraint c_{ij} be represented by the CHR constraint `c(I,J,R)` where I and J are the variables and R are the primitive constraints. The basic operation of path consistency, $c_{ij} := c_{ij} \oplus (c_{ik} \otimes c_{kj})$, can be implemented directly by a single rule.

```
path_consistency @
c(I,K,R1), c(K,J,R2) \ c(I,J,R3) <=>
      composition(R1,R2,R12), intersection(R12,R3,R123),
      R123\==R3 |
      c(I,J,R123).
```

The built-ins `composition` and `intersection` implement the corresponding constraint operations. This one rule suffices to implement an incremental concurrent path consistency algorithm for complete networks. The exhaustive application of the rule will make the constraints of the query path consistent.

Termination and complexity. Because of the properties of intersection and the guard check R123=\=R3, the number of primitive constraints of R123 must be strictly less than that of R3. Thus, every rule application removes at least one primitive constraint from the disjunctive constraint between I and J, and so since the disjunctions are finite, termination is ensured.

If the maximum number of primitive constraints is p, then for the derivation length we have that $D_{Path} \leq cp$, i.e. the worst-case derivation length is linear in the syntactic size of the query. Since the number of primitive constraints is fixed, the built-ins for composition, intersection, and inequality checking take constant time. Hence, by the complexity meta-theorem (Theorem 5.35), the complexity is $O(cp((cp)^3(1+1)+(0+1)))$, i.e.

$$O_{Path}(c^4 p^4).$$

The actual complexity has lower exponents since we have no wake-up of constraints due to built-ins in the rule. With indexing we have only $O(c^3 p^3)$ rule tries, which leads to a complexity of

$$O(v^3 p^3).$$

This complexity was also confirmed by experiments. It matches the cubic complexity of the path consistency algorithm.

Labeling search. Maintaining path consistency is an *incomplete* algorithm that can only approximate the *minimal network*, *labeling search* over the binary constraints is employed (similar to producing unit clauses for Boolean resolution).

```
label, c(I,J,R) <=> not singleton(R) | choose(B,R), c(I,J,B), label.
```

If a *disjunctive* constraint R is not a singleton, one nondeterministically chooses a primitive constraint B from R and enforces B.

Incomplete graphs. Working with incomplete graphs can improve efficiency, because not all pairs of variables may have to be considered. Similar to computing paths in the transitive closure of a graph, we may generate constraints as needed. The properties of the solver, such as correctness, termination, confluence, and worst-case complexity, remain unchanged. Concurrency is improved.

8.2.3 Finite domain arc consistency

We solve finite domain CSPs with the *arc consistency* algorithm. This local consistency approach tries to reduce the domains of the variables by removing values that cannot participate in a solution of a binary constraint in which the variable occurs.

The *finite domain constraint* X *in* D means that the variable X takes its value from the given finite domain D. Choosing integers for values allows for arithmetic expressions as constraints. Finite domains can be explicit enumerations of possible values or intervals.

Arc consistency is defined with respect to enumeration domains.

Definition 8.4 *Let* $X_1, \ldots, X_n$ *be pairwise distinct variables. An atomic constraint* $c(X_1, \ldots, X_n)$ *is (hyper-)arc consistent with respect to a conjunction of enumeration domain constraints* X_1 *in* $D_1 \wedge \ldots \wedge X_n$ *in* D_n, *if for all* $i \in \{1, \ldots, n\}$ *and for all values* v_i *in* D_i *(* $v_i \in \{k_{1i}, \ldots, k_{li}\}$ *) the constraint* $\exists (X_1$ *in* $D_1 \wedge \ldots \wedge X_i = v_i \wedge \ldots \wedge X_n$ *in* $D_n \wedge c(X_1, \ldots, X_n))$ *is satisfiable.*

A conjunction of constraints is arc consistent if each atomic constraint in it is arc consistent.

For simplicity, we only discuss the *bounds consistency* algorithm for interval domains. The definition of arc consistency can be adapted.

Definition 8.5 *Let* $X_1, \ldots, X_n$ *be pairwise distinct variables. An atomic constraint* $c(X_1, \ldots, X_n)$ *is* bounds *(or* box*) consistent with respect to a conjunction of interval domain constraints* X_1 *in* $D_1 \wedge \ldots \wedge X_n$ *in* D_n, *where* $D_i = n_i : m_i$, *if for all* $i \in \{1, \ldots, n\}$ *and for all bounds* v_i *in* D_i *(* $v_i \in \{n_i, m_i\}$ *) the constraint* $\exists (X_1$ *in* $D_1 \wedge \ldots \wedge X_i = v_i \wedge \ldots \wedge X_n$ *in* $D_n \wedge c(X_1, \ldots, X_n))$ *is satisfiable.*

A conjunction of constraints is bounds consistent if each atomic constraint in it is bounds consistent.

The difference between an interval domain and an enumeration domain is in their algorithmic use. In the former, constraint simplification is performed only on the interval bounds, while in the latter each element in the enumeration is considered.

The implementation of bounds consistency is based on interval arithmetic. In the following solver, `in`, `le`, `eq`, `ne`, and `add` are CHR constraints, the inequalities are built-in arithmetic constraints. `X in A:B` constrains `X` to be in the interval `A:B`. The rules for local consistency affect the interval constraints (`in`) only, the other constraints remain unaffected.

```
inconsistency @ X in A:B <=> A>B | false.
intersection  @ X in A:B, X in C:D <=> X in max(A,C):min(B,D).
```

```
le @ X le Y, X in A:B, Y in C:D <=> B>D |
      X le Y, X in A:D, Y in C:D.
le @ X le Y, X in A:B, Y in C:D <=> C<A |
      X le Y, X in A:B, Y in A:D.


eq @ X eq Y, X in A:B, Y in C:D <=> A=\=C |
      X eq Y, X in max(A,C):B, Y in max(C,A):D.
eq @ X eq Y, X in A:B, Y in C:D <=> B=\=D |
       X eq Y, X in A:min(B,D), Y in C:min(D,B).
```

The CHR constraint `X le Y` means that `X` is less than or equal to `Y`. Hence, `X` cannot be larger than the upper bound `D` of `Y`. Therefore, if the upper bound `B` of `X` is larger than `D`, we can replace `B` by `D` without removing any solutions. Analogously, one can reason on the lower bounds to tighten the interval for `Y`. The `eq` constraint causes the intersection of the interval domains of its variables provided the bounds are not yet the same.

Here is a sample computation involving `le`:

```
U in 2:3, V in 1:2, U le V     ↦le
V in 1:2, U le V, U in 2:2     ↦le
U le V, U in 2:2, V in 2:2.
```

Finally, $X+Y=Z$ is represented as `add(X,Y,Z)`.

```
add @ add(X,Y,Z), X in A:B, Y in C:D, Z in E:F <=>
       not (A>=E-D,B=<F-C,C>=E-B,D=<F-A,E>=A+C,F=<B+D) |
       add(X,Y,Z),
       X in max(A,E-D):min(B,F-C),
       Y in max(C,E-B):min(D,F-A),
       Z in max(E,A+C):min(F,B+D).
```

For addition, we use interval addition and subtraction to compute the interval of one variable from the intervals of the other two variables. The guard ensures that at least one interval becomes smaller whenever the rule is applied.

Here is a sample computation involving `add`:

```
U in 1:3, V in 2:4, W in 0:4, add(U,V,W)     ↦add
add(U,V,W), U in 1:2, V in 2:3, W in 3:4.
```

The solver is confluent, provided the intervals are given. The solver also works with intervals of real numbers of a chosen *granularity*. To ensure termination then, rules are not applied anymore to domains which are considered too small.

Termination and complexity. We rank finite domain constraints by the width (size) of their intervals:

$width(A\!:\!B) = 1 + B - A$ if $A \leq B$
$width(A\!:\!B) = 1$ otherwise.

We assume that each variable in a query is associated with exactly one interval domain constraint and that in each atomic constraint, all variables are pairwise different. Let w be the maximum rank of an interval constraint in a query and let v be the number of different variables in the query. Then the derivation length is bounded by $D_{Intv} = vw$ since with each rule application, at least one interval gets smaller (or is removed).

We assume that the arithmetic built-in constraints take constant time to compute. All guards and all bodies take constant time. By Theorem 5.35, the complexity is $O(vw((c + vw)^4(1 + 1) + (1 + 1)))$.

Each rule application will generate a fixed number of new interval domain constraints. What is the cost of processing a new interval constraint? Its variable may appear in all c constraints, so there may be up to $O(c)$ rule tries (rule application attempts). Each rule try has constant cost. So the worst-case time complexity with indexing is

$$O(cvw).$$

This complexity was also confirmed by experiments.

Enumeration domains. The rules for enumeration domains are analogous to those for interval domains and implement arc consistency, for example:

```
inconsistency @ X in [] <=> false.
intersect@ X in L1, X in L2 <=> intersect(L1,L2,L3) | X in L3.

eq @ X eq Y, X in L1, Y in L2 <=> L1\==L2 | intersection(L1,L2,L3),
      X eq Y, X in L3, Y in L3.
```

To implement the rule for an arithmetic operation like **add**, we have to apply the operation to all combinations of possible values to see which values should be ruled out.

Search. We implement the *search routine (procedure)* using the constraints **enum** as before and a specific **indomain** constraint. For interval domains, we split intervals in half. This splitting is repeated until the bounds of the interval are the same.

```
indomain(X), X in A:B <=> A<B |
            (X in A:((A+B)//2), indomain(X) ;
             X in ((A+B)//2+1):B, indomain(X)).
```

The guard ensures termination. For enumeration domains, each value in the domain (implemented as a list) is tried. $X=V$ is expressed as X in [V] in this solver program.

```
indomain(X), X in [V|L] <=> L=[_|_] |
            (X in [V] ; X in L, indomain(X)).
```

The guard ensures termination.

Example 8.2.1 *The famous n-queens problem asks us to place n queens* $q_1, \ldots, q_n$ *on an $n \times n$ chess board, such that they do not attack each other. The problem can be solved with a CHR program, where N is the size of the chess board and Qs is a list of N queen position variables.*

```
solve(N,Qs) <=> makedomains(N,Qs), queens(Qs), enum(Qs).
queens([Q|Qs]) <=> safe(Q,Qs,1), queens(Qs).
safe(X,[Y|Qs],N) <=> noattack(X,Y,N), safe(X,Qs,N+1).
```

We can implement noattack directly:

```
noattack(X,Y,N), X in [V], Y in D <=>
          remove(D,[V,V+N,V-N],D1) | Y in D1.
noattack(Y,X,N), X in [V], Y in D <=>
          remove(D,[V,V+N,V-N],D1) | Y in D1.
```

The constraint between three lists remove(D,L,D1) holds if D1 is D without the values in L and at least one value has been removed.

8.2.4 Temporal reasoning with path consistency

In this section, temporal reasoning is seen as a constraint satisfaction problem about the location of temporal variables along the time line. The temporal CSP is solved using path consistency and search. The framework integrates most forms of temporal relations–qualitative and quantitative (metric) over time points and intervals. We give an example before we introduce these kinds of temporal constraints. The primitive relation $a{:}b$ restricts the distance of two time points X and Y to be in the interval $a{:}b$.

Example 8.2.2 The constraints on time points U and V and on time intervals Y and Z

c(U,V,[0:1,3:4]), c(V,Y,[pbefore,pstarts]),
c(Y,Z,[before,contains]), c(Z,U,[pcontains,pstarted_by])

turn out to be inconsistent. The two occurrences of the time point U cannot be the same in the time line.

Qualitative point constraints. Variables represent time points and there are three primitive constraints $<, =, >$. Composition of a constraint with itself or equality yields the constraint again, any other composition yields the redundant constraint $\{<, =, >\}$.

Quantitative point constraints. The primitive constraint relation $X\,a{:}b\,Y$ means $a \leq (Y-X) \leq b$, where X and Y are time points and a and b are integers or ∞. Unlike assumed before, there is an infinite number of primitive quantitative constraints and they can overlap. The composition of the interval $a{:}b$ with $c{:}d$ results in $(a + c){:}(b + d)$, and the intersection in $max(a, c){:}min(b, d)$. Intersection and composition of disjunctive constraints have to merge overlapping intervals.

Interval constraints. There are 13 primitive constraints possible between two intervals: equality and six other relations with their *converses*. These constraints can be defined in terms of the end-points of the intervals. Let I=X:Y, J=U:V be intervals and X,Y,U,V be time points. In the constraint theory, we abbreviate chains of (in)equalities between variables:

I equals J $\leftrightarrow X = U < Y = V$.　　I before J $\leftrightarrow X < Y < U < V$.
I during J $\leftrightarrow U < X < Y < V$.　　I overlaps J $\leftrightarrow X < U < Y < V$.
I meets J $\leftrightarrow X < Y - U < V$.　　I starts J $\leftrightarrow X = U < Y < V$.
I finishes J $\leftrightarrow U < X < Y = V$.

The relations equals, after, contains, overlapped_by, started_by, finished_by are the converses of these relations.

Point–interval constraints. There are five possible primitive constraints between a point and an interval. Let X be a point, and J=U:V be an interval.

X pbefore J $\leftrightarrow X < U < V$.
X pafter J $\leftrightarrow U < V < X$.　　X pduring J $\leftrightarrow U < X < V$.
X pstarts J $\leftrightarrow X = U < V$.　　X pfinishes J $\leftrightarrow U < X = V$.

The converses express interval–point constraints.

Relating constraints of different types. If we solve heterogeneous constraints over the same variables, we have to translate between the different types of temporal constraints. Qualitative time point constraints can be mapped into quantitative point constraints, while quantitative constraints can only be approximated by qualitative constraints. For example, if $X = Y$ then $X\ 0{:}0\ Y$ exactly represents it. If $X\ a{:}b\ Y\ (a, b > 0)$ then $X\ \texttt{<}\ Y$ approximates it.

Points can be represented by end-points of intervals and interval constraints can be approximated by constraints on their end-points. Let $\texttt{I=X:Y}$, $\texttt{J=U:V}$ be intervals and $\texttt{X,Y,U,V}$ be time points. For example, if $X\ \texttt{eq}\ U$ then $\texttt{I \{equals,starts,started\_by\} J}$ exactly represents it. If $\texttt{I \{equals, before\} J}$ then $(X < Y \leq V \wedge U \neq Y \wedge X \leq U < V)$ approximates it.

Constraint solver. It suffices to instantiate the generic path consistency solver by defining the intersection and composition operations for temporal constraints.

8.3 Exercises

8.1 Translate the rewrite rules for De Morgan's law of propositional logic into CHR simplification rules:

```
not(and(X,Y)) -> or(not(X),not(Y)).
not(and(X,Y)) -> or(not(X),not(Y)).
```

8.2 Extend the Boolean solver with rules in order to cope with equivalence (similar to the ones already defined), i.e. implement simplifications for a CHR constraint `equiv(X,Y,Z)` which obey the given truth table.

X	Y	Z
0	0	1
0	1	0
1	0	0
1	1	1

8.3 Find out who lies using Boolean constraints:

> Lehmann says Mueller lies.
> Mueller says Schulze does not tell the truth.
> Schulze says both lie.

Write a constraint `tellTruth(Lehmann,Mueller,Schulze)` which succeeds iff the three arguments are a valid interpretation of the given statements by Lehmann, Mueller, and Schulze. Use Boolean constraints `and, neg, ...`

Hint: Lehman's statement can be modeled by `Lehmann=MuellerLies`, or using equivalence, with `MuellerLies` being the negation of `Mueller`.

8.4 A *cross circuit* exchanges two wires (signals) with the help of a logic circuit without crossing them physically. For the input pins (X, Y) and the output pins (A, B) we have $A = Y$ and $B = X$. Write a CHR constraint `cross(X,Y,A,B)`, which implements a cross circuit by means of Boolean constraints.

Queries: `cross(1,0,A,B)`, `cross(1,Y,1,B)`, and `cross(0,Y,A,B)`.

8.5 Show confluence of rules for the `and` constraint of the Boolean solver 8.1.

8.6 Extend the finite domain constraint solver.

(a) Implement rules to let the `leq`, `eq`, and `neq` constraints interact with the given solver.
Tests should include `X leq Y, Y leq Z, X in [0,3], Y in [-1,2], Z in [0,1,2,3]`.

(b) Introduce the `maximum(X,Y,Z)` constraint to the given solver, where Z is the maximum of X and Y. Tests should include `maximum(X,Y,Z), X in [0,1], Y in [2,4], Z in [3,5]`.

(c) The constraint `allneq(List)` succeeds, iff the variables in `List` are (pairwise) distinct. Test your implementation `allneq` with three variables, s.t. the answer is **no** for one and **yes** for a second query.

(d) Implement a `label(List)`-constraint to bind the variables in `List`. An easy test case is e.g. `X in [0,1], Y in [0,1], X leq Y, label([X])`.

8.7 Solve the following crypto-arithmetic puzzle using finite domain constraints. Replace distinct letters by distinct digits, s.t. each number is the absolute difference of the two numbers below (e.g. $D = |G - H|$), and the numbers are the positive integers from 1 to 15.

$$
\begin{array}{ccccc}
 & & A & & \\
 & B & & C & \\
 & D & E & & F \\
G & & H & I & & J \\
K & L & M & N & & O
\end{array}
$$

Answer:

```
pyramid(VariableStrategy,ValueStrategy) <=>
    V = [a,b,c,d,e,f,g,h,i,j,k,l,m,n,o],
    domain(V,1,15),
    allneq(V),
    abs(a,b,c),abs(b,d,e),abs(c,e,f),abs(d,g,h),abs(e,h,i),
    abs(f,i,j),abs(g,k,l),abs(h,l,m),abs(i,m,n),abs(j,n,o),
    label(V,VariableStrategy,ValueStrategy).
```

8.8 Implement in CHR the game Sudoku (number place), a logic-based placement puzzle on a 9×9 board. Fill in the grid so that every row, every column, and every 3×3 box contains the digits 1 through 9.

Answer:

```
fillone(N), f(A,B,C,D,N2,L)#Id <=> N2=N |
    member(V,L), f(A,B,C,D,V), fillone(1) pragma passive(Id).
fillone(N) <=> N < 9 | N1 is N+1, fillone(N1).
fillone(_) <=> true.

f(A,B,C,D,_) \ f(A,B,C,D,_,_)#Id <=> true pragma passive(Id).

f(_,B,_,D,V) \ f(A,B,C,D,N,L)#Id <=> select(V,L,LL) |
    N1 is N-1, N1>0, f(A,B,C,D,N1,LL) pragma passive(Id).
f(A,_,C,_,V) \ f(A,B,C,D,N,L)#Id <=> select(V,L,LL) |
    N1 is N-1, N1>0, f(A,B,C,D,N1,LL) pragma passive(Id).
f(A,B,_,_,V) \ f(A,B,C,D,N,L)#Id <=> select(V,L,LL) |
    N1 is N-1, N1>0, f(A,B,C,D,N1,LL) pragma passive(Id).

solve <=> init_board, init_data, solve.

init_board <=> fill1(a), fill1(b), fill1(c).
fill1(X) <=> fill2(X,a),fill2(X,b),fill2(X,c).
fill2(X,Y) <=> fill3(X,Y,1), fill3(X,Y,2), fill3(X,Y,3).
fill3(A,B,C) <=> fill4(A,B,C,1), fill4(A,B,C,2), fill4(A,B,C,3).
fill4(A,B,C,D) <=> f(A,B,C,D,9,[1,2,3,4,5,6,7,8,9]).

init_data <=> f(a,a,1,1,1), ..., f(c,c,3,3,9).

solve <=> fillone(1).
```

8.9 Solve the famous Zebra puzzle using finite domains. Five men with different nationalities live in the first five houses of a street. They practice five distinct professions, and each of them has a favorite animal and a favorite drink, all of them different. The five houses are painted in different colors. You have the following information:

The Englishman lives in the red house. The Spaniard owns a dog. The Japanese is a painter. The Italian drinks tea. The Norwegian lives in the first house on the left. The owner of the green house drinks coffee. The green house is next to the white and on the right of it. The sculptor breeds snails. The diplomat lives in the yellow house. Milk is drunk in the middle house. The Norwegian's house is next to the blue one. The violinist drinks fruit juice. The fox is in a house next to that of the doctor. The horse is in a house next to that of the diplomat.

Answer the question: who owns a zebra, and who drinks water?

Answer:

```
zebra(VariableStrategy,ValueStrategy) <=>
   V=[englishman,spaniard,japanese,italian,norwegian,
       red,green,white,blue,yellow,
       dog,snails,horse,fox,zebra,
       tea,coffee,milk,juice,water,
       painter,sculptor,diplomat,violinist,doctor],
   domain(V,1,5),
   allneq([englishman,spaniard,japanese,italian,norwegian]),
   allneq([red,green,white,blue,yellow]),
   allneq([dog,snails,horse,fox,zebra]),
   allneq([tea,coffee,milk,juice,water]),
   allneq([painter,sculptor,diplomat,violinist,doctor]),
   englishman eq red,
   spaniard   eq dog,
   japanese   eq painter,
   italian    eq tea,
   norwegian  in [1],
   green      eq coffee,
   white      leq green, white next green,
   sculptor   eq snails,
   diplomat   eq yellow,
   milk       in [3],
   norwegian  next blue,
   violinist  eq juice,
   fox        next doctor,
   horse      next diplomat,
   label(V,VariableStrategy,ValueStrategy).
```

8.4 Bibliographic remarks

We introduced some constraint solvers written in CHR, for more (classical) solvers see [Frü06a, FA03]. The experiments we referred to are documented in [Frü02a].

Boolean algebra (propositional logic) constraints can be solved by different techniques [MSSA93]. The propagation-based Boolean constraint solver appeared in [FA03]. More variants of resolution and in particular of the Davis–Putnam procedure [DP60] implemented in CHR can be found in [Dum95].

The arc and path consistency algorithms are discussed in [MF85, MH86, Mac77]. Variants of the CHR implementation, also with incomplete graphs and optimizations are discussed in detail in [Frü94].

Influential early CLP languages with finite domains are CHIP [DHS+88], clp(FD) [CD96], and cc(FD) [HSD95]. Bounds consistency (interval reasoning) is used in [HDT92, BO97]. Interval-based nonlinear equation solving over the reals in CHR is presented in [KSD06].

Temporal constraints are discussed in [Kou06]. A framework for temporal reasoning is presented in [Mei91]. It integrates:

- qualitative time point constraints [MV86]
- quantitative time point constraints [DMP91]
- time interval constraints [All83]
- point–interval constraints [Mei91]
- mappings between constraints of different types [KL91].

The implementation of this framework is described in detail and with variations in [Frü94]. CHR applications in temporal reasoning include [Don93, ET96, ET98, AM00, Bja96, MD06].

9

Infinite domain constraint solvers

In this chapter, we present constraint solvers for constraints over variables that have infinite domains. The first domain is the numbers, and we solve linear polynomial equations. The second domain is some ordered set of values that we extend to a lexicographic order, which we consider as a constraint on a sequence of variables. The third domain is the objects that occur in knowledge representation with description logics. Reasoning in these logics is reducible to consistency checking. The fourth domain is the universal data structure of logical terms where we consider the unification problem as equation solving.

9.1 Linear polynomial equation solving

Typically, in arithmetic constraint solvers, *incremental* variants of classical *variable elimination* algorithms like Gaussian elimination for equations and Dantzig's Simplex algorithm for equations are implemented. Gaussian elimination has cubic complexity in the number of different variables in a problem. The Simplex algorithm has exponential worst-case time complexity but is polynomial on average.

Similar to Gaussian elimination, we solve linear polynomial equations by eliminating variables, one at a time. For solving inequations, the rules for Fourier's algorithm turn out to be very similar to those for equation solving.

9.1.1 Variable elimination

We define the syntax of the equations and show the principle of eliminating a variable.

Definition 9.1 *A* linear polynomial equation *is of the form* $p + b = 0$ *where b is a constant and the polynomial p is the sum of monomials of the form $a_i * x_i$ with coefficient $a_i \neq 0$ and x_i is a variable. Constants and coefficients are numbers. Variables are totally ordered. In an equation $a_1 * x_1 + \ldots + a_n * x_n + b = 0$, variables appear in strictly descending order.*

A set of equations is in solved (normal) form *if the left-most variable of each equation is the only left-most occurrence of this variable.*

This simple solved form can exhibit inconsistency. Variables are ordered. If the solved form exists, we can give a value to the smallest left-most variable so that the equation in which it occurs is satisfied. All other equations are simplified using that value for the variable. In all other equations, there are other, larger left-most variables. We can continue with the next larger left-most variable until no equations are left and always give it a value that satisfies the equation where it occurs left-most.

To compute the solved form by *variable elimination*, we eliminate multiple occurrences of left-most variables:

1. Choose an equation $a_1 * X_1 + \ldots + a_n * X_n + b = 0$.
2. Make its left-most variable (the *pivot variable*) explicit: $X_1 = -(a_2 * X_2 + \ldots + a_n * X_n + b)/a_1$.
3. Replace the left-most occurrences of the pivot X_1 in the other equations by $-(a_2 * X_2 + \ldots + a_n * X_n + b)/a_1$.
4. Normalize the resulting equations.
5. Repeat from step 1 until in solved form.

9.1.2 Gaussian-style elimination

For solving linear polynomial equations, a minimalistic but powerful variant of variable elimination is employed. Since constraints are typically processed incrementally, we do not eliminate a variable in *all* other equations at once, but rather consider the other equations one by one. Also, we do not need to make a variable explicit using pivoting, but keep the original equation.

Two rules suffice for the solver, where eq is a binary CHR constraint for arithmetic equality in infix notation:

```
eliminate @ A1*X+P1 eq 0 \ A2*X+P2 eq 0 <=>
                    normalize(A2*(-P1/A1)+P2,P3),
                    P3 eq 0.


constant  @ B eq 0 <=> number(B) | zero(B).
```

The `eliminate` rule takes two equations with the same left-most variable. The first equation is left unaffected, it is used to eliminate the occurrence of the common variable in the second equation. The rule is similar to the merge–sort rule (Section 2.4.4). The auxiliary built-in `normalize` simplifies a polynomial arithmetic expression into a new polynomial. The `constant` rule says that if the polynomial contains no more variables, the constant B must be zero.

Example 9.1.1 The two equations

`1*X+3*Y+5 eq 0, 3*X+2*Y+8 eq 0`

match the `eliminate` rule, the variable X in the second equation is removed with the help of

    normalize(3*(-(3*Y+5)/1) + (2*Y+8), P3)

that computes P3 to be `-7*Y+-7`. The resulting equations are

`1*X+3*Y+5 eq 0, -7*Y+(-7) eq 0.`

The equation `-7*Y+(-7) eq 0` can be simplified to `Y=(-1)` and thus `X=(-2)`. The solver can be extended with rules to treat such determined variables.

Termination and complexity. Consider a problem with c equations and v different variables. The complexity is dominated by the cost of applying the `eliminate` rule. Each application of the rule `eliminate` removes the left-most, i.e. largest, occurrence of a variable from the second equation (but may introduce several strictly smaller variables). This holds since the variables in each polynomial equation are ordered in strictly descending order and since the constraint `normalize` does not introduce new variables (but may eliminate occurrences of some). Hence there are at most cv rule applications. By the meta-complexity Theorem 5.35 we arrive at $O_\Re(cv * ((c+cv)^2(v+0) + (v+1))) = O_\Re(c^3v^4)$.

  With indexing on the left-most variable of each equation, the `eliminate` rule can find a partner constraint in constant time. If the rule is applied, `normalize` causes a cost linear in v. Since there are at most cv variables to eliminate, the overall complexity is

$$O((cv)v) = O(cv^2).$$

If $c \approx v$, the complexity is cubic, $O(v^3)$, as for Gaussian elimination. The cubic complexity also holds, if no indexing is used, since there may be at most v constraints to try for partner. This complexity was also confirmed by experiments.

Logical reading and correctness. The first-order logic reading correctly reflects the intended meaning of the program. The solver produces the solved form, as can be shown by contradiction: if a set of equations is not in solved form, then the `eliminate` rule is applicable. The solver is *satisfaction-complete*, so no search is necessary.

Confluence, anytime and online algorithm, concurrency and parallelism. The solver is not confluent due to the `eliminate` rule: consider two equations with the same left-most variable, then the rule can be applied in two different ways resulting in different new equations in general.

Intermediate results will contain fewer and fewer occurrences of variables. We can add equations while the program runs without performance penalty.

In the solver, no variable is made explicit, i.e. no pivoting is performed. Any two equations with the same first variable can react with each other. Therefore, the solver is highly concurrent. By weak parallelism, it can reduce pairs of equations in parallel. By strong parallelism, it eliminates the occurrence of a variable in all other equations in one parallel computation step.

9.1.3 Fourier's algorithm

We would like to treat inequations as well. An idea borrowed from the Simplex algorithm is to replace an arbitrary inequation by an equation and a simple inequation on a so-called *slack variable*. For example, $P \geq 0$ is rewritten into $P = S \wedge S \geq 0$. Rules for the simple inequalities have to be added to the solver.

We can also solve inequations directly by variable elimination. Even though it is inefficient, the classical Fourier's algorithm for solving inequations deserves mention. It is a transitive closure algorithm similar to *resolution* and can be useful when specialized, e.g. for interval reasoning. For simplicity, we restrict ourselves to one type of inequality, $\geq$, written `geq` in CHR.

```
propagate @ A1*X+P1 geq 0, A2*X+P2 geq 0 ==>
                         A2/A1<0 |
                         normalize(A2*(-P1/A1)+P2,P3),
                         P3 eq 0.
```

The **propagate** rule generates a new inequation from the inequations by eliminating the left-most variable. This is only correct if the coefficients of that variable have opposite sign (as tested in the guard).

To improve efficiency, we introduce some rules that should be placed first in the resulting program. We start with a generalization of *duplicate elimination*: if there are two inequations whose coefficients differ only by a constant positive factor, then one of the inequations is redundant. The built-in `normalize` is used in the guard to compute the result of variable elimination, which must be 0 in that case.

```
redundant @ A1*X+P1 geq 0 \ A2*X+P2 geq 0 <=> A2/A1>0,
            normalize(A2*(-P1/A1)+P2,P3), number(P3), P3>=0 |
                true.
```

If the factor is negative, then both inequations together are equivalent to an equality. We can then use the much more efficient `eliminate` rule for equations.

```
simplify  @ A1*X+P1 geq 0 , A2*X+P2 geq 0 <=> A2/A1<0,
                normalize(A2*(-P1/A1)+P2,P3), zero(P3) |
                A1*X+P1 eq 0.
```

We also define a rule for the interaction between an equation and an inequation, where we eliminate the variable from the inequation.

```
eliminate_geq @ A1*X+P1 eq 0 \ A2*X+P2 geq 0 <=>
                normalize(A2*(-P1/A1)+P2,P3),
                P3 geq 0.
```

As one can see, all these rules have the same basic structure.

Termination and complexity. Assume v variables and c inequation constraints. The `propagate` rule dominates the complexity. Like the variable elimination rule `eliminate` for equations, it terminates because the leftmost, largest variable is removed in the inequation that is added. Each time we generate all implied inequations for a variable with the `propagate` rule, their number can grow by the square of the number of initial inequations. The repetition of this process for each variable leads to *double exponential time complexity* in the worst case,

$$O(c^{2^v}).$$

If we limit the number of variables in each inequation, we can achieve polynomial complexity. Since we can simplify inequations efficiently with equations using the additional rule `eliminate_geq`, sufficiently determined problems (where there are at least as many equations as variables) can potentially be solved with polynomial complexity as well.

9.2 Lexicographic order global constraint

Lexicographic orders are common in everyday life as the alphabetical sorting order used in dictionaries and listings (e.g. "zappa" comes before "zilch"). In computer science, lexicographic orders also play a central role in termination analysis, for example for rewrite systems. In constraint programming, these orders have raised interest because of their use in symmetry breaking and in modeling preferences among solutions.

A lexicographic order constraint $\preceq_l$ (lex) allows us to compare sequences by comparing the elements of the sequences proceeding from start to end. It is a global constraint since it admits an arbitrary number of variables.

Definition 9.2 *Given two sequences l_1 and l_2 of variables of the same length n, $[x_1, \ldots, x_n]$ and $[y_1, \ldots, y_n]$, then $l_1 \preceq_l l_2$ if and only if $n=0$ or $x_1 < y_1$ or $x_1 = y_1$ and $[x_2, \ldots, x_n] \preceq_l [y_2, \ldots, y_n]$.*

The corresponding logical specification of the constraint is thus

$$
\begin{aligned}
l_1 \preceq_l l_2 \quad \leftrightarrow \quad & (l_1 = [] \wedge l_2 = []) \vee \\
& (l_1 = [x | l_1'] \wedge l_2 = [y | l_2'] \wedge x < y) \vee \\
& (l_1 = [x | l_1'] \wedge l_2 = [y | l_2'] \wedge x = y \wedge l_1' \preceq_l l_2').
\end{aligned}
$$

Six CHR rules correctly and efficiently specify and implement an incremental and concurrent, logical algorithm to maintain consistency of the lexicographic order constraint. There is a direct recursive decomposition of the problem that does not need additional constraints and performs all possible propagations. The CHR solver is independent of the underlying built-in constraints, while the earlier approaches consider the case of finite domain constraints and arc consistency algorithms only.

9.2.1 Stepwise implementation

In this section we develop an efficient solver for the lexicographic order constraint by stepwise refinement.

Basic implementation. We rewrite the logical specification into CHR rules for the lexicographic order constraint, written as lex in infix notation. We assume that the lists to be compared are given, while their elements are variables or constants. Since the three disjuncts of the specification are mutually exclusive, we can turn each clause into a CHR simplification rule where the guards ensure the mutual exclusion.

```
l1 @ [] lex [] <=> true.
l2 @ [X|L1] lex [Y|L2] <=> X<Y | true.
l3 @ [X|L1] lex [Y|L2] <=> X=Y | L1 lex L2.
```

These rules will apply when the lists are empty or when the relationship between the leading list elements X and Y is sufficiently known. The built-ins X<Y and X=Y are in the guards, so they check if the appropriate relationship between the variables holds. For example, the queries [1] lex [2], [X] lex [X] and [X] lex [Y], X<Y will all reduce to true. To the queries [X] lex [Y], [X] lex [Y], X>=Y and [X] lex [Y], X>Y no rules are applicable. Clearly, the last rule should fail.

Adding constraint propagation. While the program is correct, the rules do not propagate any constraints except the trivial true. We must do better than that. We can derive a common consequence of the last two clauses,

$$(l_1=[x|l_1'] \land l_2=[y|l_2'] \land x<y) \lor (l_1=[x|l_1'] \land l_2=[y|l_2'] \land x=y \land l_1' \preceq l_2') \quad \rightarrow$$

$$l_1=[x|l_1'] \land l_2=[y|l_2'] \land x \leq y,$$

and implement it as a CHR propagation rule, where the built-in inequality constraint appears in the rule body and is thus enforced when the rule is applied.

14 @ [X|L1] lex [Y|L2] ==> X=<Y.

With this new rule 14, the query [X] lex [Y] leads to [X] lex [Y], X=<Y and the query [X] lex [Y], X>Y fails. To the query [R|Rs] lex [T|Ts], R≡T only the propagation rule is applicable and adds R=<T. This leads to [R|Rs] lex [T|Ts], R<T after simplification of the built-ins for inequality. Now rule 12 is applicable, the lex-constraint is removed and the result is the remaining R<T.

However, the four rules are still not sufficient, more propagations are possible. For example, consider [R1,R2,R3] lex [T1,T2,T3], R2=T2, R3>T3. The only way to satisfy this constraint is by imposing R1<T1, since the remaining elements cannot be ordered in the right way if R1>=T1.

In order to perform such reasoning, we have to look forward, at the next level of recursion. If the recursive call fails, the base case for nonempty sequences must hold. If the recursive call proceeds to the next recursion, because the two variables are equal, we can ignore (i.e. remove) this pair of variables.

15 @ [X,U|L1] lex [Y,V|L2] <=> U>V | X<Y.
16 @ [X,U|L1] lex [Y,V|L2] <=> U=V | [X|L1] lex [Y|L2].

Our example, [R1,R2,R3] lex [T1,T2,T3], R2=T2, R3>T3, can now be handled. First, since R2=T2, rule 16 is applicable, and its result is R2=T2,

R3>T3, [R1,R3] lex [T1,T3]. Now rule 15 is applied, and we arrive at
R2=T2, R3>T3, R1<T1 as desired.

There are still situations that are not covered by the current set of rules.
Just replace R2=T2 in the above example by R2>=T2. The same propagation
should take place as before, but the two rules that we have added cannot be
applied, their guards are too strict.

In these situations, the current pair of variables is followed by a sequence
of variables which are pairwise related by >=, which each could turn into
a strict inequation later on. This can be covered by modifying rule 16 into a
propagation rule and weakening its guard:

```
16'@ [X,U|L1] lex [Y,V|L2] ==> U>=V | [X|L1] lex [Y|L2].
```

The six rules (11 to 15 and 16') implement a complete constraint solver
for the nonstrict lexicographic order constraint for comparing sequences of
the same, given length.

The rules are terminating. The recursions involve the lex-constraint only.
Each recursive call proceeds with shorter lists (with one element less each).
But the solver is not as efficient as it could be.

Improving time complexity – adding simplification. A cascade of
propagation rule applications together with the subsequent simplification of
the constraints produced can lead to a quadratic time behavior with simple
CHR implementations. This happens if, after exhaustive propagation with
rule 16', the resulting $O(n^2)$ variable pairs are removed one by one by
rule 13.

In order to improve the time complexity, we start from a translation of
propagation rule 16' into a logically equivalent but nonterminating simplification rule.

```
16'' @ [X,U|L1] lex [Y,V|L2] <=> U>=V |
       [X,U|L1] lex [Y,V|L2], [X|L1] lex [Y|L2].
```

The rule body shows repeated occurrences of the subsequences L1 and
L2. As it turns out, removing L1 and L2 from the constraint [X,U|L1]
lex [Y,V|L2] preserves correctness. Together with requiring nonempty
sequences L1 (and L2) in the guard, time complexity is improved to linear (under reasonable assumptions).

9.2.2 Constraint solver

The final solver consists of three pairs of rules, the first two corresponding to base cases of the recursion (garbage collection), then two rules performing forward reasoning (recursive traversal and implied inequality), and finally two for backward reasoning, covering a special case when the lexicographic constraint has a unique solution.

```
11 @ [] lex [] <=> true.
12 @ [X|L1] lex [Y|L2] <=> X<Y | true.
13 @ [X|L1] lex [Y|L2] <=> X=Y | L1 lex L2.
14 @ [X|L1] lex [Y|L2] ==> X=<Y.


15 @ [X,U|L1] lex [Y,V|L2] <=> U>V | X<Y.
16f@ [X,U|L1] lex [Y,V|L2] <=> U>=V, L1=[_|_] |
                          [X,U] lex [Y,V], [X|L1] lex [Y|L2].
```

The first three rules 11, 12 and 13 were derived directly from the three disjuncts of the logical specification. The three rules will apply when the lists are empty or when the relationship between the leading list elements X and Y is sufficiently known. The propagation rule 14 implements a common consequence of the last two disjuncts of the logical specification.

Rule 15 deals with the special case where the elements of the second pair of the sequence are related by a strict inequality in the wrong way such that the only (way to a) solution is to enforce a strict inequality on the first two elements. Rules 14 and 15 are the only ones that impose a built-in constraint directly. Rule 16f seems to use double recursion, but note that the first recursive lex constraint has a *fixed*, small list length. The rule deals with the case where the wrong inequality treated in 15 is further down the lists. The additional condition L1=[_|_] in the guard of rule 16f avoids nontermination in case L1=[]. It means that the rule can only apply to lists with at least three elements.

If the two arguments of lex are identical lists, then the constraint will succeed by repeated application of rule 13 and finally 11. This shows reflexivity of the lexicographic order relation. Some interaction between several lex constraints is possible. Antisymmetry can be shown: let A and B be two given lists with first elements X and Y respectively. Consider a query A lex B, B lex A. Applying the propagation rule 14 to each constraint leads to A lex B, B lex A, X=<Y, Y=<X. Since now X=Y holds, both constraints can be simplified with rule 13. This process can be repeated until the empty list is reached and reduced to true. Transitivity cannot be shown in this way.

9.2.3 Worst-case time complexity

We would like to give a complexity result that is independent from the constraint system in which the built-in constraints (inequalities) are defined. The reason is that most constraint systems, such as Booleans, finite domains, and linear polynomials, admit these inequalities, but the typical algorithms used have different time complexities and achieve different degrees of completeness. We therefore give our complexity result in the number of atomic built-ins that are checked and imposed, respectively.

We show now that the list length of a `lex` constraint is an upper bound on the number of rule applications and on the number of built-in constraints checked and asserted.

One can show that the derivation length of a single `lex` constraint is linear in the length of the list arguments of the constraint:

$$rank(l_1 \text{ lex } l_2) = 1 + 4 * length(l_1 + l_2).$$

Thus, the derivation length for a single `lex` constraint is $O(n)$. Given c `lex` constraints with maximum list length n, the derivation length is bounded by $O(cn)$.

Due to the simplicity of the propagation rule, the meta-complexity Theorem 5.35 for simplification rules is still applicable. All rules have one head CHR constraint, so $n = 1$. We leave the costs for checking and imposing built-in constraints, O_G and O_B, unspecified. By the complexity meta-theorem (Theorem 5.35), this gives $O_{lex}(cn(cn^1(1 + O_G) + (O_C + 1)))$, i.e. a quadratic complexity

$$O_{lex}(c^2 n^2 O_G + cn O_C).$$

We give an example of a query with a single `lex` constraint that exhibits quadratic complexity.

`[X,U1,...Un] lex [Y,V1,...Vn], U1>=V1,...,Un>=Vn.`

Exhaustive application of rule **16f** generates n `lex` constraints:

`[X,U1] lex [Y,V1],...[X,Un] lex [Y,Vn], X=<Y, U1>=V1,...,Un>=Vn.`

Then n times `X=<Y` is imposed by the propagation rule **14**. In simple CHR implementations, each time all `lex` constraints will be woken and reconsidered. However, optimized CHR implementations do not wake up any CHR constraints if the same built-in constraint is imposed again. Therefore the linear complexity is achieved in practice.

With several `lex` constraints, however, quadratic complexity cannot be avoided. Consider the query:

```
[X1,X0] lex [Y1,Y0], [Y2,Y1,Y0] lex [X2,X1,X0],
[X3,X2,X1,X0] lex [Y3,Y2,Y1,Y0], ...,
[Y2n,...,Y0] lex [X2n,...,X0], Y0<X0.
```

The built-in Y0<X0 will wake all lex constraints, but only the first one can reduce with rule 15. This imposes X1<Y1. Again, this built-in will wake all remaining CHR constraints but only reduce one with 15. The answer to this query will be

```
Y0<X0, X1<Y1, Y2<X2, X3<Y3,...Y2n<X2n.
```

Experimental evaluation. We compared the CHR implementation of lex with the built-in lex_chain constraint of the Sicstus clpfd constraint library. This was the only available implementation. Like the other previous approaches, it is restricted to finite domains. We considered lists up to 40 000 elements. Garbage collection was never performed by the system. In the experiments, both lexicographic constraints show a complete propagation behavior and linear time complexity. Run-times were less than a second for the CHR lex constraint for simpler test cases. While forward propagation in CHR was just 3 times slower than the built-in lex_chain constraint, backward propagation proved to be an order of magnitude slower (possibly because the recursive decomposition in the CHR solver generates many small lex constraints).

9.2.4 Confluence

Rule 11 cannot give rise to any critical pair (c.p.). It does not overlap with any other rule, since it is the only one dealing with empty lists. Rules 12 and 13 are mutually exclusive. There are overlaps between all the remaining pairs of rules, which are all joinable. Thus, the solver is confluent.

Example 9.2.1 Consider the overlap between the rules

```
13 @ [X|L1] lex [Y|L2] <=> X=Y | L1 lex L2.
15 @ [X,U|L1] lex [Y,V|L2] <=> U>V | X<Y.
```

which is [X,U|L1] lex [Y,V|L2], U>V, X=Y and which leads to the confluence check:

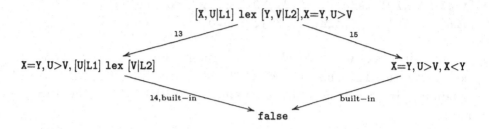

Another confluence check involves the rules 15 and 16f.

```
15 @ [X,U|L1] lex [Y,V|L2] <=> U>V | X<Y.
16f@ [X,U|L1] lex [Y,V|L2] <=> U>=V, L1=[_|_] |
                             [X,U] lex [Y,V], [X|L1] lex [Y|L2].
```

Their overlap is [X,U|L1] lex [Y,V|L2], U>V, L1=[_|_]. The resulting confluence check is

```
[X,U|L1] lex [Y,V|L2], U>V, L1=[_|_]
     | 15                | 16
     |    U>V, L1=[_|_], [X,U] lex [Y,V], [X|L1] lex [Y|L2]
     |                   | 15
     |    U>V, L1=[_|_], X<Y, [X|L1] lex [Y|L2]
     |                   | 12
   U>V, L1=[_|_], X<Y
```

If rule 12 or rule 14 is dropped, the solver becomes nonconfluent, while the other rules can be dropped without affecting the confluence.

9.2.5 Logical correctness

The logical reading of the six rules for the lexicographic order constraint solver is

$$
\begin{aligned}
&([]\preceq_l[]) \\
X<Y \to\ &([X|L1]\preceq_l[Y|L2]) \\
X=Y \to\ &([X|L1]\preceq_l[Y|L2] &&\leftrightarrow L1\preceq_l L2) \\
&([X|L1]\preceq_l[Y|L2] &&\to X\leq Y) \\
U>V \to\ &([X,U|L1]\preceq_l[Y,V|L2] &&\leftrightarrow X<Y) \\
(U\geq V \wedge L1=[\_|\_]) \to\ &([X,U|L1]\preceq_l[Y,V|L2] &&\leftrightarrow \\
&\quad ([X,U]\preceq_l[Y,V] \wedge [X|L1]\preceq_l[Y|L2])).
\end{aligned}
$$

For logical correctness, we have to show that these formulas are logical consequences of the logical specification given by

$$l_1 \preceq_l l_2 \quad \leftrightarrow \quad \begin{aligned} &(l_1=[\,] \wedge l_2=[\,]) \vee \\ &(l_1=[x|l_1'] \wedge l_2=[y|l_2'] \wedge x<y) \vee \\ &(l_1=[x|l_1'] \wedge l_2=[y|l_2'] \wedge x=y \wedge l_1' \preceq_l l_2') \end{aligned}$$

For example, the logical reading of the rule 14 is a common consequence of the last two disjuncts of the specification,

$$(l_1=[x|l_1'] \wedge l_2=[y|l_2'] \wedge x<y) \vee (l_1=[x|l_1'] \wedge l_2=[y|l_2'] \wedge x=y \wedge l_1' \preceq_l l_2') \quad \rightarrow$$

$$l_1=[x|l_1'] \wedge l_2=[y|l_2'] \wedge x \leq y.$$

Example 9.2.2 As a more involved example, we prove that the logical reading of propagation rule 16f is a logical consequence of the specification. From the specification it follows

$$[X|L1] \preceq_l [Y|L2] \leftrightarrow (X<Y \vee X=Y \wedge L1 \preceq_l L2).$$

For the rule 16f, we will actually prove a slightly stronger result by removing $L1-[\_|\_]$ from the precondition. Instead of $\forall (C \rightarrow (H \leftrightarrow B))$ we use the logically equivalent $(\forall (H \wedge C) \leftrightarrow (C \wedge B)))$. To show the equivalence of the l.h.s. and r.h.s. of that formula, we will now replace the lex constraints in the logical reading of the rule according to the specification, distribute conjunction over disjunction, and simplify by removing unsatisfiable disjuncts.

$(H \wedge C)$
$\leftrightarrow [X,U|L1] \preceq_l [Y,V|L2] \wedge U \geq V$
$\leftrightarrow U \geq V \wedge (X<Y \vee X=Y \wedge U<V \vee X=Y \wedge U=V \wedge L1 \preceq_l L2)$
$\leftrightarrow$
$(U \geq V \wedge X<Y \vee X=Y \wedge U=V \wedge L1 \preceq_l L2)$
$\leftrightarrow U \geq V \wedge (U \geq V \wedge X<Y \vee X=Y \wedge U=V) \wedge (U \geq V \wedge X<Y \vee U \geq V \wedge X=Y \wedge L1 \preceq_l L2)$
$\leftrightarrow U \geq V \wedge (X<Y \vee X=Y \wedge U<V \vee X=Y \wedge U=V) \wedge (X<Y \vee X=Y \wedge L1 \preceq_l L2)$
$\leftrightarrow U \geq V \wedge [X,U] \preceq_l [Y,V] \wedge [X|L1] \preceq_l [Y|L2]$
$\leftrightarrow (C \wedge B).$

9.2.6 Completeness

We already know that the solver is terminating, correct, and confluent. Correctness means it cannot propagate incorrect constraints. Confluence means that starting from a given query it will always propagate the same constraints, no matter which of the applicable rules are applied. What is left to show for completeness is that all possible propagations are performed, not just a few. We check if all inequalities that logically follow from the `lex` constraint and some given inequalities are produced by the rules.

The completeness result is relative to the built-in constraint solver. In particular, if its entailment check is too weak to detect all cases where guard inequalities are implied, the `lex` constraint solver will also become incomplete. This is the case for finite domains, since the underlying arc consistency algorithm only provides local consistency.

Recall the logical specification of the lexicographic order constraint:

$$l_1 \preceq_l l_2 \quad \leftrightarrow \quad (l_1=[] \wedge l_2=[]) \vee$$
$$(l_1=[x|l_1'] \wedge l_2=[y|l_2'] \wedge x<y) \vee$$
$$(l_1=[x|l_1'] \wedge l_2=[y|l_2'] \wedge x=y \wedge l_1' \preceq_l l_2').$$

If we add a built-in constraint, disjuncts may become unsatisfiable and the remaining disjuncts may imply an inequality. The three disjuncts by themselves do not imply anything. We continue by considering the two last disjuncts only that expect nonempty lists.

For two nonempty lists, the formula implies

$$l_1 \preceq_l l_2 \wedge l_1=[x|l_1'] \wedge l_2=[y|l_2'] \rightarrow x \leq y$$

and there is no tighter implied inequality. This implication is covered by the propagation rule **14**.

If we add inequalities to rule out one disjunct, the other disjunct and its inequality are implied. To rule a disjunct, it suffices to add an inequality that implies a negated conjunct of the disjunct. So if the inequality added implies $x \geq y$, the first disjunct is ruled out and the second disjunct must hold. This is achieved by rule **13** together with rule **14**.

If the inequality implies $x \neq y$, we must use the first disjunct. This is achieved by rule **13** together with rule **14**. The second disjunct is also ruled out, if $\neg l_1' \preceq_l l_2'$ is implied. We have to find the inequalities that imply this negated constraint. By negating the specification of $\preceq$ for two nonempty lists of the same length, we arrive after some simplification at the formula

$$\neg l_1 \preceq_l l_2 \wedge l_1=[x|l_1'] \wedge l_2=[y|l_2'] \leftrightarrow (x<y \vee (x \geq y \wedge \neg l_1' \preceq_l l_2')).$$

The first disjunct is handled by rule **15**, the second disjunct $(x \geq y \wedge \neg l_1' \preceq_l l_2')$ by rule **16f** together with rule **15**.

Rules **11** and **12** are not needed for completeness of propagation, simply because they do not propagate anything except the trivial *true*. (But the two rules are useful for garbage collection and **12** is also needed for confluence.)

9.3 Description logic

Description logic (DL) is used to represent the terminological knowledge of a particular problem domain on an abstract logical level. One starts with atomic concepts and roles, and then defines new concepts and their relationships in terms of existing concepts and roles. Concepts can be considered as unary relations, similar to types. By default, concepts do not exclude each other. Roles correspond to binary relations over objects.

Typical applications of DL are reasoning about the contents of the semantic web, representation of medical knowledge, and configuration of technical systems.

9.3.1 Syntax and semantics

We use a basic variant of description logic, *ALC*. *Concept terms* are defined inductively. Their syntax avoids the use of variables.

Definition 9.3 *Every* concept (name) *c is a concept term. If s and t are concept terms and r is a* role (name), *then the following expressions are also concept terms:*

    not *s (negation, complement),*
    s and *t (conjunction, intersection),*
    s or *t (disjunction, union),*
    all *r* is *s (universal quantification, value restriction),*
    some *r* is *s (existential quantification, exists-in restriction).*

There are two kinds of knowledge in description logics.

Definition 9.4 Objects (individuals) *are constants or variables. Let a, b be objects. Then a : s is a* membership assertion (constraint) *and (a, b) : r is a* role-filler assertion (constraint).

An A-box (assertional knowledge) *is a conjunction of membership and role-filler assertions.*

A T-box (terminological knowledge) *is a finite set of acyclic concept definitions of the form c* isa *s.*

The *T-box* specifies the general background knowledge of the application domain. Therefore it does not refer to individuals. It uses an intensional representation similar to a database scheme. Concepts are defined in terms of other concepts and restrictions on roles using logical connectives.

Each concept has at most one definition. In the basic formalism we assume that a concept cannot be defined in terms of itself directly or indirectly, i.e. concept definitions are acyclic. This implies that there are concepts without definition, they are called *primitive*.

The *A-box* specifies the concrete problem-specific knowledge. It contains statements about the existence of concepts and roles of individuals (objects). It uses an extensional representation similar to a database extension. The A-box is checked against the T-box for consistency.

Example 9.3.1 A classical DL example is family relationships. We generate the CHR rules for the T-box from concept definitions such as:

```
male isa not female.
parent isa human and some child is human.
mother isa parent and female.
proud_parent isa parent and all child is phd.
grandmother isa mother and some child is parent.
motherofsons isa mother and all child is male.
```

We can see that the primitive concepts are **female**, **human**, and phd. Adding **female isa not male** would result in a cyclic definition that causes non-termination.

The definitions induce an implicit concept hierarchy (taxonomy) with multiple inheritance, e.g.

```
parent<human, mother<parent, mother<female, proud_parent<parent
```

The definition of **parent** uses an exists-in restriction to ensure that there is at least one child. A value restriction would only ensure that *if* there is a child, then it is human, but would allow parents without children.

Constraint theory. Basic description logics have a straightforward embedding in the decidable two-variable fragment of first-order logic (FOL). The theory for $\mathcal{ALC}$ with T-boxes is given in Figure 9.1.

Note that already with primitive concepts, their complement and disjunction alone we can encode propositional logic problems in a straightforward way using clausal syntax. No roles are needed.

9.3.2 Constraint solver

Reasoning problems of description logics include consistency of assertions, query answering, checking if an individual is an instance of a concept term and classification of concepts by subsumption. Subsumption and consistency

$$I : not\ S \leftrightarrow \neg(I : S)$$
$$I : S_1\ and\ S_2 \leftrightarrow I : S_1 \wedge I : S_2$$
$$I : S_1\ or\ S_2 \leftrightarrow I : S_1 \vee I : S_2$$
$$I : some\ R\ is\ S \leftrightarrow \exists J((I, J) : R \wedge J : S)$$
$$I : all\ R\ is\ S \leftrightarrow ((I, J) : R \rightarrow J : S)$$
$$C\ isa\ S \leftrightarrow (I : C \leftrightarrow I : S)$$

Fig. 9.1. FOL constraint theory for $\mathcal{ALC}$

can express each other. Usually, one reduces such reasoning services to consistency checking (satisfiability).

The CHR constraint solver for description logics is a direct implementation of the constraint theory, where the axioms and T-box definitions are translated into CHR rules. (We could also represent the T-box by constraints that are added incrementally.) The solver simplifies and propagates assertions in the A-box by decomposing concept terms and by using the definitions in the T-box to unfold them. Contradictions of the form X:C and X:not C lead to failure. During this process, only membership assertions change.

We first decompose concept terms and propagate membership constraints:

```
and   @ I:S1 and S2 <=> I:S1, I:S2.
some  @ I:some R is S <=> (I,J):R, J:S.
all   @ I:all R is S, (I,J):R ==> J:S.
or    @ I:S1 or S2 <=> (I:S1 ; I:S2).
```

The conjunction rule generates two new, smaller assertions. An exists-in restriction implicitly generates a new variable J in the rule body. This variable serves as a witness for the restriction. A value restriction is propagated to all role fillers using a propagation rule all. To achieve completeness of disjunction, search is employed by splitting I:S or T into two cases in rule or.

The duplicate removal rule removes multiple occurrences of assertions.

```
duplicate @ I:C \ I:C <=> concept_name(C) | true.
```

The *clash* rule detects inconsistency (contradiction).

```
clash  @ I:not C, I:C <=> concept_name(C) | false.
```

For efficiency, these rule are only applied to concept names.

To ensure completeness, we need rules that turn an arbitrary concept term into one in negation normal form (NNF). The simplification rules push the complement operator **not** down to the leaves of a concept term:

```
I:not (not S) <=> I:S.
I:not (S1 and S2)    <=> I:not S1 or not S2.
I:not (S1 or S2)     <=> I:not S1 and not S2.
I:not (some R is S) <=> I:all R is not S.
I:not (all R is S)  <=> I:some R is not S.
```

For each concept definition C *isa* S of the T-box we generate two so-called *unfolding* rules that replace the concept name C by its definitions S, and the negated concept name by the negation of its definition.

```
I:C <=> I:S.
I:not C <=> I:not S.
```

Example 9.3.2 Here is a sample computation for our family relationship example:

```
sue:proud_parent, (sue,joe):child, joe:not phd.
```
Unfold concept definition **proud_parent**
```
sue:parent and all child is phd,...
```
Unfold concept definition **parent** and decompose **and**
```
sue:human, sue:some child is human, sue:all child is phd,...
```
Simplify *exists-in restriction* **some**
```
sue:human, (sue,X):child, X:human, sue:all child is phd,...
```
Propagate *value restriction* **all**
```
X:phd, joe:phd, sue:human, (sue,X):child, X:human,
    sue:all child is phd, (sue,joe):child, joe:not phd.
```
Clash between **joe:phd** and **joe:not phd** leads to failure.

Note that the variable **X** may be **joe**, but need not to be.

Logical correctness. The logical reading of the CHR rules immediately shows their logical correctness as logical consequences of the constraint theory.

The *solved (normal) form* is either **false** (inconsistent), **true** (tautological), or a conjunction with constraints of the form

```
I:C, I:not C, I:all R is S, (I,J):R,
```

where **C** is a primitive concept name. There are no clashes (not both **I:C** and **I:not C**) and value restrictions have been propagated to every successor object. Exhaustive application of the CHR rules produces this normal form.

Confluence, anytime and online algorithm property, parallelism and concurrency. There are overlaps between the `clash` and `duplicate` rules and the rules generated from concept definitions. These overlaps lead to critical pairs that are easily joinable.

We can stop the computation and restart it anytime while we get closer to the solved form, and we can add assertions while the program runs without affecting correctness.

Since the rules only consider one membership assertion at a time in their rule heads, membership assertions can be executed in parallel. The only synchronization necessary is when the clash rule or the duplicate removal rule applies. But since the program is confluent, it does not matter when the rule applies. Moreover, given enough processors, all applicable propagation rules for `all` can be applied simultaneously.

Termination. The only CHR constraints that are rewritten by the rules are membership assertions. Hence, for termination it suffices to show that in each rule, the membership assertions in the body are strictly smaller than the ones in the head. In that case, the propagation rule for value restrictions can only generate a finite number of smaller and smaller membership assertions. A concept term is larger than its proper subterms, and an atomic concept is larger than its defining concept term. Primitive concept terms are smallest. Since concept definitions are finite and acyclic by definition, the order is well-founded.

Complexity. The worst-case time complexity is at least exponential for several reasons: disjunction in the rule `or`, the propagation rule `all`, and repeated unfolding of the same nonprimitive concept.

For example, consider n T-box definitions of the form

C_i `isa some r is` a_i `and some r is` b_i `and all r is` C_{i-1} $(1 \leq i \leq n)$,

where C_0 is a primitive concept name, subject to the query $I : C_n$. In the answer, the role fillers form a binary tree of depth n where, for each node, one child node is of concept `a` and the other one is of concept `b`. This tree can only be generated by an exponential number of rule applications.

The same effect can be achieved without a T-box, using a nested concept term as query where the C_i are unfolded:

$I :$ `some r is` a_i `and some r is` b_i `and all r is` `(some r is` a_i
`and ...).`

We can also do without the value restriction, relying on duplicate occurrences of a concept name in the T-box definitions:

C_i `isa some r is` (a_i `and` C_{i-1}) `and some r is` (`b and` C_{i-1}).

Despite this intractability, experiments on random problems without disjunction show a very low complexity due to indexing and the improbability of difficult cases: the worst observed time complexity was just linear.

9.3.3 Extensions

In Figure 9.2 we list some standard extensions of description logic languages. We assume that = is a built-in equality constraint. Some extensions will use additional built-ins, namely **transitive/1, feature/1, distinct/1, primitive/1**. (These built-ins could also be implemented as CHR constraints by modifying the rules accordingly, i.e. by moving the constraints from the guard to the rule head.)

Top (universal) and bottom (empty) concepts:
`X:top <=> true.`   `X:bot <=> false.`

Allsome quantifiers, e.g. **parent isa allsome child is human**:
`I:allsome R is S <=> I:all R is S, I:some R is S`

Role chains (nested roles), e.g. **grandfather isa father of father**:
`(I,J):A of B <=> (I,K):A, (K,J):B`

Inverse Roles
`(I,J):inv(R) <=> (J,I):R.`

Transitive Roles, e.g. **transitive(ancestor)**
`(I,K):R, (K,J):R ==> transitive(R) | (I,J):R`

Functional roles (features, attributes), e.g. F=age
`(I,J):F \ (I,K):F <=> feature(F) | J=K.`

Distinct, disjoint primitive concepts
`I:C1 \ I:C2 <=> distinct(C1), primitive(C2) | C1=C2.`

Nominals (named individuals, singleton concepts)
`X:{I1,I2,...,In} ==> (X=I1;X=I2;...;X=In)`

Concrete domains (constraints from other domains)
`(I,J):smaller ==> I<J.`
`(I,J):not smaller ==> I>=J.`
`(I,A):flight_from, (I,B):flight_to ==> flight(I,A,B).`

T-box axioms of inclusion between concept terms, written $C \sqsubseteq S$
`I:C ==> I:S.`

Fig. 9.2. Common extensions of $\mathcal{ALC}$ and their CHR rules

9.3.4 Description logic with rules

There are several proposals to combine DL with logic-based rules to achieve more expressiveness based on their common first-order logic semantics. The gain in expressiveness is mainly due to allowing for polyadic predicates and arbitrary conjunctions of DL assertions in definitions. This allows for role-filler assertions that do not have a tree structure. A typical example is the definition of the uncle role as a male sibling of a person's father.

Integration of DL with rules in the context of the semantic web usually starts from the OWL family of DL languages. OWL has three layers of languages with increasing expressiveness and difficulty: the classic DL reasoning problems are in EXPTIME for OWL-Lite and NEXPTIME for OWL-DL while OWL-Full is undecidable. OWL-DL is an expressive DL with full negation, disjunction, and restricted forms of universal and existential quantification of variables.

In the Semantic Web Rule Language (SWRL), OWL is extended with material first-order implication between conjunctions of assertions to provide for rules. SWRL has no disjunction, negation, no predicates other than those from DL, no nonmonotonic features such as negation-as-failure or defaults. Still, SWRL is already undecidable since it can simulate role value maps. SWRL goes beyond Horn clauses because it allows existentials in the conclusion part of the implication. Together with equality and disequality, the SWRL implications are strictly more general than concept inclusion axioms. For example, they can express the uncle definition. There is also an extension of SWRL for OWL-DL where non-DL atoms can also occur in a rule.

For mapping these languages into CHR, we basically translate implications of the form

$$A_1 \vee \ldots \vee A_n \leftarrow B1 \wedge \ldots B_m,$$

where the A's and B's are atoms, into propagation rules with disjunction,

```
B1,...Bn ==> (A1 ; ...; An).
```

The uncle example yields the CHR rule:

```
Z:male, (Y,Z):hassibling, (X,Y):hasparent ==> (X,Z):hasuncle.
```

A single propagation rule may be too weak to completely express the desired computational behavior, because unlike logical implications, CHR lacks reasoning with contrapositives and only applies rules from left to right. But these can be expressed by additional rules as required. For example, consider a concept definition in CHR$^\vee$:

```
X:uncle <=> (Y,X):hasuncle.
```

It can only be used to simplify `uncle` to `hasuncle`, but cannot draw conclusions the other way round. But if we replace the CHR rule by two propagation rules, we regain that reasoning power:

```
X:uncle ==> (Y,X):hasuncle.
```

```
(Y,X):hasuncle ==> X:uncle.
```

The other example from the DL literature concerns the rule

```
X:beer ==> sean:happy.
```

where we can add the contrapositive

```
sean:not happy ==> X:not beer.
```

In summary, current rule-based DL approaches basically translate to CHR propagation rules. With such rules, CHR basically performs a bottom-up closure. While the operational semantics of CHR rules is relatively straightforward, the rule extension proposals for DL use sophisticated translations into FOL and related logics that are subjected to a theorem prover. This makes reasoning about such rule programs probably more difficult than in CHR.

9.4 Rational trees

Unification is an essential problem in symbolic computing, in particular in theorem proving and declarative programming languages. Logic programming languages like Prolog rely on unification to treat logical variables, term rewriting systems need it for confluence testing, CHR for both, and functional languages like ML for type checking.

Unification (cf. Section 3.1) is concerned with making first-order logic terms *syntactically equivalent* by *substituting* terms for variables. For example, the terms $h(a, f(Y))$ and $h(Y, f(a))$ can be made identical by substituting the variable Y by a. In constraint programming, unification of terms is understood as solving equations. For example, the equation $h(a, f(Y)) = h(Y, f(a))$ will simplify to $Y=a$. Syntactic equality is an essential ingredient of constraint logic programming, since terms are the universal data structure and equalities can be used to build, access, and take apart terms.

The equation $X=f(X)$ has no solution, because the term resulting from repeated substitutions, $f(f(f(\ldots)))$, would be infinite (but only contains itself). We can allow for such infinite terms.

Reflexivity:	$\forall(true \rightarrow x=x)$
Symmetry:	$\forall(x=y \rightarrow y=x)$
Transitivity:	$\forall(x=y \land y=z \rightarrow x=z)$
Compatibility:	$\forall(x_1=y_1 \land \ldots \land x_n=y_n \rightarrow f(x_1,\ldots,x_n)=f(y_1,\ldots,y_n))$
Decomposition:	$\forall(f(x_1,\ldots,x_n)=f(y_1,\ldots,y_n) \rightarrow x_1=y_1 \land \ldots \land x_n=y_n)$
Contradiction:	$\forall(f(x_1,\ldots,x_n)=g(y_1,\ldots,y_m) \rightarrow false)$ if $f \neq g$ or $n \neq m$

Fig. 9.3. Rational tree equality theory *RT*

Definition 9.5 *A rational tree is a (possibly infinite) finitely branching tree which has a finite set of subtrees.*

A rational tree has a finite representation as an equality constraint and as a directed (possibly cyclic) graph by merging all nodes with common subtrees.

Constraint theory *RT*. The constraint theory *RT* is a variant of Clark's Equality Theory (CET). The theory *RT* admits rational trees by dropping the *acyclicity condition (occur check)* of CET. Like CET, it assumes an infinite set of function symbols. It is defined by the axiom scheme given in Figure 9.3. The first three formulas are the usual equality axioms. The axioms *Compatibility* and *Decomposition* define equality of terms to be equivalent to equivalence of their arguments. Finally, *Contradiction (or: Clash)* defines that two terms with different function symbols are not syntactically equivalent. The theory *RT* is *satisfaction-complete*, for completeness one would have to add a *uniqueness axiom*, which mandates uniqueness of solutions and so handles implied equalities.

Definition 9.6 *Let X_i be variables and t_j be arbitrary terms $(1 \leq i,j \leq n)$. A conjunction of equations is in* solved (normal) form *if it is of the form*

$$X_1=t_2 \land X_2=t_3 \land \ldots \land X_{n-1}=t_n \quad (n \geq 0),$$

where $X_i \neq X_j$ and $X_i \neq t_j$ for all $(1 \leq i < j \leq n)$.

In words, if a variable occurs on the l.h.s. of an equation, it does not occur as the l.h.s. or r.h.s. of any subsequent equation.

For example, the equation $f(X,b)=f(a,Y)$, the equations $X=t \land X=s$, $X=Y \land Y=X$ are all not in solved form, while $X=Z \land Y=Z \land Z=t$ and $Y=X \land X=f(Y)$ are solved. The solved form is not unique, e.g. $X=Y$ and $Y=X$ are logically equivalent but syntactically different solved forms, as are $X=f(X)$ and $X=f(f(X))$.

9.4.1 Constraint solver

The following CHR program solves rational tree equations. Unlike most other *unification* algorithms it uses *variable elimination* (by *substitution*) only in a very limited way. However, this simplification of the algorithm makes termination and complexity analysis harder.

```
reflexivity   @ X eq X <=> var(X) | true.
orientation   @ T eq X <=> var(X),X<<T | X eq T.
decomposition @ T1 eq T2 <=> nonvar(T1),nonvar(T2) |
                 same_functor(T1,T2),
                 same_args(T1,T2).
confrontation @ X eq T1 \ X eq T2 <=> var(X),X<<T1,T1=<<T2 |
                 T1 eq T2.
```

The rule **reflexivity** removes trivial equations between identical variables. The rule **orientation** reverses the arguments of an equation so that the (smaller) variable comes first. The order check in the guard makes sure that the rule is applicable at most once to a given equation. The rule **decomposition** applies to *function terms*. When there is a clash, **same_functor** will lead to **false**. Otherwise, the initial equation between two function terms will be replaced by equations between the corresponding arguments of the terms by the auxiliary constraint **same_args**. The rule **confrontation** replaces the variable in the second equation by the term equated to that variable according to the first equation. It performs a limited amount of variable elimination by only considering the l.h.s. of equations. This rule duplicates the term **T1**. For termination it is ensured by the guard that **T1** is not larger than **T2**.

The implementation relies on a total order on terms, expressed by the built-in **X<<Y**. (The Prolog built-in **@<** will not work.) In that order, terms of smaller size are smaller. The *size of a term* is the number of occurrences of function symbols and variables in the term:

$$size(f(t_1,\ldots,t_n)) = 1 + size(t_1) + \ldots + size(t_n)$$
$$size(X) = 1 \text{ if } X \text{ is a variable.}$$

To analyze complexity, we will also need the *depth of a term*:

$$depth(f(t_1,\ldots,t_n)) = 1 + max(depth(t_1),\ldots,depth(t_n))$$
$$depth(X) = 0 \text{ if } X \text{ is a variable.}$$

The built-in **X=<<Y** holds if and only if **Y<<X** does not hold.

Example 9.4.1 We equate two terms. For readability, we do not show the intermediate states involving the auxiliary CHR constraint `same_args`.

```
                              h(Y,f(a),g(X,a)) eq h(f(U),Y,g(h(Y),U)))
↦decomposition↦*             Y eq f(U), f(a) eq Y, g(X,a) eq g(h(Y),U)
↦orientation                 Y eq f(U), Y eq f(a), g(X,a) eq g(h(Y),U)
↦decomposition↦*             Y eq f(U), Y eq f(a), X eq h(Y), a eq U
↦orientation                 Y eq f(U), Y eq f(a), X eq h(Y), U eq a
↦confrontation               Y eq f(U), f(U) eq f(a), X eq h(Y), U eq a
↦decomposition↦*             Y eq f(U), U eq a, X eq h(Y), U eq a
↦confrontation               Y eq f(U), U eq a, X eq h(Y), a eq a
↦decomposition↦*             Y eq f(U), U eq a, X eq h(Y)
```

Example 9.4.2 Here is a simple example involving infinite rational trees.

```
                              X eq f(X), X eq f(f(X))
↦confrontation               X eq f(X), f(X) eq f(f(X))
↦decomposition↦*             X eq f(X), X eq f(X)
↦confrontation               X eq f(X), f(X) eq f(X)
↦decomposition↦*             X eq f(X), X eq X
↦reflexivity                 X eq f(X)
```

This means that the second constraint was redundant.

Logical correctness. The logical readings of the rules **reflexivity** and **orientation** are consequences of the corresponding axioms *Reflexivity* and *Symmetry* in the constraint theory *RT*. The rule **decomposition** follows from the axioms *Compatibility*, *Decomposition*, and *Contradiction (Clash)*. The rule **confrontation** is a consequence of *Transitivity* and *Symmetry*.

If $RT \models \neg \exists C$, then the solver is *satisfaction-complete*. The conditions for the solved form can be restated as $X_i \prec X_{i+1}$ and $X_i \prec T_{i+1}$ (for $1 \leq i < n$) since any strict total order is transitive and asymmetric. The solver computes the *solved form*: as long as a conjunction of constraints is not in solved form, at least one rule is applicable. If it is in solved form, no rule is applicable.

Confluence. There are no overlaps between different rules since the guards are disjoint. However, there are overlaps of the **confrontation** rule with itself.

```
confrontation @ X eq T1 \ X eq T2 <=> var(X),X<<T1,T1=<<T2 |
                                                        T1 eq T2.
```

Note that the `confrontation` rule is analogous to the merge–sort rule (Section 2.4.4),

```
A -> B \ A -> C <=> A<B, B=<C | B -> C.
```

Hence the overlaps and critical pairs are also similar. The only difference is that we require that `X` is a variable `var(X)`, which leads to one more nonjoinable critical pair.

The overlap between second and first rule head instances `X eq A,X eq B,X eq C, var(X),X<<A,A=<<B, var(X),X<<B,B=<<C` has the two computations for the *critical pair* (where the built-in constraints have been simplified):

```
        X eq A,X eq B,X eq C, var(X),X<<A,A=<<B,B=<<C
                    /                             \
X eq A,A eq B,X eq C, var(X),X<<A,A=<<B,B=<<C      |
                    |                             |
X eq A,A eq B,A eq C, var(X),X<<A,A=<<B,B=<<C      |
                                                  |
        X eq A,X eq B,B eq C, var(X),X<<A,A=<<B,B=<<C
                                                  |
        X eq A,A eq B,B eq C, var(X),X<<A,A=<<B,B=<<C
```

In the first final state we cannot apply the `confrontation` rule to `A eq B`, `A eq C` since we do not know if `A` is a variable or not. The final states differ, hence the critical pair is not joinable and the program is not confluent. For the intended use of the solver, the computation can proceed further than in the nonjoinable critical pairs, since the terms are known.

Termination. The rules `reflexivity` and `orientation` are applicable at most once to an equation. Application of `decomposition` produces equations between the arguments of the functions of the initial equations. Thus, the new equations have arguments of smaller size. Application of `confrontation` replaces one occurrence of `X` by `T1`. The guard ensures that `X << T1 =<< T2`. Therefore, as long as $T1$ is a variable, it gets closer from below to T2 but can never exceed it. If $T1$ is a function term, then so must be T2, and then only `decomposition` is applicable to the new equation `T1 eq T2` produced by `confrontation`. The resulting equations will only contain terms that are strictly smaller than T2. There is only a finite number of variables and subterms in a given problem. The term order is thus well-founded. So the `confrontation` rule cannot be applied infinitely often. Hence the solver terminates.

Nontermination would occur without the proper guards in the `confrontation` rule:

$$\frac{\texttt{X eq f(X), X eq f(f(X))}}{}$$

$\longmapsto_{\texttt{wrong-confrontation}}$ `f(f(X)) eq f(X), X eq f(f(X))`

$\longmapsto_{\texttt{decomposition}} \longmapsto^*$ `f(X) eq X, X eq f(f(X))`

$\longmapsto_{\texttt{orientation}}$ `X eq f(X), X eq f(f(X))`

To formally show termination, we give an exponential ranking:

$$rank(T_1 \ eq \ T_2) = esize(T_1) + 2\,esize(T_2) \qquad T_1 \text{ var., } T_2 \text{ nonvar.}$$
$$rank(T_1 \ eq \ T_2) = 2\,esize(T_1) + 2\,esize(T_2) \qquad T_1 \text{ nonvar., } T_2 \text{ var.}$$
$$rank(T_1 \ eq \ T_2) = esize(T_1) + 2\,esize(T_2) \qquad T_1 \text{ var., } T_2 \text{ var.}$$
$$rank(T_1 \ eq \ T_2) = esize(T_1) + esize(T_2) \qquad T_1 \text{ nonvar., } T_2 \text{ nonvar.}$$

$$esize(f(t_1, \ldots, t_n)) = 1 + 2\sum_i esize(t_i)$$
$$esize(X_i) = i \text{ if } X_i \text{ is a variable.}$$

Variables are ranked from 1 to v, where v is the number of variables. We require that the order `<<` used in the solver satisfies two conditions: for two variables, X`<<`Y iff $esize(X)$>$esize(Y)$. For two function terms, $T1$`<<`$T2$ iff $esize(T1)$<$esize(T2)$. This means that function terms are `<<`-ordered by their $esize$-rank, while variables are ordered in the opposite direction as the rank prescribes.

For the rank of an equation, the inequality holds:

$$rank(T_1 \ eq \ T_2) \leq 2(esize(T_1) + esize(T_2)).$$

The rank of a variable is always smaller than the rank of a function term. The rank is exponential in the depth of the term:

$$esize(t) \leq v \ size(t) \ 2^{depth(t)}.$$

The factor v comes in because the largest rank of a variable is v, while the term size only assigns 1 to each variable. This inequation can be shown by induction on the term depth.

We can show that the ranking condition for termination holds for the rules in the program.

Complexity. The intricate interaction between the `decomposition` rule and the `confrontation` rule can lead to exponential complexity. Since with indexing, rules can be tried and applied in constant time (the cost of `same_args` can be attributed to the equations it produces), the ranking gives us the complexity:

$$v \; size(t) \; 2^{depth(t)}.$$

This complexity is only exhibited in rare cases, typically the complexity is polynomial.

Polynomial complexity can be guaranteed if we fix the depth of the terms. A term can be *flattened* by replacing each subterm with a new variable that is equated with the replaced term. Flattening (cf. Section 6.2) produces equations with term depth 1. We translate each equation

$$T_1 \; eq \; T_2$$

into two equations to which the flattening function [.] (Definition 6.7) is applied:

$$[X \; eq \; S] \wedge [X \; eq \; T]$$

where X is a new variable.

Since flattening increases the size of the terms by a constant factor only, the resulting complexity is now quadratic in the term size in the worst case (since $v \leq size(t)$):

$$O(v \; size(t)) = O(size(t)^2).$$

9.5 Feature terms

Feature terms FT come out of knowledge representation in computational linguistics. It is a particularly simple yet expressive constraint system providing a universal, flexible data structure. While rational trees RT access subterms by position, feature terms access them by name. FT allows us to model records in logic.

Constraint system FT. Feature terms are conjunctions of unary and binary relations.

Definition 9.7 *Feature term constraints are unary sort constraints $s(X)$, binary feature constraints $X.f.Y$, and (syntactic) equality $X=Y$, where X and Y are variables or constants, also called* individuals, *s is called* sort *(type) and f is called* feature *(attribute, label, constructor, argument selector).*

A feature term X is a conjunction of feature term constraints $s(X) \wedge X.f_1.Y_1 \wedge \ldots \wedge X.f_n.Y_n (0 \leq i \leq n)$ where the f_i are pairwise disjoint.

A more compact notation for a feature term X is $X : s(f_1=Y_1, \ldots, f_n=Y_n)$, where the sort s may be dropped, $n \geq 0$ and the Y_i are feature terms in turn. Feature terms can also be represented as a graph where nodes are labeled by variables together with their sorts and arcs are labeled by features.

Another representation of feature terms is typically used for linguistic knowledge:

$$X = \exists Y \begin{bmatrix} \text{Person} \\ \text{office} : Y \\ \text{home} : Y \\ \text{name} : \begin{bmatrix} \text{first} : Leo \\ \text{last} : Smith \end{bmatrix} \end{bmatrix}$$

Cyclic structures can be represented with feature terms, for example:

$person(X) \wedge X.spouse.Y \wedge person(Y) \wedge Y.spouse.X.$

Feature terms are in a sense weaker than rational trees, because they can be incomplete. For example, to express that a geometric object is red, we write the constraint $X.color.red$, but we do not have to specify if the object is of sort square, circle, or rectangle.

Constraint theory. The constraint theory for FT assumes infinitely many constants for individuals, sorts, and features. Besides the axioms for equality (reflexivity, symmetry, and transitivity), the theory consists of two axioms for sorts and features and a uniqueness axiom:

$X.f.Y \wedge X.f.Z \Rightarrow Y=Z$
$s(X) \wedge r(X) \Rightarrow false$ if $s \neq r$
$\exists! \bar{y}(\mathcal{F}(\bar{y})),$

where $\mathcal{F}(\bar{y})$ is a conjunction of feature terms for the variables in $\bar{y}$. The uniqueness axiom says that feature terms are uniquely determined by their components (i.e. sort and feature constraints). Features behave like unary functions and sorts are pairwise disjoint. Note that this restrictive approach is the opposite of the approach in description logic, where the binary relations are not restricted to functions, where all sorts can intersect, and where a rich set of extensions exists.

A conjunction of feature term constraints is in solved (normal) form if it is either $false$ or a conjunction of feature terms for pairwise different variables.

Constraint solver. In the solver, the feature term equality constraint $X=Y$ is written as X **eq** Y, the sort constraint $s(X)$ as X:s, the feature constraint $X.f.Y$ as X.f.Y. We use built-in syntactic equality =.

```
variable_elimination  @ X eq Y <=> X=Y.
feature_decomposition @ X.F.Y \ X.F.Z <=> Y=Z.
sort_intersection     @ X:S \ X:R <=> S=R.
```

In the rules, the built-in equality is used to implement equality, and to enforce functional dependency and sort disjointness. The uniqueness axiom is not needed for satisfaction-completeness.

For example, to the query `X:person, X.name.Y, Y=leo, X.livesin.Z, Z:munich, X.name.sepp` the rule `feature_decomposition` removes `X.name. Y`, adds `Y=sepp`, which is inconsistent with `Y=leo` and thus fails with *false*.

Complexity and confluence. Termination is obvious, since each rule removes one CHR constraint. If indexing is used for sorts and variable–feature pairs, rule applications take constant time. Then the number of rule trials and applications is linear in the number of CHR constraints, and thus the overall complexity is linear as well.

There are no overlaps between different rules, but the sort and feature rules can overlap with themselves. The resulting critical pairs are joinable. For example, `X.F.Y, X.F.Z` yields either `X.F.Y,Y=Z` or `X.F.Z,Z=Y`, and these states are equivalent.

Extensions

We discuss two common extensions of feature term constraints.

Negation. We may negate atomic feature term constraints. We write $\neg X{=}Y$ as `X neq Y`, the negated sort $\neg s(X)$ as `X:not s`, and $\forall Y \neg (X.f.Y))$ as `not X.f`. The constraint solver is extended by clash rules:

```
X neq X <=> false.
X:S, X:not S <=> false.
X.F.Z, not X.F <=> false.
```

(The clash rule for sorts is redundant since different sorts never intersect.)

Arity constraints. A rational tree $X = g(Y, Z)$ can be written as a feature term $g(X) \land X.1.Y \land X.2.Z$. To complete the isomorphism, we have to forbid additional arguments like $X.3.V$. We do this by explicitly stating allowed features using a so-called *arity constraint*, here $X\{1,2\}$). In general, arity constraints are useful to define records, e.g. $X\{livesIn, name\}$. The extension of FT by the *arity constraint* $X\{f_1, \ldots, f_n\}$ is called CFT and subsumes rational trees RT.

The constraint theory is extended by the axioms:

$$X.F \wedge X.G \Rightarrow false \text{ if } F \neq G$$
$$X.\{f_1, \ldots, f_i, \ldots, f_n\} \Rightarrow \exists Y X.f_i.Y$$
$$X.F \wedge X.f.Y \Rightarrow f \in F.$$

The additional rules of constraint solver are (assuming the feature sets such as FS and Gs have a unique representation, e.g. as an ordered list):

```
X in Fs \ X in Gs <=> Fs=Gs.
X in Fs, X.F.Y ==> member(F,Fs).
```

It may be more practical to associate arity constraints with sorts instead of individuals.

9.6 Exercises

9.1 Implement the addition of natural numbers in the usual way using a ternary constraint add(X,Y,Z) that holds if the sum of X and Y is Z. Implement the addition as a constraint solver for a single **add** constraint, i.e. try to find as many simplifications as possible. For example, you may include the rule:

```
add(X,Y,Y) <=> X=0.
```

9.2 Consider the following scenario and express it in DL constraints.

- Furniture is goods.
- Vehicles can use traffic routes.
- Transporters are vehicles that can transport goods.
- Automobiles are vehicles that are driven by a motor and that use roads (only).
- Trucks are automobiles that can transport goods.
- Trains are vehicles that use rails (only).
- Freight trains are trains that can transport goods.
- Furniture trucks are trucks to transport furniture (only).
- Bulli is a furniture truck.
- Bulli transports G112 and G235.
- G112 and G235 are goods.
- Z521 is a train.
- Z521 transports bananas and coals.
  Do the following:
  (a) Identify the primitive concepts. Identify the roles. Separate T-box from A-box knowledge.

(b) Add the T-box to the constraint solver. Test the T-box with queries like X::transporter.

(c) Add the A-box as CHR constraints. Explain the answer to the goal z521::train. Use labeling. Adapt (if necessary) your T-box, s.t. z521 does not use the road!

(d) Explain the answers when unfolding the following concept terms. Use labeling.

(1) Train and not a transporter.

(2) Freight train and not a vehicle.

9.3 With numbers in successor notation, where zero is replaced by a variable, say X, the rational tree equation solver RT can compute the greatest common divisor (gcd) of n and m as follows: X=s^n(X), X=s^m(X). Compare this with the behavior of s^n(X)=s^m(X).

9.4 Consider the rational tree equation solver RT. Implement the CHR constraint X eq Y that succeeds iff $CET \models$ X=Y.

Clark's equality theory CET should be coded naturally, i.e. implement the axioms as propagation rules (whenever possible).

Hints:

- f(X1,...,XN)=..[f|X1,...,XN].
- Rules leading to immediate contradiction should go first in the program text.
- For termination reasons remove duplicate constraint.

Queries: Equate each pair of atomic formulas:

(a) $p(a, X, c, Y, Z)$ and $p(Y, X, c, a, W)$
(b) $p(Y, g(Y, f(Y)), g(X, a))$ and $p(f(U), V, g(h(U, V, W), U))$
(c) $p(g(X), h(a, X), h(Y, Y))$ and $p(U, h(a, g(V)), h(V, g(U)))$
(d) $p(h(f(X), a), X, h(f(f(X)), f(f(X))))$ and $p(h(V, a), U, h(W, f(V)))$

Extend your implementation, such that queries like X eq f(Y), Y eq f(X) can be treated (using the occur-check).

Hint: A simple solution introduces rule(s) for variable substitution.

Answer:

```
duplicate    @ X eq Y \ X eq Y <=> true.

reflexivity @ X eq X ==> true.
symmetry     @ X eq Y ==> Y eq X.
acyclicit    @ X eq T ==> var(X),nonvar(T),T=..[F|A],in(X,A) | fail.

transitivity @ X eq Y, Y eq Z ==> X eq Z.
```

```
decompostion  @ T1 eq T2 ==> nonvar(T1),nonvar(T2),
                                same_functor(T1,T2) |
                                T1=..[F|A1], T2=..[F|A2],
                                eq_list(A1,A2).
contradiction @ T1 eq T2 ==> nonvar(T1),nonvar(T2),
                                not_same_functor(T1,T2) |
                                fail.


%rule variant with help of built-in syntactic equality
substitution @ Y eq TX \ X eq T <=>
                var(X),nonvar(TX), in(X,TX) | X=T.
%rule variant using explicit substitution
substitution @ X eq T \ Y eq TX <=>
                var(X),var(Y),nonvar(TX), in(X,TX) |
                substitute(X,T,TX,T2T1), Y eq T2T1.
```

9.5 The constraint theory CT should define the (purely) syntactic inequality $\neq$ between two terms along the lines of CET:

irreflexivity	$\forall(x \neq x \rightarrow \bot)$
symmetry	$\forall(x \neq y \rightarrow y \neq x)$
compatibility	$\forall(x_1 \neq y_1 \vee \ldots \vee x_n \neq y_n \rightarrow f(x_1,\ldots,x_n) \neq f(y_1,\ldots,y_n))$
decomposition	$\forall(f(x_1,\ldots,x_n) \neq f(y_1,\ldots,y_n) \rightarrow x_1 \neq y_1 \vee \ldots \vee x_n \neq y_n)$
distinctness	$\forall(\top \rightarrow f(x_1,\ldots,x_n) \neq g(y_1,\ldots,y_m))$ iff $f \neq g$ or $n \neq m$
cylicity	$\forall(\top \rightarrow x \neq t)$ if t is not a variable and x appears in t

Implement a CHR constraint X **neq** Y that succeeds iff $CT \models$ X$\neq$Y. Disjunction, needed for implementing axioms *compatibility* and *decomposition*, should be implemented by a $\mathrm{CHR}^\vee$ constraint **one_neq/2** as negated **same_args/** constraint. The two arguments of **one_neq/2** are lists of the same length and the $\mathrm{CHR}^\vee$ should succeed iff at least one pair of list elements is not equal.

Queries: X **neq** f(X), f(a,X) **neq** f(X,Y), f(g(X),a) **neq** f(Y,X).

9.6 Use the rational tree equation solver RT as a polynomial equation solver by only changing the body of the **con+dec** rule to handle linear polynomial equations. The resulting equation T1 minus T2 is computed in normal form. An equation is in normal form if X **eq** A + B*Y + ... for variables, X, Y, ... and numbers A, B, ...

Answer:

```
decompostion  @ T1 eq T2 <=> nonvar(T1), nonvar(T2) |
     compute(T1,T2,T),
```

```
     (number(T) -> T=:=0  ;
      T=TP+E*X, normalize(TP,E,TN) , X eq TN
      ).
   confrontation @ X eq T1 \ X eq T2 <=>
                        var(X),X<<T1,T1=<<T2 | T1 eq T2.

   compute(C1,C2,C)    <=> number(C1), number(C2) | C is C1-C2.
   compute(T1,T2+A2*X,R+A*X) <=> remove(T1,A1*X,R1), A1=\=A2 |
                                 A is A1-A2, compute(R1,T2,R).
   compute(T1,T2+A2*X,R)    <=> remove(T1,A1*X,R1), A1=:=A2 |
                                 compute(R1,T2,R).
   compute(T1,T2+A2*X,R+A*X) <=> A is -A2, compute(T1,T2,R).

   normalize(C,E,C1)         <=> number(C), C1 is -C/E.
   normalize(T+A*Y,E,T1+A1*Y) <=> A1 is -A/E, normalize(T,E,T1).
```

9.7 Specialize the propagation rule of Fourier's algorithm to the case where one inequation contains only one variable.

9.8 Based on the polynomial equation solver $\Re$, use Fourier variable elimination and the rule combining the variable elimination approaches for equations and inequations containing only slack variables.

9.7 Bibliographic remarks

The linear polynomial solver for equations and inequations is described in [FA03]. The paper [Imb05] reviews constraint-related algorithms for equation solving.

Lexicographic orders are applied in symmetry breaking (e.g. [HKW04]) and for solution preferences (e.g. [FLS93]). Earlier approaches presented algorithms for the lexicographic order constraint in pseudo-code [FHK+02] that seems hard to analyze or use an automata formalism that seems hard to re-implement [CB04, BCP04], while the CHR solver [Frü06c] for the constraint is simple, short, concise, and directly executable. The paper [Frü06c] also contains another completeness proof and compares the CHR implementation of lex with the built-in lex_chain constraint [CB04] of the Sicstus clpfd constraint library.

A CHR solver for DL [BCM+07, SSS91, BDS93] is described in [FH95]. In the Semantic Web Rule Language (SWRL) [HPSB04] extends the DL OWL [BHH04] and is in turn generalized in [MSS04].

The CHR rational tree solver was one of the first CHR programs written [Frü98, FA03, MF06]. The underlying algorithm is similar to that in [Col82]. The last paper shows an exponential ranking and complexity of the original solver. In 1930, Herbrand [Her30] gave an informal description of a unification algorithm. Robinson [Rob65] rediscovered a similar algorithm when he introduced the resolution procedure for first-order logic in 1965. Since the late 1970s, there have been quasi-linear time algorithms for unification. For finite trees (Herbrand terms), see [MR84] and [PW78]. For rational trees, see [Hue80] and [Col82]. These algorithms can be understood as extensions of the union-find algorithm [TL84] from constants to trees. For an exposition of unification algorithms see [BN98] and for a multidisciplinary survey of unification see [Kni89]. A complete theory for rational trees occurred in [Mah88].

The constraint system *CFT* [ST94] extends feature trees with the arity constraint and in this way subsumes rational trees *RT*.

10
Union-find algorithm

The classical union-find (also: disjoint set union) (UF) algorithm was introduced by Tarjan in the 1970s. This essential algorithm efficiently solves the problem of maintaining a collection of disjoint sets under the operation of union. It is the basis for many graph algorithms (e.g. efficient computation of spanning trees). By definition of set operations, a union operator working on representatives of sets is an equivalence relation, i.e. we can view sets as equivalence classes and deal with equality.

We give concise CHR programs for the union-find algorithm and some variants that have best-known time and space complexity. This is believed impossible in other pure declarative programming languages due to their lack of *destructive assignment* which is needed for efficient update of graph data structures. Our program benefits from the guaranteed properties of well-behaved CHR programs such as the anytime and online algorithm property. This makes our implementation particularly well-suited for use in constraint solvers.

Using CHR analysis techniques we study logical correctness and confluence of these programs. We observe the essential update of the algorithm which makes it nonconfluent and nonmonotonic but efficient. Based on the confluence analysis, we are able to parallelize the UF algorithm. This is considered to be hard in the literature. When the UF algorithm is extended to deal with function terms (rational trees), the algorithm can be used for optimal complexity *unification*. Last but not least, we discuss a generalization of UF that yields novel algorithms for simple Boolean and linear equations that are well-suited for constraint solving.

10.1 Union-find algorithm

The UF algorithm maintains disjoint sets under union. Each set is represented by a rooted tree, whose nodes are the elements of the set. The root is called the *representative* of the tree. The representative may change when the tree is updated by a union operation. With the algorithm come three operations:

- `make(X)`: introduce X by creating a new tree with the only node X, i.e. X is the root.
- `find(X)`: return the representative of the tree in which X is contained: follow the path from the node X to the root of the tree by repeatedly going to the parent node of the current node until the root is reached.
- `union(X,Y)`: to join the two trees, find the representatives of X and Y (they are roots). If the roots are different, `link` them by making one point to the other (possibly changing the representative).

In an *allowed (valid) query* each element (node) is first introduced by a single `make` operation (before being subject to `find` and `union` operations). The second argument of a `find` must be a new variable. Nodes are typically constants. Each node is introduced by one `make`, before being subject to `find` and `union` operations.

10.1.1 Basic union-find

The CHR program implements the operations and data structures of the basic union-find algorithm as CHR constraints.

```
make      @ make(A) <=> root(A).
union     @ union(A,B) <=> find(A,X), find(B,Y), link(X,Y).

findNode  @ A -> B \ find(A,X) <=> find(B,X).
findRoot  @ root(A) \ find(A,X) <=> X=A.

linkEq    @ link(A,A) <=> true.
link      @ link(A,B), root(A), root(B) <=> B -> A, root(A).
```

The *data constraints* `root/1` and `->/2` ("points to") represent the tree data structure. The constraints `make/1`, `union/2`, `find/2`, and `link/2` define the *operations*. The find operation is implemented as a relation `find/2` whose second argument returns the result. The use of the built-in constraint `=` in the rule `findRoot` is restricted to returning the node A in the parameter X by binding it to A. `link/2` is an auxiliary operation for performing union of two roots. The rule `link` can be interpreted as performing *abduction*. If the nodes A and B are not equivalent, introduce the minimal assumption B -> A so that they are equivalent (such that performing a union afterwards leads to application of rule `linkEq`).

The relation between the variables and operations in the rules defining union and `link` can be depicted by the diagram

```
        A - union - B
        |           |
      find        find
        |           |
        X - link -- Y
```

Logical reading and correctness

The logical reading of our basic union-find CHR program is:

make	$make(A) \Leftrightarrow root(A)$
union	$union(A, B) \Leftrightarrow \exists XY (find(A, X) \land find(B, Y) \land link(X, Y))$
findNode	$find(A, X) \land A{\to}B \Leftrightarrow find(B, X) \land A{\to}B$
findRoot	$root(A) \land find(A, X) \Leftrightarrow root(A) \land X{=}A$
linkEq	$link(A, A) \Leftrightarrow true$
link	$link(A, B) \land root(A) \land root(B) \Leftrightarrow B{\to}A \land root(A)$

From the logical reading of the rule `link`, it follows that

$$B{\to}A \land root(A) \Rightarrow root(B),$$

i.e. *root* holds for every node in the tree, not only for root nodes. Indeed, we cannot adequately model the update from a root node to an inner node in first-order logic, since first-order logic is monotonic, i.e. formulas that hold cannot cease to hold. In other words, the link step is where the UF algorithm is *nonmonotonic* since it requires a destructive update in order to make the algorithm efficient. However, linear logic can give a declarative semantics that captures these updates (Section 3.4.2).

Union as equivalence relation. The program is also logically correct in first-order logic if we ignore the root constraints. By definition of set operations, a union operator working on representatives of sets is an equivalence relation observing the usual axioms:

reflexivity	$union(A, A) \Leftrightarrow true$
symmetry	$union(A, B) \Leftrightarrow union(B, A)$
transitivity	$union(A, B) \land union(B, C) \Rightarrow union(A, C)$

To show that these axioms hold for the logical reading of the program, we can use the following observations. Since the unary constraints **make** and **root** must hold for any node in the logical reading, we can ignore them. By the rule **findRoot**, the constraint **find** must be an equivalence. Hence its occurrences can be replaced by equality (=). Now **union** is defined in terms of **link**, which is reflexive by rule **linkEq** and logically equivalent to -> by rule **link**. But -> must be an equivalence like **find** because of rule **findNode**. Hence all binary constraints define the same equivalence relation. After renaming the constraints accordingly, we arrive at the theory:

union	$A=B \Leftrightarrow \exists XY(A=X \wedge B=Y \wedge X=Y)$
findNode	$A=X \wedge A=B \Leftrightarrow B=X \wedge A=B$
findRoot	$A=X \Leftrightarrow X=A$
linkEq	$A=A \Leftrightarrow true$
link	$A=B \Leftrightarrow B=A$

These formulas are logically equivalent to the axioms for equality, hence the program is logically correct as a logical consequence of the equality axioms.

UF as equation solver. We can now understand the behavior of the UF algorithm as efficient incremental equation solving. The union operation equates its two arguments. From the resulting tree data constraints we can read off the solution: each interior tree node is equated with its root node. This relationship is computed by the find operation. We can even find out if an equation is implied (entailed) by the existing equations: this is the case if the corresponding union operation would result in a link operation of two identical nodes (that does not change the tree). It therefore suffices for entailment to use the find operation on the arguments of the equation and to check if their roots are identical. These operations are discussed in more detail for the generalization of the UF algorithm (cf. Section 10.4).

Confluence

The union-find program is not confluent. Different orders of find and union operations may result in different trees (that represent the same set, of course). This behavior is inherent in the UF algorithm due to its updates of the tree structure.

Since there is a combinatorial explosion in the number of critical pairs with program size, it is important to filter out trivial nonjoinable critical pairs that either stem from overlaps that are not possible for allowed (valid) queries or that have answer states that we would like to consider equivalent for our purposes. We also take the refined operational semantics into account that rules out certain computations possible under the abstract semantics. States that are possible in computations for valid queries can be described by an invariant and confluence analysis restricted to them using observable confluence.

In particular, for the variants of the UF algorithm we implement here, we distinguish three cases of states in nonjoinable critical pairs that do not bother us:

- States cannot be reached by *allowed queries*. In UF, the states contain incompatible tree constraints.
- States that are considered *equivalent*. In UF, tree constraints that describe the same sets are equivalent.
- States that cannot be reached under the *refined operational semantics*. In UF, states with competing and pending concurrent link operations and with reordered find and link operations.

We have analyzed confluence of the UF implementation with a small confluence checker written in Prolog and CHR. For the basic UF implementation, we have found eight nonjoinable critical pairs (c.p.s). We found one essential nonjoinable critical pair (inherent to UF), three that feature incompatible tree constraints (that cannot occur when computing with allowed queries), and four that feature pending link constraints (that cannot occur under the refined semantics).

The nonjoinable critical pairs involve these rules of the basic UF program:

```
findNode   @ A -> B \ find(A,X) <=> find(B,X).
findRoot   @ root(A) \ find(A,X) <=> X=A.
link       @ link(A,B), root(A), root(B) <=> B -> A, root(A).
```

Inherent nonjoinable critical pair. The nonjoinable c.p. between the rule findRoot and link exhibits that the relative order of find and link operations matters.

```
                find(B,A),root(B),root(C),link(C,B)
      findRoot /                              \ link
          link /                               \ findNode
             /                                  \ findRoot
root(C),B->C,A=B                          root(C),B->C,A=C
```

Find returns the interior node instead of root. Under the refined semantics, however, this node was still the root since the find operation occurred before

the link operation. It is not surprising that a `find` after a `link` operation
has a different outcome if linking updated the root. Also, the trees in both
states represent the same set of elements (nodes), B and C.

Incompatible tree constraints. The two nonjoinable critical pairs for
`find` correspond to queries where a `find` operation is confronted with two
tree constraints to which it could apply.

```
            A->B,A->D,find(A,C)
  findNode /                      \ findNode
A->B,A->D,find(B,C)      A->B,A->D,find(D,C)
```

```
            root(A),A->B,find(A,X)
  findRoot /                      \ findNode
root(A),A->B,X=A         root(A),A->B,find(B,X)
```

Also the nonjoinable c.p. involving the rule `linkEq` features incompatible
tree constraints.

```
            root(A),root(A),link(A,A)
    linkEq /                      \ link
root(A),root(A)          root(A),A->A
```

The conjunctions (`A->B`, `A->D`), (`root(A)`, `A->B`), (`root(A)`, `A->A`), and
(`root(A)`, `root(A)`) in the overlaps and nonjoinable c.p.s violate the definition of a tree. We show by contradiction the invariant that the four
conjunctions cannot occur in a computation of an allowed query. Only the
rule `make` produces a `root`, and only the rule `link` produces a `->`. It needs
`root(A)` and `root(B)` to produce A `->` B. To produce one of the first three
conjunctions, the link operations need duplicate `root` constraints to start
from. Only a query containing identical copies of `make` can produce duplicate root constraints (as in the fourth conjunction). But duplicate `make`
operations are not part of an allowed query.

Pending links. The remaining four nonjoinable critical pairs correspond
to queries where two `link` operations have at least one node in common
such that when one link is performed, at least one node in the other link
operation is not a root anymore.

```
            root(A),root(B),link(B,A),link(A,B)
    link /                             \ link
root(B),A->B,link(A,B)      root(A),link(B,A),B->A
```

```
root(A),root(B),root(C),link(B,A),link(C,B)
      link /                          \ link
root(C),A->B,B->C    root(A),root(C),link(B,A),B->C


root(A),root(B),root(C),link(B,A),link(A,C)
      link /                          \ link
root(B),root(C),A->B,link(A,C)    root(B),C->A,A->B


root(A),root(B),root(C),link(B,A),link(C,A)
      link /                          \ link
root(B),root(C),A->B,link(C,A)   root(B),root(C),link(B,A),A->C
```

The c.p.s can never arise for an allowed query under the refined semantics. link is an internal operation, it can only be called by a union. In the union, the link constraint gets its arguments from two find operations. Under the refined semantics, no other operations will be performed between these operations. Hence the results from the find constraints will still be roots when the link constraint receives them.

10.1.2 Optimized union-find

With two independent optimizations that keep the tree shallow and balanced, one can achieve logarithmic worst-case and quasi-constant (i.e. almost constant) amortized running time per operation.

The first optimization is *path compression* for the find operation. It moves nodes closer to the root after a find. We make every node on the path from X to the root point directly to the root. The second optimization is *union-by-rank* for the link operation. It keeps the tree shallow by pointing the root of the smaller tree to the root of the larger tree. Here, *rank* refers to an upper bound of the tree depth (tree height).

For each optimization alone, for a sequence of m operations on n nodes $(m \geq n)$, the worst-case time complexity is $\mathcal{O}(m log(n))$. When both optimizations are used, the complexity improves to $\mathcal{O}(m + n log(n))$. In this case, the amortized complexity is quasi-linear, $\mathcal{O}(m + n\alpha(n))$, where $\alpha(n)$ is an inverse of the Ackermann function and is less than 5 for all practical n, since $n \leq 2^{65536} \Rightarrow \alpha(n) \leq 5$.

CHR program. We implement these optimizations as follows. The first two rules, make and union, will stay the same for all remaining programs in this section, they are therefore omitted from now on.

```
make      @ make(A) <=> root(A,0).
union     @ union(A,B) <=> find(A,X), find(B,Y), link(X,Y).

findNode  @ A -> B, find(A,X) <=> find(B,X), A -> X.
findRoot  @ root(A,_) \ find(A,X) <=> X=A.

linkEq    @ link(A,A) <=> true.
linkLeft  @ link(A,B), root(A,N), root(B,M) <=> N>=M |
                 B -> A, root(A,max(N,M+1)).
linkRight @ link(B,A), root(A,N), root(B,M) <=> N>=M |
                 B -> A, root(A,max(N,M+1)).
```

When compared to the basic version, we see that `root` has been extended
with a second argument that holds the rank of the tree. The rule `findNode`
has been extended for immediate path compression: the logical variable
X serves as a placeholder for the result of the find operation. The `link` rule
has been split into two rules `linkLeft` and `linkRight` to reflect the optimization of union-by-rank: the smaller ranked tree is added to the larger
ranked tree without changing its rank. When the ranks are the same, either
tree is chosen (both rules are applicable) and only then the rank is incremented (`max(N,M+1)`). Note that these two rules just differ by the exchanged
arguments of the `link` constraint to achieve their aim.

Confluence

The nonjoinable critical pairs are in principle analogous to the ones
discussed for the basic program in Section 5.2, but their numbers increase
significantly due to the optimizations. The confluence checker found 73
nonjoinable critical pairs. The number of critical pairs is dominated by
those 68 of the link rules. Each c.p. involving `linkLeft` has a corresponding analogous c.p. involving `linkRight`.

The c.p.s between `findRoot` and a link rule are inherent to UF as in the
basic program. Unlike the basic versions, in the optimized algorithm, two
`findNode` rule applications on the same node will interact, because one will
compress, and then the other cannot proceed until the first find operation
has finished:

```
                 find(B,A),B->C,find(B,D)
           findNode /                \ findNode
find(A,D),find(C,A),B->D    find(D,A),find(C,D),B->A
```

We see that A and D are interchanged in the states of the critical pair. In the first state of the c.p., since the result of `find(C,A)` is A, the `find(A,D)` can eventually only reduce to A=D. Analogously for the second state. But under A=D the two states of the c.p. are identical. The other two c.p.s involving a `findNode` rule feature incompatible tree constraints.

All critical pairs between link rules only, except those for `linkEq`, consist of pairs of states that have the same constraints and variables, but that differ in the tree that is represented. Just as in the case of the basic program, the problem of pending links occurs without a left-to-right execution order.

10.1.3 Complexity

We establish the optimal time complexity of our CHR programs by showing that they are operationally equivalent to the respective imperative algorithms and that all computation steps in the CHR program have the same complexity as their imperative counterparts.

Operational equivalence. In the refined operational semantics of CHR, the constraints in a goal are evaluated from left to right, just as is the case for equivalent calls for the imperative program.

It is clear from the CHR program and the refined operational semantics that there is only ever at most one operation constraint in the constraint store. Moreover, whenever a data constraint is executed, the operation constraint has already been removed. Thus, a data constraint will never trigger any rule, because of lack of the necessary partner constraint.

Moreover, the recursion depth for the `find/2` constraint is equal to the path from the initial node to the root, just like in the imperative algorithm. The syntactic equality in the body of the `findRoot` rule cannot wake up any constraints, since the variable involved does not occur in any other constraint processed so far and since it will be bound to a constant.

Time complexity equivalence. We show that the time complexities of the computation steps are also the same. Based on the refined semantics of CHR (Section 3.3.4), CHR implementations exist (e.g. some K.U. Leuven CHR systems) where all of the following operations take *constant time*:

- Finding all constraints one by one with a particular value in a given argument position (with indexing).
- Matching of constants and variables in the rule head (given a bounded reference chain length).
- Checking and solving simple built-in constraints (like =, =<, + and `max`).
- Adding and deleting CHR constraints.

It is further assumed that storing the (data) constraints and their indexes takes constant space per constraint and variable.

From these assumptions it is clear that rules can be tried and applied in constant time. Hence our CHR implementation has the same time complexity properties as the imperative algorithm.

Experimental evaluation. The CHR program for optimized UF was run using the K.U. Leuven CHR system. This CHR system uses hashtables as constraint stores for look-ups on shared variables that are ground. By adding the appropriate mode declarations to our program, the system establishes the groundness of shared variables. These hashtables allow for efficient look-up, insertion, and deletion of constraints.

By initializing the hashtables to the appropriate sizes and choosing the used constants appropriately, it is possible to avoid hashtable collisions. Even in the presence of collisions, all hashtable operations can be supported in amortized constant time on average per operation, which is sufficient for our complexity analysis. The optimal time amortized quasi-linear time complexity was confirmed by the experimental evaluation.

10.2 Rational tree unification with union-find

We combine the union-find program with the solver for rational trees. The former will deal with all equations between variables, the latter only needs to handle the function terms. We assume that equations are in flat normal form, i.e. the l.h.s. is a variable and the r.h.s. is either a variable or a function symbol applied to variables. Recall the original program of the *RT* solver:

```
reflexivity    @ X eq X <=> var(X) | true.
orientation    @ T eq X <=> var(X),X<<T | X eq T.
decomposition @ T1 eq T2 <=> nonvar(T1),nonvar(T2) |
               same_functor(T1,T2),
               same_args(T1,T2).
confrontation @ X eq T1 \ X eq T2 <=> var(X),X<<T1,T1=<<T2 |
               T1 eq T2.
```

In the first new rule we replace equations between two variables by a union operation:

```
union @ X eq Y <=> var(X),var(Y) | union(X,Y).
```

Hence only equations between a variable and a flattened function term remain. The rules **reflexivity** and **orientation** become obsolete. We consider three cases for the rule **confrontation**, according to whether T1 and T2 are variables or function terms (X must be a variable always):

- If T1 and T2 are variables, we have two equations between variables that are already handled by the union operation.
- If T1 and T2 are function terms, the body equation T1 eq T2 will immediately be taken apart by an application of rule **decomposition**. We therefore move the decomposition into the body of the confrontation rule. The guard can be simplified, because the order =<< between flat terms T1 and T2 does not matter. The result is the rule con+dec:

```
con+dec @ X eq T1 \ X eq T2 <=> var(X),nonvar(T1),nonvar(T2) |
                same_functor(T1,T2), same_args(T1,T2).
```

- If T1 is a variable and T2 is a function term, then the first equation X eq T1 has already been removed by the union rule. The equation is reflected in a data constraint -> of the UF algorithm. We can therefore rewrite the rule as follows:

```
root1 @ X -> Y \ X eq T <=> Y eq T.
```

This ensures that the l.h.s. variable of an equation is always a root. However, the rule accesses the internal data structure of the UF algorithm. It is preferable to use the find operation to find the root. We have to trigger that operation whenever a node becomes an interior node. We assume that in the link rules of the UF solver, a constraint noroot is emitted in that case. Overall, this yields the rule

```
root @ noroot(X) \ X eq T <=> find(X,Y), Y eq T.
```

After these program transformations, we arrive at the program:

```
union    @ X eq Y <=> var(X),var(Y) | union(X,Y).
con+dec @ X eq T1 \ X eq T2 <=> var(X),nonvar(T1),nonvar(T2) |
                same_functor(T1,T2), same_args(T1,T2).
root    @ noroot(X) \ X eq T <=> find(X,Y), Y eq T.
```

10.3 Parallelizing union-find

We parallelize basic and optimal sequential versions of the classical union-find algorithm with the help of confluence analysis. The resulting program is close to the original one and promises to be as efficient, even though it is acknowledged in the literature that this is hard to achieve due to the inherent sequential nature of the algorithm when it comes to tree updates. Its worst-case time complexity can get worse upon parallelization if the sequential algorithm is used as a basis. Thus, often other data structures and algorithms are used for the parallel union-find problem.

10.3.1 Basic union-find

The operations make, union, and find can always proceed at their own speed. We can accommodate different find operations on the same node, since the tree constraints are not altered by a find. The link operation has to wait for the result of the find operations. Moreover, when we are about to apply the `link` rule, another link operation may remove one of the roots that we need for linking.

Confluent analysis identifies those states where the order of the constraints matters. There are eight nonjoinable critical pairs (cf. Section 10.1.2). Three nonjoinable c.p.s feature incompatible tree constraints. We avoid the other nontrivial c.p.s by modifying the given program. The c.p. between `findRoot` and `link` reveals that the *relative order of find and link* operations matters for the outcome of the find. The remaining nonjoinable c.p.s feature *pending competing links*. When one link is performed, at least one node in the other link operation is not a root anymore, and so this link operation will *deadlock*.

Avoiding the inherent nonjoinable critical pair. We first handle the critical pair between `findRoot` and `link`.

```
              find(B,A),root(B),root(C),link(C,B)
     findRoot /                          \ link
         link /                           \ findNode
             /                             \ findRoot
root(C),B->C,A=B                    root(C),B->C,A=C
```

We replace the culprit built-in equality constraint `=/2` by a new CHR constraint `found/2`, that we can tailor to our needs. In the `findRoot` rule, `X=A` becomes `found(A,X)`. It holds the result of the find operation in the first argument.

The `link` rules are modified by replacing instances of `link(A,B)` in the rule head by the proper instances of the conjunction `link(X,Y)`, `found(A,X)`, `found(B,Y)`. The new rule for `found` mimics the rule `findNode`: the `found` constraint keeps track of the updates of the tree so that its result argument is always a root.

```
findNode    @ A -> B  \ find(A,X) <=> find(B,X).
findRoot1   @ root(A) \ find(A,X) <=> found(A,X).

found       @ A -> B \ found(A,X) <=> found(B,X).

linkEq1     @ link(X,Y), found(A,X), found(A,Y) <=> true.
link1       @ link(X,Y), found(A,X), found(B,Y),
                      root(A), root(B) <=> B -> A, root(A).
```

With found we can join the corresponding critical pair.

```
                find(B,A),root(B),root(C),link(C,B)
     findRoot /                               \ link
        link /                                 \ findNode
       found /                                  \ findRoot
root(C),B->C,found(C,A)                  root(C),B->C,found(C,A)
```

There are now many (89) nonjoinable critical pairs, because the introduction of the found constraints gives rise to many possible overlaps for the link rules (84). All critical pairs are trivial now, because they either cannot occur for allowed queries or they feature different tree constraints that represent the same set of nodes.

10.3.2 Optimized union-find

We first introduce found into the program of optimal UF as for the basic algorithm. The critical pairs for the find rules tell us that parallel finds have to wait for the result of path compression from one of the finds. In the worst case, if that find process fails, other finds will deadlock (which was not the case in the basic version of the algorithm). As a remedy we introduce an *explicit compression* operation compr/2 that runs in parallel to the other operations. We modify the findNode rule to call compr(A,X) instead of immediately producing a tree data constraint that points to a yet unbound variable. Analogously we add compression for found.

A problem acknowledged in the literature is the interference between different compressions along the same subpath in the tree, because roots change and because compression destroys paths. Competing compressions may destroy the tree. Different solutions have been proposed, like comparing certain counters for nodes or time-stamps, or using a different compression technique like path halving.

Our solution is to compress the nodes of a path to the root that was used for linking. So compression is performed *after* the corresponding linking operation. The rule `compress` now uses its own `found` named `foundc`. The program will leave the `foundc` constraints in the store, but the program can also be modified to remove the `foundc` constraints.

```
findNode1 @ A -> B \ find(A,X) <=> find(B,X), compr(A,X).
findRoot1 @ root(A,_) \ find(A,X) <=> found(A,X).


found1    @ A -> B \ found(A,X) <=> found(B,X), compr(A,X).


compress  @ foundc(C,X) \ A -> B, compr(A,X) <=> A -> C.


linkEq1c   @ found(A,X), found(A,Y), link(X,Y) <=>
                    foundc(A,X), foundc(A,Y).
linkLeft1c @ found(A,X), found(B,Y), link(X,Y),
                    root(A,N), root(B,M) <=> N>=M |
                    foundc(A,X), foundc(B,Y),
                    B -> A, N1 is max(N,M+1), root(A,N1).
linkRight1c @ found(A,X), found(B,Y), link(Y,X),
                    root(A,N), root(B,M) <=> N>=M |
                    foundc(A,X), foundc(B,Y),
                    B -> A, N1 is max(N,M+1), root(A,N1).
```

Confluence of parallelized optimal union-find. The confluence analysis of this program finds 386 nonjoinable critical pairs, of the same nature as for the parallel basic version. 371 critical pairs are between the rules for the link operations. 35 of them are joinable modulo equivalence of the nodes in the trees that are produced. All but one of the remaining critical pairs can be shown not to occur for allowed queries. In this only nontrivial critical pair, competing compressions may produce different trees, but the nodes are the same, as the nodes A, B, C, and D must be on the same path, in the given order.

```
         foundc(C,X),compr(A,X), A->B, foundc(D,Y),compr(A,Y)
   compress /                               \ compress
   compress /                               \ compress
foundc(C,X),foundc(D,Y),A->D      foundc(C,X),foundc(D,Y),A->C
```

10.3.3 Correctness and complexity

We show that the new parallel CHR implementation and the optimal sequential implementation *simulate each other* by mapping computations between the two. The only exception is that not all computations involving competing compressions can be mapped into a sequential execution.

We map between states (constraints) and between computation steps (rule applications). The mapping follows the program transformation that we have performed to arrive at the parallel program. First, introduction of `found` that behaves like `find`. Second, replacement of implicit immediate path compression by an explicit one with `compr` that relies on `foundc`.

Sequential to parallel. The mapping from a sequential to a parallel execution is as follows. Immediate path compression by rule `findNode` is replaced by explicit path compression with `compr` constraints. The built-in equality constraints produced by `findRoot` in the sequential computation are replaced by `found` constraints until they are involved in a link operation. Immediately after linking, the equalities are replaced by `foundc` and we insert applications of the `compress` rule into the resulting parallel computation, so that compression is actually performed and removes all `compr` constraints.

Parallel to sequential. Parallel executions without competing compressions can be simulated by the sequential program: we map constraints `A->B,compr(A,X)` into `A->X` to achieve immediate compression. As a consequence, the `compress` rule applications become obsolete, because they do not change any constraints under the mapping.

We also map `found` into `find` constraints and thus applications of the rule `found1` into applications of `findNode`. Under the mapping, applications of the rule `findRoot1` do not change constraints, they become obsolete. Just before a link rule is applied, we insert applications of the rule `findRoot` that applies to the two involved `find` constraints that come from mapping `found`. Finally, we map `foundc` constraints into built-in equalities.

Complexity. We showed that each rule application in one program corresponds to a rule application in the other program, with exception of the `compress` rule applications that only occur in the parallel program. But their number is bounded by the number of `findNode` rule applications. Hence if rule tries and applications take constant time as in the sequential program, the optimal worst-case time complexity is preserved. Since find operations and linking for disjoint node pairs can run in parallel, we can expect a reduction in latency for simultaneous queries and updates. The parallel speed-up was confirmed experimentally.

10.4 Generalizing union-find

The union-find algorithm can be seen as solving simple equations between variables or constants. With a few lines of changed code, we generalize its implementation in CHR from equality to arbitrary binary relations. By choosing the appropriate relations, we can derive fast algorithms for solving certain propositional logic (SAT) problems as well as certain polynomial equations in two variables.

While linear-time algorithms are known to check satisfiability and to exhibit certain solutions of these problems, our algorithms are simple instances of the generic algorithm and have additional properties that make them suitable for incorporation into constraint solvers: from classical union-find, they inherit simplicity and quasi-linear time and space. By nature of CHR, they are anytime and online algorithms. They can be parallelized. They solve and simplify the constraints in the problem, and can test them for entailment, even when the constraints arrive incrementally, one after the other.

10.4.1 Generalized union-find

The idea of generalizing union-find is to replace equalities by binary relations. The generalized union-find (GUF) algorithm then maintains relations between elements (variables) under the operation of adding relations.

Operations on relations. We need some standard operations on relations from relational algebra and a nonstandard one, `combine`. The operations are implemented by built-in constraints as follows, where *id* is the identity function:

- `compose`(r_1, r_2, r_3) iff $r_3 := r_1 \circ r_2$
- `invert`(r_1, r_2) iff $r_2 := r_1^{-1}$
- `equal`(r_1) iff $r_1 = id$
- `combine`(r_1, r_2, r_3, r_4) iff $r_4 := r_1^{-1} \circ r_3 \circ r_2$.

The commutative diagram below shows the relations between the four relations that are arguments of `combine`.

```
X -- R1 -- A
|          |
R3         R4
|          |
Y -- R2 -- B
```

CHR program. We extend the CHR implementation of optimal UF by additional arguments (the relations) and by additional constraints on them (the operations on relations). In the program, these additions are underlined. The operation constraints union, find, link and the data constraint -> get an additional argument to hold the relation. The operation union now asserts a given relation between its two variables, find finds the relation between a given variable and the root of the tree in which it occurs. The operation link stores the relation in the tree data constraint. The data constraint -> in the tree is labeled by relations now.

```
make      @ make(X) <=> root(X,0).
union     @ union(X,XY,Y) <=> find(X,XA,A), find(Y,YB,B),
                     combine(XA,YB,XY,AB), link(A,AB,B).


findNode @ X-XY->Y, find(X,XR,R) <=> find(Y,YR,R),
                     compose(XY,YR,XR), X-XR->R.
findRoot @ root(X,N), find(X,XR,R) <=> root(X,N),equal(XR),X=R.


linkEq    @ link(X,XX,X) <=> equal(XX).
linkLeft  @ link(X,XY,Y), root(X,RX), root(Y,RY) <=> RX>=RY |
              invert(XY,YX), Y-YX->X, root(X,max(RX,RY+1)).
linkRight@ link(X,XY,Y), root(Y,RY), root(X,RX) <=> RY>=RX |
                     X-XY->Y, root(Y,max(RY,RX+1)).
```

The operation constraint union(X,XY,Y) enforces relation XY between X and Y. The operation find returns the root for a given node, but also the relation that holds between the node and the root. The relation AB in rule union must hold between the roots that are to be linked given the relation specified in the union. The built-in combine computes the relation AB from the initial relation XY and the relations XA and YB resulting from the two find operations.

In the linkEq rule, the link operation now tests if the relation XX given between two identical variables X is the identity relation. If this is not the case, the overall computation will fail. For example, this happens if we try to union the same two variables twice with different, incompatible relations between them.

In all allowed queries, all relations are given. Then the find operation returns a relation, the operations on relations compose, combine, and invert compute a relation (the last argument) from given relations, and finally equal checks a given relation.

Normalization and entailment checking. By using the find operation, the results can be normalized: for each variable in the problem, we issue a find operation. For implementation, we can use an *auxiliary dummy constraint* normalize.

```
normalize, X-XY-Y ==> find(X,XR,R).
```

The find operation will return the relation to the root variable and as a side-effect the tree will be compressed to have a direct pointer between the two variables. So afterwards, the solved form contains data constraints of the form X_i-XR->R_j, where all X_i are different (and the R_j are root variables only).

We can also *check for entailment*, i.e. ask if a given relation holds between two given variables. This is the case if their roots are the same (otherwise they are unrelated) and if asserting the relation using union would not change the tree. That is, a given relation already holds between two variables if the union operation leads to a link operation that does not update the tree. This is the case if the linkEq rule is applicable. Therefore a special instance of the union rule suffices for entailment of a relation (X XY Y):

```
unioned?(X,XY,Y) <=>
  find(X,XA,A),find(Y,YB,B), combine(XA,YB,XY,AB), A==B, equal(AB).
```

A==B checks if A and B are identical and equal(AB) checks if AB is the identity relation. These checks are inherited from the linkEq rule.

The query associated with the entailment test can also be modified to find out what relation between two given variables X and Y holds. In that case we replace combine(XA,YB,XY,AB) according to its definition so that it computes XY from XA, YB and AB (which must be the identity). We get the rule:

```
related?(X,XY,Y) <=>
  find(X,XA,A),find(Y,YB,B), A==B, invert(YB,BY),compose(XA,BY,XY).
```

where just X and Y are given and XY is computed.

Complexity

Our algorithm is a canonical extension (proper generalization) of the optimized UF algorithm in CHR: we added arguments holding the relations to existing CHR constraints. In the rules, these additional arguments for the relations are variables. In the head of each rule, these variables are all distinct. The guards have not been changed. The additional constraints in the rule bodies only involve variables for relations. Moreover, if we specialize our algorithm to the case where the only relation is identity `id`, we get back the original program. These observations are an indication that we can preserve the complexity and correctness results of the original algorithm – under certain conditions as we will see.

Our complexity proof is based on a mapping from computations in the generalized algorithm to computation in the original UF.

Theorem 10.1 The GUF algorithm in CHR has the same time and space complexity as the original optimized UF algorithm if the introduced operations on relations (`combine, compose, equal, invert`) take constant time and space.

Proof. We show that any computation in the generalized algorithm can be mapped into a computation of the original optimized UF algorithm where computation lengths are linearly related. This claim is shown by induction on length of the computation and case analysis of the rules applicable in a computation step. Since each rule application takes constant time and space in both algorithms, if the operations on relations take constant time and space, this proves our theorem.

We map transitions of the GUF algorithm to transitions of the optimized UF algorithm. The mapping simply removes the additional arguments holding the relations and additional constraints for the operations on the relations.

The operations on relations give rise to **Solve** transitions where the source and target state in the mapped transition are identical. Such transitions are therefore mapped to empty transitions (computation steps of length 0). Since we required that these operations take constant time and space and since these operations occur only in rule bodies, their execution causes only a constant time overhead for each rule application of our algorithm.

We also have to consider inconsistency errors caused by execution of `equal` caused by the application of a `linkeq` rule. In that case, the computation stops in the GUF algorithm, while in the corresponding mapped transition, `equal` is mapped to true and the computation can possibly proceed. Clearly it needs less time and space to stop a computation early.

Logical reading

By logical correctness of a program we mean that the logical reading of the rules of a program is a logical consequence of a specification given as a logical theory. Since the GUF algorithm maintains relations between elements under the operation of adding relations, the specification is a theory for these relations. Since our program should work with arbitrary relations, we expect the logical reading of its rules to follow from the empty theory, i.e. to be tautologies. We will see that this is not the case for all rules.

In the logical reading of our rules, we replace union, find, link, and -> as intended by the binary relations between their variables, and the constraints for operations on relations by their definitions using functional notation. Even though the first-order logical reading of UF does not reflect the intended meaning of the root data constraint, the logical reading suffices for our purposes.

(make)   make(X) ⇔ root(X,0).
(union)   (X XY Y) ⇔ ∃XA,A,YB,B,AB ((X XA A) ∧ (Y YB B) ∧
                         XA^−1∘XY∘YB=AB ∧ (A AB B))

(findNode) (X XY Y) ∧ (X XR R) ⇔
                ∃YR ((Y YR R) ∧ XY∘YR=XR ∧ (X XR R))
(findRoot) root(X,N) ∧ (X XR R) ⇔ root(X,N) ∧ XR=id ∧ X=R

(linkEq)   (X XX X) ⇔ XX=id
(linkLeft) RX>=RY ⇒ ((X XY Y) ∧ root(X,RX) ∧ root(Y,RY) ⇔
                ∃YX (XY^−1=YX ∧ (Y YX X) ∧ root(X,max(RX,RY+1)))))
(linkRight) RY>=RX ⇒ ((X XY Y) ∧ root(Y,RY) ∧ root(X,RX) ⇔
                (X XY Y) ∧ root(Y,max(RY,RX+1))))

Most rules lead to formulas that do not impose any restriction on the binary relations involved. The logical reading of the findRoot rule is flawed, because root wrongly holds for any node. More importantly, the logical reading of linkEq implies that the only relation that is allowed to hold between identical variables is the identity function *id*. Most importantly, the meaning of the findNode rule is a logical equivalence, that is not a tautology and restricts the involved relations. For example, it does not hold for ≤=XR=YR=XY even though ≤ ∘ ≤=≤.

Logical correctness

We now show that our implementation is correct if the involved relations are bijective functions. In that case, the composition operation is precise enough in that it allows us to derive any of the three involved relations from the other two. For most other types of relations, GUF is not correct, since it loses information due to composition.

Definition 10.2 *A function f is* bijective *if the function is injective and surjective, i.e.* $f(\bar{x}) = y \wedge f(\bar{u}) = v \wedge (\bar{x} = \bar{u} \vee y = v) \rightarrow \bar{x} = \bar{u} \wedge y = v.$

Bijective functions are closed under inverse and composition. Thus, a unary function $f(x) = y$ is bijective if for every x there is exactly one y and vice versa.

We first show that when the identity function id is one of the relations, then all relations must be bijective.

Theorem 10.3 The logical reading of the rules of the GUF algorithm implies that all relations are bijective if the allowed relations include the identity function.

Proof. In the formula for rule findNode,

(X XR R) $\wedge$ (X XY Y) $\Leftrightarrow$ (X XR R) $\wedge$ (Y YR R) where XY∘YR=XR,

we consider two cases in which we replace either relation XY or relation YR by the identity function id. This leads to the two formulas

(X XR R) $\wedge$ (X id Y) $\Leftrightarrow$ (X XR R) $\wedge$ (Y XR R) and
(X XR R) $\wedge$ (X XR Y) $\Leftrightarrow$ (X XR R) $\wedge$ (Y id R).

The former formula means that any relation XR used must be surjective, the latter means that any relation XR must be injective. Hence any relation must be bijective.

Bijective functions may seem a strong restriction. On the other hand, permutations, isomorphisms, and many other mappings (such as encodings in cryptography) are bijective functions. Indeed, for a domain of size n, there exist $n!$ different bijective functions, i.e. more than exponentially many. Also, most arithmetic functions are at least piecewise bijective, since they are piecewise monotone.

Theorem 10.4 The logical reading of the rules of the GUF algorithm is a consequence of a theory for the relations if these relations are bijective functions.
Proof. We observe:

- The identity function id referred to by the rules findRoot and linkEq is a bijective function.

- The `findNode` rule leads to the nontautological formula,

  (X XR R) ∧ (X XY Y) ⇔ (X XR R) ∧ (Y YR R) where XY∘YR=XR.

This condition is satisfied if the involved relations are bijective functions. Then, for any value given to one of the three variables `X`, `Y`, `Z`, the values for the other two variables are uniquely determined on both sides of the logical equivalence. Given such a triple of values `(X,Y,Z)`, there cannot be another triple of values that has any value in common in the same component.

All other rules are tautologies.

The two instances of GUF that we will discuss next involve bijective functions only.

10.4.2 Boolean equations

With the GUF algorithm, we can solve inequations between Boolean variables (propositions), i.e. certain 2-SAT problems. This instance features thus a (small) finite domain and a finite number of relations. In the CHR implementation, the relations are `eq` for = and `ne` for ≠, and the truth values are 0 for false and 1 for true. The `ne` relation holds if the Boolean exclusive-or function (`xor`) returns true. The operations on relations can be defined by the rules:

```
compose(eq,R,S) <=> S=R.          invert(R,S) <=> S=R.
compose(R,eq,S) <=> S=R.
compose(R,R,S) <=> S=eq.          equal(S) <=> S=eq.
```

```
combine(XA,YB,XY,AB) <=>
  compose(XY,YB,XB), invert(XA,AX), compose(AX,XB,AB).
```

Here is a simple example of a query for Booleans. Note that we introduce the truth values 0 and 1 by `make` and add `union(0,ne,1)` to enforce that they are distinct. This suffices to solve this type of Boolean inequations.

```
make(0),make(1),union(0,ne,1),
   make(A),make(B),union(A,eq,B),union(A,ne,0),union(B,eq,1).
root(A,2), B-eq->A, 0-ne->A, 1-eq->A.
```

The result of the query shows that `A` is also equal to 1.

10.4.3 Linear polynomials

Another instance of the GUF algorithm deals with linear polynomial equations in two variables. It features an infinite domain and an infinite number of relations. In this instance, the CHR data constraint X-A#B->Y (with A≠0) means X=A*Y+B. The operations on relations are defined as follows:

```
compose(A#B,C#D,S) <=> S = A*C # A*D+B.
invert(A#B,S) <=> S = 1/A # -B/A.          equal(S) <=> S = 1#0.
```

```
combine(XA,YB,XY,AB) <=>
          compose(XY,YB,XB), invert(XA,AX), compose(AX,XB,AB).
```

Again, an example illustrates the behavior of this instance:

```
make(X),make(Y),make(Z),make(W),
   union(X,2#3,Y),union(Y,0.5#2,Z),union(X,1#6,W).
root(X,1), Y-0.5#(-1.5)->X, Z-1.0#(-7.0)->X, W-1.0#(-6.0)->X.
```

Note that the generalized linkEq rule asserts that the relation XX in link(X,XX,X) must be the identity function. Thus, link(X,1#0,X) is fine, but all other equations of the form link(X,A#B,X) with A#B different from 1#0 will lead to an inconsistency error. While this is correct for link(X,1#1,X), the equation link(X,2#1,X) should not fail, since it has the solution X=-1. Indeed, in our program, an inconsistency will occur whenever a variable is fixed, i.e. determined to take a unique value. Our implementation succeeds exactly when the set of equations has infinitely many solutions.

We now introduce concrete numeric values and extend the program to solve for determined variables. We express numbers as multiples of the number 1. To make sure that the number 1 always stays the root, so that it can always be found by the find operation, we add root(1,∞) (instead of make(1)) to the beginning of a query.

We split the linkEq rule into two rules. The first restricts applicability of the generalized linkEq rule to the case where A=1, the second applies otherwise, i.e. to equations that determine their variable (A=\=1). It normalizes the equation such that the coefficient is 1 and the second occurrence of the variable is replaced by 1.

```
linkEq1 @ link(X,A#B,X) <=> A=:=1 | B=:=0.
linkEq2 @ link(X,A#B,X) <=> A=\=1 | link(X,1#B/(1-A)-1,1).
```

The example illustrates the behavior of the two new rules (∞ is chosen to be 9):

```
root(1,9), make(X),make(Y), union(X,2#3,Y),union(X,4#1,1).
root(1,9), X-4#1->1, Y-0.5#(-1.5)->X.
```

We add another rule that propagates values for determined variables down the tree data structure and so binds all determined variables in linear time:

```
X-A#B->N <=> number(N) | X=A*N+B.
```

The above query now yields as answer `root(1,9), X=5, Y=1`.

10.5 Bibliographic remarks

The optimal implementation of the classical union-find (also: disjoint set union) algorithm [TL84, GI91] is given in [SF06] and analyzed in [SF05]. Effective Prolog-based implementations of CHR are the SICStus [AAB$^+$93], HAL [HdlBSD05] and K.U. Leuven [SD04] CHR systems.

We combined the union-find program with the solver for rational trees in [MF06]. In [MF07] the combination is further extended to handle existentially quantified conjunctions of equations in the theory of rational trees in almost-linear time. Existential (auxiliary) variables are introduced when we flatten equations or during computations. In [MF07] it is shown that with rule `root`, equations in *RT* can be solved in amortized quasi-linear time.

It is considered hard to parallelize the union-find algorithm [AW91]. Thus, often other data structures and algorithms are used for the parallel union-find problem [PCD96]. Our implementation is based on the original sequential algorithm [Frü05]. A parallel speed-up of our basic CHR implementation was confirmed experimentally in [LS08].

Generalized union-find. The generalization of UF [Frü06b] yields novel algorithms for simple Boolean and linear equations that are well-suited for constraint solving.

It is well known that 2-SAT (conjunctions of disjunctions of at most two literals) [APT79] and Horn-SAT (conjunctions of disjunctions with at most one positive literal, i.e. propositional Horn clauses) [BB79, WFD84, Min88] can be checked for satisfiability in linear time. The class of Boolean equations and inequations we can deal with is a proper subset of 2-SAT, but not of Horn-SAT.

These two classical linear-time SAT algorithms are not incremental. They assume that the problem and its graph representation are initially known, because it has to be traversed along its edges. The 2-SAT algorithm computes maximal strongly connected components, and then proceeds component-wise by value propagation. The algorithms only check for satisfiability and can report one possible solution, but they do not simplify or solve the given problem in a general way, so the results are less informative than ours.

[AS80] gives a linear time algorithm that is similar to ours, but is more complicated. Equations correspond to directed arcs in a graph. Like the 2-SAT algorithm, it computes maximal strongly connected components, and then proceeds component-wise.

References

[AAB+93] Johan Andersson, Stefan Andersson, Kent Boortz, Mats Carlsson, Hans Nilsson, Thomas Sjöland, and Johan Widen. *SICStus Prolog User Manual.* Technical report, European Research Consortium for Informatics and Mathematics at SICS, 1993.

[Abd97] Slim Abdennadher. Operational semantics and confluence of constraint propagation rules. In *Third International Conference on Principles and Practice of Constraint Programming*, volume 1330 of *Lecture Notes in Computer Science*, pages 252–266. Springer, 1997.

[ADT+04] Marco Alberti, Davide Daolio, Paolo Torroni, Marco Gavanelli, Evelina Lamma, and Paola Mello. Specification and verification of agent interaction protocols in a logic-based system. In *2004 ACM Symposium on Applied Computing*, pages 72–78. ACM, 2004.

[AF98] Slim Abdennadher and Thom Frühwirth. On completion of constraint handling rules. In *Fourth International Conference on Principles and Practice of Constraint Programming*, volume 1520 of *Lecture Notes in Computer Science*, pages 25–39. Springer, 1998.

[AF99] Slim Abdennadher and Thom Frühwirth. Operational equivalence of CHR programs and constraints. In *Fifth International Conference on Principles and Practice of Constraint Programming*, volume 1713 of *Lecture Notes in Computer Science*, pages 43–57. Springer, 1999.

[AF03] Slim Abdennadher and Thom Frühwirth. Integration and optimization of rule-based constraint solvers. In *Revised Selected Papers of the 13th International Symposium on Logic Based Program Synthesis and Transformation*, volume 3018 of *Lecture Notes in Computer Science*, pages 198–213. Springer, 2003.

[AFH05] Slim Abdennadher, Thom Frühwirth, and C. Holzbaur. Editors, Special Issue on Constraint Handling Rules. *Journal on Theory and Practice of Logic Programming*, 5(4–5), 2005.

[AFM99] Slim Abdennadher, Thom Frühwirth, and Holger Meuss. Confluence and semantics of constraint simplification rules. *Constraints*, 4(2):133–165, 1999.

[All83] James F. Allen. Maintaining knowledge about temporal intervals. *Communications of the ACM*, 26(11):832–843, 1983.

[AM00] Slim Abdennadher and Michael Marte. University course timetabling using constraint handling rules. In C. Holzbaur and Th. Frühwirth, editors, Special Issue on Constraint Handling Rules, volume 14(4) of *Journal of Applied Artificial Intelligence*, pages 311–325. Taylor & Francis, 2000.

[AP90] J.-M. Andreoli and R. Pareschi. Linear objects: logical processes with built-in inheritance. In *Seventh International Conference on Logic Programming*, pages 495–510. MIT Press, 1990.

[APT79] B. Aspvall, M. F. Plass, and R. E. Tarjan. A linear time algorithm for testing the truth of certain quantied Boolean formulas. *Information Processing*, 8:121–123, 1979.

[AS80] Bengt Aspvall and Yossi Shiloach. A fast algorithm for solving systems of linear equations with two variables per equation. *Linear Algebra and its Applications*, 34:117–124, 1980.

[AS97] S. Abdennadher and H. Schütz. Model generation with existentially quantified variables and constraints. In *Sixth International Conference on Algebraic and Logic Programming*, volume 1298 of *Lecture Notes in Computer Science*, pages 256–272. Springer, 1997.

[AS98] S. Abdennadher and H. Schütz. CHRv: a flexible query language. In *Third International Conference on Flexible Query Answering Systems*, volume 1495 of *Lecture Notes in Computer Science*, pages 1–14. Springer, 1998.

[AW91] Richard J. Anderson and Heather Woll. Wait-free parallel algorithms for the union-find problem. In *23rd Annual ACM Symposium on Theory of Computing*, pages 370–380. ACM, 1991.

[BB79] Catriel Beeri and Philip A. Bernstein. Computational problems related to the design of normal form relational schemas. *ACM Transactions on Database Systems*, 4(1), 1979.

[BB92] Gérard Berry and Gérard Boudol. The chemical abstract machine. *Theoretical Computer Science*, 96(1):217–248, 1992.

[BCM88] Jean-Pierre Banâtre, Anne Coutant, and Daniel Le Metayer. A parallel machine for multiset transformation and its programming style. *Future Generation Computer Systems*, 4(2):133–144, 1988.

[BCM+07] Franz Baader, Diego Calvanese, Deborah L. McGuinness, Daniele Nardi, and Peter F. Patel-Schneider. *The Description Logic Handbook*. Cambridge University Press, 2007.

[BCP04] Nicolas Beldiceanu, Mats Carlsson, and Thierry Petit. Deriving filtering algorithms from constraint checkers. In *Tenth International Conference on Principles and Practice of Constraint Programming*, volume 3258 of *Lecture Notes in Computer Science*, pages 107–122. Springer, 2004.

[BDS93] M. Buchheit, F. M. Donini, and A. Schaerf. Decidable reasoning in terminological knowledge representation systems. *Journal of Artificial Intelligence Research*, 1:109–138, 1993.

[Bet07] Hariolf Betz. Relating coloured Petri nets to constraint handling rules. In *Fourth Workshop on Constraint Handling Rules*, pages 32–46, 2007.

[BF05] Hariolf Betz and Thom Frühwirth. A linear-logic semantics for constraint handling rules. In *11th International Conference on Principles and Practice of Constraint Programming*, volume 3709 of *Lecture Notes in Computer Science*, pages 137–151. Springer, 2005.

[BFKM85] Lee Brownston, Robert Farrell, Elaine Kant, and Nancy Martin. *Programming Expert Systems in OPS5: An Introduction to Rule-based Programming*. Addison-Wesley, 1985.

[BG98] Stephane Bressan and Cheng Hian Goh. Answering queries in context. In *Third International Conference on Flexible Query Answering Systems*, volume 1495 of *Lecture Notes in Computer Science*, page 68. Springer, 1998.

[BH92] Maria Paola Bonacina and Jieh Hsiang. On rewrite programs: semantics and relationship with PROLOG. *Journal of Logic Programming*, 14(1–2):155–180, 1992.

[BHH04] Sean Bechhofer, Frank Van Harmelen, and Jim Hendler. OWL Web Ontology Language Reference. http://www.w3.org/TR/owl-ref/, 2004.

[Bja96] M. Bjareland. Proving Consistency in K-IA chronicles–An Implementation of PMON. Master's thesis, Dept. of Information and Computer Science, Linkoepings Universitet, 1996.

[BKK⁺96] Peter Borovanski, Claude Kirchner, Helene Kirchner, Pierre-Etienne Moreaua, and Marian Vittek. Elan: a logical framework based on computational systems. In *First International Workshop on Rewriting Logic and its Applications*, volume 4 of *Electronic Notes in Theoretical Computer Science*, pages 35–50. Elsevier, 1996.

[BM93] Jean-Pierre Banâtre and Daniel Le Métayer. Programming by multiset transformation. *Communications of the ACM*, 36(1):98–111, 1993.

[BN98] Franz Baader and Tobias Nipkow. *Term Rewriting and All That*. Cambridge University Press, 1998.

[BO97] Frederic Benhamou and William J. Older. Applying interval arithmetic to real, integer, and Boolean constraints. *The Journal of Logic Programming*, 32(1):1–24, 1997.

[BTH04] Liviu Badea, Doina Tilivea, and Anca Hotaran. Semantic web reasoning for ontology-based integration of resources. In *Second International Workshop on Principles and Practice of Semantic Web Reasoning*, volume 3208 of *Lecture Notes in Computer Science*, pages 61–75. Springer, 2004.

[CB04] Mats Carlsson and Nicolas Beldiceanu. From constraints to finite automata to filtering algorithms. In *13th European Symposium on Programming Languages and Systems*, volume 2986 of *Lecture Notes in Computer Science*, pages 94–108. Springer, 2004.

[CCKP06] Wei-Ngan Chin, Florin Craciun, Siau-Cheng Khoo, and Corneliu Popeea. A flow-based approach for variant parametric types. In *21st Annual ACM SIGPLAN Conference on Object-Oriented Programming Systems, Languages, and Applications*, pages 273–290. ACM, 2006.

[CD96] Philippe Codognet and Daniel Diaz. Compiling constraints in clp(FD). *The Journal of Logic Programming*, 27(3):185–226, 1996.

[CDE⁺02] M. Clavel, F. Durn, S. Eker, P. Lincoln, N. Mart–Oliet, J. Meseguer, and J. F. Quesada. Maude: specification and programming in rewriting logic. *Theoretical Computer Science*, 285(2):187–243, 2002.

[CGT89] S. Ceri, G. Gottlob, and L. Tanca. What you always wanted to know about datalog (and never dared to ask). *IEEE Transaction on Knowledge and Data Engineering*, 1(1):146–166, 1989.

[Cla78] Keith L. Clark. Negations as failure. In *Logic and Databases*, pages 293–322. Plenum Press, 1978.

[Col82] A. Colmerauer. Prolog and infite trees. In K. L. Clark and S.-A. Tärnlund, editors, *Logic Programming*, pages 231–251. Academic Press, 1982.

[CR93] Alain Colmerauer and Philippe Roussel. The birth of Prolog. In *Second ACM SIGPLAN Conference on History of Programming Languages*, pages 37–52. ACM, 1993.

[Der87] Nachum Dershowitz. Termination of rewriting. *Journal of Symbolic Computation*, 3(1–2):69–116, 1987.

[DGM05] Giorgio Delzanno, Maurizio Gabbrielli, and Maria Chiara Meo. A compositional semantics for CHR. In *Seventh ACM SIGPLAN International Conference on Principles and Practice of Declarative Programming*, pages 209–217. ACM, 2005.

[DHS+88] M. Dincbas, P. Van Hentenryck, H. Simonis, A. Aggoun, T. Graf, and F. Berthier. The constraint logic programming language CHIP. In *International Conference on Fifth Generation Computer Systems*, pages 693–702, Tokyo, Japan, 1988. Institute for New Generation Computer Technology.

[DJ84] N. Dershowitz and N. A. Josephson. Logic programming by completion. In *Second International Conference on Logic Programming*, pages 313–320, Uppsala, Sweden, 1984. University Uppsala.

[DMP91] Rina Dechter, Itay Meiri, and Judea Pearl. Temporal constraint networks. *Journal of Artificial Intelligence*, 49(1–3):61–95, 1991.

[Don93] G. Dondosolla. A constraint-based implementation of the GRF. ESPRIT Project no. 2409 EQUATOR Report, 1993.

[DP60] Martin Davis and Hilary Putnam. A computing procedure for quantification theory. *Journal of the ACM*, 7(3):201–215, 1960.

[DSB06] Gregory J. Duck, Peter J. Stuckey, and Sebastian Brand. ACD term rewriting. In *22nd International Conference on Logic Programming*, volume 4079 of *Lecture Notes in Computer Science*, pages 117–131. Springer, 2006.

[DSdlBH03] Gregory J. Duck, Peter J. Stuckey, Maria Garcia de la Banda, and Christian Holzbaur. Extending arbitrary solvers with constraint handling rules. In *Fifth ACM SIGPLAN International Conference on Principles and Practice of Declaritive Programming*, pages 79–90. ACM, 2003.

[DSdlBH04] G. J. Duck, P. J. Stuckey, M. García de la Banda, and C. Holzbaur. The refined operational semantics of constraint handling rules. In *20th International Conference on Logic Programming*, volume 3132 of *Lecture Notes in Computer Science*, pages 90–104. Springer, 2004.

[DSS07] Gregory J. Duck, Peter J. Stuckey, and Martin Sulzmann. Observable confluence for constraint handling rules. In *23rd International Conference on Logic Programming*, volume 4670 of *Lecture Notes in Computer Science*, pages 224–239. Springer, 2007.

[Dum95] Edd Dumbill. Application of Resolution and Backtracking to the Solution of Constraint Satisfaction Problems. Project report, 1995.

[EEUT06] H. Ehrig, K. Ehrig, U. Prange, and G. Taentzer. *Fundamentals of Algebraic Graph Transformation*. Springer, 2006.

[ET96] M. T. Escrig and F. Toledo. Qualitative spatial orientation with constraint handling rules. In *12th European Conference on Artificial Intelligence*. John Wiley & Sons, 1996.

[ET98] M. T. Escrig and F. Toledo. *Qualitative Spatial Reasoning: Theory and Practice*. IOS Press, 1998.

[FA03] Thom Frühwirth and Slim Abdennadher. *Essentials of Constraint Programming*. Springer, 2003.

[FAM96] Thom Frühwirth, Slim Abdennadher, and Holger Meuss. On confluence of constraint handling rules. In *Second International Conference on Principles and Practice of Constraint Programming*, volume 1118 of *Lecture Notes in Computer Science*, pages 1–15. Springer, 1996.

[FdPW02] Thom Frühwirth, Alessandra di Pierro, and Herbert Wiklicky. Probabilistic constraint handling rules. In *11th International Workshop on Functional and (Constraint) Logic Programming*, volume 76 of *Electronic Notes in Theoretical Computer Science*, pages 115–130, 2002.

[FH95] T. Frühwirth and P. Hanschke. Terminological reasoning with constraint handling rules. In P. Van Hentenryck and V. J. Saraswat, editors, *Principles and Practice of Constraint Programming*. MIT Press, 1995.

[FH03] E. Friedman-Hill. *Jess in Action*. Manning Publications, 2003.

[FHK⁺02] Alan Frisch, Brahim Hnich, Zeynep Kiziltan, Ian Miguel, and Toby Walsh. Global constraints for lexicographic orderings. In *Eighth International Conference on Principles and Practice of Constraint Programming*, volume 2470 of *Lecture Notes in Computer Science*, pages 179–203. Springer, 2002.

[FLS93] H. Fargier, J. Lang, and T. Schiex. Selecting preferred solutions in fuzzy constraint satisfaction problems. In *First European Congress on Fuzzy and Intelligent Technologies*, 1993.

[FMS06] Thom Frühwirth, Laurent Michel, and Christian Schulte. Constraints in procedural and concurrent languages. In Francesca Rossi, Peter Van Beek, and Toby Walsh, editors, *Handbook of Constraint Programming*, chapter 19, pages 453–494. Elsevier, 2006.

[For83] Charles L. Forgy. Rete: a fast algorithm for the many pattern/many object pattern match problem. *Artifical Intelligence*, 19:17–37, 1983.

[Frü94] Thom Frühwirth. Temporal Reasoning with Constraint Simplification Rules. Technical report ECRC-94-05, ECRC, Munich, 1994.

[Frü95] Thom Frühwirth. Constraint handling rules. In *Constraint Programming: Basics and Trends*, volume 910 of *Lecture Notes in Computer Science*, pages 90–107. Springer, 1995.

[Frü98] Thom Frühwirth. Theory and practice of constraint handling rules. Special Issue on Constraint Logic Programming. *Journal of Logic Programming*, 37(1–3):95–138, 1998.

[Frü00] Thom Frühwirth. Proving termination of constraint solver programs. In *Selected Papers from the Joint ERCIM/Compulog Net Workshop on New Trends in Contraints*, volume 1865 of *Lecture Notes in Computer Science*, pages 298–317. Springer, 2000.

[Frü01] Thom Frühwirth. On the number of rule applications in constraint programs. *Electronic Notes in Theoretical Computer Science*, 48:147–166, 2001.

[Frü02a] Thom Frühwirth. As time goes by: automatic complexity analysis of simplification rules. In *Eighth International Conference on Principles of Knowledge Representation and Reasoning*, San Francisco, CA, USA, 2002. Morgan Kaufmann.

[Frü02b] Thom Frühwirth. As time goes by II: more automatic complexity analysis of concurrent rule programs. *Electronic Notes in Theoretical Computer Science*, 59(3):185–206, 2002.

[Frü05] Thom Frühwirth. Parallelizing union-find in constraint handling rules using confluence analysis. In *21st International Conference on Logic Programming*, volume 3668 of *Lecture Notes in Computer Science*, pages 113–127. Springer, 2005.

[Frü06a] T. Frühwirth. Constraint systems and solvers for constraint programming. *Special Issue of Archives of Control Sciences (ACS) on Constraint Programming for Decision and Control*, 2006.

[Frü06b] T. Frühwirth. Deriving linear-time algorithms from union-find in CHR. In T. Schrijvers and T. Frühwirth, editors, *Third Workshop on Constraint Handling Rules*, Venice, Italy, July 2006.

[Frü06c] Thom Frühwirth. Complete propagation rules for lexicographic order constraints over arbitrary domains. In *Joint ERCIM/CoLogNET International Workshop on Constraint Solving and Constraint Logic Programming*, volume 3978 of *Lecture Notes in Computer Science*, pages 14–28. Springer, 2006.

[GA01] Harald Ganzinger and David Mc Allester. A new meta-complexity theorem for bottom-up logic programs. In *First International Joint Conference on Automated Reasoning*, volume 2083 of *Lecture Notes in Computer Science*, pages 514–528. Springer, 2001.

[GI91] Zvi Galil and Giuseppe F. Italiano. Data structures and algorithms for disjoint set union problems. *ACM Computer Survey*, 23(3):319–344, 1991.

[Gir87] Jean-Yves Girard. Linear logic. *Theoretical Computer Science*, 50(1):1–102, 1987.

[Gir95] Jean-Yves Girard. Linear logic: its syntax and semantics. In *Workshop on Advances in Linear Logic*, pages 1–42. Cambridge University Press, 1995.

[GKK+88] Joseph Goguen, Claude Kirchner, Helene Kirchner, Aristide Megrelis, Jose Meseguer, and Timothy Winkler. An introduction to OBJ 3. In *First International Workshop on Conditional Term Rewriting Systems*, volume 308 of *Lecture Notes in Computer Science*, pages 258–263. Springer, 1988.

[GM02] H. Ganzinger and D. McAllester. Logical algorithms. In *18th International Conference on Logic Programming*, volume 2401 of *Lecture Notes in Computer Science*, pages 31–42. Springer, 2002.

[GOH01] J. Geurts, J. Van Ossenbruggen, and L. Hardman. Application-specific constraints for multimedia presentation generation. In *8th International Conference on Multimedia Modeling*, pages 247–266, 2001.

[GR94] Joseph C. Giarratano and Gary Riley. *Expert Systems: Principles and Programming*. PWS Publishing, 1994.

[Gra89] T. Graf. *Raisonnement sur les contraintes en programmation en logique*. PhD thesis, Universite de Nice, Nice, France, June 1989.

[HdlBSD05] Christian Holzbauer, Maria Garcia de la Banda, Peter J. Stuckey, and Gergory J. Duck. Optimizing compilation of constraint handling rules in HAL. *Theory and Practice of Logic Programming*, 5:503–531, 2005.

[HDT92] Pascal Van Hentenryck, Yves Deville, and Choh-Man Teng. A generic arc-consistency algorithm and its specializations. *Artificial Intelligence*, 57(2–3):291–321, 1992.

[Hen89] Pascal Van Hentenryck. *Constraint Satisfaction in Logic Programming*. Logic Programming Series. MIT Press, 1989.

[Hen91] Pascal Van Hentenryck. Constraint logic programming. *Knowledge Engineering Review*, 6:151–194, 1991.

[Her30] Jacques Herbrand. *Recherches sur la Theorie de la Demonstration*. PhD thesis, Universite de Paris, Paris, France, 1930.

[HF00] Christian Holzbaur and Thom Frühwirth. Editors, Special Issue on Constraint Handling Rules. *Applied Artificial Intelligence*, 14(4), 2000.

[HKW04] B. Hnich, Z. Kiziltan, and T. Walsh. Combining symmetry breaking with other constraints: lexicographic ordering with sums. In *Eighth International Symposium on Artificial Intelligence and Mathematics*, 2004.

[HPSB04] Ian Horrocks, Peter F. Patel-Schneider, and Harold Boley. SWRL: a semantic web rule language combining OWL and RuleML. W3C Member Submission, 2004.

[HSD95] Pascal Van Hentenryck, Vijay Saraswat, and Yves Deville. Design, implementation, and evaluation of the constraint language cc(FD). In *Constraint*

Programming: Basics and Trends, volume 910 of *Lecture Notes in Computer Science*, pages 293–316. Springer, 1995.

[Hue80] Gérard Huet. Confluent reductions: abstract properties and applications to term rewriting systems: abstract properties and applications to term rewriting systems. *Journal of the ACM*, 27(4):797–821, 1980.

[Imb05] Jean Louis J. Imbert. Linear constraint solving in CLP-languages. In *Constraint Programming: Basics and Trends*, volume 910 of *Lecture Notes in Computer Science*, pages 108–127. Springer, 2005.

[JL87] J. Jaffar and J.-L. Lassez. Constraint logic programming. In *14th ACM SIGACT-SIGPLAN Symposium on Principles of Programming Languages*, pages 111–119. ACM, 1987.

[JM94] Joxan Jaffar and Micheal J. Maher. Constraint logic programming: a survey. *Journal of Logic Programming*, 19/20:503–581, 1994.

[KL91] Henry A. Kautz and Peter B. Ladkin. Integrating metric and qualitative temporal reasoning. In *Ninth National Conference on Artificial Intelligence*, pages 241–246. AAAI Press, 1991.

[Kni89] Kevin Knight. Unification: a multidisciplinary survey. *ACM Computing Surveys*, 21(1):93–124, 1989.

[Kou06] Manolis Koubarakis. Temporal CSPs. In Francesca Rossi, Peter Van Beek, and Toby Walsh, editors, *Handbook of Constraint Programming*, chapter 19, pages 665–698. Elsevier, 2006.

[Kow86] Robert Kowalski. *Logic for Problem-solving*. North-Holland, 1986.

[KSD06] Leslie De Koninck, Tom Schrijvers, and Bart Demoen. INCLP(R)–interval-based nonlinear constraint logic programming over the reals. In *20th Workshop on Logic Programming*, volume 1843-06-02 of *INFSYS Research Report*, pages 81–90, Vienna, Austria, 2006. Technische Universitt Wien.

[KSD07a] Leslie De Koninck, Tom Schrijvers, and Bart Demoen. The correspondence between the logical algorithms language and CHR. In *23rd International Conference on Logic Programming*, volume 4670 of *Lecture Notes in Computer Science*, pages 209–223. Springer, 2007.

[KSD07b] Leslie De Koninck, Tom Schrijvers, and Bart Demoen. User-definable rule priorities for CHR. In *Ninth ACM SIGPLAN International Conference on Principles and Practice of Declarative Programming*, pages 25–36. ACM, 2007.

[Lel88] William Leler. *Constraint Programming Languages: Their Specification and Generation*. Addison-Wesley, 1988.

[LS08] Edmund S. L. Lam and Martin Sulzmann. Parallel execution of multi-set constraint rewrite rules. In *Tenth International ACM SIGPLAN Symposium on Principles and Practice of Declarative Programming*. ACM, 2008.

[Mac77] Alan K. Mackworth. Consistency in networks of relations. *Artificial Intelligence*, 8(1):99–118, 1977.

[Mah87] Michael J. Maher. Logic semantics for a class of committed-choice programs. In *Fourth International Conference on Logic Programming*, pages 858–876. MIT Press, 1987.

[Mah88] Michael J. Maher. Complete axiomatizations of the algebras of finite, rational and infinite trees. In *Third Annual Symposium on Logic in Computer Science*, pages 348–357. IEEE Computer Society, 1988.

[MD06] Martin Magnusson and Patrick Doherty. Deductive planning with temporal constraints using TAL. In *International Symposium on Practical Cognitive Agents and Robots*, pages 141–152. ACM, 2006.

[MDR07] Marc Meister, Khalil Djelloul, and Jacques Robin. A unified semantics for constraint handling rules in transaction logic. In *Ninth International Conference on Logic Programming and Nonmonotonic Reasoning*, volume 4483 of *Lecture Notes in Computer Science*, pages 201–213. Springer, 2007.

[Mei91] Itay Meiri. Combining qualitative and quantitative constraints in temporal reasoning. In *Ninth National Conference on Artificial Intelligence*, pages 260–267. AAAI Press, 1991.

[Mei07] Marc Meister. Concurrency of the preflow-push algorithm in constraint handling rules. In *12th Annual ERCIM Workshop on Constraint Solving and Constraint Logic Programming*, pages 160–169, Rocquencourt, France, 2007.

[Mes92] José Meseguer. Conditional rewriting logic as a unified model of concurrency. *Theoretical Computer Science*, 96(1):73–155, 1992.

[MF85] Alan K. Mackworth and Eugene C. Freuder. The complexity of some polynomial network consistency algorithms for constraint satisfaction problems. *Artificial Intelligence*, 25(1):65–74, 1985.

[MF06] Marc Meister and Thom Frühwirth. Complexity of the CHR rational tree equation solver. In *Third Workshop on Constraint Handling Rules*, pages 77–92, Leuven, Belgium, 2006. K. U. Leuven.

[MF07] Marc Meister and Thom Frühwirth. Reconstructing almost-linear tree equation solving algorithms in CHR. In *12th Annual ERCIM Workshop on Constraint Solving and Constraint Logic Programming*, pages 123–137, 2007.

[MH86] Roger Mohr and Thomas C. Henderson. Arc and path consistence revisited. *Artificial Intelligence*, 28(2):225–233, 1986.

[Min88] M. Minoux. LTUR: a simplified linear-time unit resolution algorithm for Horn formulae and computer implementation. *Information Processing Letters*, 29(1):1–12, 1988.

[Mir87] D.P. Miranker. TREAT: a better match algorithm for AI production systems. In *Sixth National Conference on Artificial Intelligence*, pages 42–47. AAAI Press, 1987.

[MR84] Alberto Martelli and Gianfranco Rossi. Efficient unification with infinite terms in logic programming. In *International Conference on Fifth Generation Computer Systems*, pages 202–209. North-Holland, 1984.

[MS98] Kim Marriott and Peter J. Stuckey. *Programming with Constraints: An Introduction*. MIT Press, 1998.

[MSS04] Boris Motik, Ulrike Sattler, and Rudi Studer. Query answering for OWL-DL with rules. In *Third International Semantic Web Conference*, volume 3298 of *Lecture Notes in Computer Science*, pages 549–563. Springer, 2004.

[MSSA93] Satoshi Menju, Kô Sakai, Yosuke Sato, and Akira Aiba. A study on Boolean constraint solvers. *Constraint Logic Programming: Selected Research*, pages 253–267, 1993.

[MV86] H. Kautz M. Vilain. Constraint propagation algorithms for temporal reasoning. In *Fifth National Conference on Artificial Intelligence*, pages 377–382. AAAI Press, 1986.

[New42] M. H. A. Newman. On theories with a combinatorial definition of equivalence. *Annals of Mathematics*, 43, 1942.

[PCD96] Maria Cristina Pinotti, Vincenzo A. Crupi, and Sajal K. Das. A parallel solution to the extended set union problem with unlimited backtracking. In *10th International Parallel Processing Symposium*, pages 182–186. IEEE Computer Society, 1996.

[Pet62] C. A. Petri. *Kommunikation mit Automaten*. PhD thesis, Universität Bonn, Institut für Instrumentelle Mathematik, Bonn, Germany, 1962.

[PW78] M. S. Paterson and M. N. Wegman. Linear unification. *Journal of Computer and System Sciences*, 16(2):158–167, 1978.

[Rai07] Frank Raiser. Graph transformation systems in CHR. In *23rd International Conference on Logic Programming*, volume 4670 of *Lecture Notes in Computer Science*, pages 240–254. Springer, 2007.

[RBW06] Francesca Rossi, Peter Van Beek, and Toby Walsh, editors. *Handbook of Constraint Programming*. Elsevier, 2006.

[RH04] Peter Van Roy and Seif Haridi. *Concepts, Techniques, and Models of Computer Programming*. MIT Press, 2004.

[Rob65] J. A. Robinson. A machine-oriented logic based on the resolution principle. *Journal of the ACM*, 12(1):23–41, 1965.

[San94] E. Sandewall. *Features and Fluents: The Representation of Knowledge about Dynamical Systems*, volume 1. Oxford University Press, 1994.

[Sar93] Vijay A. Saraswat. *Concurrent Constraint Programming*. MIT Press, 1993.

[SB06] Tom Schrijvers and Maurice Bruynooghe. Polymorphic algebraic data type reconstruction. In *Eighth ACM SIGPLAN International Conference on Principles and Practice of Declarative Programming*, pages 85–96. ACM, 2006.

[SBB02] C. Seitz, B. Bauer, and M. Berger. Multi agent systems using constraint handling rules for problem solving. In *International Conference on Artificial Intelligence*, pages 295–301. CSREA Press, 2002.

[Sch05] Tom Schrijvers. *Analyses, Optimizations and Extensions of Constraint Handling Rules*. PhD thesis, K. U. Leuven, Leuven, Belgium, 2005.

[SD04] T. Schrijvers and B. Demoen. The K. U. Leuven CHR system: implementation and application. In *Selected Contribution of the First Workshop on Constraint Handling Rules*, Ulmer Informatik-Berichte, pages 8–12, Ulm, Germany, 2004. Universität Ulm.

[SDD+06] Tom Schrijvers, Bart Demoen, Gregory Duck, Peter Stuckey, and Thom Frühwirth. Automatic implication checking for CHR constraints. In *Sixth International Workshop on Rule-Based Programming*, volume 147 of *Electronic Notes in Theoretical Computer Science*, pages 93–111. Elsevier, 2006.

[SdlBM+05] Peter J. Stuckey, Maria Garcia de la Banda, Michael Maher, Kim Marriott, John Slaney, Zoltan Somogyi, Mark Wallace, and Toby Walsh. The G12 project: mapping solver independent models to efficient solutions. In *21st International Conference on Logic Programming*, volume 3668 of *Lecture Notes in Computer Science*, pages 9–13. Springer, 2005.

[SF05] T. Schrijvers and T. Frühwirth. Analysing the CHR implementation of union-find. In *19th Workshop on (Constraint) Logic Programming*, number 2005-01 in Ulmer Informatik-Berichte, pages 135–146. University of Ulm, 2005.

[SF06] Tom Schrijvers and Thom Frühwirth. Optimal union-find in constraint handling rules. *Theory and Practice of Logic Programming*, 6(1–2):213–224, 2006.

[Sha89] Ehud Shapiro. The family of concurrent logic programming languages. *ACM Computing Surveys*, 21(3):413–510, 1989.

[SK95] Fariba Sadri and Robert A. Kowalski. Variants of the event calculus. In *12th International Conference on Logic Programming*, pages 67–81. MIT Press, 1995.

[Smo95] Gert Smolka. The Oz programming model. In *Computer Science Today*, volume 1000 of *Lecture Notes in Computer Science*, pages 324–343. Springer, 1995.

[SR90] Vijay A. Saraswat and Martin Rinard. Concurrent constraint programming. In *17th ACM SIGPLAN Symposium on Principles of Programming Languages*, pages 232–245. ACM, 1990.

[SRP91] Vijay A. Saraswat, Martin Rinard, and Prakash Panangaden. The semantic foundations of concurrent constraint programming. In *18th ACM SIGPLAN Symposium on Principles of Programming Languages*, pages 333–352. ACM, 1991.

[SS05] Peter J. Stuckey and Martin Sulzmann. A theory of overloading. *ACM Transactions on Programming Languages and Systems*, 27(6):1216–1269, 2005.

[SSD05a] Tom Schrijvers, Peter J. Stuckey, and Gregory J. Duck. Abstract interpretation for constraint handling rules. In *Seventh ACM SIGPLAN International Conference on Principles and Practice of Declarative Programming*, pages 218–229. ACM, 2005.

[SSD05b] J. Sneyers, T. Schrijvers, and B. Demoen. The computational power and complexity of constraint handling rules. In *Second Workshop on Constraint Handling Rules*, Report CW421, pages 3–18, Leuven, Belgium, 2005. K. U. Leuven.

[SSD06] Jon Sneyers, Tom Schrijvers, and Bart Demoen. Dijkstra's algorithm with Fibonacci heaps: an executable description in CHR. In *20th Workshop on Logic Programming*, volume 1843-06-02 of *INFSYS Research Report*, pages 182–191, Vienna, Austria, 2006. Technische Universität Wien.

[SSR07] Beata Sarna-Starosta and C. R. Ramakrishnan. Compiling constraint handling rules for efficient tabled evaluation. In *Practical Aspects of Declarative Languages*, volume 4354 of *Lecture Notes in Computer Science*, pages 170–184. Springer, 2007.

[SSS91] Manfred Schmidt-Schauß and Gert Smolka. Attributive concept descriptions with complements. *Artificial Intelligence*, 48(1):1–26, 1991.

[ST94] Gert Smolka and Ralf Treinen. Records for logic programming. *Journal of Logic Programming*, 18(3):229–258, 1994.

[ST07] Stephan Schiffel and Michael Thielscher. Fluxplayer: a successful general game player. In *22nd Conference on Artificial Intelligence*, pages 1191–1196. AAAI Press, 2007.

[SWSK08] Jon Sneyers, Peter Van Weert, Tom Schrijvers, and Leslie De Koninck. As time goes by: constraint handling rules, a survey of CHR research from 1998 to 2007. Submitted, 2008.

[Thi05] Michael Thielscher. FLUX: a logic programming method for reasoning agents. *Theory and Practice of Logic Programming*, 5:533–565, 2005.

[TL84] Robert E. Tarjan and Jan Van Leeuwen. Worst-case analysis of set union algorithms. *Journal of the ACM*, 31(2):245–281, 1984.

[Ued88] K. Ueda. Guarded Horn clauses. In *Concurrent Prolog*, pages 140–156. MIT Press, 1988.

[WFD84] J. H. Gallier W. F. Dowling. Linear-time algorithms for testing the satisfiability of propositional Horn formulae. *Journal of Logic Programming*, 1(3):267–284, 1984.

[Wol01] Armin Wolf. Adaptive constraint handling with CHR in Java. In *Seventh International Conference on Principles and Practice of Constraint Programming*, volume 2239 of *Lecture Notes in Computer Science*, pages 256–270. Springer, 2001.

[WSSD06] P. Van Weert, J. Sneyers, T. Schrijvers, and B. Demoen. Extending CHR with negation as absence. In *Third Workshop on Constraint Handling Rules*, pages 125–140, Leuven, Belgium, 2006. K. U. Leuven.

Index

Index

Printed in the United States
By Bookmasters